COLLINS GEM
ANTIQUE MARKS

D0635584

GEM

CARD

COLLINS GEM
CRICKET

COLLINS GEM
DIETING
FAT

COLLINS GEM
DOGS

COLLINS GEM
FIRST AID

COLLINS GEM
INTERNET

COLLINS GEM
PREDICTING

COLLINS GEM
Ready REFERENCE

COLLINS GEM
SHARKS

COLLINS GEM
WHALES & DOLPHINS

COLLINS GEM
WHISKY

COLLINS GEM
WORD PROCESSING

COLLINS GEM
Your PC

COLLINS GEM

Dictionary of
QUOTATIONS

HarperCollins*Publishers*

HarperCollins Publishers
PO Box, Glasgow G4 0NB

First published 1961
Third edition published 1997
This edition published 1999

Reprint 10 9 8 7 6 5 4 3 2 1

ISBN 0 00 472287-6

Printed in Italy by Amadeus S.p.A.

INTRODUCTION

'By necessity, by proclivity, and by delight, we all quote,' wrote Emerson over a century ago, and dictionaries of quotations continue to fascinate, entertain and inform in equal measure. In this new edition of *Collins Gem Quotations* the reader will find old favourites from classical authors and the great poets and playwrights alongside observations on contemporary life from today's authors, artists, sports personalities and politicians. Many of the best quotations seem to express in a few memorable words the essence of human experience - the joys and sufferings, hopes and anxieties which are common to us all. Others offer unexpected insights or challenging ideas which open up new perspectives on the familiar. And no selection of quotations would be complete without a chorus of voices from past and present commenting on the absurdity of the human condition.

The quotations in this selection are presented thematically for ease of reference. Within each subject the entries are arranged alphabetically by author. Quotations from languages other than English appear in English translation, unless they are sufficiently well known to be familiar to the reader in their original language. Writers of speeches will find the thematic arrangement of immense value, and those readers who wish to find quotes from specific authors can easily do so by consulting the index of sources. In those few instances where there are quotations by two authors of the same name, dates of birth and death have been included in the index to differentiate them.

Every care has been taken to verify the quotations, and where the source cannot be identified with certainty the quote appears as an attribution. We welcome letters from readers and if anyone can add to our knowledge of sources, or indeed wishes to send in favourite quotations for inclusion in a later edition, we would be delighted to hear from them.

Particular thanks are due to Brian Glancey, Elaine Henderson and Hazel Mills for their patience and commitment in the preparation of this edition.

Edwin Moore
Managing Editor

CONTENTS

ACTION

AMIEL, Henri-Frédéric (1821–1881)
Action is but coarsened thought – thought become concrete, obscure and unconscious.

[*Journal* (1850)]

BEERBOHM, Sir Max (1872–1956)
Anything that is worth doing has been done frequently. Things hitherto undone should be given, I suspect, a wide berth.

[*Mainly on the Air* (1946)]

CARLYLE, Thomas (1795–1881)
The end of man is an Action and not a Thought, though it were the noblest.

[*Sartor Resartus* (1834)]

CORNFORD, F.M. (1874–1943)
Every public action which is not customary, either is wrong, or if it is right, is a dangerous precedent. It follows that nothing should ever be done for the first time.

[*Microcosmographia Academica* (1908)]

DE GAULLE, Charles (1890–1970)
Deliberation is the work of many men. Action, of one alone.

[*War Memoirs*]

ELIOT, George (1819–1880)
Our deeds determine us, as much as we determine our deeds.

[*Adam Bede* (1859)]

EMERSON, Ralph Waldo (1803–1882)
We are taught by great actions that the universe is the property of every individual in it.

[*Nature* (1836)]

The reward of a thing well done, is to have done it.

['New England Reformers' (1844)]

JOWETT, Benjamin (1817–1893)
The way to get things done is not to mind who gets the credit for them.

[Attr.]

KANT, Immanuel (1724–1804)
I should always act in such a way that I may want my maxim to become a general law.

[*Outline of the Metaphysics of Morals* (1785)]

**KEMPIS, Thomas à
(c. 1380–1471)**
Truly when the day of judgement comes, it will not be a question of what we have read but what we have done.
[*De Imitatione Christi*]

**LA ROCHEFOUCAULD
(1613–1680)**
We would often be ashamed of our finest actions if the world could see the motives behind them.
[*Maximes* (1678)]

SZASZ, Thomas (1920–)
Men are rewarded and punished not for what they do, but rather for how their actions are defined. This is why men are more interested in better justifying themselves than in better behaving themselves.
[*The Second Sin* (1973)]

ACTORS

ANONYMOUS
[On a performance of Cleopatra by Sarah Bernhardt]
How different, how very different from the home life of our own dear Queen!
[Remark]

The whole world plays the actor.
[Motto of Globe playhouse]

**BENCHLEY, Robert
(1889–1945)**
[Suggesting an epitaph for an actress]
She sleeps alone at last.
[Attr.]

BRANDO, Marlon (1924–)
An actor's a guy who, if you ain't talking about him, ain't listening.
[*The Observer*, 1956]

**COLERIDGE, Samuel Taylor
(1772–1834)**
[Of Edmund Kean]
To see him act is like reading Shakespeare by flashes of lightning.
[*Table Talk* (1835)]

**COWARD, Sir Noël
(1899–1973)**
[Comment on a child star, in a long-winded play]
Two things should be cut: the second act and the child's throat.
[In Richards, *The Wit of Noël Coward*]

DUNDY, Elaine (1927–)
The question actors most often get asked is how they can bear saying the same things over and over again night after night, but God

knows the answer to that is, don't we all anyway; might as well get paid for it.

[*The Dud Avocado* (1958)]

FIELD, Eugene (1850–1895)
[Of Creston Clarke as King Lear]
He played the King as though under momentary apprehension that someone else was about to play the ace.

[Attr.]

FORD, John (1895–1973)
It is easier to get an actor to be a cowboy than to get a cowboy to be an actor.

[Attr.]

HITCHCOCK, Alfred (1899–1980)
Nobody can really like an actor.

[*The New Yorker*, 1992]

I deny that I ever said that actors are cattle. What I said was, 'Actors should be treated like cattle'.

[Attr.]

KAUFMANN, George S. (1889–1961)
[On Raymond Massey's interpretation of Abraham Lincoln]
Massey won't be satisfied until somebody assassinates him.

[In Meredith, *George S.*

Kaufmann and the Algonquin Round Table (1974)]

LEVANT, Oscar (1906–1972)
Romance on the High Seas was Doris Day's first picture; that was before she became a virgin.

[*Memoirs of an Amnesiac* (1965)]

MALOUF, David (1934–)
Actors don't pretend to be other people; they become themselves by finding other people inside them.

[*Harland's Half Acre,* (1984)]

PARKER, Dorothy (1893–1967)
[Remark on a performance by Katherine Hepburn]
She ran the whole gamut of emotions from A to B.

[In Carey, *Katherine Hepburn* (1985)]

TYNAN, Kenneth (1927–1980)
What, when drunk, one sees in other women, one sees in Garbo sober.

[*The Sunday Times* 1963]

WILLIAMSON, Nicol
[Of Sean Connery]
Guys like him and Caine talk about acting as if they knew what it was.

[Interview, *Daily Mail*, 1996]

WINCHELL, Walter (1897–1972)
[Referring to a show starring Earl Carroll]
I saw it at a disadvantage – the curtain was up.
[In Whiteman, *Come to Judgement*]

See THEATRE

ADULTERY

AUSTEN, Jane (1775–1817)
I am proud to say that I have a very good eye at an Adultress, for tho' repeatedly assured that another in the same party was the She, I fixed upon the right one from the first.
[*Letter*, 1801]

BENCHLEY, Robert (1889–1945)
[Comment on an office shared with Dorothy Parker]
One cubic foot less of space and it would have constituted adultery.
[Attr.]

BYRON, Lord (1788–1824)
What men call gallantry, and gods call adultery,
Is much more common when the climate's sultry.
[*Don Juan* (1824)]

Merely innocent flirtation.
Not quite adultery, but adulteration.
[*Don Juan* (1824)]

HUXLEY, Aldous (1894–1963)
There are few who would rather not be taken in adultery than in provincialism.
[*Antic Hay* (1923)]

JOHN PAUL II (1920–)
Adultery in your heart is committed not only when you look with excessive sexual desire at a woman who is not your wife, but also if you look in the same manner at your wife.
[*The Observer*, 1990]

MAUGHAM, William Somerset (1874–1965)
You know, of course, that the Tasmanians, who never committed adultery, are now extinct.
[*The Bread-Winner*]

RICHELIEU, Duc de (1766–1822)
[On discovering his wife with her lover]
Madame, you must really be more careful. Suppose it had been someone else who had found you like this.
[In Wallechinsky, *The Book of Lists* (1977)]

**SHAKESPEARE, William
(1564–1616)**
Adultery?
Thou shalt not die. Die for
   adultery?
No.
The wren goes to't, and the
   small gilded fly
Does lecher in my sight.
Let copulation thrive.
[*King Lear*, IV.vi]

See MARRIAGE; SEX

ADULTS

HARRIS, Sydney J. (1917–)
We have not passed that
subtle line between childhood
and adulthood until we move
from the passive voice to the
active voice – that is until we
have stopped saying 'It got
lost', and say 'I lost it'.
[Attr.]

**MILLAY, Edna St Vincent
(1892–1950)**
Was it for this I uttered
prayers,
And sobbed and cursed and
kicked the stairs,
That now, domestic as a
plate,
I should retire at half-past
eight?
['Grown-up' (1920)]

**ROSTAND, Jean
(1894–1977)**
To be an adult is to be alone.
[*Thoughts of a Biologist*
(1939)]

**SHAKESPEARE, William
(1564–1616)**
Your lordship, though not
clean past your youth, hath
yet some smack of age in
you, some relish of the salt-
ness of time.
[*Henry IV, Part 2*, I.ii]

SZASZ, Thomas (1920–)
A child becomes an adult
when he realizes that he has
a right not only to be right but
also to be wrong.
[*The Second Sin* (1973)]

ADVERTISING

**DOUGLAS, Norman
(1868–1952)**
You can tell the ideals of a
nation by its advertisements.
[*South Wind* (1917)]

**HUXLEY, Aldous
(1894–1963)**
It is far easier to write ten
passably effective sonnets,
good enough to take in the
not too inquiring critic, than
one effective advertisement
that will take in a few thou-

sand of the uncritical buying public.

[*On the Margin* (1923)]

JEFFERSON, Thomas (1743–1826)
Advertisements contain the only truths to be relied on in a newspaper.

[Letter, 1819]

LEACOCK, Stephen Butler (1869–1944)
Advertising may be described as the science of arresting the human intelligence long enough to get money from it.

[In Prochow, *The Public Speaker's Treasure Chest*]

MCLUHAN, Marshall (1911–1980)
Ads are the cave art of the twentieth century.

[*Culture Is Our Business* (1970)]

NASH, Ogden (1902–1971)
Beneath this slab
John Brown is stowed.
He watched the ads,
And not the road.

['Lather as You Go' (1942)]

BIERCE, Ambrose (1842–c. 1914)
Advice: The smallest current coin.

[*The Cynic's Word Book* (1906)]

BISMARCK, Prince Otto von (1815–1898)
To youth I have but three words of counsel – work, work, work.

[Attr.]

BURTON, Richard (1577–1640)
Who cannot give good counsel? 'tis cheap, it costs them nothing.

[*Anatomy of Melancholy* (1621)]

EMERSON, Ralph Waldo (1803–1882)
It was a high counsel that I once heard given to a young person, – 'Always do what you are afraid to do.

[*Essays, First Series* (1841)]

HARRIS, George (1844–1922)
[In his address to students at the beginning of a new academic year]
I intended to give you some advice but now I remember

how much is left over from last year unused.
[*Braude's Second Encyclopedia* (1957)]

LA ROCHEFOUCAULD (1613–1680)
One gives nothing so generously as advice.
[*Maximes* (1678)]

THOREAU, Henry (1817–1862)
I have lived some thirty years on this planet, and I have yet to hear the first syllable of valuable or even earnest advice from my seniors.
[*Walden* (1854)]

AGE

ADAMS, John Quincy (1767–1848)
I inhabit a weak, frail, decayed tenement; battered by the winds and broken in on by the storms, and, from all I can learn, the landlord does not intend to repair.
[Attr.]

ADENAUER, Konrad (1876–1967)
[To his doctor]
I haven't asked you to make me young again. All I want is to go on getting older.
[Attr.]

ALLEN, Dave (1936–)
I still think of myself as I was 25 years ago. Then I look in a mirror and see an old bastard and I realise it's me.
[*The Independent*, 1993]

ALLEN, Woody, (1935–)
I recently turned sixty. Practically a third of my life is over.
[*The Observer Review*, 1996]

BINYON, Laurence (1869–1943)
They shall not grow old, as we that are left grow old: Age shall not weary them, nor the years condemn. At the going down of the sun and in the morning We will remember them.
['For the Fallen' (1914)]

BLAKE, Eubie (1883–1983)
[He died five days after his hundredth birthday]
If I'd known I was going to live this long, I'd have taken better care of myself.
[*The Observer*, 1983]

BRENAN, Gerald (1894–1987)
Old age takes away from us what we have inherited and gives us what we have earned.
[*Thoughts in a Dry Season* (1978)]

**BYRON, Lord
(1788–1824)**
Years steal
Fire from the mind as vigour
from the limb;
And life's enchanted cup
but sparkles near the brim.
[*Childe Harolde's Pilgrimage*
(1818)]

CALMENT, Jeanne (1875–)
[Reply to someone who asked
her what she would like for
her 121st birthday]
Respect.
[*The Mail on Sunday*, 1996]

**CAMPBELL, Joseph
(1879–1944)**
As a white candle
In a holy place,
So is the beauty
of an aged face.
['The Old Woman' (1913)]

**COLLINS, Mortimer
(1827–1876)**
A man is as old as he is feel-
ing,
A woman as old as she looks.
['The Unknown Quantity']

**DEWEY, John
(1859–1952)**
It is strange that the one thing
that every person looks forward to, namely old age, is
the one thing for which no
preparation is made.
[Attr.]

**DISRAELI, Benjamin
(1804–1881)**
When a man fell into his
anecdotage it was a sign for
him to retire from the world.
[*Lothair* (1870)]

**EMERSON, Ralph Waldo
(1803–1882)**
Spring still makes spring in
the mind,
When sixty years are told.
[*Poems* (1847)]

ESTIENNE, Henri (1531–1598)
If only youth knew; if only
age could.
[*Les Prémices* (1594)]

**FRANKLIN, Benjamin
(1706–1790)**
At twenty years of age, the
will reigns; at thirty, the wit;
and at forty, the judgement.
[*Poor Richard's Almanac*
(1741)]

GONNE, Maude (1865–1953)
Oh how you hate old age –
well so do I . . . but I, who am
more a rebel against man
than you, rebel less against
nature, and accept the
inevitable and go with it
gently into the unknown.
[Letter to W.B. Yeats]

**HILTON, James
(1900–1954)**
Anno domini . . . that's the

most fatal complaint of all, in the end.

[*Goodbye, Mr Chips* (1934)]

HOLMES, Oliver Wendell, Jr. (1841–1935)
[At the age of 86, on seeing a pretty girl]
Oh, to be seventy again!

[In Fadiman, *The American Treasury*]

IRVING, Washington (1783–1859)
Whenever a man's friends begin to compliment him about looking young, he may be sure they think he is growing old.

[*Bracebridge Hall* (1822)]

LANG, Andrew (1844–1912)
Our hearts are young 'neath wrinkled rind:
Life's more amusing than we thought.

['Ballade of Middle Age']

LARKIN, Philip (1922–1985)
Perhaps being old is having lighted rooms
Inside your head, and people in them, acting.
People you know, yet can't quite name.

['The Old Fools' (1974)]

NASH, Ogden (1902–1971)
Do you think my mind is simply maturing late,
Or simply rotted early?

['Lines on Facing Forty' (1942)]

NAYLOR, James Ball (1860–1945)
King David and King Solomon
Led merry, merry lives,
With many, many lady friends
And many, many wives;
But when old age crept over them,
With many, many qualms,
King Solomon wrote the Proverbs
And King David wrote the Psalms.

['King David and King Solomon' (1935)]

ORWELL, George (1903–1950)
At 50, everyone has the face he deserves.

[*Notebook*, 1949]

PICASSO, Pablo (1881–1973)
Age only matters when one is ageing. Now that I have arrived at a great age, I might just as well be twenty.

[In J. Richardson, *Picasso in Private*]

POWELL, Anthony (1905–)
Growing old is like being increasingly penalized for a crime you did not commit.

[*A Dance to the Music of Time* (1973)]

REAGAN, Ronald
(1911–)
I am delighted to be with you. In fact, at my age, I'm delighted to be anywhere.
[Speech at the Oxford Union, 1992]

RUBINSTEIN, Helena
(c. 1872–1965)
I have always felt that a woman has a right to treat the subject of her age with ambiguity until, perhaps, she passes into the realm of over ninety. Then it is better she be candid with herself and with the world.
[My Life for Beauty (1965)]

SANTAYANA, George
(1863–1952)
The young man who has not wept is a savage, and the old man who will not laugh is a fool.
[Dialogues in Limbo (1925)]

SARTON, May
(1912–)
Old age is not an illness, it is a timeless ascent. As power diminishes, we grow toward the light.
[Ms magazine, 1982]

SEXTON, Anne
(1928–1974)
In a dream you are never eighty.
['Old' (1962)]

SHAKESPEARE, William
(1564–1616)
Unregarded age in corners thrown.
[As You Like It, II.iii]

Crabbed age and youth cannot live together:
Youth is full of pleasance, age is full of care . . .

Age, I do abhor thee; youth I do adore thee.
[The Passionate Pilgrim, xii]

SHAW, George Bernard
(1856–1950)
Old men are dangerous: it doesn't matter to them what is going to happen to the world.
[Heartbreak House (1919)]

SMITH, Logan Pearsall
(1865–1946)
There is more felicity on the far side of baldness than young men can possibly imagine.
['Last Words' (1933)]

SOLON
(c. 638–c. 559)
I grow old ever learning many things.
[In Bergk (ed.), Poetae Lyrici Graeci]

THOMAS, Dylan (1914–1953)
Do not go gentle into that
good night,
Old age should burn and rage
at close of day;
Rage, rage against the dying
of the light.
['Do Not Go Gentle into that
Good Night' (1952)]

TROTSKY, Leon (1879–1940)
Old age is the most unexpected of all the things that
happen to a man.
[*Diary in Exile,* 8 May 1935]

**WALPOLE, Horace
(1717–1797)**
What has one to do, when
one grows tired of the world,
as we both do, but to draw
nearer and nearer, and gently
waste the remains of life with
friends with whom one began
it?
[Letter to George Montagu,
1765]

WHITMAN, Walt (1819–1892)
Women sit and move to and
fro, some old, some young.
The young are beautiful - but
the old are more beautiful
than the young.
['Beautiful Women' (1871)]

WILDE, Oscar (1854–1900)
I delight in men over seventy.
They always offer one the

devotion of a lifetime.
[*A Woman of No Importance*
(1893)]

The old believe everything:
the middle-aged suspect
everything: the young know
everything.
[*The Chameleon,* 1894]

**WILLIAMS, William Carlos
(1883–1963)**
In old age
the mind
casts off
rebelliously
an eagle
from its crag.
[*Paterson* (1946–1958)]

**WODEHOUSE, P.G.
(1881–1975)**
He was either a man of about a
hundred and fifty who was
rather young for his years or a
man of about a hundred and ten
who had been aged by trouble.
[In Usborne, *Wodehouse at
Work to the End* (1976)]

**WORDSWORTH, William
(1770-1850)**
The wiser mind
Mourns less for what age
takes away
Than what it leaves behind.
['The Fountain' (1800)]

YEATS, W.B. (1865–1939)
I thought no more was needed

Youth to prolong
Than dumb-bell and foil
To keep the body young.
O who could have foretold
That the heart grows old?

['A Song' 1918]

AMBITION

**BROWNING, Robert
(1906–1963)**
'Tis not what man does which
exalts him, but what a man
would do!

['Saul' (1855)]

BURKE, Edmund (1729–1797)
Well is it known that ambition
can creep as well as soar.

[*Third Letter . . . on the
Proposals for Peace with the
Regicide Directory of France*
(1797)]

**CAESAR, Gaius Julius
(c. 102–44 BC)**
I would rather be the first
man here (in Gaul) than
second in Rome.

[Attr. in Plutarch, *Lives*]

CONRAD, Joseph (1857–1924)
All ambitions are lawful
except those which climb
upward on the miseries or
credulities of mankind.

[*A Personal Record* (1912)]

GILBERT, W.S. (1836–1911)
If you wish in this world to
advance
Your merits you're bound to
enhance,
You must stir it and stump it,
And blow your own trumpet,
Or, trust me, you haven't a
chance!

[*Ruddigore* (1887)]

KENEALLY, Thomas (1935–)
It's only when you abandon
your ambitions that they
become possible.

[*Australian,* 1983]

**SHAKESPEARE, William
(1564–1616)**
I charge thee, fling away
ambition:
By that sin fell the angels.
How can man then,
The image of his Maker,
hope to win by it?

[*Henry VIII,* III.ii]

'Tis a common proof
That lowliness is young
ambition's ladder,
Whereto the climber-upward
turns his face;
But when he once attains the
upmost round,
He then unto the ladder turns
his back,
Looks in the clouds, scorning
the base degrees
By which he did ascend.

[*Julius Caesar,* II.i]

I have no spur
To prick the sides of my
intent, but only
Vaulting ambition, which
o'er-leaps itself,
And falls on th' other.
[*Macbeth*, I.vii]

**SHAW, George Bernard
(1856–1950)**
The Gospel of Getting On.
[*Mrs Warren's Profession*,
(1898), IV]

**WEBSTER, Daniel
(1782–1852)**
[On being advised not to
enter the overcrowded legal
profession]
There is always room at the
top.
[Attr.]

AMERICA

ANONYMOUS
Overpaid, overfed, oversexed
and over here.
[Of GIs in Britain during
World War II]

AUDEN, W.H. (1907–1973)
God bless the U.S.A., so large,
so friendly and so rich.
['On the Circuit']

AYKROYD, Dan (1952–)
What the American public

doesn't know is what makes
it the American public.
[*Tommy Boy*, film, 1995]

**CLEMENCEAU, Georges
(1841–1929)**
America is the only nation in
history which miraculously
has gone directly from bar-
barism to degeneration without the usual intervention of
civilization.
[Attr.]

COOLIDGE, Calvin (1872–1929)
The business of America is
business.
[Speech, 1925]

DIAZ, Porfirio (1830–1915)
Poor Mexico, so far from God
and so near to the United
States!
[Attr.]

**EDWARD VIII (Later Duke of
Windsor) (1894–1972)**
The thing that impresses me
most about America is the
way parents obey their children.
[In *Look*, 1957]

**EISENHOWER, Dwight D.
(1890–1969)**
Whatever America hopes to
bring to pass in this world
must first come to pass in the
heart of America.
[Inaugural address, 1953]

**EMERSON, Ralph Waldo
(1803–1882)**
The Americans have little
faith. They rely on the power
of the dollar.
[Lecture, 1841, 'Man the
Reformer']

**FITZGERALD, F. Scott
(1896–1940)**
Americans, while willing,
even eager, to be serfs, have
always been obstinate about
being peasantry.
[*The Great Gatsby* (1926)]

FORD, Gerald R. (1913–)
[On becoming President]
I guess it proves that in
America anyone can be
President.
[In Reeves, *A Ford Not a
Lincoln*]

**JOHNSON, Samuel
(1709–1784)**
I am willing to love all
mankind, *except an American*.
[In Boswell, *The Life of Samuel
Johnson* (1791)]

**KENNEDY, John F.
(1917–1963)**
And so, my fellow Americans:
ask not what your country
can do for you – ask what you
can do for your country. My
fellow citizens of the world:
ask not what America will do
for you, but what together we
can do for the freedom of
man.
[Inaugural address, 1961]

**McCARTHY, Senator Joseph
(1908–1957)**
McCarthyism is Americanism
with its sleeves rolled.
[Speech, 1952]

**MADARIAGA, Salvador de
(1886–1978)**
First, the sweetheart of the
nation, then her aunt, woman
governs America because
America is a land where boys
refuse to grow up.
['Americans are Boys']

**MENCKEN, H.L.
(1880–1956)**
No-one ever went broke
underestimating the intelligence of the American people.
[Attr.]

**MINIFIE, James M.
(1900–1974)**
The United States is the glory,
jest, and terror of mankind.
[In Purdy (ed.), *The New
Romans* (1988)]

**ROOSEVELT, Theodore
(1858–1919)**
There is no room in this
country for hyphenated
Americanism.
[Speech, 1915]

**RUSSELL, Bertrand
(1872–1970)**
In America everybody is of
the opinion that he has no
social superiors, since all men
are equal, but he does not
admit that he has no social
inferiors.
        ['Ideas that have harmed
                    mankind' (1950)]

**STAPLEDON, Olaf
(1886–1950)**
That strange blend of the
commercial traveller, the mis-
sionary, and the barbarian
conqueror, which was the
American abroad
        [*Last and First Men* (1930)]

STEIN, Gertrude (1874–1946)
In the United States there is
more space where nobody is
than where anybody is. That is
what makes America what it is.
        [*The Geographical History of
                    America* (1936)]

TALLEYRAND (1754–1838)
[Of America]
I found there a country with
thirty-two religions and only
one sauce.
        [In Pedrazzini, *Autant en
                    apportent les mots*]

**TOYNBEE, Arnold
(1889–1975)**
America is a large, friendly
dog in a very small room.

Every time it wags its tail, it
knocks over a chair.
        [Broadcast news summary,
                            1954]

WELLS, H.G.(1866–1946)
Every time Europe looks
across the Atlantic to see the
American eagle, it observes
only the rear end of an ostrich.
                        [*America*]

**WILDE, Oscar
(1854–1900)**
Of course, America had often
been discovered before, but it
had always been hushed up.
        [*Personal Impressions of
                    America* (1883)]

The youth of America is their
oldest tradition. It has been
going on now for over three
hundred years.
        [*A Woman of No Importance*
                            (1893)]

**WILSON, Woodrow
(1856–1924)**
America is the only idealistic
nation in the world.
                    [Speech, 1919]

**ZANGWILL, Israel
(1864–1926)**
America is God's Crucible, the
Great Melting Pot where all
the races of Europe are melting and re-forming!
        [*The Melting Pot* (1908)]

ANGER

BACON, Francis (1561–1626)
Anger makes dull men witty,
but it keeps them poor.
['Apophthegms' (1679)]

THE BIBLE (KING JAMES VERSION)
A soft answer turneth away
wrath.
[Proverbs, 15:1]

Be ye angry, and sin not; let
not the sun go down upon
your wrath.
[Ephesians, 4:26]

BLAKE, William (1757–1827)
I was angry with my friend:
I told my wrath, my wrath did
end.
I was angry with my foe:
I told it not, my wrath did grow.
[Songs of Experience (1794)]

CONGREVE, William (1670–1729)
Heav'n has no rage, like love
to hatred turned,
Nor Hell a fury, like a woman
scorn'd.
[The Mourning Bride (1697)]

CONNOLLY, Cyril (1903–1974)
There is no fury like an ex-wife
searching for a new lover.
[The Unquiet Grave (1944)]

DILLER, Phyllis (1917–1974)
Never go to bed mad. Stay up
and fight.
[Housekeeping Hints]

DRYDEN, John (1631–1700)
Beware the fury of a patient
man.
[Absalom and Achitophel (1681)]

FULLER, Thomas (1608–1661)
Anger is one of the sinews of
the soul; he that wants it hath
a maimed one.
[The Holy State and the
Profane State (1642)]

HALIFAX, Lord (1633–1695)
Anger is never without an
Argument, but seldom with a
good one.
[Thoughts and Reflections
(1750)]

IRVING, Washington (1783–1859)
A tart temper never mellows
with age, and a sharp tongue is
the only edged tool that grows
keener with constant use.
['Rip Van Winkle' (1820)]

SHAW, George Bernard (1856–1950)
Beware of the man who does
not return your blow: he
neither forgives you nor
allows you to forgive yourself.
[Man and Superman (1903)]

COLLINS GEM
BABIES' names
a ? z
a mine of information

COLLINS GEM
BEER
a mine of information

COLLINS GEM
BIRDS
a mine of information

COLLINS GEM
CALORIE Counter
a mine of information

COLLINS GEM
FACT FILE
a mine of information

COLLINS GEM
FENG SHUI
a mine of information

COLLINS GEM
FLAGS
a mine of information

COLLINS GEM
Healthy EATING
a mine of information

COLLINS GEM
QUOTATIONS
a mine of information

COLLINS GEM
SAS Self-Defence
a mine of information

COLLINS GEM
SAS Survival Guide
a mine of information

COLLINS GEM
SEASHORE
a mine of information

COLLINS GEM
TREES
a mine of information

COLLINS GEM
Understanding DREAMS
a mine of information

COLLINS GEM
WILD flowers
a mine of information

COLLINS GEM
WINE Dictionary
a mine of information

ANIMALS

**BLAKE, William
(1757–1827)**
Tyger Tyger, burning bright
In the forests of the night:
what immortal hand or eye
Could frame thy fearful symmetry?
['The Tyger' (1794)]

ELIOT, George (1819–1880)
Animals are such agreeable
friends – they ask no questions, they pass no criticisms.
[*Scenes of Clerical Life* (1858)]

**FROUDE, James Anthony
(1818–1894)**
Wild animals never kill for
sport. Man is the only one to
whom the torture and death
of his fellow creatures is
amusing in itself.
[*Oceana* (1886)]

**GOLDSMITH, Oliver
(c. 1728–1774)**
Brutes never meet in bloody
fray,
Nor cut each other's throats
for pay.
['Logicians Refuted' (1759)]

**PEACOCK, Thomas Love
(1785–1866)**
Nothing can be more obvious
than that all animals were
created solely and exclusively
for the use of man.
[*Headlong Hall* (1816)]

**SHAKESPEARE, William
(1564–1616)**
No beast so fierce but knows
some touch of pity.
[*Richard III*, I.ii]

**SOLZHENITSYN, Alexander
(1918–)**
Nowadays we don't think
much of a man's love for an
animal; we mock people who
are attached to cats. But if we
stop loving animals, aren't we
bound to stop loving humans
too?
[*Cancer Ward* (1968)]

**SPENCER, Herbert
(1820–1903)**
People are beginning to see
that the first requisite to success in life, is to be a good
animal.
[*Education* (1861)]

**VOLTAIRE
(1694–1778)**
There are two things for
which animals are to be
envied: they know nothing of
future evils, or of what people
say about them.
[Letter, 1739]

See CATS; DOGS

ARGUMENT

**ADDISON, Joseph
(1672–1719)**
Our disputants put me in
mind of the scuttle fish, that
when he is unable to extri-
cate himself, blackens all the
water about him, till he
becomes invisible.
[*The Spectator* (1712)]

ANONYMOUS
This is a rotten argument, but
it should be good enough for
their lordships on a hot summer afternoon.
[Note in ministerial brief]

BILLINGS, Josh (1818–1885)
Thrice is he armed that hath
his quarrel just,
But four times he who gets
his blow in fust.
[*Josh Billings, his Sayings*
(1865)]

**FERGUSSON, Sir James
(1832–1907)**
I have heard many arguments
which influenced my opinion,
but never one which influenced my vote.
[Attr.]

**GAY, John
(1685–1732)**
Those, who in quarrels
interpose,

Must often wipe a bloody
nose.
[*Fables* (1727)]

**INGE, William Ralph
(1860–1954)**
It takes in reality only one to
make a quarrel. It is useless
for the sheep to pass resolu-
tions in favour of vegetarian-
ism while the wolf remains of
a different opinion.
[*Outspoken Essays* (1919)]

**JOHNSON, Samuel
(1709–1784)**
Though we cannot out-vote
them we will out-argue them.
[In Boswell, *The Life of Samuel
Johnson* (1791)]

**LA ROCHEFOUCAULD
(1613–1680)**
Quarrels would not last long
if the fault were on one side
only.
[*Maximes* (1678)]

**LOWELL, James Russell
(1819–1891)**
There is no good in arguing
with the inevitable. The only
argument available with an
east wind is to put on your
overcoat.
[*Democracy and Other
Addresses* (1887)]

ROSTAND, Jean (1894–1977)
A married couple are well

suited when both partners usually feel the need for a quarrel at the same time.

[*Le Mariage*]

YEATS, W.B. (1865–1939)
We make out of the quarrel with others, rhetoric; but, of the quarrel with ourselves, poetry.

['Anima Hominis' (1917)]

ARISTOCRACY

AILESBURY, Maria, Marchioness of (d. 1893)
My dear, my dear, you never know when any beautiful young lady may not blossom into a Duchess!

[In Portland, *Men, Women, and Things* (1937)]

BURKE, Edmund (1729–1797)
Nobility is a graceful ornament to the civil order. It is the Corinthian capital of polished society.

[*Reflections on the Revolution in France . . .* (1709)]

HOPE, Anthony (1863–1933)
'Bourgeois,' I observed, 'is an epithet which the riff-raff apply to what is respectable, and the aristocracy to what is decent.'

[*The Dolly Dialogues* (1894)]

LEVIS, Duc de (1764–1830)
Noblesse oblige.
Nobility has its obligations.

[*Maximes et réflexions* (1812)]

LLOYD GEORGE, David (1863–1945)
A fully equipped duke costs as much to keep up as two Dreadnoughts; and dukes are just as great a terror and they last longer.

[Speech, 1909]

MACHIAVELLI (1469–1527)
For titles do not reflect honour on men, but rather men on their titles.

[*Dei Discorsi*]

MANNERS, Lord John (1818–1906)
Let wealth and commerce, laws and learning die, But leave us still our old nobility!

[*England's Trust* (1841)]

MITFORD, Nancy (1904–1973)
An aristocracy in a republic is like a chicken whose head has been cut off: it may run about in a lively way, but in fact it is dead.

[*Noblesse Oblige* (1956)]

NORTHCLIFFE, Lord (1865–1922)
When I want a peerage, I

shall buy one like an honest man.

[Attr.]

PEARSON, Hesketh (1887–1964)
There is no stronger craving in the world than that of the rich for titles, except that of the titled for riches.

[Attr.]

SHAW, George Bernard (1856–1950)
Titles distinguish the mediocre, embarrass the superior, and are disgraced by the inferior.

[*Man and Superman* (1903)]

TENNYSON, Alfred, Lord (1809–1892)
Kind hearts are more than coronets,
And simple faith than Norman blood.

['Lady Clara Vere de Vere' (c. 1835)]

THACKERAY, William Makepeace (1811–1863)
Nothing like blood, sir, in hosses, dawgs, and men.

[*Vanity Fair* (1848)]

WELLINGTON, Duke of (1769–1852)
I believe I forgot to tell you I was made a Duke.

[Postscript to a letter to his nephew, 1814]

WOOLF, Virginia (1882–1941)
Those comfortable padded lunatic asylums which are known, euphemistically, as the stately homes of England.

[*The Common Reader* (1925)]

See Class

THE ARMY

ANONYMOUS
Any officer who shall behave in a scandalous manner, unbecoming the character of an officer and a gentleman shall . . . be CASHIERED.

[Articles of War]

BAXTER, James K. (1926–1972)
The boy who volunteered at seventeen
At twenty-three is heavy on the booze.

['Returned Soldier' (1946)]

BRODSKY, Joseph (1940–1996)
It is the army that finally makes a citizen of you; without it, you still have a chance, however slim, to remain a human being.

['Less Than One' (1986)]

CHURCHILL, Sir Winston (1874–1965)
You may take the most gallant sailor, the most intrepid

airman, or the most audacious soldier, put them at a table together – what do you get? The sum of their fears.

[In Macmillan, *The Blast of War*]

FREDERICK THE GREAT (1712–1786)
An army, like a serpent, goes on its belly.

[Attr.]

GERRISH, Theodore
The ties that bound us together were of the most sacred nature: they had been gotten in hardship and baptised in blood.

[*Army Life* (1812)]

GREEN, Michael (1927–)
Fortunately, the army has had much practice in ignoring impossible instructions.

[*The Boy Who Shot Down an Airship* (1988)]

HELLER, Joseph (1923–)
I had examined myself pretty thoroughly and discovered that I was unfit for military service.

[*Catch-22* (1961)]

HOFFMANN, Max (1869–1927)
[Of the British army in World War I]
Ludendorff: The English soldiers fight like lions.

Hoffmann: True. But don't we know that they are lions led by donkeys.

[In Falkenhayn, *Memoirs*]

HULL, General Sir Richard (1907–)
National Service did the country a lot of good but it darned near killed the army.

[Attr.]

KISSINGER, Henry (1923–)
The conventional army loses if it does not win. The guerrilla wins if it does not lose.

[*Foreign Affairs*, XIII (1969)]

MANNING, Frederic (1882–1935)
[Of the men in his battalion]
These apparently rude and brutal natures comforted, encouraged, and reconciled each other to fate, with a tenderness and tact which was more moving than anything in life.

[*Her Privates We* (1929)]

MILLIGAN, Spike (1918–)
The Army works like this: if a man dies when you hang him, keep hanging him until he gets used to it.

[Attr.]

MORAN, Lord (1924–)
A man of character in peace is a man of courage in war.

[*The Anatomy of Courage* (1945)]

NAPOLEON III (1808–1873)
The army is the true nobility of our country.
[*Speech*, March 1855]

PATTON, General George S. (1885–1945)
Untutored courage is useless in the face of educated bullets.
[*Cavalry Journal*, 1922]

QUARLES, Francis (1592–1644)
Our God and soldiers we alike adore
E'vn at the brink of danger; not before:
After deliverance, both alike requited,
Our God's forgotten, and our soldiers slighted.
['Of Common Devotion' (1632)]

SASSOON, Siegfried (1886–1967)
Soldiers are citizens of death's gray land.
['Dreamers' 1917]

SELLAR, Walter (1898–1951) and YEATMAN, Robert (1897–1968)
Napoleon's armies always used to march on their stomachs, shouting: 'Vive l'Interieur!' and so moved about very slowly.
[*1066 And All That* (1930)]

SHAKESPEARE, William (1564–1616)
That in the captain's but a choleric word
Which in the soldier is flat blasphemy.
[*Measure for Measure*, II.ii]

SHAW, George Bernard (1856–1950)
You can always tell an old soldier by the inside of his holsters and cartridge boxes. The young ones carry pistols and cartridges: the old ones, grub.
[*Arms and the Man* (1898)]

TRUMAN, Harry S. (1884–1972)
[Of General MacArthur] I didn't fire him because he was a dumb son of a bitch, although he was, but that's not against the law for generals. If it was, half to three-quarters of them would be in gaol.
[In Miller, *Plain Speaking* (1974)]

TUCHMAN, Barbara W. (1912–1989)
Dead battles, like dead generals, hold the military mind in their dead grip.
[*August 1914* (1962)]

TUCHOLSKY, Kurt (1890–1935)
The French soldier is a civilian

in disguise, the German civilian is a soldier in disguise.
['Ocean of Pain' (1973)]

USTINOV, Sir Peter (1921–)
As for being a General, well, at the age of four with paper hats and wooden swords we're all Generals. Only some of us never grow out of it.
[*Romanoff and Juliet* (1956)]

WELLINGTON, Duke of (1769–1852)
I don't know what effect these men will have upon the enemy, but, by God, they frighten me.
[Attr.]

WILDE, Lady Jane (1826–1896)
There's a proud array of soldiers –
what do they round your door?
They guard our master's granaries
from the thin hands of the poor.
['The Famine Years']

See NAVY; WAR

ART

ANOUILH, Jean (1910–1987)
Life is very nice, but it has no shape. It is the purpose of art to give it shape.
[*The Rehearsal* (1950)]

BELLOW, Saul (1915–)
I feel that art has someting to do with achievement of stillness in the midst of chaos. A stillness which characterizes prayer, too, and the eye of the storm. I think that art has something to do with an arrest of attention in the midst of distraction.
[In Plimpton (ed.), *Writers at Work* (1967)]

BRACK, (Cecil) John (1920–)
I know all about art, but I don't know what I like.
[*The Dictionary of Australian Quotations*]

BRAQUE, Georges (1882–1963)
Art is meant to disturb, science reassures.
[*Day and Night, Notebooks* (1952)]

BRODSKY, Joseph (1940–1996)
Art is not a better, but an alternative existence; it is not an attempt to escape reality but the opposite, an attempt to animate it. It is a spirit seeking flesh but finding words.
[*Less Than One* (1986)]

**CHEKHOV, Anton
(1860–1904)**
The artist may not be a judge
of his characters, only a dis-
passionate witness.

[Attr.]

**CHESTERTON, G.K.
(1874–1936)**
The artistic temperament is a
disease that afflicts amateurs.

[*Heretics* (1905)]

**CONNOLLY, Cyril
(1903–1974)**
There is no more sombre
enemy of good art than the
pram in the hall.

[*Enemies of Promise* (1938)]

**CONSTANT, Benjamin
(1767–1834)**
Art for art's sake, without a
purpose; every purpose dis-
torts the true nature of art.
But art achieves a purpose
which it does not have.

[*Journal intime*, 1804]

**DEBUSSY, Claude
(1862–1918)**
Art is the most beautiful of all
lies.

[*Monsieur Croche,
antidilettante*]

**DEGAS, Edgar
(1834–1917)**
Art is vice. You don't marry it
legitimately, you rape it.

[In Paul Lafond, *Degas* (1918)]

ELIOT, T.S. (1888–1965)
No poet, no artist of any sort,
has his complete meaning
alone. His significance, his
appreciation is the appreciation of his relation to the
dead poets and artists.

['Tradition and the Individual
Talent' (1919)]

No artist produces great art
by a deliberate attempt to
express his own personality.

['Four Elizabethan
Dramatists' (1924)]

**EMERSON, Ralph Waldo
(1803–1882)**
Art is a jealous mistress, and,
if a man have a genius for
painting, poetry, music, architecture, or philosophy, he
makes a bad husband and an
ill provider.

[*Conduct of Life* (1860)]

**FLAUBERT, Gustave
(1821–1880)**
The artist must be in his work
as God is in creation, invisible
and all-powerful; his presence should be felt everywhere, but he should never
be seen.

[Letter, 1857]

FORSTER, E.M. (1879–1979)
Works of art, in my opinion,
are the only objects in the

material universe to possess internal order, and that is why, though I don't believe that only art matters, I do believe in Art for Art's sake.

[*Two Cheers for Democracy* (1951)]

FRY, Roger (1866–1934)
Art is significant deformity.

[In Virginia Woolf, *Roger Fry* (1940)]

GOETHE (1749–1832)
Classicism I call health, and romanticism disease.

[*Gespräche mit Eckermann*, 1829]

HEPWORTH, Dame Barbara (1903–1975)
I rarely draw what I see. I draw what I feel in my body.

[Attr.]

HERBERT, Sir A.P. (1890–1971)
As my poor father used to say
In 1863,
Once people start on all this Art
Good-bye, moralitee!
And what my father used to say
is good enough for me.

['Lines for a Worthy Person' (1930)]

HIRST, Damien (1965–)
[On winning the Turner Prize]

It's amazing what you can do with an E in A-level art, twisted imagination and a chain-saw.

[*The Observer Review*, 1995]

HOCKNEY, David (1937–)
It is very good advice to believe only what an artist does, rather than what he says he does.

[*David Hockney* (1976)]

HUXLEY, Aldous (1894–1963)
In the upper and the lower churches of St Francis, Giotto and Cimabue showed that art had once worshipped something other than itself.

[*Those Barren Leaves* (1925)]

INGRES, J.A.D. (1780–1867)
Drawing is the true test of art.

[*Pensées d'Ingres* (1922)]

KEATS, John (1795–1921)
The excellence of every art is its intensity, capable of making all disagreeables evaporate, from their being in close relationship with Beauty and Truth.

[Letter, 1817]

KLEE, Paul (1879–1940)
Art does not reproduce what is visible; it makes things visible.

['Creative Credo' (1920)]

KRAUS, Karl (1874–1936)
The only person who is an artist is the one that can make a puzzle out of the solution.

[*By Night* (1919)]

LOW, Sir David (1891–1963)
I do not know whether he draws a line himself. But I assume that his is the direction . . . It makes Disney the most significant figure in graphic art since Leonardo.

[In R. Schickel, *Walt Disney*]

MARON, Monika (1941–)
The artist as a citizen can be a democrat, just as well and as badly as everybody else. The artist as an artist may not be a democrat.

[Interview in *Der Spiegel*, 1994]

MAYAKOVSKY, Vladimir (1893–1930)
Art is not a mirror to reflect the world, but a hammer with which to shape it.

[*The Guardian*, 1974]

MOORE, George (1852–1933)
Art must be parochial in the beginning to be cosmopolitan in the end.

[*Hail and Farewell: Ave* (1911)]

MOSES, Grandma (1860–1961)
[Of painting]
I don't advise any one to take it up as a business proposition, unless they really have talent, and are crippled so as to deprive them of physical labor.

[Attr.]

NOLAN, Sir Sidney Robert (1917–)
A successful artist would have no trouble being a successful member of the Mafia.

[*Good Weekend*, 1985]

PATER, Walter (1839–1894)
All art constantly aspires towards the condition of music.

[*Studies in the History of the Renaissance* (1873)]

PICASSO, Pablo (1881–1973)
[Remark made at an exhibition of children's drawings]
When I was their age, I could draw like Raphael, but it took me a lifetime to learn to draw like them.

[In Penrose, *Picasso: His Life and Work* (1958)]

RENOIR, Pierre-Auguste (1841–1919)
[On why he still painted although he had arthritis of his hands]
The pain passes, but the beauty remains.

[Attr.]

RUSKIN, John (1819–1900)
Fine art is that in which the hand, the head, and the heart of man go together.
[*The Two Paths* (1859)]

[Of one of Whistler's works] I have seen, and heard, much of Cockney impudence before now; but never expected to hear a coxcomb ask two hundred guineas for flinging a pot of paint in the public's face.
[*Fors Clavigera*, 1877]

SAND, George (1804–1876)
Art is not a study of positive reality; it is a search for ideal truth.
[*The Devil's Pond* (1846)]

SARGENT, John Singer (1856–1925)
Every time I paint a portrait I lose a friend.
[In Bentley and Esar, *Treasury of Humorous Quotations* (1951)]

SHAHN, Ben (1898–1969)
[Outlining the difference between professional and amateur painters]
An amateur is an artist who supports himself with outside jobs which enable him to paint. A professional is someone whose wife works to enable him to paint.
[Attr.]

SONTAG, Susan (1933–)
A photograph is not only an image (as a painting is an image), an interpretation of the real; it is also a trace, something directly stencilled off the real, like a footprint or a death mask.
[*New York Review of Books*, 1977]

SPALDING, Julian (1948–)
The professional art world is becoming a conspiracy against the public.
[*The Daily Mail*, 1996]

STOPPARD, Tom (1937–)
Skill without imagination is craftsmanship and gives us many useful objects such as wickerwork picnic baskets. Imagination without skill gives us modern art.
[*Artist Descending a Staircase* (1973)]

What is an artist? For every thousand people there's nine hundred doing the work, ninety doing well, nine doing good and one lucky bastard who's the artist
[*Travesties* (1975)]

TOLSTOY, Leo (1828–1910)
Art is a human activity which has as its purpose the transmission to others of the highest and best feelings to which

men have risen.
[*What is Art?* (1898)]

**USTINOV, Sir Peter
(1921–)**
If Botticelli were alive today
he'd be working for Vogue.
[*The Observer*, 1962]

VIDAL, Gore (1925–)
He will lie even when it is
inconvenient, the sign of the
true artist.
[*Two Sisters* (1970)]

**WHARTON, Edith
(1862–1937)**
Another unsettling element in
modern art is that common
symptom of immaturity, the
dread of doing what has been
done before.
[*The Writing of Fiction* (1925)]

**WHISTLER, James McNeill
(1834–1903)**
[Replying to the question 'For
two days labour, you ask two
hundred guineas?']
No, I ask it for the knowledge
of a lifetime.
[In Sietz, *Whistler Stories* (1913)]

**WHITEHEAD, A.N.
(1861–1947)**
Art is the imposing of a pattern on experience, and our
aesthetic enjoyment is recognition of the pattern.
[*Dialogues* (1954)]

WILDE, Oscar (1854–1900)
All art is quite useless.
[*The Picture of Dorian Gray*
(1891)]

WYLLIE, George (1921–)
Public art is art that the public
can't avoid.
[Attr.]

ATHEISM

BACON, Francis (1561–1626)
I had rather believe all the
fables in the legend, and the
Talmud, and the Alcoran,
than that this universal frame
is without a mind.
['Of Atheism' (1625)]

God never wrought miracle to
convince atheism, because
his ordinary works convince it.
['Of Atheism' (1625)]

BUCHAN, John (1875–1940)
An atheist is a man who has
no invisible means of support.
[Attr.]

BUÑUEL, Luis (1900–1983)
I am still an atheist, thank God.
[Attr.]

BURKE, Edmund (1729–1797)
Man is by his constitution a
religious animal . . . atheism
is against, not only our rea-

son, but our instincts.
[*Reflections on the Revolution in France . . .* (1790)]

DIDEROT, Denis (1713–1784)
See this egg. It is with this that one overturns all the schools of theology and all the temples on earth.
[*Le Rêve de d'Alembert* (1769)]

ORWELL, George (1903–1950)
He was an embittered atheist (the sort of atheist who does not so much disbelieve in God as personally dislike Him).
[*Down and Out in Paris and London* (1933)]

OTWAY, Thomas (1652–1685)
These are rogues that pretend to be of a religion now! Well, all I say is, honest atheism for my money.
[*The Atheist* (1683)]

ROSSETTI, Dante Gabriel (1828–1882)
The worst moment for the atheist is when he is really thankful and has nobody to thank.
[Attr.]

SARTRE, Jean-Paul (1905–1980)
She didn't believe in anything; only her scepticism kept her from being an atheist.
[*Words* (1964)]

TURGENEV, Ivan (1818–1883)
The courage to believe in nothing.
[*Fathers and Sons* (1862)]

YOUNG, Edward (1683–1765)
By Night an Atheist half believes a God.
[*Night-Thoughts on Life, Death and Immortality*]

BEAUTY

BLAKE, William (1757–1827)
Exuberance is Beauty.
['Proverbs of Hell' (1793)]

BUCK, Pearl S. (1892–1973)
It is better to be first with an ugly woman than the hundredth with a beauty.
[*The Good Earth* (1931)]

BYRON, Lord (1788–1824)
She walks in beauty, like the night
Of cloudless climes and starry skies;
And all that's best of dark and bright
Meet in her aspect and her eyes.
['She Walks in Beauty' (1815)]

CONFUCIUS (c. 550–c. 478 BC)
Everything has its beauty but not everyone sees it.
[*Analects*]

CONSTABLE, John (1776–1837)
There is nothing ugly; *I never saw an ugly thing in my life*: for let the form of an object be what it may, – light, shade, and perspective will always make it beautiful.
[In C.R. Leslie, *Memoirs of the Life of John Constable* (1843)]

ELLIS, Havelock (1859–1939)
The absence of flaw in beauty is itself a flaw.
[*Impressions and Comments* (1914)]

EMERSON, Ralph Waldo (1803–1882)
Though we travel the world over to find the beautiful we must carry it with us or we find it not.
[*Essays, First Series* (1841)]

GALSWORTHY, John (1867–1933)
He was afflicted by the thought that where Beauty was, nothing ever ran quite straight, which, no doubt, was why so many people looked on it as immoral.
[*In Chancery* (1920)]

HUGO, Victor (1802–1885)
Beauty is as useful as usefulness. Maybe more so.
[*Les Misérables* (1862)]

HUME, David (1711–1776)
Beauty is no quality in things themselves: It exists merely in the mind which contemplates them; and each mind perceives a different beauty.
[*Essays, Moral, Political, and Literary* (1742)]

KEATS, John (1795–1821)
A thing of beauty is a joy for
ever:
Its loveliness increases; it will
never
Pass into nothingness; but
still will keep
A bower quiet for us, and a
sleep
Full of sweet dreams, and
health, and quiet breathing.
['Endymion' (1818)]

**PHILIPS, Ambrose
(c. 1675–1749)**
The flowers anew, returning
seasons bring!
But beauty faded has no
second spring.
[*The First Pastoral* (1710)]

PICASSO, Pablo (1881–1973)
What *is* beauty, anyway?
There's no such thing.
[In Gilot and Lake, *Life with
Picasso* (1964)]

RUSKIN, John (1819–1900)
Remember that the most
beautiful things in the world
are the most useless; peacocks
and lilies for instance.
[*The Stones of Venice* (1851)]

SAKI (1870–1916)
I always say beauty is only
sin deep.
['Reginald's Choir Treat'
(1904)]

**SAPPHO
(fl. 7th–6th centuries BC)**
Beauty endures for only as
long as it can be seen; goodness, beautiful today, will
remain so tomorrow.
[In Naim Attallah, *Women*
(1987)]

TOLSTOY, Leo (1828–1910)
It is amazing how complete is
the delusion that beauty is
goodness.
[*The Kreutzer Sonata* (1890)]

**WOLLSTONECRAFT, Mary
(1759–1797)**
Taught from their infancy that
beauty is woman's sceptre,
the mind shapes itself to the
body, and roaming round its
gilt cage, only seeks to adorn
its prison.
[*A Vindication of the Rights of
Woman* (1792)]

See ART

BELIEF

**AMIEL, Henri-Frédéric
(1821–1881)**
A belief is not true because it
is useful.
[*Journal*, 1876]

BAGEHOT, Walter (1826–1877)
So long as there are earnest

believers in the world, they will always wish to punish opinions, even if their judgement tells them it is unwise, and their conscience that it is wrong.

[*Literary Studies* (1879)]

THE BIBLE (KING JAMES VERSION)
Lord, I believe; help thou mine unbelief.

[*Mark*, 9:24]

Faith is the substance of things hoped for, the evidence of things not seen.

[*Hebrews*, 11:1]

Faith without works is dead.

[*James*, 2:20]

BUCK, Pearl S. (1892–1973)
I feel no need for any other faith than my faith in human beings.

[*I Believe* (1939)]

CAESAR, Gaius Julius (c. 102–44 BC)
Men generally believe what they wish.

[*De Bello Gallico*]

CARROLL, Lewis (1832–1898)
'There's no use trying,' she said: 'one *can't* believe impossible things.' 'I dare say you haven't had much practice,' said the Queen. 'When I was your age, I always did it for half an hour a day. Why, sometimes I've believed as many as six impossible things before breakfast.'

[*Through the Looking-Glass* (1872)]

CHESTERTON, G.K. (1874–1936)
Reason is itself a matter of faith. It is an act of faith to assert that our thoughts have any relation to reality at all.

[*Orthodoxy* (1908)]

FRANK, Anne (1929–1945)
In spite of everything I still believe that people are good at heart.

[*The Diary of Anne Frank* (1947)]

JENKINS, David (1925–)
As I get older I seem to believe less and less and yet to believe what I do believe more and more.

[*The Observer*, 1988]

JOWETT, Benjamin (1817–1893)
My dear child, you must believe in God in spite of what the clergy tell you.

[In M. Asquith, *Autobiography* (1922)]

**KANT, Immanuel
(1724–1804)**
There is only one (true)
religion; but there can be
many different kinds of belief.
[*Religion within the Boundaries
of Mere Reason* (1793)]

**MENCKEN, H.L.
(1880–1956)**
Faith may be defined briefly
as an illogical belief in the
occurrence of the improbable.
[*Prejudices* (1927)]

**NEWMAN, Cardinal
(1801–1890)**
It is as absurd to argue men,
as to torture them, into
believing.

[Sermon, 1831]

*We can believe what we
choose.* We are answerable
for what we choose to
believe.

[Letter to Mrs Froude, 1848]

**RUSSELL, Bertrand
(1872–1970)**
Every man, wherever he
goes, is encompassed by a
cloud of comforting convic-
tions, which move with him
like flies on a summer day.

[*Sceptical Essays* (1928)]

[On being asked if he would
be willing to die for his
beliefs]

Of course not. After all, I may
be wrong.

[Attr.]

**UNAMUNO, Miguel de
(1864–1936)**
To believe in God is to yearn
for his existence and, moreover, it is to behave as if he
did exist.

[*The Tragic Sense of Life*
(1913)]

BENEFACTORS

BAGEHOT, Walter (1826–1877)
The most melancholy of
human reflections, perhaps, is
that, on the whole, it is a
question whether the benevo-
lence of mankind does most
good or harm.

[*Physics and Politics* (1872)]

**COMPTON-BURNETT, Dame
Ivy (1884–1969)**
At any time you might act for
my good. When people do
that, it kills something
precious between them.

[*Manservant and Maidservant*
(1947)]

**CREIGHTON, Mandell
(1843–1901)**
No people do so much harm
as those who go about doing

good.
> [*The Life and Letters of
> Mandell Creighton* (1904)]

GILBERT, W.S. (1836–1911)
I love my fellow creatures – I
do all the good I can –
Yet everybody says I'm such a
disagreeable man!
> [*Princess Ida* (1884)]

GOLDSMITH, Oliver (c. 1728–1774)
And learn the luxury of doing
good.
> ['The Traveller' (1764)]

MACHIAVELLI (1469–1527)
It is the nature of men to be
bound by the benefits they
confer as much as by those
they receive.
> [*The Prince* (1532)]

TITUS VESPASIANUS (39–81)
Recalling once after dinner
that he had done nothing to
help anyone all that day, he
gave voice to that memorable
and praiseworthy remark:
'Friends, I have lost a day.'
> [In Suetonius, *Lives of the
> Caesars*]

WORDSWORTH, William (1770–1850)
On that best portion of a
good man's life;
His little, nameless, unre-

membered acts
Of kindness and of love.
> ['Tintern Abbey' (1798)]

See GOODNESS

BIOGRAPHY

AMIS, Martin (1949–)
[Of biography]
To be more interested in the
writer than the writing is just
eternal human vulgarity.
> [*The Observer Review,* 1996]

ARBUTHNOT, John (1667–1735)
[Of biography]
One of the new terrors of
death.
> [In Carruthers, *Life of Pope*
> (1857)]

CARLYLE, Thomas (1795–1881)
A well-written Life is almost
as rare as a well-spent one.
> [*Essays* (1839)]

DAVIES, Robertson (1913–1995)
Biography at its best is a form
of fiction.
> [*The Lyre of Orpheus* (1988)]

DISRAELI, Benjamin (1804–1881)
Read no history: nothing but

biography, for that is life without theory.

[*Contarini Fleming* (1832)]

FRYE, Northrop (1912–1991)
There's only one story, the story of your life.
[In Ayre, *Northrop Frye* (1989)]

GRANT, Cary (1904–1986)
Nobody is ever truthful about his own life. There are always ambiguities.
[*The Observer*, 1981]

GUEDALLA, Philip (1889–1944)
Biography, like big-game hunting, is one of the recognized forms of sport, and it is as unfair as only sport can be.
[*Supers and Supermen* (1920)]

LEE, Robert E. (1807–1870)
[Refusing to write his memoirs]
I should be trading on the blood of my men.
[In M. Ringo, *Nobody Said It Better*]

SALINGER, J.D. (1919–)
If you really want to hear about it, the first thing you'll probably want to know is where I was born and what my lousy childhood was like, and how my parents were occupied and all before they had me, and all that David Copperfield kind of crap.
[*The Catcher in the Rye* (1951)]

TROLLOPE, Anthony (1815–1882)
In these days a man is nobody unless his biography is kept so far posted up that it may be ready for the national breakfast-table on the morning after his demise.
[*Doctor Thorne* (1858)]

WILDE, Oscar (1854–1900)
Every great man has his disciples, but it is always Judas who writes the biography.
[Attr.]

BOOKS

AUDEN, W.H. (1907–1973)
Some books are undeservedly forgotten; none are undeservedly remembered.
[*The Dyer's Hand* (1963)]

BACON, Francis (1561–1626)
Some books are to be tasted, others to be swallowed, and some few to be chewed and digested; that is, some books are to be read only in parts; others to be read but not curiously; and some few to be read wholly, and with diligence and attention.
['Of Studies' (1625)]

BELLOC, Hilaire (1870–1953)
When I am dead, I hope it

may be said:
'His sins were scarlet, but his books were read.'

[*Sonnets and Verse* (1923)]

BURGESS, Anthony (1917–1993)

The possession of a book becomes a substitute for reading it.

[*The New York Times Book Review*]

BYRON, Lord (1788–1824)

'Tis pleasant, sure, to see one's name in print;
A Book's a Book, altho' there is nothing in't.

[*English Bards and Scotch Reviewers* (1809)]

CHANDLER, Raymond (1888–1959)

If my books had been any worse I should not have been invited to Hollywood, and . . . if they had been any better, I should not have come.

[Letter to C.W. Morton, 1945]

DAVIES, Robertson (1913–1995)

A truly great book should be read in youth, again in maturity, and once more in old age, as a fine building should be seen by morning light, at noon, and by moonlight.

[In Grant, *The Enthusiasms of Robertson Davies*]

DESCARTES, René (1596–1650)

The reading of all good books is like a conversation with the finest men of past centuries.

[*Discours de la Méthode* (1637)]

DIODORUS SICULUS (c. 1st century BC)

[Inscription over library door in Alexandria]
Medicine for the soul.

[*History*]

FORSTER, E.M. (1879–1970)

I suggest that the only books that influence us are those for which we are ready, and which have gone a little farther down our particular path than we have yet got ourselves.

[*Two Cheers for Democracy* (1951)]

FRYE, Northrop (1912–1991)

The book is the world's most patient medium.

[*The Scholar in Society*, film, 1984]

FULLER, Thomas (1608–1661)

Learning hath gained most by those books by which the printers have lost.

[*The Holy State and the Profane State* (1642)]

**GOLDSMITH, Oliver
(c. 1728–1774)**
A book may be amusing with
numerous errors, or it may be
very dull without a single
absurdity.
[*The Vicar of Wakefield* (1766)]

HORACE (65–8 BC)
You can destroy what you
haven't published; the word
once out cannot be recalled.
[*Ars Poetica*]

**HUXLEY, Aldous
(1894–1963)**
The proper study of mankind
is books.
[*Crome Yellow* (1921)]

JAMES, Brian (1892–1972)
The book of my enemy has
been remaindered
And I am pleased.
['The Book of My Enemy Has
Been Remaindered']

KAFKA, Franz (1883–1924)
I think you should only read
those books which bite and
sting you.
[Letter to Oskar Pollak, 1904]

. . . a book must be the axe
for the frozen sea within us.
[Letter to Oskar Pollak, 1904]

KORAN
Every age hath its book.
[Chapter 13]

**LA BRUYERE, Jean de
(1645–1696)**
The making of a book, like
the making of a clock, is a
craft; it takes more than wit
to be an author.
[*Les caractères ou les moeurs
de ce siècle* (1688)]

LARKIN, Philip (1922–1985)
Get stewed:
Books are a load of crap.
['A Study of Reading Habits'
(1964)]

**LICHTENBERG, Georg
(1742–1799)**
There can hardly be a
stranger commodity in the
world than books. Printed by
people who don't understand
them; sold by people who
don't understand them;
bound, criticized and read by
people who don't understand
them, and now even written
by people who don't understand them.
[*A Doctrine of Scattered
Occasions*]

**MACAULAY, Dame Rose
(1881–1958)**
It was a book to kill time for
those who like it better dead.
[Attr.]

**MAUGHAM, William
Somerset (1874–1965)**
There is an impression
abroad that everyone had it in

him to write one book; but if by this is implied a good book the impression is false.

[*The Summing Up* (1938)]

SAMUEL, Lord (1870–1963)
A library is thought in cold storage.

[*A Book of Quotations* (1947)]

SMITH, Logan Pearsall (1865–1946)
A best-seller is the gilded tomb of a mediocre talent.

[*Afterthoughts* (1931)]

SMITH, Sydney (1771–1845)
No furniture so charming as books, even if you never open them, or read a single word.

[In Holland, *A Memoir of the Reverend Sydney Smith* (1855)]

STEVENSON, Robert Louis (1850–1894)
Books are good enough in their own way, but they are a mighty bloodless substitute for life.

[*Virginibus Puerisque* (1881)]

TUPPER, Martin (1810–1889)
A good book is the best of friends, the same today and for ever.

[*Proverbial Philosophy* (1838)]

WAUGH, Evelyn (1903–1966)
Particularly against books the Home Secretary is. If we can't stamp out literature in the country, we can at least stop it being brought in from outside.

[*Vile Bodies* (1930)]

WESLEY, John (1703–1791)
Beware you be not swallowed up in books! An ounce of love is worth a pound of knowledge.

[In Southey, *Life of Wesley* (1820)]

WILDE, Oscar (1854–1900)
There is no such thing as a moral or an immoral book. Books are well written, or badly written. That is all.

[*The Picture of Dorian Gray* (1891)]

WODEHOUSE, P.G. (1881–1975)
[Dedication]
To my daughter Leonora without whose never-failing sympathy and encouragement this book would have been finished in half the time.

[*The Heart of a Goof* (1926)]

See CENSORSHIP; FICTION; LITERATURE; READING; WRITERS; WRITING

BOREDOM

AUSTIN, Warren Robinson (1877–1962)
[On being asked if he found long debates at the UN tiring]
It is better for aged diplomats to be bored than for young men to die.

[Attr.]

BIERCE, Ambrose (1842–c. 1914)
Bore: A person who talks when you wish him to listen.

[*The Cynic's Word Book* (1906)]

BYRON, Lord (1788–1824)
Society is now one polish'd horde,
Form'd of two mighty tribes, the *Bores* and *Bored*.

[*Don Juan* (1824)]

CHESTERTON, G.K. (1874–1936)
There is no such thing on earth as an uninteresting subject; the only thing that can exist is an uninterested person.

[*Heretics* (1905)]

DE VRIES, Peter (1910–)
I wanted to be bored to death, as good a way to go as any.

[*Comfort me with Apples* (1956)]

FREUD, Clement (1924–)
If you resolve to give up smoking, drinking and loving, you don't actually live longer; it just seems longer.

[*The Observer*, 1964]

GAUTIER, Théophile (1811–1872)
Sooner barbarity than boredom.

[Attr.]

HOWELLS, W.D. (1837–1920)
Some people can stay longer in an hour than others can in a week.

[In Esar, *Treasury of Humorous Quotations* (1951)]

HUXLEY, Aldous (1894–1963)
I can sympathize with people's pains, but not with their pleasures. There is something curiously boring about somebody else's happiness.

[*Limbo* (1920)]

INGE, William Ralph (1860–1954)
The effect of boredom on a large scale in history is underestimated. It is a main cause of revolutions, and would soon bring to an end all the static Utopias and the farmyard civilization of the Fabians.

[*End of an Age* (1948)]

SHAKESPEARE, William (1564–1616)

Life is as tedious as a twice-told tale
Vexing the dull ear of a drowsy man.

[*King John*, III.iv]

TAYLOR, Bert Leston (1866–1921)

A bore is a man who, when you ask him how he is, tells you.

[*The So-Called Human Race* (1922)]

THOMAS, Dylan (1914–1953)

Dylan talked copiously, then stopped.
'Somebody's boring me,' he said, 'I think it's me.'

[In Heppenstall, *Four Absentees* (1960)]

UPDIKE, John (1932–)

A healthy male adult bore consumes one and a half times his own weight in other people's patience.

[*Assorted Prose* (1965)]

VOLTAIRE (1694–1778)

The secret of being boring is to say everything.

[*Discours en vers sur l'homme* (1737)]

ATTLEE, Clement (1883–1967)

I think the British have the distinction above all other nations of being able to put new wine into old bottles without bursting them.

[*Hansard*, 1950]

BULLOCK, Alan (1914–)

The people Hitler never understood, and whose actions continued to exasperate him to the end of his life, were the British.

[*Hitler, A Study in Tyranny* (1952)]

CAMP, William (1926–)

What annoys me about Britain is the rugged will to lose.

[Attr.]

CASSON, Sir Hugh (1910–)

The British love permanence more than they love beauty.

[*The Observer*, 1964]

EDMOND, James (1859–1933)

I had been told by Jimmy Edmond in Australia that there were only three things against living in Britain: the place, the climate and the people.

[In Low, *Low Autobiography*]

GAITSKELL, Hugh (1906–1963)
[On Britain's joining the European Community]
It does mean, if this is the idea, the end of Britain as an independent European state . . . it means the end of a thousand years of history.
[Speech, 1962]

HARLECH, Lord (1918–1985)
In the end it may well be that Britain will be honoured by historians more for the way she disposed of an empire than for the way in which she acquired it.
[*New York Times*, 1962]

LLOYD GEORGE, David (1863–1945)
What is our task? To make Britain a fit country for heroes to live in.
[Speech, 1918]

THOMSON, James (1700–1748)
Rule, Britannia, rule the waves;
Britons never will be slaves.
[*Alfred: A Masque* (1740)]

WAUGH, Evelyn (1903–1966)
Other nations use 'force'; we Britons alone use 'Might'.
[*Scoop* (1938)]

ACHESON, Dean (1893–1971)
A memorandum is written not to inform the reader but to protect the writer.
[Attr.]

ADENAUER, Konrad (1876–1967)
There's nothing which cannot be made a mess of again by officials.
[*Der Spiegel*, 1975]

ANONYMOUS
A committee is a cul-de-sac down which ideas are lured and then quietly strangled.
[*New Scientist*, 1973]

A camel is a horse designed by a committee.

FONDA, Jane (1937–)
You can run the office without a boss, but you can't run an office without the secretaries.
[*The Observer*, 1981]

GOWERS, Sir Ernest (1880–1966)
It is not easy nowadays to remember anything so contrary to all appearances as that officials are the servants of the public; and the official must try not to foster the il-

lusion that it is the other way round.

[*Plain Words*]

HUXLEY, Aldous (1894–1963)

Official dignity tends to increase in inverse ratio to the importance of the country in which the office is held.

[*Beyond the Mexique Bay* (1934)]

MCCARTHY, Mary (1912–1989)

Bureaucracy, the rule of no one, has become the modern form of despotism.

[*The New Yorker*, 1958]

SAMPSON, Anthony (1926–)

[Of the Civil service]
Members rise from CMG (known sometimes in Whitehall as 'Call Me God') to the KCMG ('Kindly Call Me God') to . . . the GCMG ('God Calls Me God').

[*The Anatomy of Britain* (1962)]

SAMUEL, Lord (1870–1963)

[Referring to the Civil Service]
A difficulty for every solution.

[Attr.]

SANTAYANA, George (1863–1952)

The working of great institutions is mainly the result of a vast mass of routine, petty malice, self interest, carelessness, and sheer mistake. Only a residual fraction is thought.

[*The Crime of Galileo*]

THOMAS, Gwyn (1913–1981)

My life's been a meeting, Dad, one long meeting. Even on the few committees I don't yet belong to, the agenda winks at me when I pass.

[*The Keep* (1961)]

TREE, Sir Herbert Beerbohm (1853–1917)

A committee should consist of three men, two of whom are absent.

[In Pearson, *Beerbohm Tree*]

BUSINESS

ANONYMOUS

A Company for carrying on an undertaking of Great Advantage, but no one to know what it is.

[The South Sea Company Prospectus]

AUSTEN, Jane (1775–1817)

Business, you know, may bring money, but friendship hardly ever does.

[*Emma* (1816)]

**BARNUM, Phineas T.
(1810–1891)**
Every crowd has a silver lining.
[Attr.]

**BETJEMAN, Sir John
(1906–1984)**
You ask me what it is I do.
Well actually, you know,
I'm partly a liaison man and
partly P.R.O.
Essentially I integrate the cur-
rent export drive
And basically I'm viable from
ten o'clock till five.
['Executive' (1974)]

**CHARLES, Prince of Wales
(1948–)**
British management doesn't
seem to understand the importance of the human factor.
[Speech, 1979]

**COHEN, Sir Jack
(1898–1979)**
Pile it high, sell it cheap.
[Business motto]

DENNIS, C.J. (1876–1938)
It takes one hen to lay an
egg,
But seven men to sell it.
['The Regimental Hen']

**FRANKLIN, Benjamin
(1706–1790)**
No nation was ever ruined by
trade.
[Essays]

GALBRAITH, J.K. (1908–)
The salary of the chief executive of the large corporation is
not a market award for
achievement. It is frequently
in the nature of a warm personal gesture by the individual to himself.
[Annals of an Abiding Liberal
(1980)]

**GOLDWYN, Samuel
(1882–1974)**
Chaplin is no business man –
all he knows is that he can't
take anything less.
[Attr.]

**LLOYD GEORGE, David
(1863–1945)**
Love your neighbour is not
merely sound Christianity; it
is good business.
[The Observer, 1921]

**MENCKEN, H.L.
(1880–1956)**
[Referring to the business-
man]
He is the only man who is
ever apologizing for his occupation.
[Prejudices (1927)]

**NAPOLEON I
(1769–1821)**
England is a nation of shop-
keepers.
[In O'Meara, Napoleon in Exile
(1822)]

**ONASSIS, Aristotle
(1906–1975)**
The secret of business is to
know something that nobody
else knows.
[*The Economist,* 1991]

PUZO, Mario (1920–)
He's a businessman. I'll make
him an offer he can't refuse.
[*The Godfather* (1969)]

**REVSON, Charles
(1906–1975)**
In the factory we make cos-
metics. In the store we sell
hope.
[In Tobias, *Fire and Ice* (1976)]

**SHEEN, J. Fulton
(1895–1979)**
[Referring to his contract for a
television appearance]
The big print giveth and the
fine print taketh away.
[Attr.]

SMITH, Adam (1723–1790)
People of the same trade seldom meet together, even for
merriment and diversion, but
the conversation ends in a
conspiracy against the public,
or in some contrivance to
raise prices.
[*Wealth of Nations* (1776)]

**THURLOW, Edward
(1731–1806)**
Did you ever expect a corporation to have a
conscience, when it has no
soul to be damned, and no
body to be kicked?
[Attr.]

**WILSON, Charles E.
(1890–1961)**
What is good for the country
is good for General Motors,
and vice versa.
[Remark to Congressional
Committee, 1953]

**See ECONOMICS; MONEY
AND WEALTH**

CAPITALISM

ANONYMOUS
Capitalism is the exploitation of man by man. Communism is the complete opposite.
[Described by Laurence J. Peter as a 'Polish proverb']

CONNOLLY, James (1868–1916)
Governments in a capitalist society are but committees of the rich to manage the affairs of the capitalist class.
[*Irish Worker*, 1914]

HAMPTON, Christopher (1946–)
If I had to give a definition of capitalism I would say: the process whereby American girls turn into American women.
[*Savages* (1973)]

HEATH, Sir Edward (1916–)
[On the Lonrho affair (involving tax avoidance)]
The unpleasant and unacceptable face of capitalism.
[Speech, House of Commons, 1973]

ILLICH, Ivan (1926–)
In a consumer society there are inevitably two kinds of slaves: the prisoners of addiction and the prisoners of envy.
[*Tools for Conviviality* (1973)]

KELLER, Helen (1880–1968)
Militarism . . . is one of the chief bulwarks of capitalism, and the day that militarism is undermined, capitalism will fail.
[*The Story of My Life* (1902)]

KEYNES, John Maynard (1883–1946)
I think that Capitalism, wisely managed, can probably be made more efficient for attaining economic ends than any alternative system yet in sight, but that in itself it is in many ways extremely objectionable.
['The End of Laissez-Faire' (1926)]

LENIN, V.I. (1870–1924)
Under capitalism we have a state in the proper sense of the word, that is, a special machine for the suppression of one class by another.
[*The State and Revolution* (1917)]

SAKI (1870–1916)
When she inveighed eloquently against the evils of capitalism at drawing-room meetings and Fabian conferences she was conscious of a comfortable feeling that the

system, with all its inequalities and iniquities, would probably last her time. It is one of the consolations of middle-aged reformers that the good they inculcate must live after them if it is to live at all.

[*Beasts and Super-Beasts* (1914)]

STRETTON, Hugh (1924–)
Is it really good for policy-makers to act as if everything has its price, and as if policies should be judged chiefly by their effects in delivering material benefits to selfish citizens? . . . It does not ask those individuals whether they also have other values which are not revealed by their shopping.

[*Capitalism, Socialism and the Environment* (1976)]

WAUGH, Evelyn (1903–1966)
Pappenhacker says that every time you are polite to a proletarian you are helping to bolster up the capitalist system.

[*Scoop* (1938)]

CATS

ARNOLD, Matthew (1822–1888)
Cruel, but composed and bland,
Dumb, inscrutable and grand,
So Tiberius might have sat,
Had Tiberius been a cat.

['Poor Matthias']

ELIOT, T.S. (1888–1965)
Macavity, Macavity, there's no one like Macavity,
There never was a Cat of such deceitfulness and suavity.
He always has an alibi, and one or two to spare:
At whatever time the deed took place - MACAVITY WASN'T THERE!

['Macavity: the Mystery Cat' (1939)]

MONTAIGNE, Michel de (1533–1592)
When I play with my cat, who knows whether she isn't amusing herself with me more than I am with her?

[*Essais* (1580)]

ROWBOTHAM, David (1924–)
Let some of the tranquillity of the cat
Curl into me.

['The Creature in the Chair']

SACKVILLE-WEST, Vita (1892–1962)
The greater cats with golden eyes
Stare out between the bars.

Deserts are there, and different skies,
And night with different stars.
[*The King's Daughter* (1929)]

SMART, Christopher (1722–1771)
[On his cat]
For he counteracts the powers of darkness by his electrical skin and glaring eyes.
For he counteracts the Devil, who is death, by brisking about the life.
[*Jubilate Agno*]

SMITH, Stevie (1902–1971)
Oh I am a cat that likes to Gallop about doing good.
['The Galloping Cat' (1972)]

TESSIMOND, A.S.J. (1902–1962)
Cats, no less liquid than their shadows,
Offer no angles to the wind.
They slip, diminished, neat, through loopholes
Less than themselves.
['Cats' (1934)]

CAUTION

ANONYMOUS
Whatever you do, do it warily, and take account of the end.
[*Gesta Romanorum*]

ARMSTRONG, Dr John (1709–1779)
Distrust yourself, and sleep before you fight.
'Tis not too late tomorrow to be brave.
[*The Art of Preserving Health* (1744)]

BELLOC, Hilaire (1870–1953)
And always keep a-hold of Nurse
For fear of finding something worse.
[*Cautionary Tales* (1907)]

DRYDEN, John (1631–1700)
But now the world's o'er stocked with prudent men.
[*The Medal* (1682)]

LINCOLN, Abraham (1809–1865)
When you have got an elephant by the hind leg, and he is trying to run away, it's best to let him run.
[Remark, 1865]

SHAW, George Bernard (1856–1950)
Self-denial is not a virtue: it is only the effect of prudence on rascality.
[*Man and Superman* (1903)]

CENSORSHIP

BOROVOY, A. Alan
It is usually better to permit a piece of trash than to suppress a work of art.
[*When Freedoms Collide* (1988)]

EMERSON, Ralph Waldo (1803–1882)
Every burned book enlightens the world.
[Attr.]

GRIFFITH-JONES, Mervyn (1909–1979)
[At the trial of *Lady Chatterley's Lover*]
Is it a book you would even wish your wife or your servants to read?
[*The Times*, 1960]

HEINE, Heinrich (1797–1856)
It is there, where they
Burn books, that eventually they burn people too.
[*Almansor: A Tragedy* (1821)]

PINTER, Harold (1930–)
[On the execution of Nigerian writer Ken Saro-Wiwa]
Murder is the most brutal form of censorship.
[*The Observer*, 1995]

RUSHDIE, Salman (1946–)
Means of artistic expression that require large quantities of finance and sophisticated technology – films, plays, records – become, by virtue of that dependence, easy to censor and to control. But what one writer can make in the solitude of one room is something no power can easily destroy.
[*Index on Censorship*, 1996]

CHANGE

ANONYMOUS
Tempora mutantur, et nos mutamur in illis.
Times change, and we change with them.
[In Harrison, *Description of Britain* (1577)]

BACON, Francis (1561–1626)
That all things are changed, and that nothing really perishes, and that the sum of matter remains exactly the same, is sufficiently certain.
[*Thoughts on the Nature of Things* (1604)]

BEAUVOIR, Simone de (1908–1986)
If you live long enough, you'll find that every victory turns into a defeat.
[*All Men are Mortal* (1955)]

**BRITTAIN, Vera
(1893–1970)
It is probably true to say that the largest scope for change still lies in men's attitude to women, and in women's attitude to themselves.

[*Lady into Woman* (1953)]

**CAMBRIDGE, Duke of
(1819–1904)
It is said I am against change. I am not against change. I am in favour of change in the right circumstances. And those circumstances are when it can no longer be resisted.

[Attr. by Paul Johnson in *The Spectator,* 1996]

**CHESTERTON, G.K.
(1874–1936)
All conservatism is based upon the idea that if you leave things alone you leave them as they are. But you do not. If you leave a thing alone you leave it to a torrent of change.

[*Orthodoxy* (1908)]

**CONFUCIUS
(c. 550–c. 478 BC)
They must often change who would be constant in happiness or wisdom.

[*Analects*]

**FALKLAND, Viscount
(c. 1610–1643)
When it is not necessary to change, it is necessary not to change.

[Speech, 1641]

**HERACLITUS
(c. 540–c. 480 BC)
You cannot step twice into the same river.

[In Plato, *Cratylus*]

**HOOKER, Richard
(c. 1554–1600)
Change is not made without inconvenience, even from worse to better.

[In Johnson, *Dictionary of the English Language* (1755)]

**IRVING, Washington
(1783–1859)
There is a certain relief in change, even though it be from bad to worse; as I have found in travelling in a stagecoach, that it is often a comfort to shift one's position and be bruised in a new place.

[*Tales of a Traveller* (1824)]

**KARR, Alphonse
(1808–1890)
Plus ça change, plus c'est la même chose.
The more things change the more they remain the same.

[*Les Guêpes* (1849)]

LUCRETIUS (c. 95–55 BC)
Some groups increase, others
diminish, and in a short space
the generations of living creatures are changed and like run-
ners pass on the torch of life.
[*De Rerum Natura*]

MCCARTNEY, Paul (1942–)
The issues are the same. We
wanted peace on earth, love,
and understanding between
everyone around the world.
We have learned that change
comes slowly.
[*The Observer*, 1987]

**SWIFT, Jonathan
(1667–1745)**
There is nothing in this world
constant, but inconstancy.
[*A Critical Essay upon the
Faculties of the Mind* (1709)]

**THOREAU, Henry
(1817–1862)**
Things do not change; we
change.
[*Walden* (1854)]

See TIME

CHARACTER

FRISCH, Max (1911–1991)
Every uniform corrupts one's
character.
[*Diary*, 1948]

GOETHE (1749–1832)
Talent is formed in quiet
retreat,
Character in the headlong
rush of life.
[*Torquato Tasso* (1790)]

**KARR, Alphonse
(1808–1890)**
Every man has three characters: that which he exhibits,
that which he has, and that
which he thinks he has.
[Attr.]

**LINCOLN, Abraham
(1809–1865)**
Character is like a tree and
reputation like its shadow.
The shadow is what we think
of it; the tree is the real thing.
[In Gross, *Lincoln's Own
Stories*]

MURRAY, Les A. (1938–)
In the defiance of fashion is
the beginning of character.
[*The Boy Who Stole the
Funeral* (1979)]

REAGAN, Ronald (1911–)
You can tell a lot about a fellow's character by the way he
eats jelly beans.
[*Daily Mail*, 1981]

**WILSON, Woodrow
(1856–1924)**
Character is a by-product; it
is produced in the great

manufacture of daily duty.
[*Speech*, 1915]

See REPUTATION

See REPUTATION

CHARITY

BACON, Francis (1561–1626)
In charity there is no excess.
['Of Goodness, and Goodness
of Nature' (1625)]

**BROWNE, Sir Thomas
(1605–1682)**
Charity begins at home, is the
voice of the world.
[*Religio Medici* (1643)]

**CARNEGIE, Andrew
(1835–1919)**
Of every thousand dollars
spent in so-called charity
today, it is probable that nine
hundred and fifty dollars is
unwisely spent.
['Wealth' (1889)]

**FULLER, Thomas
(1608–1661)**
He that feeds upon charity
has a cold dinner and no supper.
[Attr.]

**POPE, Alexander
(1688–1744)**
In Faith and Hope the world
will disagree,
But all Mankind's concern is
Charity.
[*Essay on Man* (1733)]

**ROUSSEAU, Jean-Jacques
(1712–1778)**
The feigned charity of the rich
man is for him no more than
another luxury; he feeds the
poor as he feeds dogs and
horses.
[Letter to M. Moulton]

**SHERIDAN, Richard Brinsley
(1751–1816)**
Rowley: I believe there is no
sentiment he has more faith
in than that 'charity begins at
home'.
Sir Oliver Surface: And his, I
presume, is of that domestic
sort which never stirs abroad
at all.
[*The School for Scandal*
(1777)]

VOLTAIRE (1694–1778)
The man who leaves money
to charity in his will is only
giving away what no longer
belongs to him.
[Letter, 1769]

CHARM

BARRIE, Sir J.M. (1860–1937)
[On charm]
It's a sort of bloom on a

woman. If you have it, you don't need to have anything else; and if you don't have it, it doesn't much matter what else you have.

[*What Every Woman Knows*
(1908)]

**BIERCE, Ambrose
(1842–c. 1914)**
Please: To lay the foundation for a superstructure of imposition.

[*The Enlarged Devil's
Dictionary* (1961)]

**CONNOLLY, Cyril
(1903–1974)**
All charming people have something to conceal, usually their total dependence on the appreciation of others.

[*Enemies of Promise* (1938)]

**FARQUHAR, George
(1678–1707)**
Charming women can true converts make,
We love the precepts for the teacher's sake.

[*The Constant Couple* (1699)]

**LERNER, Alan Jay
(1918–1986)**
Oozing charm from every pore,
He oiled his way around the floor.

[*My Fair Lady* (1956)]

**MACNALLY, Leonard
(1752–1820)**
On Richmond Hill there lives a lass,
More sweet than May day morn,
Whose charms all other maids surpass,
A rose without a thorn.

['The Lass of Richmond Hill'
(1789)]

CHILDREN

AMIS, Kingsley (1922–1995)
It was no wonder that people were so horrible when they started life as children.

[*One Fat Englishman* (1963)]

AUSTEN, Jane (1775–1817)
On every formal visit a child ought to be of the party, by way of provision for discourse.

[*Sense and Sensibility* (1811)]

**BACON, Francis
(1561–1626)**
Children sweeten labours, but they make misfortunes more bitter.

[*Essays* (1625)]

**BALDWIN, James
(1924–1987)**
Children have never been very good at listening to their

elders, but they have never failed to imitate them. They must, they have no other models.

[*Nobody Knows My Name* (1961)]

BOWEN, Elizabeth (1899–1973)
There is no end to the violations committed by children on children, quietly talking alone.

[*The House in Paris* (1935)]

CARROLL, Lewis (1832–1898)
I am fond of children (except boys).

[Letter to Kathleen Eschwege, 1879]

GEORGE V (1865–1936)
My father was frightened of his mother. I was frightened of my father, and I'm damned well going to make sure that my children are frightened of me.

[In R. Churchill, *Lord Derby – 'King of Lancashire'* (1959)]

GIBBON, Edward (1737–1794)
Few, perhaps, are the children who, after the expiration of some months or years, would sincerely rejoice in the resurrection of their parents.

[*Memoirs of My Life and Writings* (1796)]

HARWOOD, Gwen (1920–)
'It's so sweet
to hear their chatter, watch them grow and thrive,'
she says to his departing smile. Then, nursing the youngest child, sits staring at her feet.
To the wind she says, 'They have eaten me alive.'

[*Poems* (1968)]

INGE, William Ralph (1860-1954)
The proper time to influence the character of a child is about a hundred years before he is born

[*The Observer*, 1929]

JONSON, Ben (1572-1637)
Rest in soft peace, and, ask'd say here doth lye
Ben Jonson his best piece of poetrie.

['On My First Son' (1616)]

KNOX, Ronald (1888-1957)
[Definition of a baby]
A loud noise at one end and no sense of responsibility at the other.

[Attr.]

LAMB, Charles (1775-1834)
Riddle of destiny, who can show
What thy short visit meant, or

know
What thy errand here below?
['On an Infant Dying as soon
as Born']

MILLER, Alice
Society chooses to disregard
the mistreatment of children,
judging it to be altogether
normal because it is so commonplace.
[*Pictures of a Childhood*
(1986)]

**MITFORD, Nancy
(1904–1973)**
I love children – especially
when they cry, for then someone takes them away.
[Attr.]

**MONTAIGNE, Michel de
(1533–1592)**
It should be noted that children at play are not merely
playing; their games should
be seen as their most serious
actions.
[*Essais* (1580)]

NASH, Ogden (1902–1971)
Children aren't happy with
nothing to ignore,
And that's what parents were
created for.
['The Parent' (1933)]

PAVESE, Cesare (1908–1950)
One stops being a child when
one realizes that telling one's

trouble does not make it
better.
[*The Business of Living: Diaries
1935–50*]

PLATH, Sylvia (1932–1963)
[On seeing her newborn baby]
What did my fingers do
before they held him?
What did my heart do, with
its love?
I have never seen a thing so
clear.
His lids are like the lilac
flower
And soft as a moth, his
breath.
I shall not let go.
There is no guile or warp in
him. May he keep so.
['Three Women: A Poem for
Three Voices' (1962)]

**SMITH, Sir Sydney
(1883–1969)**
No child is born a criminal:
no child is born an angel: he's
just born.
[Remark]

VIDAL, Gore (1925–)
Never have children, only
grandchildren.
[*Two Sisters* (1970)]

**WILDE, Oscar
(1854–1900)**
Children begin by loving their
parents. After a time they
judge them. Rarely, if ever, do

they forgive them.
[*A Woman of No Importance*
(1893)]

See PARENTS

CHRISTIANITY

BARTON, Bruce (1886–1967)
[Jesus] picked up twelve men
from the bottom ranks of
business and forged them
into an organization that conquered the world.
[*The Man Nobody Knows: A
Discovery of the Real Jesus*
(1924)]

BRECHT, Bertolt (1898–1956)
In those days [our Lord] could
demand that men love their
neighbour, because they'd
had enough to eat. Nowadays
it's different.
[*Mother Courage and her
Children* (1941)]

BUTLER, Samuel (1835–1902)
They would have been equal-
ly horrified at hearing the
Christian religion doubted,
and at seeing it practised.
[*The Way of All Flesh* (1903)]

**CARLYLE, Thomas
(1795–1881)**
If Jesus Christ were to come
to-day, people would not
even crucify him. They would

ask him to dinner, and hear
what he had to say, and make
fun of it.
[In Wilson, *Carlyle at his
Zenith* (1927)]

**CHESTERTON, G.K.
(1874–1936)**
The Christian ideal has not
been tried and found wanting. It has been found
difficult; and left untried.
[*What's Wrong with the World*
(1910)]

**DE BLANK, Joost
(1908–1968)**
[Of South Africa]
Christ in this country would
quite likely have been arrest-
ed under the Suppression of
Communism Act.
[*The Observer,* 1963]

**DISRAELI, Benjamin
(1804–1881)**
A Protestant, if he wants aid
or advice on any matter, can
only go to his solicitor.
[*Lothair* (1870)]

ELLIS, Bob (1942–)
Show me a Wednesday
wencher and a Sunday saint,
and I'll show you a Roman
Catholic.
[*The Legend of King O'Malley*
(1974)]

**FRANCE, Anatole
(1844–1924)**
Christianity has done a great
deal for love by making a sin
of it.

[*Le Jardin d'Epicure* (1894)]

**HALE, Sir Matthew
(1609–1676)**
Christianity is part of the laws
of England.
[In Blackstone, *Commentaries
on the Laws of England*
(1769)]

LENNON, John (1940–1980)
We're more popular than
Jesus Christ now. I don't
know which will go first.
Rock and roll or Christianity.
[*The Beatles Illustrated Lyrics*]

**LUTHER, Martin
(1483–1546)**
Be a sinner and sin strongly,
but believe and rejoice in
Christ even more strongly.
[Letter to Melanchton]

MENCKEN, H.L. (1880–1956)
Puritanism – The haunting
fear that someone, some-
where, may be happy.
[*A Mencken Chrestomathy*
(1949)]

**MONTESQUIEU, Charles
(1689–1755)**
No kingdom has ever had as
many civil wars as the kingdom of Christ.

[*Lettres persanes* (1721)]

**NIETZSCHE, Friedrich
(1844–1900)**
The Christian decision to find
the world ugly and bad has
made the world ugly and bad.
[*The Gay Science*]

PENN, William (1644–1718)
No pain, no palm; no thorns,
no throne; no gall, no glory;
no cross, no crown.
[*No Cross, No Crown* (1669)]

**RUSSELL, Bertrand
(1872–1970)**
There's a Bible on that shelf
there. But I keep it next to
Voltaire – poison and anti-
dote.
[In Harris, *Kenneth Harris
Talking To:* (1971)]

**SANTAYANA, George
(1863–1952)**
The Bible is literature, not
dogma.
[Introduction to Spinoza's
Ethics]

**TEMPLE, William
(1881–1944)**
Christianity is the most ma-
terialistic of all great religions.
[*Readings in St John's Gospel*
(1939)]

TUTU, Archbishop (1931–)
For the Church in any country to retreat from politics is nothing short of heresy. Christianity is political or it is not Christianity.

[*The Observer*, 1994]

TWAIN, Mark (1835–1910)
Most people are bothered by those passages in Scripture which they cannot understand; but as for me, I always noticed that the passages in Scripture which trouble me most are those that I do understand.

[In Simcox, *Treasury of Christian Quotations on Christian Themes*]

YBARRA, Thomas Russell (1880–)
A Christian is a man who feels
Repentance on a Sunday
For what he did on Saturday
And is going to do on Monday.

['The Christian' (1909)]

THE CHURCH

ANDREWES, Bishop Lancelot (1555–1626)
The nearer the Church the further from God.

[*Sermon 15, Of the Nativity* (1629)]

AUGUSTINE, Saint (354–430)
Outside the church there is no salvation.

[*De Baptismo*]

BANCROFT, Richard (1544–1610)
Where Christ erecteth his Church, the devil in the same churchyard will have his chapel.

[Sermon, 1588]

BELLOC, Hilaire (1870–1953)
I always like to associate with a lot of priests because it makes me understand anti-clerical things so well.

[Attr.]

THE BIBLE (KING JAMES VERSION)
Thou art Peter, and upon this rock I will build my church; and the gates of hell shall not prevail against it.

[*Matthew*, 16:18]

BLAKE, William (1757–1827)
But if at the Church they would give us some Ale,
And a pleasant fire our souls to regale:
We'd sing and we'd pray all the live-long day;
Nor ever once wish from the Church to stray.

['The Little Vagabond' (1794)]

**D'ALPUGET, Blanche
(1944–)**
Convent girls never leave the church, they just become feminists. I learned that in Australia.
[*Turtle Beach* (1981)]

**DEVLIN, Bernadette
(1947–)**
Among the best traitors Ireland has ever had, Mother Church ranks at the very top, a massive obstacle in the path to equality and freedom.
[*The Price of My Soul*]

**MELBOURNE, Lord
(1779–1848)**
While I cannot be regarded as a pillar, I must be regarded as a buttress of the church, because I support it from the outside.
[Attr.]

SABIA, Laura
I'm a Roman Catholic and I take a dim view of 2,500 celibates shuffling back and forth to Rome to discuss birth control and not one woman to raise a voice.
[*The Toronto Star*, 1975]

**SWIFT, Jonathan
(1667–1745)**
I never saw, heard, nor read, that the clergy were beloved in any nation where Christianity was the religion of the country. Nothing can render them popular, but some degree of persecution.
[*Thoughts on Religion* (1765)]

**TEMPLE, William
(1881–1944)**
I believe in the Church, One Holy, Catholic and Apostolic, and I regret that it nowhere exists.
[Attr.]

**TUCHOLSKY, Kurt
(1890–1935)**
What the church can't prevent, it blesses.
[*Scraps* (1973)]

**WAUGH, Evelyn
(1903–1966)**
There is a species of person called a 'Modern Churchman' who draws the full salary of a beneficed clergyman and need not commit himself to any religious belief.
[*Decline and Fall* (1928)]

CINEMA

**ALTMAN, Robert
(1922–)**
What's a cult? It just means not enough people to make a minority.
[*The Observer*, 1981]

BROWN, Geoff (1949–)
Dictators needed a talking cinema to twist nations round their fingers: remove the sound from Mussolini and you are left with a puffing bullfrog.

[*The Times*, 1992]

DISNEY, Walt (1901–1966)
Girls bored me – they still do. I love Mickey Mouse more than any woman I've ever known.

[In Wagner, *You Must Remember This*]

GODARD, Jean-Luc (1930–)
Photography is truth. Cinema is truth twenty-four times a second.

[*Le Petit Soldat*, film, 1960]

Of course a film should have a beginning, a middle and an end. But not necessarily in that order.

[Attr.]

GOLDWYN, Samuel (1882–1974)
[Of his film *The Best Years of Our Lives*]
I don't care if it doesn't make a nickel, I just want every man, woman, and child in America to see it.

[In Zierold, *Moguls* (1969)]

Why should people go out and pay money to see bad films when they can stay at home and see bad television for nothing?

[*The Observer*, 1956]

GRIFFITH, D.W. (1874–1948)
[Said when directing an epic film]
Move those ten thousand horses a trifle to the right. And that mob out there, three feet forward.

[Attr.]

JUNG, Carl Gustav (1875–1961)
The cinema, like the detective story, makes it possible to experience without danger all the excitement, passion and desire which must be repressed in a humanitarian ordering of life.

[Attr.]

KAEL, Pauline (1919–)
Movies are so rarely great art that if we cannot appreciate the great *trash* we have very little reason to be interested in them.

[*Kiss Kiss Bang Bang* (1968)]

MARX, Groucho (1895–1977)
We in this industry know that behind every successful screenwriter stands a woman. And behind her stands his wife.

[Attr.]

ROGERS, Will (1879–1935)
The movies are the only business you can go out front and applaud yourself.
[In Halliwell, *Filmgoer's Book of Quotes* (1973)]

TRACY, Spencer (1900–1967)
[Defending his demand for equal billing with Katherine Hepburn]
This is a movie, not a lifeboat.
[Attr.]

See SHOWBUSINESS

CITIES

BURGON, John William (1813–1888)
Match me such marvel save in Eastern clime,
A rose-red city 'half as old as Time'!
['Petra' (1845)]

COLTON, Charles Caleb (c. 1780–1832)
If you would be known, and not know, vegetate in a village; if you would know, and not be known, live in a city.
[*Lacon* (1820)]

COWPER, William (1731–1800)
God made the country, and man made the town.
[*The Task* (1785)]

KIPLING, Rudyard (1865–1936)
Cities and Thrones and Powers,
Stand in Time's eye,
Almost as long as flowers,
Which daily die:
But, as new buds put forth,
To glad new men,
Out of the spent and unconsidered Earth,
The Cities rise again.
['Cities and Thrones and Powers' (1906)]

MILTON, John (1608–1674)
Towred Cities please us then,
And the busie humm of men.
['L'Allegro' (1645)]

MORRIS, Charles (1745–1838)
A house is much more to my taste than a tree,
And for groves, oh! a good grove of chimneys for me.
['Country and Town', 1840]

MORRIS, Desmond (1928–)
Clearly, then, the city is not a concrete jungle, it is a human zoo.
[*The Human Zoo* (1969)]

BOSTON

APPLETON, Thomas Gold (1812–1884)
A Boston man is the east wind made flesh.

[Attr.]

BOSSIDY, John Collins (1860–1928)
And this is good old Boston,
The home of the bean and the cod,
Where the Lowells talk only to Cabots,
And the Cabots talk only to God.

[Toast at Harvard dinner, 1910]

EMERSON, Ralph Waldo (1803–1882)
We say the cows laid out Boston. Well, there are worse surveyors.

[*Conduct of Life* (1860)]

GLASGOW

MCGONAGALL, William (c. 1830–1902)
Beautiful city of Glasgow, I now conclude my muse,
And to write in praise of thee my pen does not refuse;
And, without fear of contradiction, I will venture to say
You are the second grandest city in Scotland at the present day.

['Glasgow' (1890)]

SMITH, Alexander (1830–1867)
City! I am true son of thine . . .

Instead of shores where ocean beats,
I hear the ebb and flow of streets.
Thou hast my kith and kin:
My childhood, youth, and manhood brave;
Thou hast that unforgotten grave
Within thy central din.
A sacredness of love and death
Dwells in thy noise and smoky breath.

['Glasgow' (1857)]

LONDON

AUSTEN, Jane (1775–1817)
Nobody is healthy in London. Nobody can be.

[*Emma* (1816)]

BLAKE, William (1757–1827)
I wander thro' each charter'd street,
Near where the charter'd Thames does flow
And mark in every face I meet
Marks of weakness, marks of woe.

['London' (1794)]

COBBETT, William (1762–1835)
[Of London]
But what is to be the fate of the great wen of all? The

monster, called . . . 'the metropolis of the empire'?
['Rural Rides' (1822)]

COLMAN, the Younger, George (1762–1836)
Oh, London is a fine town,
A very famous city,
Where all the streets are paved with gold,
And all the maidens pretty.
[*The Heir at Law* (1797)]

DISRAELI, Benjamin (1804–1881)
London; a nation, not a city.
[*Lothair* (1870)]

DUNBAR, William (c. 1460–c. 1525)
London, thou art the flower of cities all!
Gemme of all joy, jasper of jocunditie.
['London' (1834)]

JOHNSON, Samuel (1709–1784)
When a man is tired of London, he is tired of life; for there is in London all that life can afford.
[In Boswell, *The Life of Samuel Johnson* (1791)]

WORDSWORTH, William (1770–1850)
Earth has not anything to show more fair;
Dull would he be of soul who

could pass by
A sight so touching in its majesty:
This city now doth, like a garment, wear

The beauty of the morning; silent, bare,
Ships, towers, domes, theatres, and temples lie
Open unto the fields, and to the sky,
All bright and glittering in the smokeless air ...

Dear God! the very houses seem asleep;
And all that mighty heart is lying still!
['Sonnet composed upon Westminster Bridge' (1807)]

MELBOURNE

BEVEN, Rodney Allan (1916–1982)
The people of Melbourne
Are frightfully well-born.
['Observation Sociologique']

BYGRAVES, Max (1922–)
[Of Melbourne]
I've always wanted to see a ghost town. You couldn't even get a parachute to open here after 10 p.m.
[Melbourne *Sun*, 1965]

NAPLES

GLADSTONE, William Ewart (1809–1898)
This is the negation of God erected into a system of government.
[*Letter to Lord Aberdeen*, 1851]

NEW YORK

GILMAN, Charlotte Perkins (1860–1935)
New York . . . that unnatural city where every one is an exile, none more so than the American.
[*The Living of Charlotte Perkins Gilman* (1935)]

MOORE, Brian (1921–)
This city was full of lunatics, people who went into muttering fits on the bus, others who shouted obscenities in automats, lost souls who walked the pavements alone, caught up in imaginary conversations.
[*An Answer From Limbo* (1962)]

SIMON, Neil (1927–)
New York . . . is not Mecca. It just smells like it.
[*California Suite* (1976)]

PARIS

ELMS, Robert
Paris is the paradise of the easily-impressed – the universal provincial mind.
[In Burchill, *Sex and Sensibility* (1992)]

HEMINGWAY, Ernest (1898–1961)
If you are lucky enough to have lived in Paris as a young man, then wherever you go for the rest of your life, it stays with you, for Paris is a moveable feast.
[*A Moveable Feast* (1964)]

See COUNTRY

CIVILIZATION

ADDAMS, Jane (1860–1935)
Civilisation is a method of living, an attitude of equal respect for all men.
[Speech, Honolulu, 1933]

ALCOTT, Bronson (1799–1888)
Civilisation degrades the many to exalt the few.
[*Table Talk* (1877)]

BAGEHOT, Walter (1826–1877)
The whole history of civiliz-

ation is strewn with creeds and institutions which were invaluable at first, and deadly afterwards.

[*Physics and Politics* (1872)]

BATES, Daisy May (1863–1951)

The Australian native can withstand all the reverses of nature, fiendish droughts and sweeping floods, horrors of thirst and enforced starvation – but he cannot withstand civilisation.

[*The Passing of the Aborigines* (1938)]

DISRAELI, Benjamin (1804–1881)

Increased means and increased leisure are the two civilizers of man.

[Speech, Manchester, 1872]

GANDHI (1869–1948)

[When asked what he thought of Western civilization]
I think it would be an excellent idea.

[Attr.]

GARROD, Heathcote William (1878–1960)

[In response to criticism that, during World War I, he was not fighting to defend civilization]
Madam, I am the civilization

they are fighting to defend.

[In Balsdon, *Oxford Now and Then* (1970)]

HILLARY, Sir Edmund (1919–)

There is precious little in civilization to appeal to a Yeti.

[*The Observer,* 1960]

KNOX, Ronald (1888–1957)

It is so stupid of modern civilization to have given up believing in the devil when he is the only explanation of it.

[Attr.]

MILL, John Stuart (1806–1873)

I am not aware that any community has a right to force another to be civilized.

[*On Liberty* (1859)]

PAGLIA, Camille (1947–)

If civilization had been left in female hands, we would still be living in grass huts.

[*Sex, Art and American Culture: Essays* (1992)]

PARK, Mungo (1771–1806)

[On finding a gibbet in an unexplored part of Africa]
The sight of it gave me infinite pleasure, as it proved that I was in a civilized society.

[Attr.]

SANTAYANA, George (1863–1952)
Civilization is perhaps approaching one of those long winters that overtake it from time to time. Romantic Christendom – picturesque, passionate, unhappy episode — may be coming to an end. Such a catastrophe would be no reason for despair.
[*Characters and Opinions in the United States*]

TREVELYAN, G.M. (1876–1962)
Disinterested intellectual curiosity is the life blood of real civilization.
[*English Social History* (1942)]

YEATS, W.B. (1865–1939)
A civilisation is a struggle to keep self-control.
[*A Vision* (1925), 'Dove or Swan']

CLASS

ARNOLD, Matthew (1822–1888)
One has often wondered whether upon the whole earth there is anything so unintelligent, so unapt to perceive how the world is really going, as an ordinary young Englishman of our upper class.
[*Culture and Anarchy* (1869)]

BRENAN, Gerald (1894–1987)
Poets and painters are outside the class system, or rather they constitute a special class of their own, like the circus people and the gipsies.
[*Thoughts in a Dry Season* (1978)]

BROUGHAM, Lord Henry (1778–1868)
The great Unwashed.
[Attr.]

BURGESS, Anthony (1917–1993)
Without class differences, England would cease to be the living theatre it is.
[Remark, 1985]

CARTLAND, Barbara (1902–)
[When asked in a radio interview whether she thought that British class barriers had broken down]
Of course they have, or I wouldn't be sitting here talking to someone like you.
[In J. Cooper, *Class* (1979)]

CURZON, Lord (1859–1925)
[On seeing some soldiers bathing]
I never knew the lower classes had such white skins.
[Attr.]

ELIZABETH, the Queen Mother (1900–)
My favourite programme is 'Mrs Dale's Diary'. I try never to miss it because it is the only way of knowing what goes on in a middle-class family.
[Attr.]

ENGELS, Friedrich (1820–1895)
The history of all hitherto existing society is the history of class struggles.
[*The Communist Manifesto* (1848)]

FRIEL, Brian (1929–)
The result is that people with a culture of poverty suffer much less repression than we of the middle-class suffer and indeed, if I may make the suggestion with due qualification, they often have a lot more fun than we have.
[*The Freedom of the City* (1973)]

HAILSHAM, Quintin Hogg, Baron (1907–)
I don't see any harm in being middle class, I've been middle class all my life and have benefited from it.
[*The Observer*, 1983]

LERNER, Alan Jay (1918–1986)
An Englishman's way of speaking absolutely classifies him.
[*My Fair Lady* (1956)]

MARX, Karl (1818–1883)
What I did that was new was prove . . . that the class struggle necessarily leads to the dictatorship of the proletariat.
[Letter, 1852]

RATTIGAN, Terence (1911–1977)
You can be in the Horse Guards and still be common, dear.
[*Separate Tables* (1955)]

SCARGILL, Arthur (1941–)
[On John Prescott's description of himself as middle class]
I have little or no time for people who aspire to be members of the middle class.
[Remark, 1996]

STANTON, Elizabeth Cady (1815–1902)
It is impossible for one class to appreciate the wrongs of another.
[In Anthony and Gage, *History of Woman Suffrage* (1881)]

THEROUX, Paul (1941–)
The ship follows Soviet custom: it is riddled with class distinctions so subtle, it takes

a trained Marxist to appreciate them.

[*The Great Railway Bazaar* (1975)]

THIERS, Louis Adolphe (1797–1877)
[Defending his social status after someone had remarked that his mother had been a cook]
She was – but I assure you that she was a very bad cook.

[Attr.]

SEE ARISTOCRACY

COMMON SENSE

DESCARTES, René (1596–1650)
Common sense is the best distributed thing in the world, for we all think we possess a good share of it.

[*Discours de la Méthode* (1637)]

EINSTEIN, Albert (1879–1955)
Common sense is the collection of prejudices acquired by age eighteen.

[Attr.]

EMERSON, Ralph Waldo (1803–1882)
Nothing astonishes men so much as common-sense and plain dealing.

['Art' (1841)]

SALISBURY, Lord (1830–1903)
No lesson seems to be so deeply inculcated by the experience of life as that you never should trust experts. If you believe the doctors, nothing is wholesome: if you believe the theologians, nothing is innocent: if you believe the soldiers, nothing is safe. They all require to have their strong wine diluted by a very large admixture of insipid common sense.

[Letter to Lord Lytton, 1877]

COMMUNISM

ATTLEE, Clement (1883–1967)
Russian Communism is the illegitimate child of Karl Marx and Catherine the Great.

[*The Observer,* 1956]

ELLIOTT, Ebenezer (1781–1849)
What is a communist? One who hath yearnings
For equal division of unequal earnings.

[Epigram, 1850]

**KHRUSHCHEV, Nikita
(1894–1971)**
[On the possibility that the
Soviet Union might one day
reject communism]
Those who wait for that must
wait until a shrimp learns to
whistle.

[Attr.]

**MCCARTHY, Senator Joseph
(1908–1957)**
[Of someone alleged to have
communist sympathies]
It makes me sick, sick, sick
way down inside.

[In Lewis, *The Fifties* (1978)]

**MORLEY, Robert
(1908–1992)**
There's no such thing in
Communist countries as a
load of old cod's wallop, the
cod's wallop is always fresh
made.

[*Punch*, 1974]

ROGERS, Will (1879–1935)
Communism is like prohibition, it's a good idea but it
won't work.

[*Weekly Articles* (1981)]

SMITH, F.E. (1872–1930)
[On Bolshevism]
Nature has no cure for this
sort of madness, though I
have known a legacy from a
rich relative work wonders.

[*Law, Life and Letters* (1927)]

**SOLZHENITSYN, Alexander
(1918–)**
For us in Russia, communism
is a dead dog, while for many
people in the West, it is still a
living lion.

[*The Listener,* 1979]

SPARK, Muriel (1918–)
Every communist has a fascist frown, every fascist a
communist smile.

[*The Girls of Slender Means*]

See CAPITALISM

COMPASSION

**THE BIBLE (KING JAMES
VERSION)**
Blessed are the merciful: for
they shall obtain mercy.

[*Matthew,* 5:7]

**BRADFORD, John
(c. 1510–1555)**
[Remark on criminals going
to the gallows]
But for the grace of God there
goes John Bradford.

[Attr.]

BURNS, Robert (1759–1796)
Then gently scan your brother
man,
Still gentler sister woman;
Tho' they may gang a kennin
wrang,

To step aside is human.
['Address to the Unco Guid'
(1786)]

ELIOT, George (1819–1880)
We hand folks over to God's
mercy, and show none ourselves.
[*Adam Bede* (1859)]

GAY, John (1685–1732)
He best can pity who has felt
the woe.
[*Dione* (1720)]

**GIBBON, Edward
(1737–1794)**
Our sympathy is cold to the
relation of distant misery.
[*Decline and Fall of the Roman
Empire* (1788)]

**HOPKINS, Gerard Manley
(1844–1889)**
My own heart let me more
have pity on; let
Me live to my sad self
hereafter kind,
Charitable; not live this
tormented mind
With this tormented mind
tormenting yet.
['My own Heart let me more
have Pity on' (c. 1885)]

**HUXLEY, Aldous
(1894–1963)**
She was a machine-gun
riddling her hostess with
sympathy.
[*Mortal Coils* (1922)]

KINNOCK, Neil (1942–)
Compassion is not a sloppy,
sentimental feeling for people
who are underprivileged or
sick . . . it is an absolutely
practical belief that, regard-
less of a person's background,
ability or ability to pay, he
should be provided with the
best that society has to offer.
[Maiden speech, House of
Commons, 1970]

LAZARUS, Emma (1849–1887)
Give me your tired, your poor,
Your huddled masses yearn-
ing to breathe free.
['The New Colossus' (1883);
verse inscribed on the Statue
of Liberty]

**SHAKESPEARE, William
(1564–1616)**
The quality of mercy is not
strain'd;
It droppeth as the gentle rain
from heaven
Upon the place beneath. It is
twice blest:
It blesseth him that gives and
him that takes.
[*The Merchant of Venice*, IV.i]

WHITE, Patrick (1912–1990)
And remember Mother's practical ethics: *one can drown in
compassion if one answers
every call it's another way of
suicide.*
[*The Eye of the Storm* (1973)]

**WILDE, Oscar
(1854–1900)**
Anybody can sympathise with
the sufferings of a friend, but
it requires a very fine nature
to sympathise with a friend's
success.
['The Soul of Man under
Socialism' (1881)]

CONSCIENCE

**DE QUINCEY, Thomas
(1785–1859)**
Better to stand ten thousand
sneers than one abiding
pang, such as time could not
abolish, of bitter self-
reproach.
[*Confessions of an English
Opium Eater* (1822)]

**HOBBES, Thomas
(1588–1679)**
A man's conscience and his
judgement is the same thing,
and as the judgement, so also
the conscience, may be
erroneous.
[Attr.]

**MENCKEN, H.L.
(1880–1956)**
Conscience is the inner voice
that warns us somebody may
be looking.
[*A Mencken Chrestomathy*
(1949)]

NASH, Ogden (1902–1971)
He who is ridden by a con-
science
Worries about a lot of non-
science;
He without benefit of scruples
His fun and income soon
quadruples.
['Reflection on the Fallibility
of Nemesis' (1940)]

**SHAKESPEARE, William
(1564–1616)**
A peace above all earthly dig-
nities,
A still and quiet conscience.
[*Henry VIII*, III.ii]

**WASHINGTON, George
(1732–1799)**
Labour to keep alive in your
breast that little spark of
celestial fire, called conscience.
[*Rules of Civility and Decent
Behaviour*]

CONTEMPT

**ASHFORD, Daisy
(1881–1972)**
Ethel patted her hair and
looked very sneery.
[*The Young Visiters* (1919)]

AUSTEN, Jane (1775–1817)
She was nothing more than a
mere good-tempered, civil

and obliging young woman; as such we could scarcely dislike her – she was only an Object of Contempt.

[*Love and Freindship* (1791)]

BIERCE, Ambrose (1842–c. 1914)

Contempt: The feeling of a prudent man for an enemy who is too formidable safely to be opposed.

[*The Enlarged Devil's Dictionary* (1961)]

CHATEAUBRIAND (1768–1848)

One is not superior merely because one sees the world in an odious light.

[Attr.]

CONGREVE, William (1670–1729)

A little disdain is not amiss; a little scorn is alluring.

[*The Way of the World* (1700)]

PROVERB

Familiarity breeds contempt.

SHAW, George Bernard (1856–1950)

I have never sneered in my life. Sneering doesn't become either the human face or the human soul.

[*Pygmalion* (1916)]

CONVERSATION

BRYAN, William Jennings (1860–1925)

An orator is a man who says what he thinks and feels what he says.

[Attr.]

CARLYLE, Thomas (1795–1881)

Speech is human, silence is divine, yet also brutish and dead: therefore we must learn both arts.

[Attr.]

CHURCHILL, Sir Winston (1874–1965)

[Of Lord Charles Beresford] He is one of those orators of whom it was well said, 'Before they get up they do not know what they are going to say; when they are speaking, they do not know what they are saying; and when they sit down, they do not know what they have said.'

[Speech, House of Commons, 1912]

To jaw-jaw is better than to war-war.

[Speech, Washington, 1954]

CONFUCIUS (c. 550–c. 478 BC)

For one word a man is often deemed to be wise, and for one word he is often deemed

to be foolish. We should be careful indeed what we say.
[*Analects*]

DISRAELI, Benjamin (1804–1881)

I grew intoxicated with my own eloquence.
[*Contarini Fleming* (1832)]

DRYDEN, John (1631–1700)

But far more numerous was the herd of such
Who think too little and who talk too much.
[*Absalom and Achitophel* (1681)]

ELIOT, George (1819–1880)

Half the sorrows of women would be averted if they could repress the speech they know to be useless; nay, the speech they have resolved not to make.
[*Felix Holt* (1866)]

HALIFAX, Lord (1633–1695)

Most Men make little other use of their Speech than to give evidence against their own Understanding.
['Of Folly and Fools' (1750)]

HOLMES, Oliver Wendell (1809–1894)

And, when you stick on conversation's burrs,
Don't strew your pathway

with those dreadful urs.
['A Rhymed Lesson' (1848)]

MACAULAY, Lord (1800–1859)

The object of oratory alone is not truth, but persuasion.
['Essay on Athenian Orators' (1898)]

O'BRIAN, Patrick

Question and answer is not a civilized form of conversation.
[*Clarissa Oakes* (1992)]

SENECA (c. 4 BC–AD 65)

Conversation has a kind of charm about it, an insinuating and insidious something that elicits secrets from us just like love or liquor.
[*Epistles*]

SHAKESPEARE, William (1564–1616)

He draweth out the thread of his verbosity finer than the staple of his argument.
[*Love's Labour Lost*, V.i]

TALLEYRAND (1754–1838)

Speech was given to man to disguise his thoughts.
[Attr.]

TANNEN, Deborah (1945–)

Each person's life is lived as a series of conversations.
[*The Observer*, 1992]

COOKERY

**FERN, Fanny
(1811–1872)**
The way to a man's heart is
through his stomach.
[*Willis Parton*]

**HARNEY, Bill
(1895–1962)**
[Advice on bush cooking]
You always want to garnish it
when it's orf.
['*Talkabout*', c.1960]

LEITH, Prue (1940–)
Cuisine is when things taste
like what they are.
[Lecture, 'The Fine Art of
Food', 1987]

**MEREDITH, George
(1828–1909)**
Kissing don't last: cookery do!
[*The Ordeal of Richard Feverel*
(1859)]

**MEREDITH, Owen
(1831–1891)**
We may live without poetry,
music and art;
We may live without con-
science, and live without
heart;
We may live without friends;
we may live without books;
But civilized man cannot live
without cooks.
['Lucile' (1860)]

POST, Emily (1873–1960)
To the old saying that man
built the house but woman
made of it a 'home' might be
added the modern supple-
ment that woman accepted
cooking as a chore but man
has made of it a recreation.
[*Etiquette* (1922)]

SAKI (1870–1916)
The cook was a good cook,
as cooks go; and as cooks go
she went.
[*Reginald* (1904)]

SLATER, Nigel
Cooking is about not cheating
yourself of pleasure.
[*Slice of Life*, BBC TV pro-
gramme]

See FOOD

THE COUNTRY

**CONGREVE, William
(1670–1729)**
I nauseate walking; 'tis a country
diversion, I loathe the country.
[*The Way of the World* (1700)]

**COWPER, William
(1731–1800)**
God made the country, and
man made the town.
[*The Task* (1785)]

DOYLE, Sir Arthur Conan (1859–1930)
It is my belief, Watson, founded upon my experience, that the lowest and vilest alleys of London do not present a more dreadful record of sin than does the smiling and beautiful countryside.
['Copper Beeches' (1892)]

HAZLITT, William (1778–1830)
There is nothing good to be had in the country, or, if there is, they will not let you have it.
[*The Round Table* (1817)]

KILVERT, Francis (1840–1879)
It is a fine thing to be out on the hills alone. A man could hardly be a beast or a fool alone on a great mountain.
[*Diary*, 1871]

SACKVILLE-WEST, Vita (1892–1962)
The country habit has me by the heart,
For he's bewitched for ever who has seen,
Not with his eyes but with his vision, Spring
Flow down the woods and stipple leaves with sun.
['Winter' (1926)]

SMITH, Sydney (1771–1845)
I have no relish for the country; it is a kind of healthy grave.
[Letter, 1838]

WILDE, Oscar (1854–1900)
Anybody can be good in the country.
[*The Picture of Dorian Gray* (1891)]

See CITIES

COURAGE

ARISTOTLE (384–322 BC)
I count him braver who overcomes his desires than him who overcomes his enemies.
[In Stobaeus, *Florilegium*]

BARRIE, Sir J.M. (1860–1937)
Courage is the thing. All goes if courage goes.
[Address, St Andrews University, 1922]

EARHART, Amelia (1898–1937)
Courage is the price that Life exacts for granting peace.
['Courage' (1927)]

HEMINGWAY, Ernest (1898–1961)
[Definition of 'guts']
Grace under pressure.
[Attr.]

HOWARD, Michael (1922–)
The important thing when you are going to do something brave is to have someone on hand to witness it.
[The Observer, 1980]

IBARRURI, Dolores ('La Pasionaria') (1895–1989)
It is better to die on your feet than to live on your knees.
[Speech, Paris, 1936]

LEACOCK, Stephen Butler (1869–1944)
It takes a good deal of physical courage to ride a horse. This, however, I have. I get it at about forty cents a flask, and take it as required.
[Literary Lapses (1910)]

NAPOLEON I (1769–1821)
As for moral courage, he said he had very rarely encountered two o'clock in the morning courage; that is, the courage of the unprepared.
[Mémorial de Sainte Hélène]

SHERIDAN, Richard Brinsley (1751–1816)
My valour is certainly going! – it is sneaking off! – I feel it oozing out as it were at the palms of my hands!
[The Rivals (1775)]

USTINOV, Sir Peter (1921–)
Courage is often lack of insight, whereas cowardice in many cases is based on good information.
[Attr.]

COWARDICE

CARROLL, Lewis (1832–1898)
'I'm very brave generally,' he went on in a low voice: 'only to-day I happen to have a headache.'
[Through the Looking-Glass (1872)]

ELIZABETH I (1533–1603)
If thy heart fails thee, climb not at all.
[In Fuller, The History of the Worthies of England (1662)]

HOUSMAN, A.E. (1859–1936)
The man that runs away
Lives to die another day.
[A Shropshire Lad (1896)]

JOHNSTON, Brian (1912–1994)
[When asked by his commanding officer what steps he would take if he came across a German battalion]
Long ones, backwards.
[Quoted in his obituary, Sunday Times]

ROCHESTER, Earl of (1647–1680)

All men would be cowards if they durst.

['A Satire Against Reason and Mankind' (1679)]

SHAW, George Bernard (1856–1950)

As an old soldier I admit the cowardice: it's as universal as sea sickness, and matters just as little.

[*Man and Superman* (1903)]

VOLTAIRE (1694–1778)

Marriage is the only adventure open to the cowardly.

[Attr.]

CRIME

ADLER, Freda (1934–)

[On rape]

Perhaps it is the only crime in which the victim becomes the accused and, in reality, it is she who must prove her good reputation, her mental soundness, and her impeccable propriety.

[*Sisters in Crime* (1975)]

ANONYMOUS

The fault is great in man or woman
Who steals a goose from off a common;
But what can plead that man's excuse
Who steals a common from a goose?

[*The Tickler Magazine*, 1821]

BACON, Francis (1561–1626)

Opportunity makes a thief.

[Letter to Essex, 1598]

THE BIBLE (KING JAMES VERSION)

Whoso sheddeth man's blood, by man shall his blood be shed.

[*Genesis*, 9:6]

BRECHT, Bertolt (1898–1956)

What is robbing a bank compared with founding a bank?

[*The Threepenny Opera* (1928)]

BULWER-LYTTON, Edward (1803–1873)

In other countries poverty is a misfortune – with us it is a crime.

[*England and the English* (1833)]

CAPONE, Al (1899–1947)

I've been accused of every death except the casualty list of the World War.

[In Allsop, *The Bootleggers* (1961)]

CHESTERTON, G.K. (1874–1936)

Thieves respect property; they merely wish the property to

become their property that
they may more perfectly
respect it.

[Attr.]

**CONGREVE, William
(1670–1729)**
He that first cries out stop
thief, is often he that has
stolen the treasure.

[*Love for Love* (1695)]

**DE QUINCEY, Thomas
(1785–1859)**
If a man once indulges himself
in murder, very soon he comes
to think little of robbing; and
from robbing he comes next to
drinking and sabbath-break-
ing, and from that to incivility
and procrastination.

['Murder Considered as One
of the Fine Arts' (1839)]

FARBER, Barry
Crime expands according to our
willingness to put up with it.

[Attr.]

FRY, Elizabeth (1780–1845)
Punishment is not for
revenge, but to lessen crime
and reform the criminal.

[Journal entry]

**GOLDMAN, Emma
(1869–1940)**
Crime is naught but misdi-
rected energy.

[*Anarchism*, 1910)]

**HAWTHORNE, Nathaniel
(1804–1864)**
By the sympathy of your
human hearts for sin ye shall
scent out all the places –
whether in church, bed-
chamber, street, field or forest
– where crime has been
committed, and shall exult to
behold the whole earth one
stain of guilt, one mighty
blood spot.

[*Young Goodman Brown*
(1835)]

**LA BRUYERE, Jean de
(1645–1696)**
If poverty is the mother of
crime, lack of intelligence is
its father.

[*Les caractères ou les moeurs
de ce siècle* (1688)]

LEWES, G.H. (1817–1878)
Murder, like talent, seems
occasionally to run in families.

[*The Physiology of Common
Life* (1859)]

**LIGHTNER, Candy
(1946–)**
Death by drunken driving is a
socially acceptable form of
homicide.

[*San José Mercury*, 1981]

RACINE, Jean (1639–1699)
Crime has its degrees, as
virtue does.

[*Phèdre* (1677)]

**RAINS, Claude
(1889–1967)**
Major Strasser has been shot.
Round up the usual suspects.
[*Casablanca*, film, 1942]

**ROOSEVELT, Theodore
(1858–1919)**
[Dismissing a cowboy who
had put Roosevelt's brand on
a steer belonging to a neighbouring ranch]
A man who will steal for me
will steal from me.
[In Hagedorn, *Roosevelt in the
Bad Lands* (1921)]

**ROSS, Nick
(1947–)**
We're barking mad about
crime in this country. We
have an obsession with
believing the worst, conning
ourselves that there was a
golden age – typically forty
years before the one we're
living in.
[*Radio Times*, 1993]

**ROSTAND, Jean
(1894–1977)**
Kill one man, and you are a
murderer. Kill millions of
men, and you are a con-
queror. Kill them all, and you
are a god.
[*Thoughts of a Biologist*
(1939)]

**SHAKESPEARE, William
(1564–1616)**
The robb'd that smiles steals
something from the thief.
[*Othello*, I.iii]

**SPENCER, Herbert
(1820–1903)**
A clever theft was praiseworthy amongst the Spartans;
and it is equally so amongst
Christians, provided it be on a
sufficiently large scale.
[*Social Statics* (1850)]

See PUNISHMENT

CRITICISM

**ARNOLD, Matthew
(1822–1888)**
I am bound by my own definition of criticism: a disinterested endeavour to learn and
propagate the best that is
known and thought in the
world.
[*Essays in Criticism* (1865)]

AUDEN, W.H. (1907–1973)
One cannot review a bad
book without showing off.
[*The Dyer's Hand* (1963)]

**BULLET, Gerald
(1893–1958)**
So, when a new book comes
his way,

By someone still alive to-day,
Our Honest John, with right
good will,
Sharpens his pencil for the
kill.

['A Reviewer']

**BURGESS, Anthony
(1917–1993)**
I know how foolish critics can
be, being one myself.

[*The Observer*, 1980]

BYRON, Lord (1788–1824)
A man must serve his time to
every trade
Save censure – critics all are
ready made.
Take hackney'd jokes from
Miller, got by rote,
With just enough of learning
to misquote.

[*English Bards and Scotch
Reviewers* (1809)]

**CHURCHILL, Charles
(1731–1764)**
Though by whim, envy, or
resentment led,
They damn those authors
whom they never read.

[*The Candidate* (1764)]

**CHURCHILL, Sir Winston
(1874–1965)**
I do not resent criticism, even
when, for the sake of empha-
sis, it parts for the time with
reality.

[Speech, 1941]

CONRAN, Shirley (1932–)
[On Julie Burchill]
I cannot take seriously the
criticism of someone who
doesn't know how to use a
semicolon.

[Attr.]

**DISRAELI, Benjamin
(1804–1881)**
This shows how much easier
it is to be critical than to be
correct.

[Speech, 1860]

Cosmopolitan critics, men
who are the friends of every
country save their own.

[Speech, 1877]

**FRANCE, Anatole
(1844–1924)**
A good critic is one who tells
of his own soul's adventures
among masterpieces.

[*La Vie Littéraire* (1888)]

FRY, Christopher (1907–)
I sometimes think
His critical judgement is so
exquisite
It leaves us nothing to admire
except his opinion.

[*The Dark is Light Enough*
(1954)]

**HAMPTON, Christopher
(1946–)**
Asking a working writer what
he thinks about critics is like

asking a lamp-post how it
feels about dogs.
[*The Sunday Times Magazine*,
1977]

HUXLEY, Aldous (1894–1963)
Parodies and caricatures are
the most penetrating of criticisms.
[*Point Counter Point* (1928)]

**JOHNSON, Samuel
(1709–1784)**
[Of literary criticism]
You *may* scold a tragedy,
though you cannot write one,
You may scold a carpenter
who has made you a bad
table, though you cannot
make a table. It is not your
trade to make tables.
[In Boswell, *The Life of Samuel
Johnson* (1791)]

The man who is asked by an
author what he thinks of his
work, is put to the torture,
and is not obliged to speak
the truth.
[In Boswell, *The Life of Samuel
Johnson* (1791)]

**LA BRUYÈRE, Jean de
(1645–1696)**
The pleasure of criticizing
takes away from us the
pleasure of being moved by
some very fine things.
[*Les caractères ou les moeurs
de ce siècle* (1688)]

**MARX, Groucho
(1895–1977)**
I was so long writing my
review that I never got
around to reading the book.
[Attr.]

**MAUGHAM, William
Somerset (1874–1965)**
People ask you for criticism,
but they only want praise.
[*Of Human Bondage* (1915)]

MOORE, George (1852–1933)
The lot of critics is to be
remembered by what they
failed to understand.
[*Impressions and Opinions*
(1891)]

**PARKER, Dorothy
(1893–1967)**
This is not a novel to be
tossed aside lightly. It should
be thrown with great force.
[In Gaines, *Wit's End*]

POPE, Alexander (1688–1744)
Nor in the Critic let the Man
be lost.
Good-nature and good-sense
must ever join;
To err is human, to forgive,
divine.
[*An Essay on Criticism* (1711)]

**PORSON, Richard
(1759–1808)**
[On Southey's poems]
Your works will be read after

Shakespeare and Milton are forgotten – and not till then.

[In Meissen, *Quotable Anecdotes*]

QUILLER-COUCH, Sir Arthur ('Q') (1863–1944)
The best is the best, though a hundred judges have declared it so.

[*Oxford Book of English Verse* (1900)]

SHAW, George Bernard (1856–1950)
You don't expect me to know what to say about a play when I don't know who the author is, do you? . . . If it's by a good author, it's a good play, naturally. That stands to reason.

[*Fanny's First Play* (1911)]

SIBELIUS, Jean (1865–1957)
Pay no attention to what the critics say. No statue has ever been put up to a critic.
[Attr.]

[In Pearson, *The Smith of Smiths* (1934)]

SONTAG, Susan (1933–)
Interpretation is the revenge of the intellect upon art.

[*Evergreen Review*, 1964]

STEINBECK, John (1902–1968)
[On critics]
Unless the bastards have the

courage to give you unqualified praise, I say ignore them.

[In J.K. Galbraith, *A Life in Our Times* (1981)]

SWIFT, Jonathan (1667–1745)
So, naturalists observe, a flea
Hath smaller fleas that on him prey;
And these have smaller fleas to bite 'em,
And so proceed *ad infinitum*.
Thus every poet, in his kind,
Is bit by him that comes behind.

['On Poetry' (1733)]

TYNAN, Kenneth (1927–1980)
A good drama critic is one who perceives what is happening in the theatre of his time. A great drama critic also perceives what is not happening.

[*Tynan Right and Left* (1967)]

VOLTAIRE (1694–1778)
[Reviewing Rousseau's poem 'Ode to Posterity']
I do not think this poem will reach its destination.

[Attr.]

WILDE, Oscar (1854–1900)
The man who sees both sides of a question is a man who

sees absolutely nothing at all.
['The Critic as Artist' (1891)]

[On a notice at a dancing saloon]
I saw the only rational method of art criticism I have ever come across . . . 'Please do not shoot the pianist. He is doing his best.'
['Impressions of America' (1906)]

CRUELTY

BLAKE, William (1757–1827)
Cruelty has a Human Heart
And Jealousy a Human Face,
Terror the Human Form Divine,
And Secrecy the Human Dress.
['A Divine Image' (c. 1832)]

COWPER, William (1731–1800)
I would not enter on my list of friends
(Tho' grac'd with polish'd manners and fine sense,
Yet wanting sensibility) the man
Who needlessly sets foot upon a worm.
[*The Task* (1785)]

FROUDE, James Anthony (1818–1894)
Fear is the parent of cruelty.
[*Short Studies on Great Subjects* (1877)]

GIDE, André (1869–1951)
Cruelty is the first of God's attributes.
[*The Counterfeiters*]

TROTSKY, Leon (1879–1940)
In a serious struggle there is no worse cruelty than to be magnanimous at an inappropriate time.
[*The History of the Russian Revolution* (1933)]

CRYING

BYRON, Lord (1788–1824)
Oh! too convincing – dangerously dear –
In woman's eye the unanswerable tear!
[*The Corsair* (1814)]

CROMPTON, Richmal (1890–1969)
Violet Elizabeth dried her tears. She saw that they were useless and she did not believe in wasting her effects. 'All right,' she said calmly, 'I'll thcream then. I'll thcream, an' thcream, an' thcream till I'm thick.'
[*Still William* (1925)]

**DICKENS, Charles
(1812–1870)**
We need never be ashamed
of our tears.
[*Great Expectations* (1861)]

'It opens the lungs, washes
the countenance, exercises
the eyes, and softens down
the temper', said Mr Bumble.
'So cry away.'
[*Oliver Twist* (1838)]

LIBERACE (1919–1987)
[Remark made after hostile
criticism]
I cried all the way to the
bank.
[*Autobiography* (1973)]

RHYS, Jean (1894–1979)
I often want to cry. That is the
only advantage women have
over men – at least they can
cry.
[*Good Morning, Midnight*
(1939)]

**SAINT–EXUPERY, Antoine
de (1900–1944)**
It is such a mysterious place,
the land of tears.
[*The Little Prince* (1943)]

**SHAKESPEARE, William
(1564–1616)**
You think I'll weep.
No, I'll not weep.
I have full cause of weeping;
but this heart
Shall break into a hundred
thousand flaws
Or ere I'll weep.
[*King Lear*, II.iv]

CULTURE

**ARNOLD, Matthew
(1822–1888)**
Culture, the acquainting ourselves with the best that has
been known and said in the
world, and thus the history of
the human spirit.
[*Literature and Dogma*]

**BANDA, Dr Hastings
(1905–)**
I wish I could bring
Stonehenge to Nyasaland to
show there was a time when
Britain had a savage culture.
[*The Observer*, 1963]

**BELLOW, Saul
(1915–)**
If culture means anything, it
means knowing what value
to set upon human life; it's
not somebody with a mortar-
board reading Greek. I know
a lot of facts, history. That's
not culture. Culture is the
openness of the individual
psyche . . . to the news of
being.
[*The Glasgow Herald*, 1985]

CULTURE

**CARLYLE, Thomas
(1795–1881)**
The great law of culture is: let each become all that he was created capable of being.
['Jean Paul Friedrich Richter' (1839)]

**DARWIN, Charles
(1809–1882)**
The highest possible stage in moral culture is when we recognize that we ought to control our thoughts.
[*The Descent of Man* (1871)]

**FRYE, Northrop
(1912–1991)**
Creative culture is infinitely porous – it absorbs influences from all over the world.
[*Maclean's*, 1991]

**GOERING, Hermann
(1893–1946)**
When I hear anyone talk of Culture, I reach for my revolver.
[Attr.]

KENNY, Mary (1944–)
Decadent cultures usually fall in the end, and robust cultures rise to replace them. Our own cultural supermarket may eventually be subject to a takeover bid: the most likely challenger being, surely, Islam.
[*Sunday Telegraph*, 1993]

**KOESTLER, Arthur
(1905–1983)**
Two half-truths do not make a truth, and two half-cultures do not make a culture.
[*The Ghost in the Machine* (1961)]

**MCLUHAN, Marshall
(1911–1980)**
In a culture like ours, long accustomed to splitting and dividing all things as a means of control, it is sometimes a bit of a shock to be reminded that, in operational and practical fact, the medium is the message.
[*Understanding Media* (1964)]

MANTEL, Hilary (1953–)
[On travel]
I saw the world as some sort of exchange scheme for my ideals, but the world deserves better than this. When you come across an alien culture you must not automatically respect it. You must sometimes pay it the compliment of hating it.
['Last Months in Al Hamra' (1987)]

**MUSSOLINI, Benito
(1883–1945)**
In a statesman so-called 'culture' is, after all, a useless luxury.
[*Il Populo d'Italia*, 1919]

**WALLACE, Edgar
(1875–1932)**
What is a highbrow? He is a man who has found something more interesting than women.
[*New York Times*, 1932]

**WHARTON, Edith
(1862–1937)**
Mrs Ballinger is one of the ladies who pursue Culture in bands, as though it were dangerous to meet it alone.
[*Xingu and Other Stories* (1916)]

CURIOSITY

**BACON, Francis
(1561-1626)**
They are ill discoverers that think there is no land, when they can see nothing but sea.
[*The Advancement of Learning* (1605)]

**BAX, Sir Arnold
(1883-1953**
One should try everything once, except incest and folk-dancing.
[*Farewell my Youth* (1943)]

THE BIBLE (KING JAMES VERSION)
Be not curious in unnecessary matters: for more things are shewed unto thee than men understand.
[Apocrypha, *Ecclesiasticus*, 3:23]

**CARROLL, Lewis
(1832–1898)**
'If everybody minded their own business,' said the Duchess in a hoarse growl, 'the world would go round a deal faster than it does.'
[*Alice's Adventures in Wonderland* (1865)]

**LAMB, Charles
(1775–1834)**
Not many sounds in life, and I include all urban and all rural sounds, exceed in interest a knock at the door.
['Valentine's Day' (1823)]

MORITA, Akio
Curiosity is the key to creativity.
[*Made in Japan* (1986)]

**PERELMAN, S.J.
(1904–1979)**
[Giving his reasons for refusing to see a priest as he lay dying]
I am curious to see what happens in the next world to one who dies unshriven.
[Attr.]

CUSTOM

**BAILLIE, Joanna
(1762–1851)**
What custom hath endear'd
We part with sadly, though
we prize it not.
[*Basil* (1798)]

**BECKETT, Samuel
(1906–1989)**
The air is full of our cries. But
habit is a great deadener.
[*Waiting for Godot* (1955)]

**CRABBE, George
(1754–1832)**
Habit with him was all the
test of truth,
'It must be right: I've done it
from my youth.'
[*The Borough* (1810)]

HUME, David (1711–1776)
Custom, then, is the great
guide of human life.
[*Philosophical Essays* (1748)]

**MORE, Hannah
(1745–1833)**
Small habits, well pursued
betimes,
May reach the dignity of
crimes.
[*Florio*, (1786)]

**PEGUY, Charles
(1873–1914)**
Memory and habit are the
harbingers of death.
[*Note conjointe sur M.
Descartes*]

**SHAKESPEARE, William
(1564–1616)**
Age cannot wither her, nor
custom stale
Her infinite variety. Other
women cloy
The appetites they feed, but
she makes hungry
Where most she satisfies.
[*Antony and Cleopatra*, II.ii]

It is a custom
More honour'd in the breach
than the observance.
[*Hamlet*, I.iv]

CYNICISM

**BIERCE, Ambrose
(1842–c. 1914)**
Cynic: A blackguard whose
faulty vision sees things as they
are, not as they ought to be.
[*The Enlarged Devil's
Dictionary* (1961)]

**CHEKHOV, Anton
(1860–1904)**
After all, the cynicism of real
life can't be outdone by any
literature: one glass won't get
someone drunk when he's
already had a whole barrel.
[*Letter*, 1887]

COZZENS, James Gould (1903–1978)
A cynic is just a man who found out when he was about ten that there wasn't any Santa Claus, and he's still upset.

[Attr.]

HARRIS, Sydney J. (1917–)
A cynic is not merely one who reads bitter lessons from the past, he is one who is prematurely disappointed in the future.

[*On the Contrary* (1962)]

HELLMAN, Lillian (1905–1984)
Cynicism is an unpleasant way of saying the truth.

[*The Little Foxes* (1939)]

HURST, Fannie (1889–1968)
It takes a clever man to turn cynic, and a wise man to be clever enough not to.

[Attr.]

WILDE, Oscar (1854–1900)
Cecil Graham: What is a cynic?
Lord Darlington: A man who knows the price of everything and the value of nothing.

[*Lady Windermere's Fan* (1892)]

DANCING

AUSTEN, Jane (1775–1817)
Fine dancing, I believe, like virtue, must be its own reward.

[*Emma* (1816)]

BANKHEAD, Tallulah (1903–1968)
[Said on dropping fifty dollars into a tambourine held out by a Salvation Army collector] Don't bother to thank me. I know what a perfectly ghastly season it's been for you Spanish dancers.

[Attr.]

BURNEY, Fanny (1752–1840)
Dancing? Oh, dreadful! How it was ever adopted in a civilized country I cannot find out; 'tis certainly a Barbarian exercise, and of savage origin.

[*Cecilia* (1782)]

CHESTERFIELD, Lord (1694–1773)
Custom has made dancing sometimes necessary for a young man; therefore mind it while you learn it, that you may learn to do it well, and not to be ridiculous, though in a ridiculous act.

[Letter to his son, 1746]

DUNCAN, Isadora (1878–1927)
I have discovered the dance. I have discovered the art which has been lost for two thousand years.

[*My Life* (1927)]

SHAKESPEARE, William (1564–1616)
You and I are past our dancing days.

[*Romeo and Juliet,* I.v]

When you do dance, I wish you
A wave o' th' sea, that you might ever do
Nothing but that; move still, still so,
And own no other function.

[*The Winter's Tale*, IV.iv]

SURTEES, R.S. (1805–1864)
These sort of boobies think that people come to balls to do nothing but dance; whereas everyone knows that the real business of a ball is either to look out for a wife, to look after a wife, or to look after somebody else's wife.

[*Mr Facey Romford's Hounds* (1865)]

YEATS, W.B. (1865–1939)
All men are dancers and their tread
Goes to the barbarous clangour of a gong.

['Nineteen Hundred and Nineteen' (1921)]

DANGER

**BURKE, Edmund
(1729–1797)**
Dangers by being despised
grow great.
[Speech on the Petition of the
Unitarians, 1792]

**CHAPMAN, George
(c. 1559–c. 1634)**
Danger (the spurre of all great
mindes) is ever
The curbe to your tame spirits.
[Revenge of Bussy D'Ambois
(1613)]

**CORNEILLE, Pierre
(1606–1684)**
When we conquer without
danger our triumph is without
glory.
[Le Cid (1637)]

**EMERSON, Ralph Waldo
(1803–1882)**
In skating over thin ice, our
safety is in our speed.
['Prudence' (1841)]

As soon as there is life there
is danger.
[Society and Solitude (1870)]

GAY, John (1685–1732)
How, like a moth, the simple
maid,
Still plays about the flame!
[The Beggar's Opera (1728)]

MACCARTHY, Cormac
There are dragons in the
wings of the world.
[The Guardian, 1995]

SALINGER, J.D. (1919–)
What I have to do, I have to
catch everybody if they start to
go over the cliff – I mean if
they're running and they don't
look where they're going I have
to come out from somewhere
and *catch* them . . . I'd just be
the catcher in the rye and all.
[The Catcher in the Rye (1951)]

**STEVENSON, Robert Louis
(1850–1894)**
The bright face of danger.
['The Lantern–Bearers' (1892)]

DEATH

AUBER, Daniel (1782–1871)
[Remark made at a funeral]
This is the last time I will take
part as an amateur.
[Attr.]

BACON, Francis (1561–1626)
Men fear death as children fear to
go in the dark; and as that natural fear in children is increased
with tales, so is the other.
['Of Death' (1625)]

BHAGAVADGITA
I am become death, the

destroyer of worlds.
[Quoted by J. Robert
Oppenheimer on seeing the
first nuclear explosion]

BOWRA, Sir Maurice (1898–1971)

Any amusing deaths lately?
[Attr.]

BUCK, Pearl S. (1892–1973)

Euthanasia is a long, smooth-
sounding word, and it
conceals its danger as long,
smooth words do, but the
danger is there, nevertheless.
[*The Child Who Never Grew*
(1950)]

BUTLER, Samuel (1835–1902)

When you have told anyone
you have left him a legacy the
only decent thing to do is to
die at once.
[In Festing Jones, *Samuel
Butler: A Memoir*]

DIBDIN, Charles (1745–1814)

What argufies pride and ambi-
tion?
Soon or late death will take
us in tow:
Each bullet has got its com-
mission,
And when our time's come
we must go.
['Each Bullet has its
Commission']

DICKINSON, Emily (1830–1886)

Because I could not stop for
Death –
He kindly stopped for me –
The Carriage held but just
Ourselves –
And Immortality.
['Because I could not stop for
Death' (c. 1863)]

DUNBAR, William (c. 1460–c. 1525)

Unto the deid gois all Estatis,
Princis, prelatis, and potesta-
tis,
Baith rich and poor of all
degree:
Timor Mortis conturbat me.
['Lament for the Makaris'
(1834)]

FONTAINE, Jean de la (1621–1695)

Death does not take the wise
man by surprise, he is always
prepared to leave.
['La Mort et le mourant']

FORSTER, E.M. (1879–1970)

Death destroys a man; the
idea of Death saves him.
[*Howard's End* (1910)]

HENLEY, W.E. (1849–1903)

Madam Life's a piece in
bloom
Death goes dogging every-
where:
She's the tenant of the room,

He's the ruffian on the stair.
[*Echoes* (1877)]

HUXLEY, Aldous (1894–1963)
Death ... It's the only thing we haven't succeeded in completely vulgarizing.
[*Eyeless in Gaza* (1936)]

HUXLEY, Henrietta (1825–1915)
And if there be no meeting past the grave,
If all is darkness, silence, yet 'tis rest.
Be not afraid ye waiting hearts that weep;
For still He giveth His beloved sleep,
And if an endless sleep He wills, so best.
[Lines on the grave of her husband, 1895]

KOESTLER, Arthur (1905–1983)
[Of the atomic bomb]
Hitherto man had to live with the idea of death as an individual; from now onward mankind will have to live with the idea of its death as a species.
[Attr.]

LARKIN, Philip (1922–1985)
[On death]
The anaesthetic from which none come round.
['Aubade' (1988)]

MANKIEWICZ, Herman J. (1897–1953)
[Of death]
It is the only disease you don't look forward to being cured of.
[*Citizen Kane*, film, 1941]

MILLAY, Edna St Vincent (1892–1950)
Down, down, down into the darkness of the grave
Gently they go, the beautiful, the tender, the kind;
Quietly they go, the intelligent, the witty, the brave.
I know. But I do not approve.
And I am not resigned.
['Dirge without Music' (1928)]

OUIDA (1839–1908)
Even of death Christianity has made a terror which was unknown to the gay calmness of the Pagan.
[*Views and Opinions* (1895)]

OWEN, Wilfred (1893–1918)
What passing-bells for these who die as cattle?
Only the monstrous anger of the guns.
Only the stuttering rifles' rapid rattle
Can patter out their hasty orisons.
['Anthem for Doomed Youth' (1917)]

PATTEN, Brian (1946–)
Death is the only grammatically correct full-stop . . .

Between himself and the grave his parents stand, monuments that will crumble.
['Schoolboy' (1990)]

POWER, Marguerite, Countess of Blessington (1789–1849)
It is better to die young than to outlive all one loved, and all that rendered one lovable.
[*The Confessions of an Elderly Gentleman* (1836)]

SAKI (1870–1916)
Waldo is one of those people who would be enormously improved by death.
[*Beasts and Super-Beasts* (1914)]

SEVIGNE, Mme de (1626–1696)
I find death so terrible that I hate life more for leading me towards it than for the thorns encountered on the way.
[Letter to Mme de Grignan, 1672]

SHAKESPEARE, William (1564–1616)
Fear no more the heat o' th' sun
Nor the furious winter's rages;
Thou thy worldly task hast done,
Home art gone, and ta'en thy wages.
Golden lads and girls all must,
As chimney-sweepers, come to dust.
[*Cymbeline*, IV.ii]

This fell sergeant Death
Is strict in his arrest.
[*Hamlet*, V.ii]

Cowards die many times before their deaths:
The valiant never taste of death but once.
[*Julius Caesar*, II.ii]

Men must endure
Their going hence, even as their coming hither:
Ripeness is all.
[*King Lear*, V.ii]

SHAW, George Bernard (1856–1950)
Life levels all men: death reveals the eminent.
[*Man and Superman* (1903)]

SHELLEY, Percy Bysshe (1792–1822)
Death is the veil which those who live call life:
They sleep, and it is lifted.
[*Prometheus Unbound* (1820)]

SHIRLEY, James (1596–1666)
The glories of our blood and

state
Are shadows, not substantial things;
There is no armour against fate;
Death lays his icy hand on kings:
Sceptre and crown
Must tumble down,
And in the dust be equal made
With the poor crooked scythe and spade.
[*The Contention of Ajax and Ulysses* (1659)]

SMITH, Stevie (1902–1971)
If there wasn't death, I think you couldn't go on.
[*The Observer*, 1969]

SOUTHEY, Robert (1774–1843)
My name is Death: the last best friend am I.
[*Carmen Nuptiale* (1816)]

THOMAS, Dylan (1914–1953)
Though they go mad they shall be sane,
Though they sink through the sea they shall rise again;
Though lovers be lost love shall not;
And death shall have no dominion.
['And death shall have no dominion' (1936)]

TWAIN, Mark (1835–1910)
The report of my death was an exaggeration.
[Cable, 1897]

WRIGHT, Judith (1915–)
Death marshals up his armies round us now.
Their footsteps crowd too near.
Lock your warm hand above the chilling heart
and for a time I live without my fear.
Grope in the night to find me and embrace,
for the dark preludes of the drums begin,
and round us, round the company of lovers,
death draws his cordons in.
['The Company of Lovers' (1946)]

YEATS, W.B. (1865–1939)
Nor dread nor hope attend
A dying animal;
A man awaits his end
Dreading and hoping all.
['Death' (1933)]

DEATH: DYING

ALLEN, Woody (1935–)
It's not that I'm afraid to die. I just don't want to be there when it happens.
[*Without Feathers* (1976)]

BACON, Francis (1561–1626)
I do not believe that any man fears to be dead, but only the stroke of death.

[*The Remaines of . . . Lord Verulam* (1648)]

BARRIE, Sir J.M. (1860–1937)
To die will be an awfully big adventure.

[*Peter Pan* (1904)]

BETJEMAN, Sir John (1906–1984)
There was sun enough for lazing upon beaches,
There was fun enough for far into the night.
But I'm dying now and done for,
What on earth was all the fun for?
For I'm old and ill and terrified and tight.

['Sun and Fun' (1954)]

BUTLER, Samuel (1835–1902)
It costs a lot of money to die comfortably.

[*The Note-Books of Samuel Butler* (1912)]

CHARLES II (1630–1685)
He had been, he said, a most unconscionable time dying; but he hoped that they would excuse it.

[In Macaulay, *The History of England* (1849)]

CHILDERS, Erskine (1870–1922)
[Writing about his imminent execution]
It seems perfectly simple and inevitable, like lying down after a long day's work.

[Prison letter to his wife]

CRASHAW, Richard (c. 1612–1649)
And when life's sweet fable ends,
Soul and body part like friends;
No quarrels, murmurs, no delay;
A kiss, a sigh, and so away.

['Temperance' (1652)]

DICKINSON, Emily (1830–1886)
I heard a Fly buzz – when I died . . .
With Blue – uncertain stumbling Buzz –
Between the light – and me –
And then the Windows failed – and then
I could not see to see.

['I heard a Fly buzz – when I died' (c. 1862)]

JOHNSON, Samuel (1709–1784)
It matters not how a man dies, but how he lives. The act of dying is not of importance, it lasts so short a time.

[In Boswell, *The Life of Samuel Johnson* (1791)]

MAUGHAM, William Somerset (1874–1965)
Dying is a very dull, dreary affair. And my advice to you is to have nothing whatever to do with it.
[In R. Maugham, *Escape from the Shadows* (1972)]

PLATH, Sylvia (1932–1963)
Dying
Is an art, like everything else.
I do it exceptionally well.
['Lady Lazarus' (1963)]

POPE, Alexander (1688–1744)
I mount! I fly!
O Grave! where is thy victory?
O Death! where is thy sting?
['The Dying Christian to his Soul' (1730)]

SHAKESPEARE, William (1564–1616)
Nothing in his life
Became him like the leaving it: he died
As one that had been studied in his death
To throw away the dearest thing he ow'd
As 'twere a careless trifle.
[*Macbeth*, I.iv]

SMITH, Logan Pearsall (1865–1946)
I cannot forgive my friends for dying; I do not find these van-
ishing acts of theirs at all amusing.
[*Afterthoughts* (1931)]

THOMAS, Dylan (1914–1953)
Do not go gentle into that good night,
Old age should burn and rave at close of day;
Rage, rage against the dying of the light.
['Do Not Go Gentle into that Good Night' (1952)]

TWAIN, Mark (1835–1910)
All say, 'How hard it is to die' – a strange complaint to come from the mouths of people who have had to live.
[*Pudd'nhead Wilson's Calendar* (1894)]

DEATH: THE DEAD

ADDISON, Joseph (1672–1719)
When I read the several dates of the tombs, of some that died yesterday, and some six hundred years ago, I consider that great day when we shall all of us be contemporaries, and make our appearance together.
[*Thoughts in Westminster Abbey*]

DICKINSON, Emily
(1830–1886)
This quiet Dust was
Gentlemen and Ladies
And Lads and Girls –
Was laughter and ability and
Sighing
And Frocks and Curls.
['This quiet Dust was
Gentlemen and Ladies'
(c. 1864)]

GRAY, Patrick, Lord
(d. 1612)
[Advocating the execution of
Mary, Queen of Scots]
A dead woman bites not.
[Oral tradition, 1587]

HENDRIX, Jimi
(1942–1970)
Once you're dead, you're
made for life.
[Attr.]

LAWRENCE, D.H.
(1885–1930)
The dead don't die. They look
on and help.
[Letter to J. Middleton Murry,
1923]

MAETERLINCK, Maurice
(1862–1949)
The living are just the dead on
holiday.
[Attr.]

SCHOPENHAUER, Arthur
(1788–1860)
After your death you will be
what you were before your
birth.
[*Parerga and Paralipomena*
(1851)]

TENNYSON, Alfred, Lord
(1809–1892)
Do we indeed desire the dead
Should still be near us at our
side?
Is there no baseness we
would hide?
No inner vileness that we
dread?
[*In Memoriam A. H. H.* (1850)]

VOLTAIRE
(1694–1778)
We owe respect to the living;
we owe nothing but truth to
the dead.
['Première Lettre sur *Oedipe*'
(1785)]

YOUNG, Edward
(1683–1765)
Life is the desert, life the
solitude;
Death joins us to the great
majority.
[*The Revenge* (1721)]

See GRIEF

DEBTS

COOLIDGE, Calvin (1872–1933)
[Of Allied war debts]
They hired the money, didn't they?
[Remark, 1925]

FOX, Henry Stephen (1791–1846)
[Remark after an illness]
I am so changed that my oldest creditors would hardly know me.
[Quoted by Byron in a letter to John Murray, 1817]

IBSEN, Henrik (1828–1906)
Home life ceases to be free and beautiful as soon as it is founded on borrowing and debt.
[*A Doll's House* (1879)]

SHERIDAN, Richard Brinsley (1751–1816)
[Handing one of his creditors an IOU]
Thank God, that's settled.
[In Shriner, *Wit, Wisdom, and Foibles of the Great* (1918)]

[After being refused a loan of £25 from a friend who asked him to repay the £500 he had already borrowed]
My dear fellow, be reasonable; the sum you ask me for is a very considerable one, whereas I only ask you for twenty-five pounds.
[Attr.]

WARD, Artemus (1834–1867)
Let us all be happy, and live within our means, even if we have to borrer the money to do it with.
['Science and Natural History']

WODEHOUSE, P.G. (1881–1975)
I don't owe a penny to a single soul – not counting tradesmen, of course.
['Jeeves and the Hard-Boiled Egg' (1919)]

DECEPTION

BERKELEY, Bishop George (1685–1753)
It is impossible that a man who is false to his friends and neighbours should be true to the public.
[*Maxims Concerning Patriotism* (1750)]

CARSWELL, Catherine (1879–1946)
It wasn't a woman who betrayed Jesus with a kiss.
[*The Savage Pilgrimage* (1932)]

**CHAUCER, Geoffrey
(c. 1340–1400)**
The smyler with the knyf
under the cloke.
[*The Canterbury Tales* (1387)]

**FONTAINE, Jean de la
(1621–1695)**
It is a double pleasure to trick
the trickster.
['Le coq et le renard']

GAY, John (1685–1732)
To cheat a man is nothing;
but the woman must have
fine parts indeed who cheats
a woman!
[*The Beggar's Opera* (1728)]

HENRY, O. (1862–1910)
It was beautiful and simple as
all truly great swindles are.
['The Octopus Marooned'
(1908)]

HILL, Joe (1879–1914)
You will eat (You will eat)
Bye and bye (Bye and bye)
In that glorious land above
the sky (Way up high)
Work and pray (Work and pray)
Live on hay (Live on hay)
You'll get pie in the sky when
you die (That's a lie.)
['The Preacher and the Slave',
song, 1911]

**SCOTT, Sir Walter
(1771–1832)**
O what a tangled web we
weave,
When first we practise to
deceive!
[*Marmion* (1808)]

**SHAKESPEARE, William
(1564–1616)**
O villain, villain, smiling,
damned villain!
My tables – meet it is I set it
down
That one may smile, and
smile, and be a villain.
[*Hamlet*, I.v]

**THURBER, James
(1894–1961)**
You can fool too many of the
people too much of the time.
[*The New Yorker*, 1939]

See HYPOCRISY

DEMOCRACY

**ATTLEE, Clement
(1883–1967)**
Democracy means govern-
ment by discussion but it is
only effective if you can stop
people talking.
[Speech, 1957]

**BEVERIDGE, William
(1879–1963)**
The trouble in modern
democracy is that men do not
approach to leadership until

they have lost the desire to lead anyone.

[*The Observer*, 1934]

CHURCHILL, Sir Winston (1874–1965)
Many forms of government have been tried, and will be tried in this world of sin and woe. No one pretends that democracy is perfect or all-wise. Indeed, it has been said that democracy is the worst form of Government except all those other forms that have been tried from time to time.

[Speech, 1947]

FLERS, Robert, Marquis de (1872–1927) and CAILLAVET, Arman de (1869–1915)
Democracy is the name we give the people whenever we need them.

[*L'habit vert*]

FO, Dario (1926–)
Correct! You said it! Scandal is the manure of democracy.

[*Accidental Death of an Anarchist* (1974)]

FORSTER, E.M. (1879–1970)
So Two cheers for Democracy: one because it admits variety and two because it permits criticism. Two cheers are quite enough: there is no occasion to give three. Only Love the Beloved Republic deserves that.

[*Two Cheers for Democracy* (1951)]

IBSEN, Henrik (1828–1906)
The most dangerous foe to truth and freedom in our midst is the compact majority. Yes, the damned, compact liberal majority.

[*An Enemy of the People* (1882)]

LINCOLN, Abraham (1809–1865)
No man is good enough to govern another man without that other's consent.

[Speech, 1854]

The ballot is stronger than the bullet.

[Speech, 1856]

NIEBUHR, Reinhold (1892–1971)
Man's capacity for justice makes democracy possible, but man's inclination to injustice makes democracy necessary.

[*The Children of Light and the Children of Darkness* (1944)]

SHAW, George Bernard (1856–1950)
Democracy substitutes election by the incompetent many for appointment by the corrupt few.

[*Man and Superman* (1903)]

**TOCQUEVILLE, Alexis de
(1805–1859)**
I sought the image of democracy, in order to learn what we have to fear and to hope from its progress.
[*De la Démocratie en Amérique (1840)*]

**WEBSTER, Daniel
(1782–1852)**
The people's government, made for the people, made by the people, and answerable to the people.

[Speech, 1830]

**WILLIAMS, Tennessee
(1911–1983)**
Knowledge – Zzzzzp! Money – Zzzzzp! – Power! That's the cycle democracy is built on!
[*The Glass Menagerie* (1945)]

**WILSON, Woodrow
(1856–1924)**
The world must be made safe for democracy.

[Speech, 1917]

See GOVERNMENT

DESPAIR

ALLEN, Woody (1935–)
More than any other time in history, mankind faces a crossroads. One path leads to despair and utter hopelessness. The other, to total extinction. Let us pray we have the wisdom to choose correctly.

[*Side Effects*]

**CAMUS, Albert
(1913–1960)**
He who despairs over an event is a coward, but he who holds hopes for the human condition is a fool.
[*The Rebel* (1951)]

**FITZGERALD, F. Scott
(1896–1940)**
In the real dark night of the soul it is always three o'clock in the morning.
[*The Crack-Up* (1945)]

**GREENE, Graham
(1904– 1991)**
Despair is the price one pays for setting oneself an impossible aim.
[*Heart of the Matter* (1948)]

**HOPKINS, Gerard Manley
(1844–1889)**
Not, I'll not, carrion comfort, Despair, not feast on thee;
Not untwist – slack they may be – these last strands of man
In me or. most weary, cry *I can no more*. I can;
Can something, hope, wish day come, not choose not to be.
['Carrion Comfort' (1885)]

ST JOHN OF THE CROSS (1542–1591)
The dark night of the soul.
[Title of poem]

KAFKA, Franz (1883–1924)
Do not despair, not even about the fact that you do not despair.
[*Diary*, 1913]

SHAKESPEARE, William (1564–1616)
I shall despair. There is no creature loves me;
And if I die no soul will pity me:
And wherefore should they, since that I myself
Find in myself no pity to myself?
[*Richard III*, V.iii]

SHAW, George Bernard (1856–1950)
He who has never hoped can never despair.
[*Caesar and Cleopatra* (1901)]

DESTINY

CLAUDIUS CAECUS, Appius (4th–3rd century BC)
Each man is the architect of his own destiny.
[In Sallust, *Ad Caesarem*]

ARNOLD, Matthew (1822–1888)
Yet they, believe me, who await
No gifts from chance, have conquered fate.
['Resignation' (1849)]

AURELIUS, Marcus (121–180)
Nothing happens to any thing which that thing is not made by nature to bear.
[*Meditations*]

BACON, Francis (1561–1626)
If a man look sharply, and attentively, he shall see Fortune: for though she be blind, yet she is not invisible.
[*Essays* (1625)]

BOWEN, Elizabeth (1899–1973)
Fate is not an eagle, it creeps like a rat.
[*The House in Paris* (1935)]

BÜCHNER, Georg (1813–1837)
We are puppets on strings worked by unknown forces; we ourselves are nothing, nothing!
[*Danton's Death* (1835)]

CHURCHILL, Sir Winston (1874–1965)
I felt as if I were walking with destiny, and that all my past life had been but a preparation for this hour and this trial.
[*The Gathering Storm*]

CRISP, Quentin (1908–)
Believe in fate, but lean forward where fate can see you.
[Attr.]

DELILLE, Abbé Jacques (1738–1813)
Relations are made by fate, friends by choice.
[*Malheur et pitié* (1803)]

ELIOT, George (1819–1880)
'Character', says Novalis, in one of his questionable aphorisms – 'character is destiny'.
[*The Mill on the Floss* (1860)]

FITZGERALD, Edward (1809–1883)
'Tis all a Chequer-board of Nights and Days
Where Destiny with Men for Pieces plays:
Hither and thither moves, and mates, and slays,
And one by one back in the Closet lays.
[*The Rubáiyát of Omar Khayyám* (1859)]

The Moving Finger writes; and, having writ,
Moves on: nor all thy Piety nor Wit
Shall lure it back to cancel half a Line,
Nor all thy Tears wash out a Word of it.
[*The Rubáiyát of Omar Khayyám* (1859)]

FORD, John (c. 1586–1639)
Tempt not the stars, young man, thou canst not play
With the severity of fate.
[*The Broken Heart* (1633)]

GAY, John (1685–1732)
'Tis a gross error, held in schools,
That Fortune always favours fools.
[*Fables* (1738)]

HARE, Maurice Evan (1886–1967)
There once was a man who said, 'Damn!
It is borne in upon me I am
An engine that moves
In predestinate grooves,
I'm not even a bus, I'm a tram.'
['Limerick', 1905]

HITLER, Adolf (1889–1945)
I go the way that Providence bids me go with the certainty of a sleepwalker.
[Speech, Munich, 1936]

JONSON, Ben (1572–1637)
Blind Fortune still
Bestows her gifts on such as cannot use them.
[*Every Man out of His Humour* (1599)]

LOOS, Anita (1893–1981)
Fate keeps on happening.
[*Gentlemen Prefer Blondes* (1925)]

MACAULAY, Lord (1800–1859)
He never would believe that Providence had sent a few men into the world ready booted and spurred to ride, and millions ready saddled and bridled to be ridden.
[*History of England* (1849)]

MACHIAVELLI (1469–1527)
Fortune, like a woman, is friendly to the young, because they show her less respect, they are more daring and command her with audacity.
[*The Prince* (1532)]

MALLARMÉ, Stéphane (1842–1898)
A throw of the dice will never eliminate chance.
[Title of work, 1897]

SCHOPENHAUER, Arthur (1788–1860)
Fate shuffles the cards and we play.
['Aphorisms for Wisdom' (1851)]

SHAKESPEARE, William (1564–1616)
Men at some time are masters of their fates:

The fault, dear Brutus, is not in our stars,
But in ourselves, that we are underlings.
[*Julius Caesar*, I.ii]

There is a tide in the affairs of men
Which, taken at the flood, leads on to fortune;
Omitted, all the voyage of their life
Is bound in shallows and in miseries.
[*Julius Caesar*, IV.iii.]

TERENCE (c. 190–159 BC)
Fortune favours the brave.
[*Phormio*]

THE DEVIL

BAUDELAIRE, Charles (1821–1867)
My dear brothers, never forget when you hear the progress of the Enlightenment praised, that the Devil's cleverest ploy is to persuade you that he doesn't exist.
[Attr.]

THE BIBLE (KING JAMES VERSION)
Resist the devil, and he will flee from you.
[*James*, 4:7]

BROWNING, Elizabeth Barrett (1806–1861)
The devil's most devilish when respectable.
[*Aurora Leigh* (1857)]

BUTLER, Samuel (1835–1902)
An apology for the devil: it must be remembered that we have heard only one side of the case; God has written all the books.
[*The Note-Books of Samuel Butler* (1912)]

DOSTOEVSKY, Fyodor (1821–1881)
I think if the devil doesn't exist, and man has created him, he has created him in his own image and likeness.
[*The Brothers Karamazov* (1880)]

HILL, Rowland (1744–1833)
[Referring to his writing of hymns]
He did not see any reason why the devil should have all the good tunes.
[In Broome, *The Rev. Rowland Hill* (1881)]

LAWRENCE, D.H. (1885–1930)
It is no good casting out devils. They belong to us, we must accept them and be at peace with them.
['The Reality of Peace' (1936)]

MILTON, John (1608–1674)
Abasht the Devil stood,
And felt how awful goodness is.
[*Paradise Lost* (1667)]

SHAKESPEARE, William (1564–1616)
The devil can cite Scripture for his purpose.
[*The Merchant of Venice*, I.iii]

DINING

BOWRA, Sir Maurice (1898–1971)
I'm a man
More dined against than dining.
[In Betjeman, *Summoned by Bells* (1960)]

EVARTS, William Maxwell (1818–1901)
[Of a dinner given by US President and temperance advocate Rutherford B. Hayes]
It was a brilliant affair; water flowed like champagne.
[Attr.]

GULBENKIAN, Nubar (1896–1972)
The best number for a dinner party is two: myself and a

damn good head waiter.
[*The Observer*, 1965]

**JOHNSON, Samuel
(1709–1784)**
This was a good dinner
enough, to be sure; but it was
not a dinner to *ask* a man to.
[In Boswell, *The Life of Samuel
Johnson* (1791)]

A man seldom thinks with
more earnestness of anything
than he does of his dinner.
[In Piozzi, *Anecdotes of the
Late Samuel Johnson* (1786)]

A man is in general better
pleased when he has a good
dinner upon his table, than
when his wife talks Greek.
[In Hawkins, *Life of Samuel
Johnson* (1787)]

**MAUGHAM, William
Somerset (1874–1965)**
At a dinner party one should
eat wisely but not too well,
and talk well but not too
wisely.
[*A Writer's Notebook* (1949)]

PEPYS, Samuel (1633–1703)
Strange to see how a good
dinner and feasting reconciles
everybody.

[*Diary*, 1665]

SWIFT, Jonathan (1667–1745)
He showed me his bill of fare
to tempt me to dine with him;
Poh, said I, I value not your
bill of fare; give me your bill
of company.
[*Journal to Stella*, 1711]

DIPLOMACY

**CROMWELL, Oliver
(1599–1658)**
A man-of-war is the best
ambassador.

[Attr.]

**PEARSON, Lester B.
(1897–1972)**
Diplomacy is letting someone
else have your way.
[*The Observer*, 1965]

**USTINOV, Sir Peter
(1921–)**
A diplomat these days is
nothing but a head-waiter
who's allowed to sit down
occasionally.
[*Romanoff and Juliet* (1956)]

**WOTTON, Sir Henry
(1568–1639)**
*Legatus est vir bonus peregre
missus ad mentiendum rei
publicae causa.*
An ambassador is an honest
man sent to lie abroad for the
good of his country.
[Written in an album, 1606]

DOGS

**BEERBOHM, Sir Max
(1872–1956)**
You will find that the woman who is really kind to dogs is always one who has failed to inspire sympathy in men.
[*Zuleika Dobson* (1911)]

**BENNETT, Alan
(1934–)**
[On dogs]
It's the one species I wouldn't mind seeing vanish from the face of the earth. I wish they were like the white rhino – six of them left in the Serengeti National Park, and all males.
[Attr.]

**ELIOT, George
(1819–1880)**
Though, as we know, she was not fond of pets that must be held in the hands or trodden on, she was always attentive to the feelings of dogs, and very polite if she had to decline their advances.
[*Middlemarch* (1872)]

**HUXLEY, Aldous
(1894–1963)**
To his dog, every man is Napoleon; hence the constant popularity of dogs.
[Attr.]

MUIR, Frank (1920–)
Dogs, like horses, are quadrupeds. That is to say, they have four rupeds, one at each corner, on which they walk.
[*You Can't Have Your Kayak and Heat It*, with Dennis Norden]

NASH, Ogden (1902–1971)
A door is what a dog is perpetually on the wrong side of.
['A Dog's Best Friend Is His Illiteracy' (1952)]

**POPE, Alexander
(1688–1744)**
[On the collar of a dog given to Frederick, Prince of Wales]
I am his Highness' dog at Kew;
Pray, tell me sir, whose dog are you?
['Epigram' (1738)]

**SPARROW, John
(1906–1992)**
That indefatigable and unsavoury engine of pollution, the dog.
[Letter to *The Times*, 1975]

**STREATFIELD, Sir Geoffrey
(1897–1978)**
I loathe people who keep dogs. They are cowards who haven't got the guts to bite people themselves.
[*A Madman's Diary*]

DOUBT

BACON, Francis (1561–1626)
If a man will begin with certainties, he shall end in doubts; but if he will be content to begin with doubts, he shall end in certainties.
[*The Advancement of Learning* (1605)]

BORGES, Jorge Luis (1899–1986)
I have known what the Greeks knew not: uncertainty.
[*The Garden of Paths which Diverge* (1941)]

BROWNING, Robert (1812–1889)
All we have gained then by our unbelief
Is a life of doubt diversified by faith,
For one of faith diversified by doubt:
We called the chess–board white, – we call it black.
['Bishop Blougram's Apology' (1855)]

BUTLER, Samuel (1835–1902)
My Lord, I do not believe. Help thou mine unbelief.
[*Samuel Butler's Notebooks* (1951)]

DARROW, Clarence (1857–1938)
[Remark during the trial of John Scopes, 1925, for teaching evolution in school]
I do not consider it an insult but rather a compliment to be called an agnostic. I do not pretend to know where many ignorant men are sure – that is all that agnosticism means.
[Attr.]

DENT, Alan (1905–1978)
This is the tragedy of a man who could not make up his mind.
[Introduction to film *Hamlet*, 1948]

HARDWICKE, Earl of (1690–1764)
[Referring to Dirleton's *Doubts*]
His doubts are better than most people's certainties.
[In Boswell, *The Life of Samuel Johnson* (1791)]

HUXLEY, T.H. (1825–1895)
I am too much of a sceptic to deny the possibility of anything.
[Letter to Herbert Spencer, 1886]

KORAN
There is no doubt in this book.
[Chapter 1]

**NEWMAN, Cardinal
(1801–1890)**
Ten thousand difficulties do
not make one doubt.
[*Apologia pro Vita Sua* (1864)]

**TENNYSON, Alfred, Lord
(1809–1892)**
There lives more faith in
honest doubt,
Believe me, than in half the
creeds.
[*In Memoriam A. H. H.* (1850)]

DREAMS

**BACON, Francis
(1561–1626)**
Dreams and predictions of
astrology . . . ought to serve
but for winter talk by the fire-
side.
[*Essays* (1625)]

**BUNN, Alfred
(1796–1860)**
I dreamt that I dwelt in marble halls,
With vassals and serfs at my
side.
[*The Bohemian Girl* (1843)]

**CALDERÓN DE LA BARCA,
Pedro (1600–1681)**
For I see, since I am asleep, that
I dream while I am awake.
[*Life is a Dream* (1636)]

**CHUANG TSE
(c. 369–286 BC)**
I do not know whether I was
then a man dreaming I was a
butterfly, or whether I am now
a butterfly dreaming I am a
man.
[*Chuang Tse* (1889), trans.
H.A. Giles]

**LAWRENCE, T.E.
(1888–1935)**
All men dream: but not equally. Those who dream by night
in the dusty recesses of their
minds wake in the day to find
that it was vanity; but the
dreamers of the day are
dangerous men, for they may
act their dream with open
eyes, to make it possible.
[*The Seven Pillars of Wisdom*
(1926)]

**MONTAIGNE, Michel de
(1533–1592)**
Those who have compared
our life to a dream were, by
chance, more right than they
thought . . . We are awake
while sleeping, and sleeping
while awake.
[*Essais* (1580)]

**POE, Edgar Allan
(1809–1849)**
All that we see or seem
Is but a dream within a dream.
['A Dream within a Dream'
(1849)]

SHAKESPEARE, William (1564–1616)
O God, I could be bounded in a nutshell and count myself a king of infinite space, were it not that I have bad dreams.
[*Hamlet*, II.ii]

We are such stuff
As dreams are made on; and our little life
Is rounded with a sleep.
[*The Tempest*, IV.i]

TENNYSON, Alfred, Lord (1809–1892)
Dreams are true while they last, and do we not live in dreams?
['The Higher Pantheism' (1867)]

YEATS, W.B. (1865–1939)
In dreams begins responsibility.
[*Responsibilities* (1914)]

DRESS

AESOP (6th century BC)
It is not only fine feathers that make fine birds.
['The Jay and the Peacock']

ASHFORD, Daisy (1881–1972)
You look rather rash my dear your colors dont quite match your face.
[*The Young Visiters* (1919)]

BONGAY, Amy
[Commenting on the fact that the fashion industry had begun to find supermodels too demanding]
It's a terrible sign. It will be the death of this profession if designers start using real people on the catwalks and in their advertising.
[*Daily Mail*, 1995]

CHANEL, Coco (1883–1971)
[On Dior's New Look]
These are clothes by a man who doesn't know women, never had one and dreams of being one.
[*Scotland on Sunday*, 1995]

CURIE, Marie (1867–1934)
[Referring to a wedding dress]
I have no dress except the one I wear every day. If you are going to be kind enough to give me one, please let it be practical and dark so that I can put it on afterwards to go to the laboratory.
[*Letter to a friend*, 1894]

DARROW, Clarence (1857–1938)
I go to a better tailor than any of you and pay more for my clothes. The only difference is

that you probably don't sleep in yours.

[In E. Fuller, *2500 Anecdotes*]

EMERSON, Ralph Waldo (1803–1882)

It is only when the mind and character slumber that the dress can be seen.

[*Letters and Social Aims* (1875)]

FARQUHAR, George (1678–1707)

A lady, if undrest at Church, looks silly,
One cannot be devout in dishabille.

[*The Stage Coach* (1704)]

FORBES, Miss C.F. (1817–1911)

The sense of being well-dressed gives a feeling of inward tranquillity which religion is powerless to bestow.

[In Emerson, *Social Aims* (1876)]

GASKELL, Elizabeth (1810–1865)

[The Cranford ladies'] dress is very independent of fashion; as they observe, 'What does it signify how we dress here at Cranford, where everybody knows us?' And if they go from home, their reason is equally cogent, 'What does it signify how we dress here, where nobody knows us?'

[*Cranford* (1853)]

HEWETT, Dorothy (1923–)

Gentlemen may remove any garment consistent with decency.
Ladies may remove any garment consistent with charm.

['Beneath the Arches']

NASH, Ogden (1902–1971)

Sure, deck your lower limbs in pants;
Yours are the limbs, my sweeting.
You look divine as you advance –
Have you seen yourself retreating?

['What's the Use?' (1940)]

PARKER, Dorothy (1893–1967)

Where's the man could ease a heart,
Like a satin gown?

['The Satin Dress' (1937)]

Brevity is the soul of lingerie.

[In Woollcott, *While Rome Burns* (1934)]

WATTS, Isaac (1674–1748)

The tulip and the butterfly
Appear in gayer coats than I:
Let me be dressed fine as I will,
Flies, worms, and flowers, exceed me still.

['Against Pride in Clothes' (1715)]

**WHITEHORN, Katherine
(1926–)**
Hats divide generally into
three classes: offensive hats,
defensive hats, and shrapnel.
[*Shouts and Murmurs* (1963)]

**WODEHOUSE, P.G.
(1881–1975)**
The Right Hon was a tubby
little chap who looked as if he
had been poured into his
clothes and had forgotten to
say 'When!'
['Jeeves and the Impending
Doom' (1930)]

DRINK

AGA KHAN III (1877–1957)
[Justifying his liking for alcohol]
I'm so holy that when I touch
wine, it turns into water.
[Attr. in Compton Miller,
Who's Really Who (1983)]

**ALDRICH, Henry
(1647–1710)**
If all be true that I do think,
There are five reasons we
should drink;
Good wine – a friend – or
being dry –
Or lest we should be by and
by –
Or any other reason why.
['Five Reasons for Drinking'
(1689)]

ANONYMOUS
Hath wine an oblivious
power?
Can it pluck out the sting from
the brain?
The draught might beguile for
an hour,
But still leaves behind it the
pain.
['Farewell to England'; sometimes attr. to Byron]

**BECON, Thomas
(1512–1567)**
For when the wine is in, the
wit is out.
[*Catechism* (1560)]

**BENCHLEY, Robert
(1889–1945)**
[Reply when asked if he
realised that drinking was a
slow death]
So who's in a hurry?
[Attr.]

BURNS, Robert (1759–1796)
Freedom and whisky gang
thegither,
Tak aff your dram!
['The Author's Earnest Cry
and Prayer' (1786)]

BYRON, Lord (1788–1824)
Man, being reasonable, must
get drunk;
The best of life is but intoxication:
Glory, the grape, love, gold, in
these are sunk

DRINK

The hopes of all men, and of every nation.

[*Don Juan* (1824)]

CHANDLER, Raymond (1888–1959)

Alcohol is like love: the first kiss is magic, the second is intimate, the third is routine. After that you just take the girl's clothes off.

[*The Long Good-bye* (1953)]

CHURCHILL, Sir Winston (1874–1965)

[Said during a lunch with the Arab leader Ibn Saud, when he heard that the king's religion forbade smoking and alcohol] I must point out that my rule of life prescribed as an absolutely sacred rite smoking cigars and also the drinking of alcohol before, after, and if need be during all meals and in the intervals between them.

[*Triumph and Tragedy*]

COPE, Wendy (1945–)

All you need is love, love or, failing that, alcohol.

[Variation on a Lennon and McCartney song]

COREN, Alan (1938–)

Apart from cheese and tulips, the main product of the country [Holland] is advocaat, a drink made from lawyers.

[*The Sanity Inspector* (1974)]

DE QUINCEY, Thomas (1785–1859)

It is most absurdly said, in popular language, of any man, that he is *disguised* in liquor; for, on the contrary, most men are disguised by sobriety.

[*Confessions of an English Opium Eater* (1822)]

DIBDIN, Charles (1745–1814)

Then trust me, there's nothing like drinking
So pleasant on this side the grave;
It keeps the unhappy from thinking,
And makes e'en the valiant more brave.

['Nothing like Grog']

DUNNE, Finley Peter (1867–1936)

There is wan thing an' on'y wan thing to be said in favour iv dhrink, an' that is that it has caused manny a lady to be loved that otherwise might've died single.

[*Mr Dooley Says* (1910)]

FITZGERALD, Edward (1809–1883)

Drink! for you know not whence you came, nor why: Drink! for you know not why you go, nor where.

[*The Rubáiyát of Omar Khayyám* (1879)]

**FITZGERALD, F. Scott
(1896–1940)**
First you take a drink, then
the drink takes a drink, then
the drink takes you.
[In Jules Feiffer, *Ackroyd*]

**FLETCHER, John
(1579–1625)**
And he that will go to bed
sober,
Falls with the leaf still in
October.
[*The Bloody Brother* (1616)]

**FRANKLIN, Benjamin
(1706–1790)**
There are more old drunkards
than old doctors.
[Attr.]

JAMES, William (1842–1910)
If merely 'feeling good' could
decide, drunkenness would be
the supremely valid human
experience.
[*Varieties of Religious
Experience* (1902)]

**JOHNSON, Samuel
(1709–1784)**
A man who exposes himself
when he is intoxicated, has
not the art of getting drunk.
[In Boswell, *The Life of Samuel
Johnson* (1791)]

JUNELL, Thomas
The Finns have a very different alcohol culture from other
European countries. Basically,
it's nothing to do with social-
ising – it's about getting
drunk.
[*Daily Mail*, 1996]

**LARDNER, Ring
(1885–1933)**
Frenchmen drink wine just
like we used to drink water
before Prohibition.
[In R.E. Drennan, *Wit's End*]

**LLOYD GEORGE, David
(1863–1945)**
[To a deputation of ship own-
ers urging prohibition during
the First World War]
We are fighting Germany,
Austria, and drink, and so far
as I can see the greatest of
these deadly foes is drink.
[Speech, 1915]

**MENCKEN, H.L.
(1880–1956)**
I've made it a rule never to
drink by daylight and never to
refuse a drink after dark.
[*New York Post*, 1945]

**NASH, Ogden
(1902–1971)**
Candy
Is dandy
But liquor
Is quicker.
['Reflections on Ice-Breaking'
(1931)]

OSLER, Sir William
[His description of alcohol]
Milk of the elderly.
[*The Globe and Mail*, 1988]

PEACOCK, Thomas Love
(1785–1866)
There are two reasons for
drinking; one is, when you are
thirsty, to cure it; the other,
when you are not thirsty, to
prevent it . . . Prevention is
better than cure.
[*Melincourt* (1817)]

PLINY THE ELDER (23–79)
In vino veritas.
Wine brings out the truth!
[*Historia Naturalis*]

POTTER, Stephen
(1900–1969)
It is WRONG to do what
everyone else does – namely,
to hold the wine list just out
of sight, look for the second
cheapest claret on the list,
and say, 'Number 22, please'.
[*One-Upmanship* (1952)]

RABELAIS, François
(c. 1494–c. 1553)
I drink for the thirst to come.
[*Gargantua* (1534)]

SHAW, George Bernard
(1856–1950)
I'm only a beer teetotaller, not
a champagne teetotaller.
[*Candida* (1898)]

SQUIRE, Sir J.C.
(1884–1958)
But I'm not so think as you
drunk I am.
['Ballade of Soporific
Absorption' (1931)]

TARKINGTON, Booth
(1869–1946)
There are two things that will
be believed of any man what-
soever, and one of them is
that he has taken to drink.
[*Penrod* (1914)]

THATCHER, Denis (1915–)
[Reply to someone who asked
if he had a drinking problem]
Yes, there's never enough.
[*Daily Mail*, 1996]

THURBER, James
(1894–1961)
It's a naïve domestic
Burgundy, without any breed-
ing, but I think you'll be
amused by its presumption.
[Cartoon caption in *The New
Yorker*, 1937]

WODEHOUSE, P.G.
(1881–1975)
It was my Uncle George who
discovered that alcohol was a
food well in advance of modern medical thought.
[*The Inimitable Jeeves* (1923)]

DUTY

ANONYMOUS

Straight is the line of Duty
Curved is the line of Beauty
Follow the first and thou
shallt see
The second ever following
thee.

**GILBERT, W.S.
(1836–1911)**

The question is, had he not
been a thing of beauty,
Would she be swayed by quite
as keen a sense of duty?

[*The Pirates of Penzance*
(1880)]

**GRANT, Ulysses S.
(1822–1885)**

No personal consideration
should stand in the way of
performing a public duty.

[Note on letter, 1875]

**HOOPER, Ellen Sturgis
(1816–1841)**

I slept, and dreamed that life
was Beauty;
I woke, and found that life
was Duty.

['Beauty and Duty' (1840)]

**IBSEN, Henrik
(1828–1906)**

What's a man's first duty? The
answer's brief: To be himself.

[*Peer Gynt* (1867)]

LEE, Robert E. (1807–1870)

Duty then is the sublimest
word in our language. Do
your duty in all things. You
cannot do more. You should
never wish to do less.

[Inscription in the Hall of
Fame]

MILNER, Alfred (1854–1925)

If we believe a thing to be
bad, and if we have a right to
prevent it, it is our duty to try
to prevent it and to damn the
consequences.

[Speech, 1909]

NELSON, Lord (1758–1805)

[Nelson's last signal at the
Battle of Trafalgar, 1805]
England expects every man to
do his duty.

[In Southey, *The Life of Nelson*
(1860)]

**PEACOCK, Thomas Love
(1785–1866)**

Sir, I have quarrelled with my
wife; and a man who has
quarrelled with his wife is
absolved from all duty to his
country.

[*Nightmare Abbey* (1818)]

**SHAKESPEARE, William
(1564–1616)**

Every subject's duty is the
King's; but every subject's
soul is his own.

[*Henry V*, IV.i]

STEVENSON, Robert Louis (1850–1894)
There is no duty we so much underrate as the duty of being happy.

[*Virginibus Puerisque* (1881)]

TENNYSON, Alfred, Lord (1809–1892)
O hard, when love and duty clash!

[*The Princess* (1847)]

WASHINGTON, George (1732–1799)
To persevere in one's duty and be silent is the best answer to calumny.

[*Moral Maxims*]

WILSON, Woodrow (1856–1924)
I fancy that it is just as hard to do your duty when men are sneering at you as when they are shooting at you.

[Speech, 1914]

ECONOMICS

**BAGEHOT, Walter
(1826–1877)**
No real English gentleman, in his secret soul, was ever sorry for the death of a political economist.
['The First Edinburgh Reviewers' (1858)]

BLAIR, Tony (1953–)
I want Britain to be a stake-holder economy where every-one has a chance to get on and succeed, where there is a clear sense of national pur-pose and where we leave behind some of the battles between Left and Right which really are not relevant in the new global economy of today.
[Speech in Singapore, 1996]

**DOUGLAS–HOME, Sir Alec
(1903–1995)**
When I have to read econ-omic documents I have to have a box of matches and start moving them into posi-tion to illustrate and simplify the points to myself.
[Interview in *The Observer*, 1962]

FRIEDMAN, Milton (1912–)
There's no such thing as a free lunch.
[Title of book]

**GALBRAITH, J.K.
(1908–)**
Economics is extremely useful as a form of employment for economists.
[Attr.]

If all else fails, immortality can always be assured by spectacular error.
[Attr.]

**GEORGE, Eddie
(1938–)**
There are three kinds of econ-omist. Those who can count and those who can't.
[*The Observer Review*, 1996]

**KEYNES, John Maynard
(1883–1946)**
It is better that a man should tyrannize over his bank balance than over his fellow-citizens.
[*The General Theory of Employment, Interest and Money* (1936)]

LEVIN, Bernard (1928–)
Inflation in the Sixties was a nuisance to be endured, like varicose veins or French for-eign policy.
[*The Pendulum Years* (1970)]

**MALTHUS, Thomas
(1766–1834)**
Population, when unchecked, increases in a geometrical

ratio. Subsistence only increases in an arithmetical ratio.

[*Essay on the Principle of Population* (1798)]

MELLON, Andrew William (1855–1937)
A nation is not in danger of financial disaster merely because it owes itself money.

[Attr.]

ROOSEVELT, Franklin Delano (1882–1945)
We have always known that heedless self-interest was bad morals; we know now that it is bad economics.

[First Inaugural Address, 1933]

RUTSKOI, Alexander (1947–)
The dollar is Russia's national currency now, the rouble is just a sweetie paper. We've handed our sword to America.

[*Newsweek*, 1994]

SCHUMACHER, E.F. (1911–1977)
Small is Beautiful. A study of economics as if people mattered.

[Title of book, 1973]

SELLAR, Walter Carruthers (1898–1951) and YEATMEN, Robert (1897–1968)
The National Debt is a very

Good Thing and it would be dangerous to pay it off, for fear of Political Economy.

[*1066 And All That* (1930)]

SHAW, George Bernard (1856–1950)
If all economists were laid end to end, they would not reach a conclusion.

[Attr.]

TRUMAN, Harry S. (1884–1972)
It's a recession when your neighbour loses his job; it's a depression when you lose your own.

[*The Observer*, 1958]

YELTSIN, Boris (1931–)
I am for the market, not for the bazaar.

[*The Times*, 1992]

EDITING

ALLEN, Fred (1894–1956)
[To writers who had heavily edited one of his scripts] Where were you fellows when the paper was blank?

[Attr.]

AUBREY, John (1626–1697)
He [Shakespeare] was wont to say that he 'never blotted out a line of his life'; said Ben Jonson, 'I wish he had blotted

out a thousand.'
[*Brief Lives* (c. 1693)]

HUBBARD, Elbert (1856–1915)
Editor: a person employed by a newspaper whose business it is to separate the wheat from the chaff and to see that the chaff is printed.
[*A Thousand and One Epigrams* (1911)]

JOHNSON, Samuel (1709–1784)
Read over your compositions, and where ever you meet with a passage which you think is particularly fine, strike it out.
[In Boswell, *The Life of Samuel Johnson* (1791)]

MAYER, Louis B. (1885–1957)
[Comment to writers who had objected to changes in their work]
The number one book of the ages was written by a committee, and it was called The Bible.
[*In Hallivell, The Filmgoer's Book of Quotes* (1973)]

EDUCATION

ARISTOTLE (384–322 BC)
The roots of education are bit-ter, but the fruit is sweet.
[In Diogenes Laertius, *Lives of Philosophers*]

BACON, Francis (1561–1626)
Reading maketh a full man; conference a ready man; and writing an exact man.
[*Essays* (1625)]

BIERCE, Ambrose (1842–c. 1914)
Education: That which discloses to the wise and disguises from the foolish their lack of understanding.
[*The Cynic's Word Book* (1906)]

BROUGHAM, Lord Henry (1778–1868)
Education makes a people easy to lead, but difficult to drive; easy to govern, but impossible to enslave.
[Attr.]

BUCHAN, John (1875–1940)
To live for a time close to great minds is the best kind of education.
[*Memory Hold the Door*]

CHESTERTON, G.K. (1874–1936)
Education is simply the soul of a society as it passes from one generation to another.
[*The Observer*, 1924]

CODY, Henry (1868–1951)
Education is casting false pearls before real swine.
[Attr.]

COOPER, Roger
[On being released after five years in an Iranian prison]
I can say that anyone who, like me, has been educated in English public schools and served in the ranks of the British Army is quite at home in a Third World prison.
[*Newsweek*, 1991]

DICKENS, Charles (1812–1870)
Now, what I want is, Facts. Teach these boys and girls nothing but Facts. Facts alone are wanted in life. Plant nothing else, and root out everything else . . . Stick to Facts, sir!
[*Hard Times* (1854)]

DIOGENES (THE CYNIC) (c. 400–325 BC)
Education is something that tempers the young and consoles the old, gives wealth to the poor and adorns the rich.
[In Diogenes Laertius, *Lives of Eminent Philosophers*]

EMERSON, Ralph Waldo (1803–1882)
I pay the schoolmaster, but 'tis the schoolboys that educate my son.
[*Journals*]

HUXLEY, Aldous (1894–1963)
The solemn foolery of scholarship for scholarship's sake.
[*The Perennial Philosophy* (1945)]

JOHNSON, Samuel (1709–1784)
All intellectual improvement arises from leisure.
[In Boswell, *The Life of Samuel Johnson* (1791)]

KRAUS, Karl (1874–1936)
Education is what most people receive, many pass on and few actually have.
[*Pro domo et mundo* (1912)]

MCIVER, Charles D. (1860–1906)
When you educate a man you educate an individual; when you educate a woman you educate a whole family.
[Address at women's college]

MORAVIA, Alberto (1907–1990)
The ratio of literacy to illiteracy is constant, but nowadays the illiterates can read and write.
[*The Observer*, 1979]

PARSONS, Tony
The death of the grammar schools – those public schools without the sodomy – resulted

in state education relinquishing its role of nurturing bright young working class kids.

[*Arena*, 1989]

ROUSSEAU, Jean-Jacques (1712–1778)

One is only curious in proportion to one's level of education.

[*Émile ou De l'éducation* (1762)]

SITWELL, Sir Osbert (1892–1969)

Educ: during the holidays from Eton.

[*Who's Who* (1929)]

SPARK, Muriel (1918–)

To me education is a leading out of what is already there in the pupil's soul. To Miss Mackay it is a putting in of something that is not there, and that is not what I call education, I call it intrusion.

[*The Prime of Miss Jean Brodie* (1961)]

STOCKS, Mary, Baroness (1891–1975)

Today we enjoy a social structure which offers equal opportunity in education. It is indeed regrettably true that there is no equal opportunity to take advantage of the equal opportunity.

[*Still More Commonplace* (1973)]

TREVELYAN, G.M. (1876–1962)

Education . . . has produced a vast population able to read but unable to distinguish what is worth reading.

[*English Social History* (1942)]

USTINOV, Sir Peter (1921–)

People at the top of the tree are those without qualifications to detain them at the bottom.

[Attr.]

See KNOWLEDGE; LEARNING; SCHOOLS; TEACHERS; UNIVERSITY

EGOISM

ADLER, Alfred (1870–1937)

[On hearing that an egocentric had fallen in love]
Against whom?

[Attr.]

ALI, Muhammad (1942–)

I am the greatest.

[Catchphrase]

BACON, Francis (1561–1626)

It was prettily devised of Aesop, 'The fly sat upon the axletree of the chariot-wheel and said, what a dust do I raise.'

['Of Vain-Glory' (1625)]

BARNES, Peter (1931–)
I know I am God because
when I pray to him I find I'm
talking to myself.
[*The Ruling Class* (1968)]

**BIERCE, Ambrose
(1842–c. 1914)**
Egotist: A person of low taste,
more interested in himself
than in me.
[*The Cynic's Word Book* (1906)]

**BULMER-THOMAS, Ivor
(1905–1993)**
[Of Harold Wilson]
If ever he went to school without any boots it was because
he was too big for them.
[Remark, 1949]

**BUTLER, Samuel
(1835–1902)**
The advantage of doing one's
praising for oneself is that one
can lay it on so thick and
exactly in the right places.
[*The Way of All Flesh* (1903)]

**CHAMFORT, Nicolas
(1741–1794)**
Someone said of a great egotist: 'He would burn your
house down to cook himself a
couple of eggs.'
[*Caractères et anecdotes*]

**DULLES, John Foster
(1888–1959)**
[Reply when asked if he had

ever been wrong]
Yes, once – many, many years
ago. I thought I had made a
wrong decision. Of course, it
turned out that I had been
right all along. But I was
wrong to have *thought* that I
was wrong.
[Attr.]

**ELIOT, George
(1819–1880)**
He was like a cock, who
thought the sun had risen to
hear him crow.
[*Adam Bede* (1859)]

**GORTON, John Grey
(1911–)**
I am always prepared to recognize that there can be two
points of view – mine, and
one that is probably wrong.
[In Trengove, *John Grey
Gorton*]

HARTLEY, L.P. (1895–1972)
'Should I call myself an ego-
ist?' Miss Johnstone mused.
'Others have called me so.
They merely meant I did not
care for them.'
[*Simonetta Perkins* (1925)]

**JEROME, Jerome K.
(1859–1927)**
Conceit is the finest armour a
man can wear.
[*Idle Thoughts of an Idle Fellow*
(1886)]

KEITH, Penelope (1940–)
Shyness is just egotism out of
its depth.

[*The Observer*, 1988]

**SITWELL, Dame Edith
(1887–1964)**
I have often wished I had time
to cultivate modesty ... But I
am too busy thinking about
myself.

[*The Observer*, 1950]

SUZUKI, D.T. (1870–1966)
The individual ego asserts
itself strongly in the West. In
the East, there is no ego. The
ego is non-existent and,
therefore, there is no ego to
be crucified.

[*Mysticism Christian and
Buddhist* (1957)]

**TROLLOPE, Anthony
(1815–1882)**
As for conceit, what man will
do any good who is not con-
ceited? Nobody holds a good
opinion of a man who has a
low opinion of himself.

[*Orley Farm* (1862)]

ENEMIES

**THE BIBLE (KING JAMES
VERSION)**
Love your enemies, bless
them that curse you, do good
to them that hate you, and
pray for them which despite-
fully use you, and persecute
you.

[*Matthew*, 5:44]

**BRETON, Nicholas
(c. 1545–c. 1626)**
I wish my deadly foe, no
worse
Than want of friends, and
empty purse.

['A Farewell to Town' (1577)]

**BURKE, Edmund
(1729–1797)**
He that wrestles with us
strengthens our nerves, and
sharpens our skill. Our antag-
onist is our helper.

[*Reflections on the Revolution
in France* (1790)]

**CONRAD, Joseph
(1857–1924)**
You shall judge of a man by
his foes as well as by his
friends.

[*Lord Jim* (1900)]

**LESAGE, Alain-René
(1668–1747)**
They made peace between us;
we embraced, and since that
time we have been mortal
enemies.

[*Le Diable boiteux*]

LINKLATER, Eric (1899–1974)
With a heavy step Sir Matthew

left the room and spent the morning designing mausoleums for his enemies.

[*Juan in America* (1931)]

MONTAGU, Lady Mary Wortley (1689–1762)
People wish their enemies dead — but I do not; I say give them the gout, give them the stone!

[Letter from Horace Walpole, 1778]

NARVÁEZ, Ramón María (1800–1868)
[On his deathbed, when asked by a priest if he forgave his enemies]
I do not have to forgive my enemies, I have had them all shot.

[Attr.]

ROOSEVELT, Franklin Delano (1882–1945)
I ask you to judge me by the enemies I have made.

[*The Observer*, 1932]

WILDE, Oscar (1854–1900)
A man cannot be too careful in the choice of his enemies.

[*The Picture of Dorian Gray* (1891)]

AGATE, James (1877–1947)
The English instinctively admire any man who has no talent and is modest about it.

[Attr.]

BAGEHOT, Walter (1826–1877)
Of all nations in the world the English are perhaps the least a nation of pure philosophers.

[*The English Constitution* (1867)]

BEHAN, Brendan (1923–1964)
He was born an Englishman and remained one for years.

[*The Hostage* (1958)]

BRADBURY, Malcolm (1932–)
I like the English. They have the most rigid code of immorality in the world.

[*Eating People is Wrong* (1954)]

BRIGHT, John (1811–1889)
England is the mother of Parliaments.

[Speech, 1865]

BROOKE, Rupert (1887–1915)
If I should die, think only this of me:
That there's some corner of a foreign field
That is for ever England.

['The Soldier' (1914)]

BROWNE, Sir Thomas (1605–1682)
All places, all airs make unto me one country; I am in England, everywhere, and under any meridian.
[*Religio Medici* (1643)]

BUTLER, Samuel (1835–1902)
The wish to spread those opinions that we hold conducive to our own welfare is so deeply rooted in the English character that few of us can escape its influence.
[*Erewhon* (1872)]

BYRON, Lord (1788–1824)
The English winter – ending in July,
To recommence in August.
[*Don Juan* (1824)]

CARLYLE, Thomas (1795–1881)
[When asked what the population of England was]
Thirty millions, mostly fools.
[Attr.]

CHESTERTON, G.K. (1874–1936)
Before the Roman came to Rye or out to Severn strode,
The rolling English drunkard made the rolling English road.
['The Rolling English Road' (1914)]

COMPTON-BURNETT, Dame Ivy (1884–1969)
Well, the English have no family feelings. That is, none of the kind you mean. They have them, and one of them is that relations must cause no expense.
[*Parents and Children* (1941)]

COWPER, William (1731–1800)
England, with all thy faults, I love thee still.
[*The Task* (1785)]

DEFOE, Daniel (c. 1661–1731)
Your Roman-Saxon-Danish-Norman English.
[*The True-Born Englishman* (1701)]

FORSTER, E.M. (1879–1970)
It is not that the Englishman can't feel – it is that he is afraid to feel. He has been taught at his public school that feeling is bad form. He must not express great joy or sorrow, or even open his mouth too wide when he talks – his pipe might fall out if he did.
[*Abinger Harvest* (1936)]

GOLDING, William (1911–1993)
We've got to have rules and obey them. After all, we're not

savages. We're English; and the English are best at everything. So we've got to do the right things.

[*Lord of the Flies* (1954)]

HERBERT, Sir A.P. (1890–1971)

The Englishman never enjoys himself except for a noble purpose.

[*Uncommon Law* (1935)]

HILL, Reginald (1936–)

Nobody has ever lost money by overestimating the superstitious credulity of an English jury.

[*Pictures of Perfection* (1994)]

HOWARD, Philip (1933–)

Every time an Englishman opens his mouth, he enables other Englishmen if not to despise him, at any rate to place him in some social and class pigeonhole.

[*The Times*, 1992]

HUGO, Victor (1802–1885)

England has two books: the Bible and Shakespeare. England made Shakespeare but the Bible made England.

[Attr.]

JOAD, C.E.M. (1891–1953)

It will be said of this generation that it found England a

land of beauty and left it a land of beauty spots.

[*The Observer*, 1953]

JOYCE, James (1882–1941)

We feel in England that we have treated you [Irish] rather unfairly. It seems history is to blame.

[*Ulysses* (1922)]

KINGSLEY, Charles (1819–1875)

'Tis the hard grey weather Breeds hard English men.

['Ode to the North-East Wind' (1854)]

KIPLING, Rudyard (1865–1936)

For Allah created the English mad – the maddest of all mankind!

[*The Five Nations* (1903)]

MACAULAY, Lord (1800–1859)

The history of England is emphatically the history of progress.

['Sir James Mackintosh' (1843)]

MACINNES, Colin (1914–1976)

England is . . . a country infested with people who love to tell us what to do, but who very rarely seem to know what's going on.

[*England, Half English*]

**MARY, Queen of Scots
(1542–1587)**
England is not all the world.
[Said at her trial, 1586]

MIKES, George (1912–1987)
An Englishman, even if he is
alone, forms an orderly queue
of one.
[*How to be an Alien* (1946)]

NAPOLEON I (1769–1821)
England is a nation of shop-
keepers.
[In O'Meara, *Napoleon in Exile*
(1822)]

NASH, Ogden (1902–1971)
Englishmen are distinguished
by their traditions and cere-
monials,
And also by their affection for
their colonies and their con-
descension to their colonials.
['England Expects' (1929)]

**O'CONNELL, Daniel
(1775–1847)**
The Englishman has all the
qualities of a poker except its
occasional warmth.
[Attr.]

PEPYS, Samuel (1633–1703)
But Lord! to see the absurd
nature of Englishmen, that
cannot forbear laughing and
jeering at everything that
looks strange.
[*Diary*, 1662]

RHODES, Cecil (1853–1902)
Remember that you are an
Englishman, and have conse-
quently won first prize in the
lottery of life.
[In Ustinov, *Dear Me* (1977)]

**SANTAYANA, George
(1863–1952)**
England is the paradise of
individuality, eccentricity,
heresy, anomalies, hobbies,
and humours.
[*Soliloquies in England* (1922)]

**SEELEY, Sir John
(1834–1895)**
We [the English] seem as it
were to have conquered and
peopled half the world in a fit
of absence of mind.
[*The Expansion of England*
(1883)]

**SHAKESPEARE, William
(1564–1616)**
This royal throne of kings, this
sceptr'd isle,
This earth of majesty, this seat
of Mars,
This other Eden, demi-par-
adise,
This fortress built by Nature
for herself
Against infection and the
hand of war,
This happy breed of men, this
little world,
This precious stone set in the
silver sea,

Which serves it in the office of a wall,
Or as a moat defensive to a house,
Against the envy of less happier lands;
This blessed plot, this earth, this realm, this England.

[*Richard II*, II.i]

SULLY, Duc de (1559–1641)
The English enjoy themselves sadly, according to the custom of their country.

[*Memoirs* (1638)]

WELLS, H.G. (1866–1946)
In England we have come to rely upon a comfortable time-lag of fifty years or a century intervening between the perception that something ought to be done and a serious attempt to do it.

[*The Work, Wealth and Happiness of Mankind* (1931)]

WILDE, Oscar (1854–1900)
The English have a miraculous power of turning wine into water.

[Attr.]

THE ENVIRONMENT

BOTTOMLEY, Gordon (1874–1948)
When you destroy a blade of grass
You poison England at her roots:
Remember no man's foot can pass
Where evermore no green life shoots.

['To Ironfounders and Others' (1912)]

CARSON, Rachel (1907–1964)
As man proceeds towards his announced goal of the conquest of nature, he has written a depressing record of destruction, directed not only against the earth he inhabits but against the life that shares it with him.

[*The Silent Spring* (1962)]

Over increasingly large areas of the United States, spring now comes unheralded by the return of the birds, and the early mornings are strangely silent where once they were filled with the beauty of bird song.

[*The Silent Spring* (1962)]

MCLEAN, Joyce
There's an old saying which goes: Once the last tree is cut and the last river poisoned, you will find you cannot eat your money.

[*The Globe and Mail*, 1989]

**MEAD, Margaret
(1901–1978)**
We are living beyond our
means. As a people we have
developed a life-style that is
draining the earth of its price-
less and irreplaceable
resources without regard for
the future of our children and
people all around the world.
[*Redbook*]

ENVY

**BEERBOHM, Sir Max
(1872–1956)**
The dullard's envy of brilliant
men is always assuaged by
the suspicion that they will
come to a bad end.
[*Zuleika Dobson* (1911)]

**THE BIBLE (KING JAMES
VERSION)**
Through envy of the devil
came death into the world.
[Apocrypha, *Wisdom of
Solomon*, 2:24]

FIELDING, Henry (1707–1754)
Some folks rail against other
folks because other folks have
what some folks would be
glad of.
[*Joseph Andrews* (1742)]

GAY, John (1685–1732)
Fools may our scorn, not envy

raise,
For envy is a kind of praise.
[*Fables* (1727)]

MOORE, Brian (1921–)
How many works of the im-
agination have been goaded
into life by envy of an untal-
ented contemporary's success.
[*An Answer from Limbo* (1962)]

**SHAKESPEARE, William
(1564–1616)**
[Of Cassius]
Such men as he be never at
heart's ease
Whiles they behold a greater
than themselves,
And therefore are they very
dangerous.
[*Julius Caesar*, I.ii]

EQUALITY

**ANTHONY, Susan B.
(1820–1906)**
There never will be complete
equality until women themselves help to make laws and
elect lawmakers.
[*The Arena*, 1897]

**BAKUNIN, Mikhail
(1814–1876)**
[Anarchist declaration, Lyon,
1870]
We wish, in a word, equality –
equality in fact as corollary, or

rather, as primordial condition of liberty. From each according to his faculties, to each according to his needs; that is what we wish sincerely and energetically.

[In J. Morrison Davidson, *The Old Order and the New* (1890)]

**BALZAC, Honoré de
(1799–1850)**
Equality may perhaps be a right, but no power on earth can ever turn it into a fact.

[*La Duchesse de Langeais* (1834)]

**BARRIE, Sir J.M.
(1860–1937)**
His Lordship may compel us to be equal upstairs, but there will never be equality in the servants' hall.

[*The Admirable Crichton* (1902)]

**BURNS, Robert
(1759–1796)**
The rank is but the guinea's stamp,
The man's the gowd for a' that . . .

For a' that, an' a' that,
It's comin yet for a' that,
That man to man the world o'er
Shall brithers be for a' that.

['A Man's a Man for a' that' (1795)]

**GILBERT, W.S.
(1836–1911)**
They all shall equal be!
The Earl, the Marquis, and the Dook,
The Groom, the Butler, and the Cook,
The Aristocrat who banks with Coutts,
The Aristocrat who cleans the boots.

[*The Gondoliers* (1889)]

**HUXLEY, Aldous
(1894–1963)**
That all men are equal is a proposition to which at ordinary times, no sane human being has ever given his assent.

[*Proper Studies* (1927)]

**JOHNSON, Samuel
(1709–1784)**
Your levellers wish to level *down* as far as themselves; but they cannot bear levelling *up* to themselves.

[In Boswell, *The Life of Samuel Johnson* (1791)]

It is better that some should be unhappy than that none should be happy, which would be the case in a general state of equality.

[In Boswell, *The Life of Samuel Johnson* (1791)]

**KING, Martin Luther
(1929–1968)**
I have a dream that one day
this nation will rise up and
live out the true meaning of
its creed: 'We hold these
truths to be self-evident, that
all men are created equal'.
[Speech, 1963]

MANDELA, Nelson (1918–)
I have fought against white
domination, and I have fought
against black domination. I
have cherished the ideal of a
democratic and free society in
which all persons will live
together in harmony and with
equal opportunities. It is an
ideal which I hope to live for
and achieve. But, if needs be,
it is an ideal for which I am
prepared to die.
[Statement in the dock, 1964]

MURDOCH, Iris (1919–)
The cry of equality pulls
everyone down.
[The Observer, 1987]

**ORWELL, George
(1903–1950)**
All animals are equal, but
some animals are more equal
than others.
[Animal Farm (1945)]

**RAINBOROWE, Thomas
(d. 1648)**
The poorest he that is in

England hath a life to live as
the greatest he.
[Speech in Army debates,
1647]

**WEDGWOOD, Josiah
(1730–1795)**
Am I not a man and a brother?
[Motto adopted by Anti-
Slavery Society]

**WILSON, Harold
(1916–1995)**
Everybody should have an
equal chance – but they
shouldn't have a flying start.
[The Observer, 1963]

ERROR

**AESCHYLUS
(525–456 BC)**
Even he who is wiser than the
wise may err.
[Fragments]

**BANVILLE, Théodore de
(1823–1891)**
Those who do nothing are
never wrong.
[Odes funambulesques]

**BOLINGBROKE, Henry
(1678–1751)**
Truth lies within a little and
certain compass, but error is
immense.
[Reflections upon Exile (1716)]

DESTOUCHES, Philippe Néricault (1680–1754)
The absent are always in the wrong.
[*L'Obstacle Imprévu* (1717)]

DRYDEN, John (1631–1700)
Errors, like straws, upon the surface flow;
He who would search for pearls must dive below.
[*All for Love* (1678)]

ELIOT, George (1819–1880)
Errors look so very ugly in persons of small means – one feels they are taking quite a liberty in going astray; whereas people of fortune may naturally indulge in a few delinquencies.
[*Scenes of Clerical Life* (1858)]

JOHNSON, Samuel (1709–1784)
[Asked the reason for a mistake in his Dictionary]
Ignorance, madam, sheer ignorance.
[In Boswell, *The Life of Samuel Johnson* (1791)]

LOCKE, John (1632–1704)
It is one thing to show a man that he is in an error, and another to put him in possession of truth.
[*Essay concerning Human Understanding* (1690)]

POPE, Alexander (1688–1744)
A man should never be ashamed to own he has been in the wrong, which is but saying, in other words, that he is wiser today than he was yesterday.
[*Miscellanies* (1727)]

REAGAN, Ronald (1911–)
You know, by the time you reach my age, you've made plenty of mistakes if you've lived your life properly.
[*The Observer*, 1987]

SCHOPENHAUER, Arthur (1788–1860)
There is only one innate error, and that is that we are here in order to be happy.
[*The World as Will and Idea* (1859)]

See TRUTH

EUROPE

BALDWIN, James (1924–1987)
Europe has what we [Americans] do not have yet, a sense of the mysterious and inexorable limits of life, a sense, in a word, of tragedy. And we have what they sorely need: a sense of life's possibilities.
[Attr.]

DELORS, Jacques (1925–)
Europe is not just about material results, it is about spirit. Europe is a state of mind.
[*The Independent*, 1994]

FANON, Frantz (1925–1961)
When I search for man in the technique and style of Europe, I see only a succession of negations of man, and an avalanche of murders.
[*The Wretched of the Earth* (1961)]

FISHER, H.A.L. (1856–1940)
Purity of race does not exist. Europe is a continent of energetic mongrels.
[*History of Europe* (1935)]

GLADSTONE, William (1809–1898)
We are part of the community of Europe, and we must do our duty as such.
[Speech, 1888]

GOLDSMITH, James (1933–)
Brussels is madness. I will fight it from within.
[*The Times*, 1994]

GOLDSMITH, Oliver (c. 1728–1774)
On whatever side we regard the history of Europe, we shall perceive it to be a tissue of crimes, follies, and misfortunes.
[*The Citizen of the World* (1762)]

HEALEY, Denis (1917–)
[Of Conservatives]
Their Europeanism is nothing but imperialism with an inferiority complex.
[*The Observer*, 1962]

HUGO, Victor (1802–1885)
I represent a party which does not exist: the party of revolution, civilization. This party will make the twentieth century. There will issue from it first the United States of Europe, then the United States of the World.
[Written on the wall of the room in which Hugo died, Paris, 1885]

LEFEVRE, Théo (1914–1973)
In Western Europe there are now only small countries – those that know it and those that don't know it yet.
[*The Observer*, 1963]

McCARTHY, Mary (1912–1989)
The immense popularity of American movies abroad demonstrates that Europe is the unfinished negative of which America is the proof.
[*On the Contrary* (1961)]

**SCANLON, Hugh
(1913–)**
[Referring to his union's attitude to the Common Market]
Here we are again with both feet firmly planted in the air.
[*The Observer*, 1973]

**SHERMAN, Alfred
(1919–)**
Britain does not wish to be ruled by a conglomerate in Europe which includes Third World nations such as the Greeks and Irish, nor for that matter the Italians and French, whose standards of political morality are not ours, and never will be.
[*The Independent*, 1990]

**THATCHER, Margaret
(1925–)**
Historians will one day look back and think it a curious folly that just as the Soviet Union was forced to recognize reality by dispersing power to its separate states and by limiting the powers of its central government, some people in Europe were trying to create a new artificial state by taking powers from national states and concentrating them at the centre.
[Speech, 1994]

ANONYMOUS
Honi soit qui mal y pense.
Evil be to him who evil thinks.
[Motto of the Order of the Garter]

**ARENDT, Hannah
(1906–1975)**
[Of Eichmann]
It was as though in those last minutes he was summing up the lessons that this long course in human wickedness had taught us – the lesson of the fearsome, word-and-thought-defying banality of evil.
[*Eichmann in Jerusalem* (1963)]

**BOILEAU-DESPREAUX,
Nicolas (1636–1711)**
The fear of one evil often leads us into a greater one.
[*L'Art Poétique* (1674)]

**BURKE, Edmund
(1729–1797)**
The only thing necessary for the triumph of evil is for good men to do nothing.
[Attr.]

**CONRAD, Joseph
(1857–1924)**
The belief in a supernatural source of evil is not necessary; men alone are

quite capable of every wickedness.
[*Under Western Eyes* (1911)]

CRISP, Quentin (1908–)
Vice is its own reward.
[*The Naked Civil Servant* (1968)]

DELBANCO, Andrew
The idea of evil is something on which the health of society depends. We have an obligation to name evil and oppose it in ourselves as well as in others.
[*The Guardian*, 1995]

HATTERSLEY, Roy (1932–)
Familiarity with evil breeds not contempt but acceptance.
[*The Guardian*, 1993]

HAZLITT, William (1778–1830)
To great evils we submit, we resent little provocations.
[*Table-Talk* (1822)]

KEMPIS, Thomas à (c. 1380–1471)
Of two evils the lesser is always to be chosen.
[*De Imitatione Christi* (1892)]

LA ROCHEFOUCAULD (1613-1680)
There is scarcely a single man clever enough to know all the evil he does.
[*Maximes* (1678)]

MCCARTHY, Mary (1912–1989)
If someone tells you he is going to make 'a realistic decision', you immediately understand that he has resolved to do something bad.
[*On the Contrary* (1961)]

NEWMAN Cardinal (1801–1890)
Whatever is the first time persons hear evil, it is quite certain that good has been beforehand with them, and they have a something within them which tells them it is evil.
[*Parochial and Plain Sermons*]

NIETZSCHE, Friedrich (1844–1900)
Whoever struggles with monsters might watch that he does not thereby become a monster. When you stare into an abyss for a long time, the abyss also stares into you.
[*Beyond Good and Evil* (1886)]

POPE, Alexander (1688–1744)
Vice is a monster of so frightful mien,
As, to be hated, needs but to be seen;
Yet soon too oft, familiar with her face,
We first endure, then pity, then embrace.
[*An Essay on Man* (1733)]

SHAKESPEARE, William (1564–1616)
How oft the sight of means to do ill deeds
Make deeds ill done!

[*King John,* IV.ii]

Through tatter'd clothes small vices do appear;
Robed and furr'd gowns hide all.

[*King Lear,* IV.vi]

WEST, Mae (1892–1980)
Whenever I'm caught between two evils, I take the one I've never tried.

[*Klondike Annie,* film, 1936]

WILDE, Oscar (1854–1900)
Wickedness is a myth invented by good people to account for the curious attractiveness of others.

[*The Chameleon,* 1894]

See GOOD AND EVIL; SIN

EVOLUTION

BLACKWELL, Antoinette Brown (1825–1921)
Mr Darwin . . . has failed to hold definitely before his mind the principle that the difference of sex, whatever it may consist in, must itself be subject to natural selection and to evolution.

[*The Sexes Throughout Nature* (1875)]

CONGREVE, William (1670–1729)
I confess freely to you, I could never look long upon a monkey, without very mortifying reflections.

[Letter to Mr Dennis, 1695]

DARWIN, Charles (1809–1882)
I have called this principle, by which each slight variation, if useful, is preserved, by the term of Natural Selection.

[*The Origin of Species* (1859)]

We must, however, acknowledge, as it seems to me, that man with all his noble qualities . . . still bears in his bodily frame the indelible stamp of his lowly origin.

[*The Descent of Man* (1871)]

DARWIN, Charles Galton (1887–1962)
The evolution of the human race will not be accomplished in the ten thousand years of tame animals, but in the million years of wild animals, because man is and will always be a wild animal.

[*The Next Ten Million Years*]

**DISRAELI, Benjamin
(1804–1881)**
Is man an ape or an angel?
Now I am on the side of the
angels.

[Speech, 1864]

**SPENCER, Herbert
(1820–1903)**
It cannot but happen . . . that
those who will survive whose functions happen to be most nearly in equilibrium with the
modified aggregate of external forces . . . This survival of
the fittest implies multiplica-
tion of the fittest.

[*The Principles of Biology*
(1864)]

**WILBERFORCE, Bishop
Samuel (1805–1873)**
[To T.H. Huxley]
And, in conclusion, I would
like to ask the gentleman . . .
whether the ape from which
he is descended was on his
grandmother's or his grandfather's side of the family.

[Speech at Oxford, 1860]

EXILE

AYTOUN, W.E. (1813–1865)
They bore within their breasts
the grief
That fame can never heal –
The deep, unutterable woe

Which none save exiles feel.
['The Island of the Scots'
(1849)]

The earth is all the home I
have,
The heavens my wide roof-
tree.
['The Wandering Jew' (1867)]

**THE BIBLE (KING JAMES
VERSION)**
I have been a stranger in a
strange land.

[*Exodus*, 2:22]

GALT, John (1779–1839)
From the lone shieling of the
misty island
Mountains divide us, and the
waste of seas –
Yet still the blood is strong,
the heart is Highland,
And we in dreams behold the
Hebrides!
[Attr. in *Blackwoods Edinburgh
Magazine*, 1829]

**GREGORY VII
(c. 1020–1085)**
[Last words]
I have loved righteousness
and hated iniquity: therefore I
die in exile.

[In Bowden, *The Life and
Pontificate of Gregory VII*
(1840)]

SPARK, Muriel (1918–)
It was Edinburgh that bred

within me the conditions of exiledom; and what have I been doing since then but moving from exile to exile? It has ceased to be a fate, it has become a calling.

['What Images Return']

EXPERIENCE

ANTRIM, Minna (1861-1950)
Experience is a good teacher, but she sends in terrific bills.
[*Naked Truth and Veiled Allusions* (1902)]

BLAKE, William (1757-1827)
What is the price of Experience? do men buy it for a song?
Or wisdom for a dance in the street?
[*Vala, or the Four Zoas*]

BOWEN, Elizabeth (1899-1973)
Experience isn't interesting till it begins to repeat itself – in fact, till it does that, it hardly *is* experience.
[*The Death of the Heart* (1938)]

EMERSON, Ralph Waldo (1803-1882)
The years teach much which the days never know.
['Experience' (1844)]

FADIMAN, Clifton (1904–)
Experience teaches you that the man who looks you straight in the eye, particularly if he adds a firm handshake, is hiding something.
[*Enter, Conversing*]

HEGEL, Georg Wilhelm (1770-1831)
What experience and history teach us, however, is this, that peoples and governments have never learned anything from history.
[*Lectures on the Philosophy of History* (1837)]

HOLMES, Oliver Wendell (1809-1894)
A moment's insight is sometimes worth a life's experience.
[*The Professor at the Breakfast-Table* (1860)]

KEATS, John (1795-1821)
Nothing ever becomes real till it is experienced – Even a Proverb is no proverb to you till your Life has illustrated it.
[Letter, 1819]

WILDE, Oscar (1854-1900)
Experience is the name every one gives to their mistakes.
[*Lady Windermere's Fan* (1892)]

FACTS

**BARRIE, Sir J.M.
(1860–1937)**
Facts were never pleasing to him. He acquired them with reluctance and got rid of them with relief. He was never on terms with them until he had stood them on their heads.
[*The Greenwood Hat* (1937)]

BURNS, Robert (1759–1796)
But facts are chiels that winna ding,
And downa be disputed.
['A Dream' (1786)]

**DOYLE, Sir Arthur Conan
(1859–1930)**
'I should have more faith,' he said; 'I ought to know by this time that when a fact appears opposed to a long train of deductions it invariably proves to be capable of bearing some other interpretation.'
[*A Study in Scarlet* (1887)]

**HUXLEY, Aldous
(1894–1963)**
Facts do not cease to exist because they are ignored.
[*Proper Studies* (1927)]

**JAMES, Henry
(1843–1916)**
The fatal futility of Fact.
[*Prefaces* (1897 edition)]

RYLE, Gilbert (1900–1976)
A myth is, of course, not a fairy story. It is the presentation of facts belonging to one category in the idioms appropriate to another. To explode a myth is accordingly not to deny the facts but to re-allocate them.
[*The Concept of Mind* (1949)]

FAILURE

**CIANO, Count Galeazzo
(1903–1944)**
As always, victory finds a hundred fathers, but defeat is an orphan.
[*Diary*, 1942]

**COWARD, Sir Noël
(1899–1973)**
[On Randolph Churchill]
Dear Randolph, utterly unspoiled by failure.
[Attr.]

HARE, Augustus (1792–1834)
Half the failures in life arise from pulling in one's horse as he is leaping.
[*Guesses at Truth* (1827)]

HELLER, Joseph (1923–)
He was a self-made man who owed his lack of success to nobody.
[*Catch-22* (1961)]

HEMINGWAY, Ernest (1898–1961)
But man is not made for defeat . . . A man can be destroyed but not defeated.
[*The Old Man and the Sea* (1952)]

KEATS, John (1795–1821)
I would sooner fail than not be among the greatest.
[Letter to James Hessey, 1818]

NEWMAN, Paul (1925–)
Show me a good loser and I'll show you a loser.
[*The Observer*, 1982]

SHAKESPEARE, William (1564–1616)
Macbeth: If we should fail?
Lady Macbeth: We fail!
But screw your courage to the sticking place,
And we'll not fail.
[*Macbeth*, I.vii]

STEVENSON, Robert Louis (1850–1894)
Here lies one who meant well, tried a little, failed much: – surely that may be his epitaph, of which he need not be ashamed.
[*Across the Plains* (1892)]

WILDE, Oscar (1854–1900)
We women adore failures. They lean on us.
[*A Woman of No Importance* (1893)]

ALLEN, Fred (1894–1956)
A celebrity is a person who works hard all his life to become known, then wears dark glasses to avoid being recognized.
[Attr.]

ANONYMOUS
Fame is a mask that eats the face.

BURKE, Edmund (1729–1797)
Passion for fame; a passion which is the instinct of all great souls.
[*Speech on American Taxation* (1774)]

BYRON, Lord (1788–1824)
[Remark on the instantaneous success of *Childe Harold*]
I awoke one morning and found myself famous.
[In Moore, *Letters and Journals of Lord Byron* (1830)]

CALDERÓN DE LA BARCA, Pedro (1600–1681)
Fame, like water, bears up the lighter things, and lets the weighty sink.
[Attr.]

**CATO THE ELDER
(234–149 BC)**
I would much rather have
men ask why I have no statue
than why I have one.
[In Plutarch, *Lives*]

**GRAINGER, James
(c. 1721–1766)**
What is fame? an empty bubble;
Gold? a transient, shining
trouble.
['Solitude' (1755)]

**HUXLEY, Aldous
(1894–1963)**
I'm afraid of losing my obscu-
rity. Genuineness only thrives
in the dark. Like celery.
[*Those Barren Leaves* (1925)]

HUXLEY, T.H. (1825–1895)
[Remark to George Howell]
Posthumous fame is not particularly attractive to me, but,
if I am to be remembered at
all, I would rather it should be
as 'a man who did his best to
help the people' than by any
other title.
[In L. Huxley, *Life and Letters
of T.H. Huxley* (1900)]

**MELBA, Dame Nellie
(1861–1931)**
[To the editor of the *Argus*]
I don't care what you say, for
me or against me, but for
heaven's sake say something

about me.
[In Thompson, *On Lips of
Living Men*]

**MONTAIGNE, Michel de
(1533–1592)**
Fame and tranquillity cannot
dwell under the same roof.
[*Essais* (1580)]

PECK, Gregory (1916–)
[On the fact that no-one in a
crowded restaurant recog-
nized him]
If you have to tell them who
you are, you aren't anybody.
[In Harris, *Pieces of Eight*]

**SITWELL, Dame Edith
(1887–1964)**
A pompous woman of his
acquaintance, complaining
that the head-waiter of a
restaurant had not shown her
and her husband immediately
to a table, said 'We had to tell
him who we were.' Gerald,
interested, enquired, 'And
who were you?'
[*Taken Care Of* (1965)]

**WARHOL, Andy
(c. 1926–1987)**
In the future everyone will be
world famous for fifteen minutes.
[Exhibition catalogue, 1968]

WILDE, Oscar (1854–1900)
There is only one thing in the

world worse than being talked about, and that is not being talked about.

[*The Picture of Dorian Gray* (1891)]

FAMILIES

BEERBOHM, Sir Max (1872–1956)
They were a tense and peculiar family, the Oedipuses, weren't they?

[Attr.]

DICKENS, Charles (1812–1870)
Accidents will occur in the best-regulated families.

[*David Copperfield* (1850)]

FREUD, Sigmund (1856–1939)
Philosophers and politicians have agreed that the bonding together in family groups is both instinctive and necessary to human welfare – and therefore essential to the health of a society. The family is the microcosm.

[Attr. in *The Times*, May 1996]

HAZLITT, William (1778–1830)
A person may be indebted for a nose or an eye, for a graceful carriage or a voluble dis-course, to a great-aunt or uncle, whose existence he has scarcely heard of.

[*London Magazine*, 1821]

JOHN PAUL II (1920–)
Treasure your families – the future of humanity passes by way of the family.

[Speech, 1982]

LEACH, Sir Edmund (1910–1989)
Far from being the basis of the good society, the family, with its narrow privacy and tawdry secrets, is the source of all our discontents.

[BBC Reith Lecture, 1967]

LINCOLN, Abraham (1809–1865)
I don't know who my grandfather was; I am much more concerned to know what his grandson will be.

[In Gross, *Lincoln's Own Stories*]

MONTAIGNE, Michel de (1533–1592)
There is scarcely any less trouble in running a family than in governing an entire state . . . and domestic matters are no less importunate for being less important.

[*Essais* (1580)]

MOONEY, Bel
[On the need for family life]
I find myself surprised at how its realism actually unites morality with – yes – romance. It is that need that draws us to nest in rows, separated by thin walls, hoping to be tolerated and loved forever – and to go on reproducing ourselves in family patterns, handing on some misery (perhaps), but untold happiness too.

[*The Times*, 1996]

NASH, Ogden (1902–1971)
One would be in less danger
From the wiles of a stranger
If one's own kin and kith
Were more fun to be with.

['Family Court' (1931)]

POUND, Ezra (1885–1972)
Oh how hideous it is
To see three generations of one house gathered together!
It is like an old tree with shoots,
And with some branches rotted and falling.

['Commission' (1916)]

THACKERAY, William Makepeace (1811–1863)
If a man's character is to be abused, say what you will, there's nobody like a relation to do the business.

[*Vanity Fair* (1848)]

TOLSTOY, Leo (1828–1910)
All happy families resemble one another, but every unhappy family is unhappy in its own way.

[*Anna Karenina* (1877)]

FASCISM

BEVAN, Aneurin (1897–1960)
Fascism is not in itself a new order of society. It is the future refusing to be born.

[Attr.]

IBÁRRURI, Dolores ('La Pasionaria') (1895–1989)
Wherever they pass, they [the fascists] sow death and desolation.

[*Speeches and Articles* (1938)]

MCKENNEY, Ruth (1911–1972)
If modern civilisation had any meaning it was displayed in the fight against Fascism.

[In Seldes, *The Great Quotations* (1960)]

MOSLEY, Sir Oswald (1896–1980)
Before the organization of the Blackshirt movement free speech did not exist in this country.

[Attr.]

MUSSOLINI, Benito (1883–1945)
[On Hitler's seizing power]
Fascism is a religion; the twentieth century will be known in history as the century of Fascism.
[In Seldes, *Sawdust Caesar*]

PLATH, Sylvia (1932–1963)
Every woman adores a Fascist,
The boot in the face, the brute
Brute heart of a brute like you.
['Daddy' (1963)]

FATHERS

THE BIBLE (KING JAMES VERSION)
The fathers have eaten sour grapes, and the children's teeth are set on edge.
[*Ezekiel*, 18:2]

BURTON, Robert (1577–1640)
Diogenes struck the father when the son swore.
[*Anatomy of Melancholy* (1621)]

CHESTERFIELD, Lord (1694–1773)
As fathers commonly go, it is seldom a misfortune to be fatherless; and considering the general run of sons, as seldom a misfortune to be childless.
[Attr.]

CODE NAPOLEON
Investigations into paternity are forbidden.
[Article 340]

RUSSELL, Bertrand (1872–1970)
The fundamental defect of fathers is that they want their children to be a credit to them.
[Attr.]

SHAKESPEARE, William (1564–1616)
It is a wise father that knows his own child.
[*The Merchant of Venice*, II.ii]

TENNYSON, Alfred, Lord (1809–1892)
How many a father have I seen,
A sober man, among his boys,
Whose youth was full of foolish noise.
[*In Memoriam A. H. H.* (1850)]

TURNBULL, Margaret (fl. 1920s–1942)
No man is responsible for his father. That is entirely his mother's affair.
[*Alabaster Lamps* (1925)]

TWAIN, Mark (1835–1910)
When I was a boy of 14 my
father was so ignorant I could
hardly stand to have the old
man around. But when I got
to be 21, I was astonished at
how much he had learned in
seven years.

[In Mackay, *The Harvest of a
Quiet Eye* (1977)]

FEAR

**BOWEN, Elizabeth
(1899–1973)**
Proust has pointed out that
the predisposition to love creates its own objects: is this
not true of fear?

[*Collected Impressions* (1950)]

**CHURCHILL, Sir Winston
(1874–1965)**
When I look back on all these
worries I remember the story
of the old man who said on
his deathbed that he had had
a lot of trouble in his life,
most of which had never happened.

[*Their Finest Hour*]

CURIE, Marie (1867–1934)
Nothing in life is to be feared, it
is only to be understood. Now
is the time to understand more,
so that we may fear less.

[Attr.]

DELANEY, Shelagh (1939–)
I'm not frightened of the darkness outside. It's the darkness
inside houses I don't like.

[*A Taste of Honey* (1959)]

**FOCH, Ferdinand
(1851–1929)**
None but a coward dares to
boast that he has never
known fear.

[Attr.]

**MTSHALI, Oswald
(1940–)**
Man is
a great wall builder . . .
but the wall
most impregnable
has a moat
flowing with fright
around his heart.

[*Sounds of a Cowhide Drum*
(1971)]

**PARRIS, Matthew
(1949–)**
Terror of discovery and fear of
reproval slip into our unconscious minds during infancy
and remain there forever,
always potent, usually unac-
knowledged.

[*The Spectator*, 1996]

**PLATO
(c. 429–347 BC)**
Nothing in the affairs of men
is worthy of great anxiety.

[*Republic*]

ROOSEVELT, Franklin Delano (1882–1945)
The only thing we have to fear is fear itself.
[First Inaugural Address, 1933]

SHAW, George Bernard (1856–1950)
There is only one universal passion: fear.
[*The Man of Destiny* (1898)]

STEPHENS, James (1882–1950)
Curiosity will conquer fear even more than bravery will.
[*The Crock of Gold* (1912)]

THOMAS, Lewis (1913–)
Worrying is the most natural and spontaneous of all human functions. It is time to acknowledge this, perhaps even to learn to do it better.
[*More Notes of a Biology Watcher*]

See DEATH

FEELINGS

ANONYMOUS
What goes on in his chest is firmly suppressed
By the weight of his old school tie.

COLMAN, the Younger, George (1762–1836)
His heart runs away with his head.
[*Who Wants a Guinea?* (1805)]

MUSSOLINI, Benito (1883–1945)
[Maxim to which he attributed his political success]
Keep your heart a desert.
[Attr.]

PASCAL, Blaise (1623–1662)
Le coeur a ses raisons que la raison ne connaît point.
The heart has its reasons which the mind knows nothing of.
[*Pensées* (1670)]

SAINT-EXUPERY, Antoine de (1900–1944)
It is only with the heart that one can see clearly. The important things are invisible to the naked eye.
[*The Little Prince* (1943)]

FEMINISM

ANTHONY, Susan B. (1820–1906)
Men their rights and nothing more; women their rights and nothing less.
[Motto of *The Revolution*, 1868]

ATKINSON, Ti-Grace
(c. 1938–)
Feminism is the theory: lesbianism is the practice.
[Attr.]

FAIRBAIRN, Sir Nicholas
(1933–1995)
[On feminism]
It's a cover for lesbian homosexuality.
[*Daily Mail*, 1993]

FAUST, Beatrice (1939–)
If the women's movement can be summed up in a single phrase, it is 'the right to choose'.
[*Women, Sex and Pornography* (1980)]

FOURIER, François
(1772-1837)
The extension of women's privileges is the basic principle of all social progress.
[*Théorie des Quatre Mouvements* (1808)]

FRIEDAN, Betty (1921–)
I hope there will come a day when you, daughter mine, or your daughter, can truly afford to say 'I'm not a feminist. I'm a person'.
[Letter to her daughter, in *Cosmopolitan*, 1978]

JOHNSTON, Jill (1929–)
Feminists who still sleep with men are delivering their most vital energies to the oppressor.
[*Lesbian Nation: The Feminist Solution* (1973)]

No one should have to dance backwards all their life.
[In Miles, *The Women's History of the World* (1988)]

KEY, Ellen (1849–1926)
The emancipation of women is practically the greatest egoistic movement of the nineteenth century, and the most intense affirmation of the right of the self that history has yet seen.
[*The Century of the Child* (1909)]

LOOS, Anita (1893–1981)
I'm furious about the Women's Liberationists. They keep getting up on soapboxes and proclaiming that women are brighter than men. That's true, but it should be kept very quiet or it ruins the whole racket.
[*The Observer*, 1973]

MARTINEAU, Harriet
(1802–1876)
Is it to be understood that the principles of the Declaration of Independence bear no relation to half of the human race?
[*Society in America* (1837)]

O'BRIEN, Edna (1936–)
The vote, I thought, means nothing to women. We should be armed.
[In Erica Jong, *Fear of Flying* (1973)]

SHAW, George Bernard (1856–1950)
Give women the vote, and in five years there will be a crushing tax on bachelors.
[Man and Superman (1903)]

SOLANAS, Valerie (1940-)
[SCUM (Society for Cutting Up Men), manifesto, 1968]
Every man, deep down, knows he's a worthless piece of shit.
[In Bassnett, *Feminist Experiences* (1986)]

STANTON, Elizabeth Cady (1815–1902)
We hold these truths to be self-evident, that all men and women are created equal.
['Declaration of Sentiments', 1848]

WOLLSTONECRAFT, Mary (1759–1797)
[Of women]
I do not wish them to have power over men; but over themselves.
[*A Vindication of the Rights of Women* (1792)]

See MEN AND WOMEN; WOMEN

FICTION

ALDISS, Brian (1925–)
Science fiction is no more written for scientists than ghost stories are written for ghosts.
[*Penguin Science Fiction* (1961)]

BARTH, John (1930–)
If you are a novelist of a certain type of temperament, then what you really want to do is re-invent the world. God wasn't too bad a novelist, except he was a Realist.
[Attr.]

CECIL, Lord David (1902–1986)
It does not matter that Dickens's world is not lifelike: it is alive.
[*Early Victorian Novelists* (1934)]

CHESTERTON, G.K. (1874–1936)
A good novel tells us the truth about its hero; but a bad novel tells us the truth about its author.
[*Heretics* (1905)]

[On fiction]
It is the art in which the conquests of woman are quite beyond controversy

. . . The novel of the nineteenth century was female.
[*The Victorian Age in Literature* (1913)]

DAVISON, Frank Dalby (1893–1970)
You need a skin as thin as a cigarette paper to write a novel and the hide of an elephant to publish it.
[*Meanjin*, 1982]

GIBBON, Edward (1737–1794)
The romance of *Tom Jones*, that exquisite picture of human manners, will outlive the palace of the Escurial and the imperial eagle of the house of Austria.
[*Memoirs of My Life and Writings* (1796)]

LARKIN, Philip (1922–1985)
[Referring to modern novels] Far too many relied on the classic formula of a beginning, a muddle, and an end.
[*New Fiction*, 1978]

LAWRENCE, D.H. (1885–1930)
The novel is the one bright book of life.
['Why the Novel Matters' (1936)]

NABOKOV, Vladimir (1899–1977)
A novelist is, like all mortals, more fully at home on the surface of the present than in the ooze of the past.
[*Strong Opinions* (1973)]

SHAW, George Bernard (1856–1950)
It is clear that a novel cannot be too bad to be worth publishing . . . It certainly is possible for a novel to be too good to be worth publishing.
[*Plays Pleasant and Unpleasant* (1898)]

STENDHAL (1783–1842)
A novel is a mirror walking along a wide road.
[*Le Rouge et le Noir* (1830)]

WILDE, Oscar (1854–1900)
The good ended happily, and the bad unhappily. That is what Fiction means.
[*The Importance of Being Earnest* (1895)]

WOOLF, Virginia (1882–1941)
A woman must have money and a room of her own if she is to write fiction.
[*A Room of One's Own* (1929)]

See BOOKS; LITERATURE; WRITERS; WRITING

FLATTERY

AUSTEN, Jane (1775–1817)
It is happy for you that you possess the talent of flattering with delicacy. May I ask whether these pleasing attentions proceed from the impulse of the moment, or are the result of previous study?
[*Pride and Prejudice* (1813)]

BIERCE, Ambrose (1842–c. 1914)
Flatter: To impress another with a sense of one's own merit.
[*The Enlarged Devil's Dictionary* (1961)]

COLTON, Charles Caleb (c. 1780–1832)
Imitation is the sincerest form of flattery.
[*Lacon* (1820)]

DUNBAR, William (c. 1460–c. 1525)
Flattery wearis ane furrit gown,
And falsett with the lord does roun,
And truth stands barrit at the dure.
['Into this World May None Assure' (1834 edition)]

FONTAINE, Jean de la (1621–1695)
My dear Monsieur, know that every flatterer lives at the expense of the one who listens to him.
['Le corbeau et le renard']

HALIFAX, Lord (1633–1695)
It is flattering some Men to endure them.
['Of Company' (1750)]

SHAW, George Bernard (1856–1950)
What really flatters a man is that you think him worth flattering.
[*John Bull's Other Island* (1907)]

FOLLY

BARNUM, Phineas T. (1810–1891)
There's a sucker born every minute.
[Attr.]

BEECHER, Henry Ward (1813–1887)
[On receiving a note containing only one word: 'Fool']
I have known many an instance of a man writing a letter and forgetting to sign his name, but this is the only instance I have ever known of a man signing his name and forgetting to write the letter.
[Attr.]

THE BIBLE (KING JAMES VERSION)
Answer a fool according to his folly.

[*Proverbs*, 26:5]

BLAKE, William (1757–1827)
If the fool would persist in his folly he would become wise.

['Proverbs of Hell' (1793)]

COWPER, William (1731–1800)
A fool must now and then be right, by chance.

['Conversation' (1782)]

CURTIZ, Michael (1888–1962)
The next time I send a damn fool for something, I go myself.

[In Zierold, *Moguls* (1969)]

FIELDING, Henry (1707–1754)
One fool at least in every married couple.

[*Amelia* (1751)]

FRANKLIN, Benjamin (1706–1790)
Experience keeps a dear school, but fools will learn in no other.

[*Poor Richard's Almanac* (1743)]

HORACE (65–8 BC)
Mix a little folly with your plans: it is sweet to be silly at the right moment.

[*Odes*]

IBSEN, Henrik (1828–1906)
Fools are in a terrible, overwhelming majority, all the wide world over.

[*An Enemy of the People* (1882)]

MOLIERE (1622–1673)
The greatest folly of all is wanting to busy oneself in setting the world to rights.

[*Le Misanthrope* (1666)]

ROWLAND, Helen (1875–1950)
The follies which a man regrets most in his life are those which he didn't commit when he had the opportunity.

[*A Guide to Men* (1922)]

SCHILLER (1759–1805)
Gods themselves struggle in vain with stupidity.

[*The Maid of Orleans* (1801)]

SHAKESPEARE, William (1564–1616)
He uses his folly like a stalking-horse, and under the presentation of that he shoots his wit.

[*As You Like It*, V.iv]

STEVENSON, Robert Louis (1850–1894)
For God's sake give me the

young man who has brains enough to make a fool of himself!

[*Virginibus Puerisque* (1881)]

SWIFT, Jonathan (1667–1745)
Hated by fools, and fools to hate,
Be that my motto and my fate.

['To Mr Delany' (1718)]

THOREAU, Henry (1817–1862)
Any fool can make a rule and every fool will mind it.

[Attr.]

TUSSER, Thomas (c. 1524–1580)
A fool and his money be soon at debate.

[*Five Hundred Points of Good Husbandry* (1557)]

YOUNG, Edward (1683–1765)
Be wise with speed;
A fool at forty is a fool indeed.

[*Love of Fame, the Universal Passion* (1728)]

FOOD

BAREHAM, Lindsey (1948–)
Good mashed potato is one of the great luxuries of life and I don't blame Elvis for eating it every night for the last year of his life.

[*In Praise of the Potato* (1989)]

CERVANTES, Miguel de (1547–1616)
Hunger is the best sauce in the world.

[*Don Quixote* (1615)]

DAHL, Roald (1916–1990)
Do you *know* what breakfast cereal is made of? It's made of all those little curly wooden shavings you find in pencil sharpeners!

[*Charlie and the Chocolate Factory* (1964)]

DAVIES, David (1742–1819)
Though the potato is an excellent root, deserving to be brought into general use, yet it seems not likely that the use of it should ever be normal in the country.

[*The Case of the Labourers in Husbandry* (1795)]

DE VRIES, Peter (1910–)
Gluttony is an emotional escape, a sign something is eating us.

[*Comfort me with Apples* (1956)]

FEUERBACH, Ludwig (1804–1872)
Man is what he eats.

[In Moleschott, *Lehre der Nahrungsmittel: Für das Volk* (1850)]

**FRANKLIN, Benjamin
(1706–1790)**
To lengthen thy life, lessen thy
meals.

[*Poor Richard's Almanac*
(1733)]

FULLER, Thomas (1608–1661)
He was a very valiant man
who first ventured on eating
of oysters.

[*The History of the Worthies of
England* (1662)]

HERBERT, George (1593–1633)
A cheerful look makes a dish
a feast.

[*Jacula Prudentum* (1640)]

**JOHNSON, Samuel
(1709–1784)**
I look upon it, that he who
does not mind his belly will
hardly mind anything else.

[In Boswell, *The Life of Samuel
Johnson* (1791)]

**LUTYENS, Sir Edwin
Landseer (1869–1944)**
[Comment made in a restaurant]
This piece of cod passes all
understanding.

[In R. Lutyens, *Sir Edwin
Lutyens* (1942)]

MOLIERE (1622–1673)
One should eat to live, not
live to eat.

[*L'Avare* (1669)]

**PETER, Laurence J.
(1919–1990)**
The noblest of all dogs is the
hot-dog; it feeds the hand that
bites it.

[*Quotations for Our Time*
(1977)]

PIGGY, Miss
Never eat anything at one sitting that you can't lift.

[*Woman's Hour*, 1992]

**POPE, Alexander
(1688–1744)**
Fame is at best an unperforming cheat;
But 'tis substantial happiness,
to *eat*.

['Prologue for Mr D'Urfey's
Last Play' (1727)]

ROUSSEAU, Emile (1929–)
Great eaters of meat are in
general more cruel and ferocious than other men. The
English are known for their
cruelty.

[Attr.]

**SHAKESPEARE, William
(1564–1616)**
Methinks sometimes I have
no more wit than a Christian
or an ordinary man has; but I
am a great eater of beef, and I
believe that does harm to my
wit.

[*Twelfth Night*, I.iii]

SHAW, George Bernard (1856–1950)
There is no love sincerer than the love of food.

[*Man and Superman* (1903)]

VOLTAIRE (1694–1778)
[On learning that coffee was considered a slow poison]
I think it must be so, for I have been drinking it for sixty-five years and I am not dead yet.

[Attr.]

WEBSTER, John (c. 1580–c. 1625)
I saw him even now going the way of all flesh, that is to say towards the kitchen.

[*Westward Hoe* (1607)]

WODEHOUSE, P.G. (1881–1975)
The lunches of fifty-seven years had caused his chest to slip down to the mezzanine floor.

[*The Heart of a Goof* (1926)]

See COOKERY; DINING

FOREIGNERS

BELLOY, P.–L.-B. du (1727–1775)
The more foreigners I saw, the more I loved my native land.

[*Le Siège de Calais* (1765)]

CRISP, Quentin (1908–)
I don't hold with abroad and think that foreigners speak English when our backs are turned.

[*The Naked Civil Servant* (1968)]

ERASMUS (c. 1466–1536)
Is not the Turk a man and a brother?

[*Querela Pacis*]

MEYNELL, Hugo (1727–1780)
For anything I see, foreigners are fools.

[In Boswell, *The Life of Samuel Johnson* (1791)]

MITFORD, Nancy (1904–1973)
Abroad is unutterably bloody and foreigners are fiends.

[*The Pursuit of Love* (1945)]

TROLLOPE, Anthony (1815–1882)
We cannot bring ourselves to believe it possible that a foreigner should in any respect be wiser than ourselves. If any such point out to us our follies, we at once claim those follies as the special evidences of our wisdom.

[*Orley Farm* (1862)]

TWAIN, Mark (1835–1910)
They spell it Vinci and pro-

nounce it Vinchy; foreigners always spell better than they pronounce.

[*The Innocents Abroad* (1869)]

See TRAVEL

FORGIVENESS

**AUSTEN, Jane
(1775–1817)**
You ought certainly to forgive them as a Christian, but never to admit them in your sight, or allow their names to be mentioned in your hearing.

[*Pride and Prejudice* (1813)]

THE BIBLE (KING JAMES VERSION)
Father, forgive them; for they know not what they do.

[*Luke*, 23:34]

**BROWNING, Robert
(1812–1889)**
Good, to forgive;
Best, to forget!
Living, we fret;
Dying, we live.

[*La Saisiaz* (1878)]

**CATHERINE THE GREAT
(1729–1796)**
I shall be an autocrat: that's my job. And the good Lord will forgive me: that's his job.

[Attr.]

**DRYDEN, John
(1631–1700)**
Forgiveness to the injured does belong;
But they ne'er pardon, who have done the wrong.

[*The Conquest of Granada* (1670)]

**FROST, Robert
(1874–1963)**
Forgive, O Lord, my little jokes on Thee
And I'll forgive Thy great big one on me.

['Cluster of Faith' (1962)]

PROVERB
To err is human; to forgive divine.

FRANCE

**CARLYLE, Thomas
(1795–1881)**
France was long a despotism tempered by epigrams.

[*History of the French Revolution* (1837)]

**DE GAULLE, Charles
(1890–1970)**
One can only unite the French under the threat of danger. One cannot simply bring together a nation that produces 265 kinds of cheese.

[Speech, 1951]

**JOHNSON, Samuel
(1709–1784)**
A Frenchman must be always
talking, whether he knows
anything of the matter or not;
an Englishman is content to
say nothing, when he has
nothing to say.
[In Boswell, *The Life of Samuel
Johnson* (1791)]

NAPOLEON I (1769–1821)
France has more need of me
than I have need of France.
[Speech, 1813]

NOVELLO, Ivor (1893–1951)
There's something Vichy
about the French.
[In Marsh, *Ambrosia and Small
Beer*]

**WALPOLE, Horace
(1717–1797)**
I do not dislike the French
from the vulgar antipathy
between neighbouring
nations, but for their insolent
and unfounded airs of superiority.
[Letter, 1787]

**WILDER, Billy
(1906–)**
France is a country where the
money falls apart in your
hands and you can't tear the
toilet paper.
[In Halliwell, *Filmgoer's Book
of Quotes* (1973)]

FREEDOM

ANONYMOUS
[Declaration sent to Pope John
XXII by the Scottish barons]
For so long as but a hundred
of us remain alive, we will in
no way yield ourselves to the
dominion of the English. For it
is not for glory, nor riches, nor
honour that we fight, but for
Freedom only, which no good
man lays down but with his
life.
[Declaration of Arbroath,
1320]

BELL, Clive (1881–1964)
Only reason can convince us
of those three fundamental
truths without a recognition of
which there can be no effective liberty: that what we
believe is not necessarily true;
that what we like is not
necessarily good; and that all
questions are open.
[*Civilization* (1928)]

BERLIN, Sir Isaiah (1909–)
Liberty is liberty, not equality
or fairness or justice or culture, or human happiness or a
quiet conscience.
[*Four Essays on Liberty* (1969)]

**BURKE, Edmund
(1729–1797)**
Freedom and not servitude is

the cure of anarchy; as religion, and not atheism, is the true remedy for superstition.

[*Speech on Conciliation with America* (1775)]

The only liberty I mean, is a liberty connected with order; that not only exists along with order and virtue, but which cannot exist at all without them.

[Speech, 1774]

BURNS, Robert (1759–1796)
Scots, wha hae wi' Wallace bled,
Scots, wham Bruce has aften led,
Welcome to your gory bed
Or to victorie! . . .

Lay the proud usurpers low!
Tyrants fall in ev'ry foe!
Liberty's in every blow!
Let us do, or die!

['Scots, Wha Hae' (1793)]

COLERIDGE, Hartley (1796–1849)
But what is Freedom? Rightly understood,
A universal licence to be good.

['Liberty' (1833)]

CONNOLLY, James (1868–1916)
Apostles of Freedom are ever idolised when dead, but cruci-

fied when alive.

[Workers Republic, 1898]

CURRAN, John Philpot (1750–1817)
The condition upon which God hath given liberty to man is eternal vigilance; which condition if he break, servitude is at once the consequence of his crime, and the punishment of his guilt.

[Speech, 1790]

DIDEROT, Denis (1713–1784)
Men will never be free until the last king is strangled with the entrails of the last priest.

[*Dithyrambe sur la Fête des Rois*]

ENGELS, Friedrich (1820–1895)
Freedom is the recognition of necessity.

[In Mackay, *The Harvest of a Quiet Eye* (1977)]

EWER, William (1885–1976)
I gave my life for freedom –
This I know:
For those who bade me fight had told me so.

['The Souls' (1917)]

GOLDWATER, Barry (1909–)
[On accepting nomination for the presidency]
Extremism in the defence of

liberty is no vice.

[Speech, 1964]

HALIFAX, Lord (1633–1695)
Power is so apt to be insolent
and Liberty to be saucy, that
they are very seldom upon
good Terms.

[*Miscellaneous Thoughts and
Reflections* (1750)]

When the people contend for
their Liberty, they seldom get
any thing by their Victory but
new Masters.

[*Miscellaneous Thoughts and
Reflections* (1750)]

HATTERSLEY, Roy (1932–)
The proposition that Muslims
are welcome in Britain if, and
only if, they stop behaving
like Muslims is incompatible
with the principles of a free
society.

[*The Independent*, 1995]

**HAZLITT, William
(1778–1830)**
The love of liberty is the love
of others; the love of power is
the love of ourselves.

['The Times Newspaper'
(1819)]

**HENRY, Patrick
(1736–1799)**
Give me liberty, or give me
death!

[Speech, 1775]

HOFFER, Eric (1902–1983)
When people are free to do as
they please, they usually imitate each other.

[*The Passionate State of Mind*
(1955)]

**JEFFERSON, Thomas
(1743–1826)**
The tree of liberty must be
refreshed from time to time
with the blood of patriots and
tyrants. It is its natural manure.

[Letter to W.S. Smith, 1787]

KAFKA, Franz (1883–1924)
It's often better to be in chains
than to be free.

[*The Trial* (1925)]

**KING, Martin Luther
(1929–1968)**
Free at last, free at last, thank
God Almighty, we are free at
last!

[Speech, 1963]

LENIN, V.I. (1870–1924)
It is true that liberty is
precious – so precious that it
must be rationed.

[In Sidney and Beatrice Webb,
Soviet Communism (1936)]

**LINCOLN, Abraham
(1809–1865)**
Those who deny freedom to
others, deserve it not for
themselves.

[Speech, 1856]

**MACAULAY, Lord
(1800–1859)**
There is only one cure for the evils which newly acquired freedom produces; and that is freedom.
[*Collected Essays* (1843)]

**MANDELA, Nelson
(1918–)**
I cannot and will not give any undertaking at a time when I, and you, the people, are not free. Your freedom and mine cannot be separated.
[Message to a rally in Soweto, 1985]

MANN, W. Edward (1918–)
A sudden access of psychological freedom often turns from sheer excitement to deep panic.
[*The Man Who Dreamed of Tomorrow* (1980)]

**MILL, John Stuart
(1806–1873)**
The sole end for which mankind are warranted, individually or collectively, in interfering with the liberty of action of any of their number, is self-protection.
[*On Liberty* (1859)]

**MILTON, John
(1608–1674)**
None can love freedom heartilie, but good men; the rest love not freedom, but licence.
[*The Tenure of Kings and Magistrates* (1649)]

MONTESQUIEU (1689–1755)
Freedom is the right to do whatever the law permits.
[*De l'esprit des lois* (1748)]

PANKHURST, Dame Christabel (1880–1958)
What we suffragettes aspire to be when we are enfranchised is ambassadors of freedom to women in other parts of the world, who are not so free as we are.
[Speech, 1915]

**ROLAND, Madame
(1754–1793)**
[Remark on mounting the scaffold]
O liberty! O liberty! how many crimes are committed in your name!
[In Lamartine, *Histoire des Girondins* (1847)]

**SARTRE, Jean-Paul
(1905–1980)**
Once freedom has exploded in the soul of a man, the gods have no more power over him.
[*The Flies* (1943)]

Man is condemned to be free.
[*Existentialism and Humanism*]

SHAW, George Bernard (1856–1950)
Liberty means responsibility. That is why most men dread it.
[*Man and Superman* (1903)]

SOLZHENITSYN, Alexander (1918–)
You only have power over people as long as you don't take *everything* away from them. But when you've robbed a man of *everything* he's no longer in your power — he's free again.
[*The First Circle* (1968)]

STEVENSON, Adlai (1900–1965)
My definition of a free society is a society where it is safe to be unpopular.
[Speech, Detroit, 1952]

TWAIN, Mark (1835–1910)
It is by the goodness of God that in our country we have those three unspeakably precious things: freedom of speech, freedom of conscience, and the prudence never to practise either of them.
[*Following the Equator* (1897)]

VOLTAIRE (1694–1778)
Liberty was born in England from the quarrels of tyrants.
[*Lettres philosophiques* (1734)]

WASHINGTON, George (1732–1799)
Liberty, when it begins to take root, is a plant of rapid growth.
[Letter, 1788]

FRIENDSHIP

ADAMS, Henry (1838–1918)
One friend in a lifetime is much; two are many; three are hardly possible. Friendship needs a certain parallelism of life, a community of thought, a rivalry of aim.
[*The Education of Henry Adams* (1918)]

ARISTOTLE (384–322 BC)
On being asked what is a friend, he said 'A single soul dwelling in two bodies.'
[In Diogenes Laertius, *Lives of Philosophers*]

BACON, Francis (1561–1626)
It is the worst solitude, to have no true friendships.
[*The Advancement of Learning* (1605)]

This communicating of a man's self to his friend works two contrary effects; for it redoubleth joys, and cutteth griefs in halves.
[*Essays* (1625)]

**BELLOC, Hilaire
(1870–1953)**
From quiet homes and first
beginning,
Out to the undiscovered ends,
There's nothing worth the
wear of winning,
But laughter and the love of
friends.
[*Verses* (1910), 'Dedicatory
Ode']

**THE BIBLE (KING JAMES
VERSION)**
A faithful friend is a sturdy
shelter: he that has found one
has found a treasure. There is
nothing so precious as a faithful friend, and no scales can
measure his excellence.
[Apocrypha, *Ecclesiasticus*]

**BIERCE, Ambrose
(1842–c. 1914)**
Antipathy: The sentiment
inspired by one's friend's
friend.
[*The Enlarged Devil's
Dictionary* (1961)]

**BRADBURY, Malcolm
(1932–)**
I've noticed your hostility
towards him . . . I ought to
have guessed you were friends.
[*The History Man* (1975)]

**BULWER-LYTTON, Edward
(1803–1873)**
There is no man so friendless

but what he can find a friend
sincere enough to tell him disagreeable truths.
[*What Will He Do With It?*
(1857)]

BYRON, Lord (1788–1824)
Friendship is Love without his
wings.
['L'amitié est l'amour sans
ailes' (1806)]

**CANNING, George
(1770–1827)**
Give me the avowed, erect
and manly foe;
Firm I can meet, perhaps
return the blow;
But of all plagues, good
Heaven, thy wrath can send,
Save me, oh, save me, from
the candid friend.
['New Morality' (1821)]

COLETTE (1873–1954)
My true friends have always
given me that supreme proof
of devotion, a spontaneous
aversion for the man I loved.
[*Break of Day* (1928)]

**COLTON, Charles Caleb
(c. 1780–1832)**
Friendship often ends in love;
but love in friendship – never.
[*Lacon* (1820)]

**EMERSON, Ralph Waldo
(1803–1882)**
Let the soul be assured that

somewhere in the universe it should rejoin its friend, and it would be content and cheerful alone for a thousand years.

['Friendship' (1841)]

The only reward of virtue is virtue; the only way to have a friend is to be one.

['Friendship' (1841)]

HUMPHRIES, Barry (1934–)
Friendship is tested in the thick years of success rather than in the thin years of struggle.

[In Green, *A Dictionary of Contemporary Quotations* (1982)]

JOHNSON, Samuel (1709–1784)
If a man does not make new acquaintance as he advances through life, he will soon find himself left alone. A man, Sir, should keep his friendship in constant repair.

[In Boswell, *The Life of Samuel Johnson* (1791)]

How few of his friends' houses would a man choose to be at when he is sick.

[In Boswell, *The Life of Samuel Johnson* (1791)]

KINGSMILL, Hugh (1889–1949)
Friends are God's apology for relations.

[In Ingrams, *God's Apology* (1977)]

LEWIS, C.S. (1898–1963)
Friendship is unnecessary, like philosophy, like art. . . . It has no survival value; rather it is one of those things that give value to survival.

[*The Four Loves* (c. 1936)]

MEDICI, Cosimo de' (1389–1464)
We read that we ought to forgive our enemies; but we do not read that we ought to forgive our friends.

[In Bacon, *Apophthegms* (1625)]

POPE, Alexander (1688–1744)
True friendship's laws are by this rule express'd,
Welcome the coming, speed the parting guest.

[*The Odyssey* (1726)]

How often are we to die before we go quite off this stage? In every friend we lose a part of ourselves, and the best part.

[Letter to Swift, 1732]

SHAKESPEARE, William (1564–1616)
Friendship is constant in all other things

Save in the office and affairs of love.

[*Much Ado About Nothing*, II.i]

TWAIN, Mark (1835–1910)

The holy passion of Friendship is of so sweet and steady and loyal and enduring a nature that it will last through a whole lifetime, if not asked to lend money.

[*Pudd'nhead Wilson's Calendar* (1894)]

VIDAL, Gore (1925–)

Whenever a friend succeeds, a little something in me dies.

[*The Sunday Times Magazine*, 1973]

WHITMAN, Walt (1819–1892)

I no doubt deserved my enemies, but I don't believe I deserved my friends.

[In Bradford, *Biography and the Human Heart*]

YEATS, W.B. (1865–1939)

Think where man's glory most begins and ends,
And say my glory was I had such friends.

['The Municipal Gallery Revisited' (1937)]

BALDWIN, James (1924–1987)

The future is . . . black.

[*The Observer*, 1963]

BALFOUR, A.J. (1848–1930)

The energies of our system will decay, the glory of the sun will be dimmed, and the earth, tideless and inert, will no longer tolerate the race which has for a moment disturbed its solitude. Man will go down into the pit, and all his thoughts will perish.

[*The Foundations of Belief* (1895)]

BIERCE, Ambrose (1842–c. 1914)

Future: That period of time in which our affairs prosper, our friends are true and our happiness is assured.

[*The Cynic's Word Book* (1906)]

CAMUS, Albert (1913–1960)

The future is the only kind of property that the masters willingly concede to slaves.

[*The Rebel* (1951)]

CHURCHILL, Sir Winston (1874–1965)

The empires of the future are empires of the mind.

[Speech, 1943]

CLARK, Lord Kenneth (1903–1983)
One may be optimistic, but one can't exactly be joyful at the prospect before us.
[End of TV series, *Civilization*]

COLERIDGE, Samuel Taylor (1772–1834)
Often do the spirits
Of great events stride on
before the events,
And in to-day already walks
to-morrow.
['Death of Wallenstein' (1800)]

CONFUCIUS (c. 550–c. 478 BC)
Study the past, if you would divine the future.
[*Analects*]

COWARD, Sir Noël (1899–1973)
I don't give a hoot about posterity. Why should I worry about what people think of me when I'm dead as a doornail anyway?
[*Present Laughter* (1943)]

DIX, Dorothy (1870–1951)
I have learned to live each day as it comes, and not to borrow trouble by dreading tomorrow. It is the dark menace of the future that makes cowards of us.
[*Dorothy Dix, Her Book* (1926)]

HILL, Reginald (1936–)
I have seen the future and it sucks.
[*Pictures of Perfection* (1994)]

HUGO, Victor (1802–1885)
In the twentieth century, war will be dead, the scaffold will be dead, hatred will be dead, frontier boundaries will be dead, dogmas will be dead; man will live. He will possess something higher than all these – a great country, the whole earth, and a great hope, the whole heaven.
[*The Future of Man*]

LEWIS, C.S. (1898–1963)
The Future is something which everyone reaches at the rate of sixty minutes an hour, whatever he does, whoever he is.
[*The Screwtape Letters* (1942)]

MITCHELL, Margaret (1900–1949)
After all, tomorrow is another day.
[*Gone with the Wind* (1936)]

ORWELL, George (1903–1950)
If you want a picture of the future, imagine a boot stamping on a human face – for ever.
[*Nineteen Eighty-Four* (1949)]

PROUST, Marcel
(1871–1922)
What we call our future is the
shadow which our past
throws in front of us.
[*A l'ombre des jeunes filles en
fleurs* (1918)]

RIFKIN, Jeremy
When the Iroquois made a
decision, they said, 'How does
it affect seven generations in
the future?'
[*The New York Times
Magazine*, 1988]

STEFFENS, Lincoln
(1866–1936)
[Remark after visiting Russia
in 1919]
I have seen the future; and it
works.
[Letter to Marie Howe, 1919]

WEIL, Simone
(1909–1943)
The future is made of the
same stuff as the present.
[*On Science, Necessity, and the
Love of God*]

WELLS, H.G.
(1866–1946)
One thousand years more.
That's all *Homo sapiens* has
before him.
[In H. Nicolson, *Diary*]

GARDENS

ADDISON, Joseph
(1672–1719)
I value my garden more for
being full of blackbirds than of
cherries, and very frankly give
them fruit for their songs.
[*The Spectator*, 1712]

BROWN, Thomas Edward
(1830–1897)
A garden is a lovesome thing,
God wot!
['My Garden' (1893)]

COWLEY, Abraham
(1618–1667)
God the first garden made,
and the first city Cain.
['The Garden' (1668)]

EMERSON, Ralph Waldo
(1803–1882)
What is a weed? A plant
whose virtues have not yet
been discovered.
[*Fortune of the Republic*
(1878)]

GURNEY, Dorothy
(1858–1932)
The kiss of the sun for pardon,
The song of the birds for
mirth,
One is nearer God's Heart in a
garden
Than anywhere else on earth.
['God's Garden' (1913)]

KIPLING, Rudyard
(1865–1936)
Oh, Adam was a gardener,
and God who made him sees
That half a proper gardener's
work is done upon his knees,
So when your work is fin-
ished, you can wash your
hands and pray
For the Glory of the Garden,
that it may not pass away!
*And the Glory of the Garden it
shall never pass away!*
['The Glory of the Garden'
(1911)]

MARVELL, Andrew
(1621–1678)
Here at the fountain's sliding
foot,
Or at some fruit-tree's mossy
root,
Casting the body's vest aside,
My soul into the boughs does
glide.
['The Garden' (1681)]

RUSSELL, Bertrand
(1872–1970)
Every time I talk to a savant I
feel quite sure that happiness
is no longer a possibility. Yet
when I talk to my gardener,
I'm convinced of the opposite.
[Attr.]

SHAKESPEARE, William
(1564–1616)
'Tis in ourselves that we are
thus or thus. Our bodies are

our gardens to the which our wills are gardeners.

[*Othello*, I.iii]

TENNYSON, Alfred, Lord (1809–1892)
Come into the garden, Maud,
For the black bat, night, has flown,
Come into the garden, Maud,
I am here at the gate alone;
And the woodbine spices are wafted abroad,
And the musk of the rose is blown.

[*Maud* (1855)]

VOLTAIRE (1694–1778)
'That is well said,' replied Candide, 'but we must cultivate our garden.'

[*Candide* (1759)]

GENEROSITY

BARRIE, Sir J.M. (1860–1937)
Never ascribe to an opponent motives meaner than your own.

[Address, 1922]

THE BIBLE (KING JAMES VERSION)
It is more blessed to give than to receive.

[*Acts of the Apostles*, 20:35]

God loveth a cheerful giver.

[*II Corinthians*, 9:7]

CORNEILLE, Pierre (1606–1684)
The manner of giving is worth more than the gift.

[*Le Menteur* (1643)]

GIBBS, Sir Philip (1877–1962)
It is better to give than to lend, and it costs about the same.

[Attr.]

TALLEYRAND (1754–1838)
Don't trust first impulses; they are always generous.

[Attr.]

GENIUS

BEERBOHM, Sir Max (1872–1956)
I have known no man of genius who had not to pay, in some affliction or defect either physical or spiritual, for what the gods had given him.

[*And Even Now* (1920)]

DALI, Salvador (1904–1989)
I'm going to live forever. Geniuses don't die.

[*The Observer*, 1986]

DOYLE, Sir Arthur Conan (1859–1930)
Mediocrity knows nothing higher than itself, but talent instantly recognizes genius.
[*The Valley of Fear* (1914)]

EDISON, Thomas Alva (1847–1931)
Genius is one per cent inspiration and ninety-nine per cent perspiration.
[*Life*, 1932]

HAZLITT, William (1778–1830)
Rules and models destroy genius and art.
['Thoughts on Taste' (1818)]

HOPE, Anthony (1863–1933)
Unless one is a genius, it is best to aim at being intelligible.
[*The Dolly Dialogues* (1894)]

HOPKINS, Jane Ellice (1836–1904)
Gift, like genius, I often think, only means an infinite capacity for taking pains.
[*Work amongst Working Men*, 1870]

HUBBARD, Elbert (1856–1915)
One machine can do the work of fifty ordinary men. No machine can do the work of one extraordinary man.
[*A Thousand and One Epigrams* (1911)]

KENNEDY, John F. (1917–1963)
[At a dinner held at the White House for Nobel prizewinners] . . . probably the greatest concentration of talent and genius in this house, except for perhaps those times when Thomas Jefferson ate alone.
[*New York Times*, 1962]

MEREDITH, Owen (1831–1891)
Genius does what it must, and Talent what it can.
['Last Words of a Sensitive Second-Rate Poet' (1868)]

SWIFT, Jonathan (1667–1745)
When a true genius appears in the world, you may know him by this sign, that the dunces are all in confederacy against him.
[*Thoughts on Various Subjects* (1711)]

WHISTLER, James McNeill (1834–1903)
[Replying to a lady inquiring whether he thought genius hereditary]
I cannot tell you that, madam. Heaven has granted me no offspring.
[In Seitz, *Whistler Stories* (1913)]

WILDE, Oscar (1854–1900)
[Spoken to André Gide]
Do you want to know the great tragedy of my life? I have put all of my genius into my life; all I've put into my works is my talent.
    [In Gide, *Oscar Wilde* (1910)]

[At the New York Customs]
I have nothing to declare except my genius.
    [In Harris, *Oscar Wilde* (1918)]

GENTLEMEN

ALLEN, Fred (1894–1956)
A gentleman is any man who wouldn't hit a woman with his hat on.
                                    [Attr.]

ANONYMOUS
When Adam delved, and Eve span,
Who was then a gentleman?
    [Attr. John Ball, 1381]

**BURKE, Edmund
(1729–1797)**
Somebody has said, that a king may make a nobleman but he cannot make a Gentleman.
    [Letter to William Smith, 1795]

CHIFLEY, Joseph (1885–1951)
My experience of gentlemen's agreements is that, when it comes to the pinch, there are rarely enough bloody gentlemen about.
    [In Crisp, *Ben Chifley* (1960)]

CURZON, Lord (1859–1925)
Gentlemen do not take soup at luncheon.
    [In Woodward, *Short Journey* (1942)]

FURPHY, Joseph (1843–1912)
For there is no such thing as a democratic gentleman; the adjective and the noun are hyphenated by a drawn sword.
    [*Such is Life* (1903)]

LINTON, W.J. (1812–1897)
For he is one of Nature's Gentlemen, the best of every time.
    [*Nature's Gentleman*]

**MATTHEWS, Brander
(1852–1929)**
A gentleman need not know Latin, but he should at least have forgotten it.
                                    [Attr.]

**NELSON, Lord
(1758–1805)**
[To his midshipmen]
Recollect that you must be a seaman to be an officer; and also, that you cannot be a good officer without being a

gentleman.

[In Southey, *The Life of Nelson* (1860)]

NEWMAN Cardinal (1801–1890)

It is almost a definition of a gentleman to say that he is one who never inflicts pain.

['Knowledge and Religious Duty' (1852)]

SHAW, George Bernard (1856–1950)

I am a gentleman: I live by robbing the poor.

[*Man and Superman* (1903)]

STEVENSON, Robert Louis (1850–1894)

Between the possibility of being hanged in all innocence, and the certainty of a public and merited disgrace, no gentleman of spirit could long hesitate.

[*The Wrong Box* (1889)]

SURTEES, R.S. (1805–1864)

The only infallible rule we know is, that the man who is always talking about being a gentleman never is one.

[*Ask Mamma* (1858)]

GLORY

ANONYMOUS

Sic transit gloria mundi.

Thus passes the glory of the world.

[Spoken during the coronation of a new Pope]

BLAKE, William (1757–1827)

The pride of the peacock is the glory of God.

['Proverbs of Hell' (c. 1793)]

BYRON, Lord (1788–1824)

Glory, like the phoenix 'midst her fires,
Exhales her odours, blazes, and expires.

[*English Bards and Scotch Reviewers* (1809)]

CAMPBELL, Thomas (1777–1844)

The combat deepens. On, ye brave,
Who rush to glory, or the grave!

['Hohenlinden']

FONTAINE, Jean de la (1621–1695)

No flowery path leads to glory.

['Les deux aventuriers et le talisman']

GRAY, Thomas (1716–1771)

The boast of heraldry, the pomp of pow'r,
And all that beauty, all that wealth e'er gave,
Awaits alike th' inevitable

hour,
The paths of glory lead but to
the grave.
['Elegy Written in a Country
Churchyard' (1751)]

**MORDAUNT, Thomas
(1730–1809)**
Sound, sound the clarion, fill
the fife,
Throughout the sensual world
proclaim,
One crowded hour of glorious
life
Is worth an age without a
name.
['Verses written during the
War, 1756–1763' (1791)]

**SHAKESPEARE, William
(1564–1616)**
Like madness is the glory of
this life.
[*Timon of Athens*, I.ii]

**WEBSTER, John
(c. 1580–c. 1625)**
Glories, like glow-worms, afar
off shine bright,
But, looked too near, have
neither heat nor light.
[*The Duchess of Malfi* (1623)]

**WORDSWORTH, William
(1770–1850)**
Not in entire forgetfulness,
And not in utter nakedness,
But trailing clouds of glory do
we come
From God, who is our home:

Heaven lies about us in our
infancy!
['Ode: Intimations of
Immortality' (1807)]

GOALS

BERLIN, Sir Isaiah (1909–)
Injustice, poverty, slavery,
ignorance – these may be
cured by reform or revolution.
But men do not live only by
fighting evils. They live by
positive goals, individual and
collective, a vast variety of
them, seldom predictable, at
times incompatible.
['Political Ideas in the
Twentieth Century' (1969)]

KAFKA, Franz (1883–1924)
There is a goal but no way of
reaching it; what we call the
way is hesitation.
[*Reflections on Sin, Sorrow,
Hope and the True Way*]

**SANTAYANA, George
(1863–1952)**
Fanaticism consists in re-
doubling your effort when you
have forgotten your aim.
[*The Life of Reason* (1906)]

**SIDNEY, Sir Philip
(1554–1586)**
Who shoots at the midday
sun, though he be sure he

shall never hit the mark, yet as sure he is he shall shoot higher than who aims but at a bush.

[*New Arcadia* (1590)]

SMITH, Logan Pearsall (1865–1946)
When people come and talk to you of their aspirations, before they leave you had better count your spoons.

[*Afterthoughts* (1931)]

STEVENSON, Robert Louis (1850–1894)
An aspiration is a joy forever.

[*Virginibus Puerisque* (1881)]

WHITE, Patrick (1912–1990)
That is men all over . . . They will aim too low. And achieve what they expect.

[*Voss* (1957)]

GOD

AGATHON (c. 445–400 BC)
Even God is deprived of this one thing only: the power to undo what has been done.

[In Aristotle, *Nicomachean Ethics*]

THE BIBLE (KING JAMES VERSION)
For the Lord seeth not as man seeth: for man looketh on the outward appearance, but the Lord looketh on the heart.

[*I Samuel,* 16:7]

BONHOEFFER, Dietrich (1906–1945)
In all important questions, man has learned to cope without recourse to God as a working hypothesis.

[Letter to a friend, 1944]

BROOKE, Rupert (1887–1915)
Because God put His adamantine fate
Between my sullen heart and its desire,
I swore that I would burst the Iron Gate,
Rise up, and curse Him on His throne of fire.

['Failure' (1905–1908)]

BROWNING, Elizabeth Barrett (1806–1861)
God answers sharp and sudden on some prayers,
And thrusts the thing we have prayed for in our face,
A gauntlet with a gift in't.

[*Aurora Leigh* (1857)]

CLOUGH, Arthur Hugh (1819–1861)
Youths green and happy in first love,
So thankful for illusion;
And men caught out in what the world

Calls guilt, in first confusion;

And almost every one when
age,
Disease, or sorrows strike
him,
Inclines to think there is a
God,
Or something very like Him.
[*Dipsychus* (1865)]

**COWPER, William
(1731–1800)**
God moves in a mysterious
way
His wonders to perform;
He plants his footsteps in the
sea,
And rides upon the storm.
[*Olney Hymns* (1779)]

DE VRIES, Peter (1910–)
It is the final proof of God's
omnipotence that he need not
exist in order to save us.
[*The Mackerel Plaza* (1958)]

**DUHAMEL, Georges
(1884–1966)**
I have too much respect for
the idea of God to make it
responsible for such an
absurd world.
[*Chronique des Pasquier*
(1948)]

**GALILEO GALILEI
(1564–1642)**
I do not feel obliged to believe
that the same God who has

endowed us with sense,
reason, and intellect has
intended us to forgo their use.
[Attr.]

HALDANE, J.B.S. (1892–1964)
[Reply when asked what infer-
ences could be drawn about
the nature of God from a
study of his works]
The Creator . . . has a special
preference for beetles.
[*Lecture*, 1951]

HUGHES, Sean (1966–)
I'd like to thank God for fucking up my life and at the same
time not existing, quite a
special skill.
[*The Independent*, 1993]

**KEMPIS, Thomas à
(c. 1380–1471)**
For man proposes, but God
disposes.
[*De Imitatione Christi* (1892)]

**KOESTLER, Arthur
(1905–1983)**
God seems to have left the
receiver off the hook, and
time is running out.
[*The Ghost in the Machine*
(1961)]

**MENCKEN, H.L.
(1880–1956)**
God is the immemorial refuge
of the incompetent, the help-
less, the miserable. They find

not only sanctuary in His arms, but also a kind of superiority, soothing to their macerated egos; He will set them above their betters.

[*Notebooks* (1956)]

It takes a long while for a naturally trustful person to reconcile himself to the idea that after all God will not help him.

[*Notebooks* (1956)]

NERVAL, Gérard de (1808–1855)

God is dead! Heaven is empty – Weep, children, you no longer have a father.

['Le Christ aux Oliviers']

OWEN, John (c. 1560–1622)

God and the doctor we alike adore
But only when in danger, not before;
The danger o'er, both are alike requited,
God is forgotten, and the Doctor slighted.

[*Epigrams*]

PASCAL, Blaise (1623–1662)

I cannot forgive Descartes; in all his philosophy he did his best to dispense with God. But he could not avoid making Him set the world in motion with a flick of His finger; after that he had no more use for God.

[*Pensées* (1670)]

SARTRE, Jean-Paul (1905–1980)

God is absence. God is the solitude of man.

[*Le Diable et le Bon Dieu* (1951)]

SHAKESPEARE, William (1564–1616)

There's a divinity that shapes our ends,
Rough-hew them how we will.

[*Hamlet*, V.ii]

As flies to wanton boys are we to th' gods –
They kill us for their sport.

[*King Lear*, IV.i]

SQUIRE, Sir J.C. (1884–1958)

God heard the embattled nations sing and shout
'Gott strafe England!' and 'God save the King!'
God this, God that, and God the other thing –
'Good God!' said God, 'I've got my work cut out.'

[*The Survival of the Fittest* (1916)]

WALKER, Alice (1944–)

I think it pisses God off if you walk by the color purple in a field somewhere and don't notice it.

[*The Color Purple*, film, 1985]

See ART; BELIEF

GOOD AND EVIL

THE BIBLE (KING JAMES VERSION)
Ye shall be as gods, knowing good and evil.

[*Genesis*, 3:5]

BURNS, Robert (1759–1796)
Whatever mitigates the woes or increases the happiness of others, this is my criterion of goodness; and whatever injures society at large, or any individual in it, this is my measure of iniquity.

[Attr.]

BUTLER, Samuel (1835–1902)
Virtue and vice are like life and death or mind and matter: things which cannot exist without being qualified by their opposite.

[*The Way of All Flesh* (1903)]

GOLDSMITH, Oliver (c. 1728–1774)
We must touch his weaknesses with a delicate hand. There are some faults so nearly allied to excellence, that we can scarce weed out the vice without eradicating the virtue.

[*The Good Natur'd Man* (1768)]

LERMONTOV, Mikhail (1814–1841)
What *is* the greatest good and evil? – two ends of an invisible chain which come closer together the further they move apart.

[*Vadim* (1834)]

SHAKESPEARE, William (1564–1616)
The evil that men do lives after them;
The good is oft interred with their bones.

[*Julius Caesar*, III.ii]

Some rise by sin, and some by virtue fall.

[*Measure for Measure*, II.i]

SURTEES, R.S. (1805–1864)
More people are flattered into virtue than bullied out of vice.

[*The Analysis of the Hunting Field* (1846)]

VANBRUGH, Sir John (1664–1726)
Belinda: Ay, but you know we must return good for evil.
Lady Brute: That may be a mistake in the translation.

[*The Provok'd Wife* (1697)]

GOODNESS

ARISTOTLE (384–322 BC)
In all things the middle state

is to be praised. But it is sometimes necessary to incline towards overshooting and sometimes to shooting short of the mark, since this is the easiest way of hitting the mean and the right course.

[*Nicomachean Ethics*]

BARTH, Karl (1886–1968)
Men have never been good, they are not good, they never will be good.

[*Time*, 1954]

BLAKE, William (1757–1827)
He who would do good to another must do it in Minute Particulars.
General Good is the plea of the Scoundrel hypocrite & flatterer.

[*Jerusalem* (1804–1820)]

BUDDHA (c. 563–483 BC)
This Ayrian Eightfold Path, that is to say: Right view, right aim, right speech, right action, right living, right effort, right mindfulness, right contemplation.

[In Woodward, *Some Sayings of the Buddha*]

BURKE, Edmund (1729–1797)
When bad men combine, the good must associate; else they will fall, one by one, an unpitied sacrifice in a contemptible struggle.

[*Thoughts on the Cause of the Present Discontents* (1770)]

CONFUCIUS (c. 550–c. 478 BC)
True goodness springs from a man's own heart. All men are born good.

[*Analects*]

GRELLET, Stephen (1773–1855)
I expect to pass through this world but once; any good thing therefore that I can do, or any kindness that I can show to any fellow-creature, let me do it now; let me not defer or neglect it, for I shall not pass this way again.

[Attr.]

HUTCHESON, Francis (1694–1746)
That action is best, which procures the greatest happiness for the greatest numbers.

[*An Inquiry into the Original of our Ideas of Beauty and Virtue* (1725)]

LANDOR, Walter Savage (1775–1864)
Goodness does not more certainly make men happy than happiness makes them good.

[*Imaginary Conversations* (1853)]

MACHIAVELLI (1469–1527)
Men never do anything good
except out of necessity.
[*Discourse*]

**SHAKESPEARE, William
(1564–1616)**
How far that little candle
throws its beams!
So shines a good deed in a
naughty world.
[*The Merchant of Venice*, V.i]

VOLTAIRE (1694–1778)
The best is the enemy of the
good.
['Art dramatique' (1770)]

WEST, Mae (1892–1980)
When I'm good I'm very good,
but when I'm bad I'm better.
[*I'm No Angel*, film, 1933]

WILDE, Oscar (1854–1900)
It is better to be beautiful than
to be good. But . . . it is better
to be good than to be ugly.
[*The Picture of Dorian Gray*
(1891)]

See BEAUTY; BENEFAC-
TORS; MORALITY; VIRTUE

GOSSIP

**BIERCE, Ambrose
(1842–c. 1914)**
Backbite: To speak of a man

as you find him when he can't
find you.
[*The Enlarged Devil's
Dictionary* (1961)]

**CHESTERFIELD, Lord
(1694–1773)**
In the case of scandal, as in
that of robbery, the receiver is
always thought as bad as the
thief.
[Letter to his son, 1748]

**CONGREVE, William
(1670–1729)**
Retired to their tea and scandal, according to their ancient
custom.
[*The Double Dealer* (1694)]

They come together like the
Coroner's Inquest, to sit upon
the murdered reputations of
the week.
[*The Way of the World* (1700)]

**FARQUHAR, George
(1678–1707)**
I believe they talked of me, for
they laughed consumedly.
[*The Beaux' Stratagem* (1707)]

**LONGWORTH, Alice
Roosevelt (1884–1980)**
[Embroidered on a cushion at
her home in Washington]
If you haven't anything nice to
say about anyone, come and
sit by me.
[*New York Times*, 1980]

OUIDA (1839–1908)
A cruel story runs on wheels, and every hand oils the wheels as they run.
[*Wisdom, Wit and Pathos*, 'Moths']

POPE, Alexander (1688–1744)
At ev'ry word a reputation dies.
[*The Rape of the Lock* (1714)]

RUSSELL, Bertrand (1872–1970)
No one gossips about other people's secret virtues.
[*On Education* (1926)]

SHERIDAN, Richard Brinsley (1751–1816)
Tale-bearers are as bad as the tale-makers.
[*The School for Scandal* (1777)]

Here is the whole set! a character dead at every word.
[*The School for Scandal* (1777)]

GOVERNMENT

ACTON, Lord (1834–1902)
The danger is not that a particular class is unfit to govern. Every class is unfit to govern.
[Letter, 1881]

BAGEHOT, Walter (1826–1877)
A severe though not unfriendly critic of our institutions said that 'the cure for admiring the House of Lords was to go and look at it.'
[*The English Constitution* (1867)]

BEVERIDGE, William (1879–1963)
The object of government in peace and in war is not the glory of rulers or of races, but the happiness of the common man.
[*Report on Social Insurance and Allied Services* (1942)]

BURKE, Edmund (1729–1797)
All government, indeed every human benefit and enjoyment, every virtue, and every prudent act, is founded on compromise and barter.
[*Speech on Conciliation with America* (1775)]

In all forms of Government the people is the true legislator.
[*Tracts on the Popery Laws* (1812)]

CAMPBELL-BANNERMAN, Sir Henry (1836–1908)
Good government could never be a substitute for govern-

ment by the people themselves.

[Speech, 1905]

GOLDWATER, Barry (1909–)
A government that is big enough to give you all you want is big enough to take it all away.

[*Bachman's Book of Freedom Quotations*]

HOBBES, Thomas (1588–1679)
They that are discontented under monarchy, call it tyranny; and they that are displeased with aristocracy, call it oligarchy . . . they which find themselves grieved under a democracy, call it anarchy.

[*Leviathan* (1651)]

JAMES VI OF SCOTLAND AND I OF ENGLAND (1566–1625)
I will govern according to the common weal, but not according to the common will.

[Remark, 1621]

JOHNSON, Samuel (1709–1784)
I would not give half a guinea to live under one form of government rather than another. It is of no moment to the happiness of an individual.

[In Boswell, *The Life of Samuel Johnson* (1791)]

KEYNES, John Maynard (1883–1946)
The important thing for government is not to do things which individuals are doing already, and to do them a little better or a little worse; but to do those things which at present are not done at all.

['The End of Laissez-Faire' (1926)]

MAISTRE, Joseph de (1753–1821)
Each country has the government it deserves.

[Letter, 1811]

MENCKEN, H.L. (1880–1956)
The worst government is the most moral. One composed of cynics is often very tolerant and human. But when fanatics are on top there is no limit to oppression.

[*Notebooks* (1956)]

O'SULLIVAN, John L. (1813–1895)
The best government is that which governs least.

[*United States Magazine and Democratic Review*, 1837]

PAINE, Thomas (1737–1809)
Man is not the enemy of Man, but through the medium of a false system of government.

[*The Rights of Man* (1791)]

RIPPON, Geoffrey (1924–)
Governments don't retreat,
they just simply advance in another direction.
[*The Observer*, 1981]

ROGERS, Will (1879–1935)
I don't make jokes – I just
watch the government and
report the facts.
[Attr.]

RUSKIN, John (1819–1900)
Government and cooperation
are in all things the laws of
life; anarchy and competition,
the laws of death.
[*Unto this Last* (1862)]

VOLTAIRE (1694–1778)
In governments there must be
both shepherds and butchers.
['The Piccini Notebooks']

See CAPITALISM;
DEMOCRACY

GREATNESS

**AMIEL, Henri-Frédéric
(1821–1881)**
The age of great men is going;
the epoch of the ant-hill, of life
in multiplicity, is beginning.
[*Journal*, 1851]

BACON, Francis (1561–1626)
All rising to great place is by a
winding stair.
['Of Great Place' (1625)]

**BEERBOHM, Sir Max
(1872–1956)**
Great men are but life-sized.
Most of them, indeed, are
rather short.
[Attr.]

**CARLYLE, Thomas
(1795–1881)**
No great man lives in vain.
The History of the world is but
the Biography of great men.
['The Hero as Divinity' (1841)]

**CHAPMAN, George
(c. 1559–c. 1634)**
They're only truly great who
are truly good.
[*Revenge for Honour* (1654)]

**EMERSON, Ralph Waldo
(1803–1882)**
Is it so bad, then, to be misunderstood? Pythagoras was
misunderstood, and Socrates,
and Jesus, and Luther, and
Copernicus, and Galileo, and
Newton, and every pure and
wise spirit that ever took
flesh. To be great is to be misunderstood.
['Self-Reliance' (1841)]

**FIELDING, Henry
(1707–1754)**
Greatness consists in bringing
all manner of mischief on

mankind, and goodness in removing it from them.
[*Jonathan Wild* (1743)]

FRAZER, Sir James (1854–1941)
The world cannot live at the level of its great men.
[*The Golden Bough* (1900)]

LA ROCHEFOUCAULD (1613–1680)
The glory of great men must always be measured by the means they have used to obtain it.
[*Maximes* (1678)]

LAW, Bonar (1858–1923)
If I am a great man, then a good many of the great men of history are frauds.
[Attr.]

SHAKESPEARE, William (1564–1616)
Be not afraid of greatness. Some are born great, some achieve greatness, and some have greatness thrust upon 'em.
[*Twelfth Night*, II.v]

SPENDER, Sir Stephen (1909–)
I think continually of those who were truly great.

The names of those who in their lives fought for life

Who wore at their hearts the fire's centre.
Born of the sun they travelled a short while towards the sun,
And left the vivid air signed with their honour.
['I think continually of those who were truly great' (1933)]

GRIEF

BYRON, Lord (1788–1824)
[A cypress]
Dark tree, still sad when others' grief is fled,
The only constant mourner o'er the dead!
['The Giaour' (1813)]

COWPER, William (1731–1800)
Grief is itself a med'cine.
['Charity' (1782)]

DICKINSON, Emily (1830–1886)
The Bustle in a House
The Morning after Death
Is solemnest of industries
Enacted upon Earth –

The Sweeping up the Heart
And putting Love away
We shall not want to use again
Until Eternity.
['The Bustle in a House' (c. 1866)]

ELLIOT, Jean (1727–1805)
I've heard them lilting, at our
yowe-milking,
Lasses a' lilting before the
dawn o' day;
But now they are moaning on
ilka green loaning –
The Flowers of the Forest are
a' wede away.
['The Flowers of the Forest'
(1756)]

FORD, John (c. 1586–1639)
They are the silent griefs
which cut the heart-strings.
[*The Broken Heart* (1633)]

**GRAVES, Robert
(1895–1985)**
His eyes are quickened so
with grief,
He can watch a grass or leaf
Every instant grow . . .

Across two counties he can
hear
And catch your words before
you speak.
The woodlouse or the mag-
got's weak
Clamour rings in his sad ear,
And noise so slight it would
surpass
Credence.
['Lost Love' (1921)]

**JOHNSON, Samuel
(1709–1784)**
Grief is a species of idleness.
[Letter to Mrs. Thrale, 1773]

MILTON, John (1608–1674)
Methought I saw my late
espoused Saint
Brought to me like Alcestis
from the grave . . .

But O as to embrace me she
enclin'd,
I wak'd, she fled, and day
brought back my night.
['Methought I saw my late
espoused Saint' (1658)]

**PROUST, Marcel
(1871–1922)**
Happiness alone is beneficial
for the body, but it is grief that
develops the powers of the
mind.
[Le Temps retrouvé (1926)]

**SHAKESPEARE, William
(1564–1616)**
Grief fills the room up of my
absent child,
Lies in his bed, walks up and
down with me,
Puts on his pretty looks,
repeats his words,
Remembers me of all his
gracious parts,
Stuffs out his vacant garments
with his form;
Then have I reason to be fond
of grief.
[*King John*, III.iv]

What, man! Ne'er pull your
hat upon your brows;
Give sorrow words. The grief

that does not speak
Whispers the o'erfraught heart
and bids it break.
                    [*Macbeth*, IV.iii]

**SHELLEY, Percy Bysshe
(1792–1822)**
Ah, woe is me! Winter is
come and gone,
But grief returns with the
revolving year.
                    [*Adonais* (1821)]

**STOWE, Harriet Beecher
(1811–1896)**
The bitterest tears shed over
graves are for words left
unsaid and deeds left undone.
                    [*Little Foxes* (1866)]

**TENNYSON, Alfred, Lord
(1809–1892)**
Death has made
His darkness beautiful with
thee.
                    [*In Memoriam A. H. H.* (1850)]

**WORDSWORTH, William
(1770–1850)**
Surprised by joy – impatient
as the Wind
I turned to share the transport
– Oh! with whom
But thee, deep buried in the
silent tomb.
                    ['Surprised by joy' (1815)]

**ARENDT, Hannah
(1906–1975)**
It is quite gratifying to feel
guilty if you haven't done anything wrong: how noble!
Whereas it is rather hard and
certainly depressing to admit
guilt and to repent.
          [*Eichmann in Jerusalem:
A Report on the Banality of Evil*
                                (1963)]

**GOLDSMITH, Oliver
(c. 1728–1774)**
When lovely woman stoops to
folly
And finds too late that men
betray,
What charm can soothe her
melancholy,
What art can wash her guilt
away?
     [*The Vicar of Wakefield* (1766)]

HORACE (65–8 BC)
This be your wall of brass, to
have nothing on your con-
science, no reason to grow
pale with guilt.
                    [*Epistles*]

MCGOUGH, Roger (1937–)
You will put on a dress of guilt
and shoes with broken high
ideals.
          ['Comeclose and Sleepnow'
                                (1967)]

RUSKIN, John (1819–1900)
Life without industry is guilt.
['The Relation of Art to Morals' (1870)]

SHAKESPEARE, William (1564–1616)
Will all great Neptune's ocean wash this blood
Clean from my hand? No; this my hand will rather
The multitudinous seas incarnadine,
Making the green one red.
[*Macbeth*, II.ii]

Out, damned spot! out, I say! One, two; why then 'tis time to do't. Hell is murky. Fie, my lord, fie! a soldier, and afeard? What need we fear who knows it, when none can call our pow'r to account? Yet who would have thought the old man to have had so much blood in him?
[*Macbeth*, V.i]

Here's the smell of the blood still. All the perfumes of Arabia will not sweeten this little hand.
[*Macbeth*, V.i]

STEVENSON, Robert Louis (1850–1894)
What hangs people . . . is the unfortunate circumstance of guilt.
[*The Wrong Box* (1889)]

ARISTOTLE (384–322 BC)
One swallow does not make a summer, neither does one fine day; similarly one day or brief time of happiness does not make a person entirely happy.
[*Nicomachean Ethics*]

BENTHAM, Jeremy (1748–1832)
[Quoting Francis Hutcheson] . . . this sacred truth – that the greatest happiness of the greatest number is the foundation of morals and legislation.
[*Works*]

BOETHIUS (c. 475–524)
Nothing is miserable unless you think it so; conversely, every lot is happy to one who is content with it.
[*De Consolatione Philosophiae*]

CAMPBELL, Thomas (1777–1844)
One moment may with bliss repay
Unnumber'd hours of pain.
['The Ritter Bann']

COLERIDGE, Samuel Taylor (1772–1834)
We ne'er can be
Made happy by compulsion.
['The Three Graves' (1809)]

DRYDEN, John (1631–1700)
Happy the man, and happy he alone,
He, who can call to-day his own:
He who, secure within, can say,
Tomorrow do thy worst, for I have lived to-day.
[*Sylvae* (1685)]

ELIOT, George (1819–1880)
The happiest women, like the happiest nations, have no history.
[*The Mill on the Floss* (1860)]

FRANKLIN, Benjamin (1706–1790)
Be in general virtuous, and you will be happy.
['On Early Marriages']

JOHNSON, Samuel (1709–1784)
There is nothing which has yet been contrived by man, by which so much happiness is produced as by a good tavern or inn.
[In Boswell, *The Life of Samuel Johnson* (1791)]

KANT, Immanuel (1724–1804)
Act in such a way that you will be worthy of being happy.
[*Critique of Pure Reason* (1787)]

**MARMION, Shackerley
(1603–1639)**
Great joys, like griefs, are
silent.

[*Holland's Leaguer* (1632)]

**ROUSSEAU, Jean-Jacques
(1712–1778)**
Happiness: a good bank
account, a good cook, and a
good digestion.

[*Treasury of Humorous
Quotations*]

SAGAN, Françoise (1935–)
What is that wall that always
rises up between human
beings and their most intimate desire, their frightening
will to be happy?

[*Le Garde du coeur* (1968)]

**SAINT-EXUPERY, Antoine de
(1900–1944)**
If you want to understand the
meaning of happiness, you
must see it as a reward and
not as a goal.

[*Carnets*]

**SHAKESPEARE, William
(1564–1616)**
O, how bitter a thing it is to
look into happiness through
another man's eyes!

[*As You Like It*, V.ii]

**SHAW, George Bernard
(1856–1950)**
We have no more right to

consume happiness without
producing it than to consume
wealth without producing it.

[*Candida* (1898)]

A lifetime of happiness! No
man alive could bear it: it
would be hell on earth.

[*Man and Superman* (1903)]

SMITH, Sydney (1771–1845)
Mankind are always happy for
having been happy, so that if
you make them happy now,
you make them happy twenty
years hence by the memory of
it.

[*Sketches of Moral Philosophy*
(1849)]

SOLON (c. 638–c. 559 BC)
Until [a man] dies, be careful
to call him not happy but
lucky.

[In Herodotus, *Histories*]

**WAUGH, Evelyn
(1903–1966)**
I can't quite explain it, but I
don't believe one can ever be
unhappy for long provided
one does just exactly what
one wants to and when one
wants to.

[*Decline and Fall* (1928)]

WELDON, Fay (1931–)
I don't believe in happiness:
why should we expect to be
happy? In such a world as

this, depression is rational,
rage reasonable.
[*The Observer*, 1995]

HATRED

BYRON, Lord (1788–1824)
Now hatred is by far the
longest pleasure;
Men love in haste, but they
detest at leisure.
[*Don Juan* (1824)]

DE VRIES, Peter (1910–)
Everybody hates me because
I'm so universally liked.
[*The Vale of Laughter* (1967)]

FIELDS, W.C. (1880–1946)
I am free of all prejudice. I
hate everyone equally.
[Attr.]

GABOR, Zsa-Zsa (1919–)
I never hated a man enough
to give him his diamonds
back.
[*The Observer*, 1957]

**HAZLITT, William
(1778–1830)**
Violent antipathies are always
suspicious, and betray a
secret affinity.
[*Table-Talk* (1822)]

HOFFER, Eric (1902–1983)
Passionate hatred can give

meaning and purpose to an
empty life.
[Attr.]

JUNG CHANG (1952–)
He [Mao Zedong] was, it
seemed to me, really a restless fight promoter by nature
and good at it. He understood
ugly human instincts such as
envy and resentment, and
knew how to mobilize them
for his ends. He ruled by getting people to hate each
other.
[*Wild Swans* (1991)]

NASH, Ogden (1902–1971)
Any kiddie in school can love
like a fool,
But hating, my boy, is an art.
['Plea for Less Malice Toward
None' (1933)]

**NIXON, Richard
(1913–1994)**
Always remember, others may
hate you, but those who hate
you don't win unless you hate
them, and then you destroy
yourself.
[Farewell speech to his staff,
1974]

ROSTEN, Leo (1908–1997)
[Of W.C. Fields; often attrib-
uted to him]
Any man who hates dogs and
babies can't be all bad.
[Speech, 1939]

**RUSSELL, Bertrand
(1872–1970)**
Few people can be happy
unless they hate some other
person, nation or creed.

[Attr.]

TACITUS (c. 56–c. 120)
It is part of human nature to
hate those whom you have
injured.

[*Agricola*]

HEALTH

BUTLER, Samuel (1835–1902)
The healthy stomach is nothing if not conservative. Few
radicals have good digestions.

[*The Note–Books of Samuel
Butler* (1912)]

DRYDEN, John (1631–1700)
Better to hunt in fields, for
health unbought,
Than fee the doctor for a
nauseous draught.
The wise, for cure, on exercise depend;
God never made his work, for
man to mend.

['To John Driden of
Chesterton' (1700)]

JUVENAL (c. 60–130)
Your prayers should be for a
healthy mind in a healthy body.

[*Satires*]

MARTIAL (c. 40–c. 104)
It is not to live but to be
healthy that makes a life.

[*Epigrammata*]

SMITH, Sydney (1771–1845)
I am convinced digestion is
the great secret of life.

[Letter to Arthur Kinglake,
1837]

**TUSSER, Thomas
(c. 1524–1580)**
Make hunger thy sauce, as a
medicine for health.

[*Five Hundred Points of Good
Husbandry* (1557)]

WALTON, Izaak (1593–1683)
Look to your health; and if
you have it, praise God, and
value it next to a good conscience; for health is the second blessing that we mortals
are capable of; a blessing
money cannot buy.

[*The Compleat Angler* (1653)]

See ILLNESS; MEDICINE

HEAVEN

**BORGES, Jorge Luis
(1899–1986)**
Let heaven exist, even if my
place be hell.

['The Library of Babel'
(1941)]

**BROWN, Helen Gurley
(1922–)**
[Promotional line for
Cosmopolitan magazine]
Good girls go to heaven, bad
girls go everywhere.

[Attr.]

**BROWNING, Robert
(1812–1889)**
On the earth the broken arcs;
in the heaven, a perfect round.

['Abt Vogler' (1864)]

**DE QUINCEY, Thomas
(1785–1859)**
Thou hast the keys of
Paradise, oh just, subtle, and
mighty opium!

[*Confessions of an English
Opium Eater* (1822)]

ELLIS, Havelock (1859–1939)
The Promised Land always
lies on the other side of a
wilderness.

[*The Dance of Life*]

**FITZGERALD, Edward
(1809–1883)**
Here with a Loaf of Bread
beneath the Bough,
A Flask of Wine, a Book of
Verse – and Thou
Beside me singing in the
Wilderness –
And Wilderness is Paradise
enow.

[*The Rubáiyát of Omar
Khayyám* (1859)]

**LICHTENBERG, Georg
(1742–1799)**
Probably no invention came
more easily to man than Heaven.

[*Aphorisms*]

**PROUST, Marcel
(1871–1922)**
The true paradises are the
paradises we have lost.

[*Le Temps retrouvé* (1926)]

**SHAKESPEARE, William
(1564–1616)**
Heaven is above all yet: there
sits a Judge
That no king can corrupt.

[*Henry VIII*, III.i]

**SHAW, George Bernard
(1856–1950)**
Heaven, as conventionally
conceived, is a place so inane,
so dull, so useless, so miserable, that nobody has ever
ventured to describe a whole
day in heaven, though plenty
of people have described a
day at the seaside.

[*Misalliance* (1914)]

SMITH, Sydney (1771–1845)
My idea of heaven is eating
pâté de foie gras to the sound
of trumpets.

[In Pearson, *The Smith of
Smiths* (1934)]

WADDELL, Helen (1889–1965)
Would you think Heaven

could be so small a thing
As a lit window on the hills at
night.
['I Shall Not Go To Heaven']

HELL

BUNYAN, John (1628–1688)
Then I saw there was a way
to Hell, even from the gates of
heaven.
[*The Pilgrim's Progress* (1678)]

**BURTON, Robert
(1577–1640)**
If there is a hell upon earth, it
is to be found in a melancholy
man's heart.
[*Anatomy of Melancholy*
(1621)]

CLARE, Dr Anthony (1942–)
Hell is when you get what you
think you want.
[*The Observer*, 1983]

ELIOT, T.S. (1888–1965)
Hell is oneself;
Hell is alone, the other figures
in it
Merely projections. There is
nothing to escape from
And nothing to escape to.
One is always alone.
[*The Cocktail Party* (1950)]

LEWIS, C.S. (1898–1963)
There is wishful thinking in

Hell as well as on earth.
[*The Screwtape Letters* (1942)]

MILTON, John (1608–1674)
Here we may reign secure,
and in my choice
To reign is worth ambition
though in Hell:
Better to reign in Hell, then
serve in Heav'n.
[*Paradise Lost* (1667)]

Long is the way
And hard, that out of Hell
leads up to Light.
[*Paradise Lost* (1667)]

**SADE, Marquis de
(1740–1814)**
There is no other hell for man
than the stupidity and wickedness of his own kind.
[*Histoire de Juliette* (1797)]

**SARTRE, Jean-Paul
(1905–1980)**
Hell is other people.
[*In Camera* (1944)]

**SHAW, George Bernard
(1856–1950)**
A perpetual holiday is a good
working definition of hell.
[Attr.]

**TEILHARD DE CHARDIN,
Pierre (1881–1955)**
You have told me, O God, to
believe in hell. But you have
forbidden me to think, with

absolute certainty, of any man as damned.

[*Le Milieu divin*]

VIRGIL (70–19 BC)
The gates of Hell are open night and day;
Smooth the descent, and easy is the way:
But to return, and view the cheerful skies,
In this the task and mighty labour lies.

[*Aeneid*, trans. Dryden]

HEROES

BRECHT, Bertolt (1898–1956)
Andrea: Unhappy the country that has no heroes!
Galileo: No. Unhappy the country that needs heroes.

[*Life of Galileo* (1939)]

CORNUEL, Madame de (1605–1694)
No man is a hero to his valet.

[In *Lettres de Mlle Aïssé à Madame C* (1787)]

GAMBETTA, Léon (1838–1882)
Heroic times have passed away.

[Saying]

HENDERSON, Hamish (1919–)
There were our own, there were the others.
Their deaths were like their lives, human and animal.
There were no gods and precious few heroes.

['First Elegy, End of a Campaign' (1948)]

LANDOR, Walter Savage (1775–1864)
Hail, ye indomitable heroes, hail!
Despite of all your generals ye prevail.

['The Crimean Heroes']

MACKENZIE, Sir Compton (1883–1972)
Ever since the first World War there has been an inclination to denigrate the heroic aspect of man.

[*On Moral Courage* (1962)]

MORELL, Thomas (1703–1784)
See, the conquering hero comes!
Sound the trumpets, beat the drums!

[*Joshua* (1748)]

ORWELL, George (1903–1950)
The high sentiments always win in the end, leaders who offer blood, toil, tears and sweat always get more out of their followers than those who offer safety and a good

time. When it comes to the pinch, human beings are heroic.

[*Horizon*, 1941]

ROGERS, Will (1879–1935)
Heroing is one of the shortest-lived professions there is.
[In Grove, *The Will Rogers Book* (1961)]

HISTORY

ANGELOU, Maya (1928–)
History, faced with courage, need not be lived again.
[Speech at the Inauguration of President Clinton, 1993]

AUSTEN, Jane (1775–1817)
Real solemn history, I cannot be interested in ... The quarrels of popes and kings, with wars or pestilences, in every page; the men all so good for nothing, and hardly any women at all, it is very tiresome.
[*Northanger Abbey* (1818)]

BALFOUR, A.J. (1848–1930)
History does not repeat itself. Historians repeat each other.
[Attr.]

BEECHAM, Sir Thomas (1879–1961)
When the history of the first

half of this century comes to be written – properly written – it will be acknowledged the most stupid and brutal in the history of civilisation.
[Attr.]

BUTLER, Samuel (1835–1902)
It has been said that though God cannot alter the past, historians can; it is perhaps because they can be useful to Him in this respect that He tolerates their existence.
[*Erewhon Revisited* (1901)]

CARLYLE, Thomas (1795–1881)
History is the essence of innumerable biographies.
['On History' (1839)]

Happy the people whose annals are blank in history –books!
[*History of Frederick the Great* (1865)]

CATHER, Willa (1873–1947)
The history of every country begins in the heart of a man or a woman.
[*O Pioneers!* (1913)]

COLERIDGE, Samuel Taylor (1772–1834)
If men could learn from history, what lessons it might teach us! But passion and

party blind our eyes, and the light which experience gives is a lantern on the stern, which shines only on the waves behind us!

[Table Talk (1835)]

EBAN, Abba (1915–)
History teaches us that men and nations behave wisely once they have exhausted all other alternatives.

[Speech, 1970]

FISHER, H.A.L. (1856–1940)
There can be . . . only one safe rule for the historian: that he should recognize in the development of human destinies the play of the contingent and the unforeseen.

[History of Europe (1935)]

FORD, Henry (1863–1947)
[Popularly remembered as 'History is bunk']
History is more or less bunk. It's tradition. We don't want tradition. We want to live in the present and the only history that is worth a tinker's damn is the history we make today.

[Chicago Tribune, 1916]

GIBBON, Edward (1737–1794)
History . . . is, indeed, little more than the register of the crimes, follies, and misfor-tunes of mankind.

[Decline and Fall of the Roman Empire (1776–88)]

JOYCE, James (1882–1941)
History is a nightmare from which I am trying to awake.

[Ulysses (1922)]

KOESTLER, Arthur (1905–1983)
The most persistent sound which reverberates through men's history is the beating of war drums.

[Janus: A Summing Up (1978)]

LANG, Ian (1940–)
History is littered with dead opinion polls.

[The Independent, 1994]

MCLUHAN, Marshall (1911–1980)
The hydrogen bomb is history's exclamation point. It ends an age-long sentence of manifest violence.

[Attr.]

POPPER, Sir Karl (1902–1994)
There is no history of man-kind, there are only many histories of all kinds of aspects of human life. And one of these is the history of political power. This is elevated into the history of the world.

[The Open Society and its Enemies (1945)]

SAKI (1870–1916)
The people of Crete unfortunately make more history than they can consume locally.
[*The Chronicles of Clovis* (1911)]

SAMUEL, Lord (1870–1963)
Hansard is history's ear, already listening.
[*The Observer*, 1949]

SELLAR, Walter (1898–1951) and YEATMAN, Robert (1897–1968)
A Bad Thing: America was thus clearly top nation, and History came to a .
[*1066 And All That* (1930)]

TAYLOR, A.J.P. (1906–1990)
[Of Napoleon III]
He was what I often think is a dangerous thing for a statesman to be – a student of history; and like most of those who study history, he learned from the mistakes of the past how to make new ones.
[*The Listener*, 1963]

TOLSTOY, Leo (1828–1910)
Historians are like deaf people who go on answering questions that no one has asked them.
[Attr.]

WELLS, H.G. (1866–1946)
Human history becomes more and more a race between education and catastrophe.
[*The Outline of History* (1920)]

YELTSIN, Boris (1931–)
[Said after the failure of the communist coup]
History will record that the twentieth century essentially ended on 19–21 August 1991.
[Article in *Newsweek*, 1994]

HOME

ACE, Jane (1905–1974)
Home wasn't built in a day.
[In G. Ace, *The Fine Art of Hypochondria* (1966)]

ANONYMOUS
Be it ever so humble there's no place like home for sending one slowly crackers.

BEAUVOIR, Simone de (1908–1986)
The ideal of happiness has always taken material form in the house, whether cottage or castle; it stands for permanence and separation from the world.
[*The Second Sex* (1949)]

CLARKE, John (fl. 1639)
Home is home, though it be

never so homely.
[*Paraemiologia Anglo-Latina*
(1639)]

**COKE, Sir Edward
(1552–1634)**
The house of everyone is to
him as his castle and fortress,
as well for his defence against
injury and violence, as for his
repose.
[*Semayne's Case*]

**DE WOLFE, Elsie
(1865–1950)**
It is the personality of the
mistress that the home
expresses. Men are forever
guests in our homes, no matter
how much happiness they
may find there.
[*The House in Good Taste*
(1920)]

**DOUGLAS, Norman
(1868–1952)**
Many a man who thinks to
found a home discovers that
he has merely opened a tavern
for his friends.
[*South Wind* (1917)]

**FLETCHER, John
(1579–1625)**
Charity and beating begins at
home.
[*Wit Without Money* (c. 1614)]

FROST, Robert (1874–1963)
Home is the place where,
when you have to go there,
They have to take you in.
['The Death of the Hired Man'
(1914)]

FULLER, Margaret
A house is no home unless it
contain food and fire for the
mind as well as for the body.
[*Woman in the Nineteenth
Century* (1845)]

**LUCE, Clare Boothe
(1903–1987)**
A man's home may seem to
be his castle on the outside;
inside, it is more often his
nursery.
[Attr.]

**MEYER, Agnes
(1887–c. 1970)**
What the nation must realise
is that the home, when both
parents work, is non-existent.
Once we have honestly faced
the fact, we must act accordingly.
[*Washington Post*, 1943]

MORE, Hannah (1745–1833)
The sober comfort, all the
peace which springs
From the large aggregate of
little things;
On these small cares of
daughter, wife, or friend,
The almost sacred joys of
home depend.
['Sensibility' (1782)]

MORRIS, William
(1834–1896)
If you want a golden rule that
will fit everybody, this is it:
Have nothing in your houses
that you do not know to be
useful, or believe to be beautiful.
[*Hopes and Fears for Art*
(1882)]

PAYNE, J.H. (1791–1852)
Mid pleasures and palaces
though we may roam,
Be it ever so humble, there's
no place like home.
['Home, Sweet Home', song,
1823]

ROWLAND, Helen
(1875–1950)
'Home' is any four walls that
enclose the right person.
[*Reflections of a Bachelor Girl*
(1909)]

SHAW, George Bernard
(1856–1950)
The great advantage of a
hotel is that it's a refuge from
home life.
[*You Never Can Tell* (1898)]

STOWE, Harriet Beecher
(1811–1896)
Home is a place not only of
strong affections, but of entire
unreserve; it is life's undress
rehearsal, its backroom, its
dressing room, from which

we go forth to more careful
and guarded intercourse,
leaving behind us much
debris of cast-off and everyday clothing.
[*Little Foxes* (1866)]

HONESTY

AUDEN, W.H. (1907–1973)
Only God can tell the saintly
from the suburban,
Counterfeit values always
resemble the true;
Neither in Life nor Art is
honesty bohemian,
The free behave much as the
respectable do.
['New Year Letter' (1941)]

BLAKE, William
(1757–1827)
Always be ready to speak
your mind, and a base man
will avoid you.
[Attr.]

BROWNE, Sir Thomas
(1605–1682)
I have tried if I could reach
that great resolution . . . to be
honest without a thought of
Heaven or Hell.
[*Religio Medici* (1643)]

CARLYLE, Thomas
(1795–1881)
Make yourself an honest man

and then you may be sure there is one rascal less in the world.

[Attr.]

CROMWELL, Oliver
(1599–1658)
A few honest men are better than numbers.

[Letter to Sir William Spring, 1643]

DEFOE, Daniel
(c. 1661–1731)
Necessity makes an honest man a knave.

[*Serious Reflections of Robinson Crusoe* (1720)]

FITZGERALD, F. Scott
(1896–1940)
I am one of the few honest people that I have ever known.

[*The Great Gatsby* (1926)]

MARQUIS, Don (1878–1937)
honesty is a good
thing but
it is not profitable to
its possessor
unless it is
kept under control.

['archygrams' (1933)]

RICHELIEU, Cardinal
(1585–1642)
If you give me six lines written by the most honest man, I will find something in them to hang him.

[Attr.]

WHATELY, Richard
(1787–1863)
Honesty is the best policy, but he who is governed by that maxim is not an honest man.

[*Apophthegms* (1854)]

HOPE

BACON, Francis
(1561–1626)
Hope is a good breakfast, but it is a bad supper.

['Apophthegms']

CHESTERTON, G.K.
(1874–1936)
Hope is the power of being cheerful in circumstances which we know to be desperate.

[*Heretics* (1905)]

FRANKLIN, Benjamin
(1706–1790)
He that lives upon hope will die fasting.

[*Poor Richard's Almanac* (1758)]

ILLICH, Ivan (1926–)
We must rediscover the distinction between hope and expectation.

[*Deschooling Society* (1971)]

KERR, Jean (1923–)
You don't seem to realize that

a poor person who is unhappy is in a better position than a rich person who is unhappy. Because the poor person has hope. He thinks money would help.

[*Poor Richard* (1963)]

Hope is the feeling you have that the feeling you have isn't permanent.

[*Finishing Touches* (1973)]

**OSBORNE, John
(1929–1994)**
[A notice in his bathroom]
Since I gave up hope I feel so much better.

[*The Independent*, 1994]

**POPE, Alexander
(1688–1744)**
Hope springs eternal in the human breast.

[*An Essay on Man* (1733)]

TERENCE (c. 190–159 BC)
Where there's life, there's hope.

[*Heauton Timoroumenos*]

See DESPAIR

HUMANITY

AUDEN, W.H. (1907–1973)
Man is a history-making creature who can neither repeat

his past nor leave it behind.

[*The Dyer's Hand* (1963)]

BEAUMARCHAIS (1732–1799)
Drinking when we're not thirsty and making love all the time, madam, that is all there is to distinguish us from other animals.

[*Le Barbier de Seville* (1775)]

**BEERBOHM, Sir Max
(1872–1956)**
Mankind is divisible into two great classes: hosts and guests.

[Attr.]

**THE BIBLE (KING JAMES
VERSION)**
Man is born unto trouble, as the sparks fly upward.

[*Job*, 5:7]

When I consider thy heavens, the work of thy fingers, the moon and the stars, which thou hast ordained;
What is man, that thou art mindful of him? and the son of man, that thou visitest him?

[*Psalms*, 8:3–4]

As for man, his days are as grass: as a flower of the field, so he flourisheth.

[*Psalms*, 103:15]

**BRONOWSKI, Jacob
(1908-1974)**
Every animal leaves traces of

what it was; man alone leaves traces of what he created.
[*The Ascent of Man* (1973)]

**BUCHNER, Georg
(1813–1837)**
We are puppets on strings worked by unknown forces; we ourselves are nothing, nothing!
[*Danton's Death* (1835)]

BURNS, Robert (1759–1796)
Man's inhumanity to man Makes countless thousands mourn!
['Man was made to Mourn, a Dirge' (1784)]

**BUTLER, Samuel
(1835–1902)**
'Man wants but little here below' but likes that little good – and not too long in coming.
[*Further Extracts from the Note-Books of Samuel Butler* (1934)]

Man is the only animal that can remain on friendly terms with the victims he intends to eat until he eats them.
[*Samuel Butler's Notebooks* (1951)]

CAMUS, Albert (1913–1960)
A single sentence will suffice for modern man: he fornicated and read the papers.
[*The Fall* (1956)]

**CHESTERTON, G.K.
(1874–1936)**
Individually, men may present a more or less rational appearance, eating, sleeping and scheming. But humanity as a whole is changeful, mystical, fickle and delightful. Men are men, but Man is a woman.
[*The Napoleon of Notting Hill* (1904)]

**DISRAELI, Benjamin
(1804–1881)**
Man is only truly great when he acts from the passions.
[*Coningsby* (1844)]

DONNE, John (1572–1631)
No man is an Island, entire of it self; every man is a piece of Continent, a part of the main . . . any man's death diminishes me, because I am involved in Mankind;
And therefore never send to know for whom the bell tolls; it tolls for thee.
[*Devotions upon Emergent Occasions* (1624)]

**ELIOT, George
(1819–1880)**
There is a great deal of unmapped country within us which would have to be taken into account in an explanation of our gusts and storms.
[*Daniel Deronda* (1876)]

FROUDE, James Anthony (1818–1894)

Wild animals never kill for sport. Man is the only one to whom the torture and death of his fellow creatures is amusing in itself.

[*Oceana* (1886)]

GOLDSMITH, Oliver (c. 1728–1774)

Man wants but little here below, Nor wants that little long.

[*The Vicar of Wakefield* (1766)]

GORKY, Maxim (1868–1936)

Man and man alone is, I believe, the creator of all things and all ideas.

[Attr.]

HAZLITT, William (1778–1830)

Man is an intellectual animal, and therefore an everlasting contradiction to himself. His senses centre in himself, his ideas reach to the ends of the universe; so that he is torn in pieces between the two, without a possibility of its ever being otherwise.

[*Characteristics* (1823)]

MONASH, Sir John (1865–1931)

Nothing man does to the animal creation is equal to the cruelties he commits on his own kind.

[*The Seals*]

MONTAIGNE, Michel de (1533–1592)

Man is quite insane. He wouldn't know how to create a maggot, yet he creates Gods by the dozen.

[*Essais* (1580)]

NIETZSCHE, Friedrich (1844–1900)

What? is man only a mistake made by God, or God only a mistake made by man?

[*Twilight of the Idols* (1889)]

PASCAL, Blaise (1623–1662)

Man is only a reed, the feeblest thing in nature; but he is a thinking reed.

[*Pensées* (1670)]

POPE, Alexander (1688–1744)

Know then thyself, presume not God to scan;
The proper study of Mankind is Man . . .

Created half to rise, and half to fall;
Great lord of all things, yet a prey to all;
Sole judge of truth, in endless error hurl'd:
The glory, jest, and riddle of the world!

[*An Essay on Man* (1733)]

ROUSSEAU, Jean-Jacques (1712–1778)

Nature made man happy and

good, but . . . society corrupts him and makes him miserable.

[*Rousseau juge de Jean-Jacques*]

RUSKIN, John (1819–1900)
No human being, however great, or powerful, was ever so free as a fish.

[*The Two Paths* (1859)]

SCHILLER (1759–1805)
Man is honoured by his heart and not by his opinions.

[*Wallensteins Tod* (1801)]

SHAKESPEARE, William (1564–1616)
What a piece of work is a man! How noble in reason! how infinite in faculties! in form and moving, how express and admirable! in action, how like an angel! in apprehension, how like a god!

[*Hamlet*, II.ii]

SHAW, George Bernard (1856–1950)
Man can climb to the highest summits; but he cannot dwell there long.

[*Candida* (1898)]

TEMPLE, William (1881–1944)
It is not the ape, nor the tiger in man that I fear, it is the donkey.

[Attr.]

TERTZ, Abram (1925–1997)
Man is always both much worse and much better than is expected of him. The fields of good are just as limitless as the wastelands of evil.

[*A Voice From the Chorus* (1973)]

TWAIN, Mark (1835–1910)
Man is the only animal that blushes. Or needs to.

[*Following the Equator* (1897)]

UNAMUNO, Miguel de (1864–1936)
Man, because he is man, because he is conscious, is, in relation to the ass or to a crab, already a diseased animal. Consciousness is a disease.

[*The Tragic Sense of Life* (1913)]

VALERY, Paul (1871–1945)
A man is infinitely more complicated than his thoughts.

[In Auden, *A Certain World*]

VOLTAIRE (1694–1778)
If God has created us in his image, we have repaid him well.

[*Le Sottisier* (c. 1778)]

YEVTUSHENKO, Yevgeny (1933–)
In the final analysis, humanity has only two ways out –

either universal destruction or universal brotherhood.

['The Spirit of Elbe' (1966)]

HUMAN NATURE

AUSTEN, Jane (1775–1817)
Human nature is so well disposed towards those who are in interesting situations, that a young person, who either marries or dies, is sure of being kindly spoken of.

[*Emma* (1816)]

BACON, Francis (1561–1626)
There is in human nature generally more of the fool than of the wise.

['Of Boldness' (1625)]

**CONFUCIUS
(c. 550–c. 478 BC)**
Men's natures are alike; it is their habits that carry them far apart.

[*Analects*]

DONLEAVY, J.P. (1926–)
I got disappointed in human nature as well and gave it up because I found it too much like my own.

[*Fairy Tales of New York* (1961)]

**JOHNSON, Samuel
(1709–1784)**
Sir, are you so grossly ignorant of human nature, as not to know that a man may be very sincere in good principles without having good practice?

[In Boswell, *Journal of a Tour to the Hebrides* (1785)]

**JUNG, Carl Gustav
(1875–1961)**
We need more understanding of human nature, because the only real danger that exists is man himself . . . We know nothing of man, far too little. His psyche should be studied because we are the origin of all coming evil.

[BBC television interview, 1959]

KEATS, John (1795–1821)
Scenery is fine – but human nature is finer.

[Letter to Benjamin Bailey, 1818]

**MACHIAVELLI
(1469–1527)**
Men sooner forget the death of their father than the loss of their possessions.

[*The Prince* (1532)]

**SARTRE, Jean-Paul
(1905–1980)**
So there is no human nature, since there is no God to conceive it.

[*Existentialism and Humanism* (1946)]

HUMOUR

ADDISON, Joseph
(1672–1719)
If we may believe our logicians, man is distinguished from all other creatures by the faculty of laughter.

[*The Spectator*, 1712]

AYCKBOURN, Alan
(1939–)
Few women care to be laughed at and men not at all, except for large sums of money.

[*The Norman Conquests* (1975)]

BARKER, Ronnie
(1929–)
The marvellous thing about a joke with a double meaning is that it can only mean one thing.

[Attr.]

BEAUMARCHAIS
(1732–1799)
I make myself laugh at everything, for fear of having to cry.

[*Le Barbier de Seville* (1775)]

BUTLER, Samuel
(1835–1902)
The most perfect humour and irony is generally quite unconscious.

[*Life and Habit* (1877)]

CARLYLE, Thomas
(1795–1881)
No man who has once heartily and wholly laughed can be altogether irreclaimably bad.

[*Sartor Resartus* (1834)]

CHESTERFIELD, Lord
(1694–1773)
In my mind, there is nothing so illiberal and so ill-bred, as audible laughter . . . I am neither of a melancholy, nor a cynical disposition; and am as willing, and as apt, to be pleased as anybody; but I am sure that, since I have had the full use of my reason, nobody has ever heard me laugh.

[Letter to his son, 1748]

COLBY, Frank Moore
(1865–1925)
Men will confess to treason, murder, arson, false teeth, or a wig. How many of them will own up to a lack of humour?

[*Essays*]

DODD, Ken
(1931–)
[Commenting on Freud's theory that a good joke will lead to great relief and elation]
The trouble with Freud is that he never played the Glasgow Empire Saturday night after Rangers and Celtic had both lost.

[TV interview, 1965]

ELIOT, George (1819–1880)
A difference of taste in jokes is a great strain on the affections.

[*Daniel Deronda* (1876)]

GRIFFITHS, Trevor (1935–)
Comedy is medicine.

[*The Comedians* (1979)]

HUMPHRIES, Barry (1934–)
The only people really keeping the spirit of irony alive in Australia are taxi-drivers and homosexuals.

[*Australian Women's Weekly*, 1983]

PRIESTLEY, J.B. (1894–1984)
Comedy, we may say, is society protecting itself – with a smile.

[*George Meredith* (1926)]

ROGERS, Will (1879–1935)
Everything is funny as long as it is happening to someone else.

[*The Illiterate Digest* (1924)]

SHAW, George Bernard (1856–1950)
My way of joking is to tell the truth. It's the funniest joke in the world.

[*John Bull's Other Island* (1907)]

STERNE, Laurence (1713–1768)
'Tis no extravagant arithmetic to say, that for every ten jokes, – thou hast got a hundred enemies.

[*Tristram Shandy*]

WALTON, Izaak (1593–1683)
I love such mirth as does not make friends ashamed to look upon one another next morning.

[*The Compleat Angler* (1653)]

WILCOX, Ella Wheeler (1850–1919)
Laugh and the world laughs with you;
Weep, and you weep alone;
For the sad old earth must borrow its mirth,
But has trouble enough of its own.

['Solitude' (1917)]

WODEHOUSE, P.G. (1881–1975)
She had a penetrating sort of laugh. Rather like a train going into a tunnel.

[*The Inimitable Jeeves* (1923)]

HYPOCRISY

BACON, Francis (1561–1626)
It is the wisdom of the crocodiles, that shed tears when they would devour.

['Of Wisdom for a Man's Self' (1625)]

HYPOCRISY

**BYRON, Lord
(1788–1824)**
Even innocence itself has
many a wile,
And will not dare to trust
itself with truth,
And love is taught hypocrisy
from youth.
[*Don Juan* (1824)]

**CHURCHILL, Charles
(1731–1764)**
Keep up appearances; there
lies the test;
The world will give thee credit
for the rest.
Outward be fair, however foul
within;
Sin if thou wilt, but then in
secret sin.
['Night' (1761)]

**DICKENS, Charles
(1812–1870)**
With affection beaming in one
eye, and calculation shining
out of the other.
[*Martin Chuzzlewit* (1844)]

GAY, John (1685–1732)
An open foe may prove a
curse,
But a pretended friend is
worse.
[*Fables* (1727)]

**LA ROCHEFOUCAULD
(1613–1680)**
Hypocrisy is a homage that
vice pays to virtue.
[*Maximes* (1678)]

**MAUGHAM, William
Somerset (1874–1965)**
Hypocrisy is the most difficult
and nerve-racking vice that
any man can pursue; it needs
an unceasing vigilance and a
rare detachment of spirit. It
cannot, like adultery or gluttony, be practised at spare
moments; it is a whole-time
job.
[*Cakes and Ale* (1930)]

**MILTON, John
(1608–1674)**
For neither Man nor Angel
can discern
Hypocrisie, the onely evil that
walks
Invisible, except to God alone.
[*Paradise Lost* (1667)]

**WILDE, Oscar
(1854–1900)**
I hope that you have not been
leading a double life, pretend-
ing to be wicked and being
really good all the time. That
would be hypocrisy.
[*The Importance of Being
Earnest* (1895)]

See DECEPTION

IDEAS

ALAIN (Emile-Auguste Chartier) (1868–1951)
Nothing is more dangerous than an idea, when you only have one idea.
[*Remarks on Religion* (1938)]

BOWEN, Elizabeth (1899–1973)
One can live in the shadow of an idea without grasping it.
[*The Heat of the Day* (1949)]

HOLMES, Oliver Wendell, Jr. (1841–1935)
Many ideas grow better when transplanted into another mind than in the one where they sprang up.
[In Bowen, *Yankee from Olympus* (1945)]

HUGO, Victor (1802–1885)
One can resist the invasion of an army; but one cannot resist the invasion of ideas.
[*Histoire d'un Crime* (1852)]

LEWIS, Wyndham (1882–1957)
'Dying for an idea,' again, sounds well enough, but why not let the idea die instead of you?
[*The Art of Being Ruled* (1926)]

MACDONALD, Ramsay (1866–1937)
Society goes on and on and on. It is the same with ideas.
[Speech, 1935]

MARQUIS, Don (1878–1937)
An idea isn't responsible for the people who believe in it.
[*New York Sun*]

MEDAWAR, Sir Peter (1915–1987)
The human mind treats a new idea the way the body treats a strange protein – it rejects it.
[Attr.]

SHAW, George Bernard (1856–1950)
This creature Man, who in his own selfish affairs is a coward to the backbone, will fight for an idea like a hero.
[*Man and Superman* (1903)]

UNAMUNO, Miguel de (1864–1936)
It is not normally our ideas which make us optimists or pessimists, but it is our optimism or our pessimism, which is perhaps of a physio-logical or pathological origin . . . which makes us our ideas.
[*The Tragic Sense of Life* (1913)]

See MIND; THOUGHT

IDLENESS & UNEMPLOYMENT

BOILEAU-DESPREAUX, Nicolas (1636–1711)
What a terrible burden it is to have nothing to do!
[*Epitres* (c. 1690)]

BRUMMEL, Beau (1778–1840)
I always like to have the morning well-aired before I get up.
[In Macfarlane, *Reminiscences of a Literary Life* (1917)]

CHESTERFIELD, Lord (1694–1773)
Idleness is only the refuge of weak minds, and the holiday of fools.
[Letter to his son, 1749]

CONRAN, Shirley (1932–)
I make no secret of the fact that I would rather lie on a sofa than sweep beneath it. But you have to be efficient if you're going to be lazy.
[*Superwoman* (1975)]

COWPER, William (1731–1800)
How various his employments, whom the world Calls idle.
[*The Task* (1785)]

EWART, Gavin (1916–1995)
After Cambridge – unemployment. No one wanted much to know.
Good degrees are good for nothing in the business world below.
['The Sentimental Education']

FITZGERALD, F. Scott (1896–1940)
'What'll we do with ourselves this afternoon?' cried Daisy, 'and the day after that, and the next thirty years?'
[*The Great Gatsby* (1925)]

FURPHY, Joseph (1843–1912)
Unemployed at last!
[*Such is Life* (1903)]

HEWETT, Dorothy (1923–)
For dole bread is bitter bread
Bitter bread and sour
There's grief in the taste of it
There's weevils in the flour.
['Weevils in the Flour']

HOOVER, Herbert (1874–1964)
When a great many people are unable to find work, unemployment results.
[In Boller, *Presidential Anecdotes* (1981)]

JEROME, Jerome K. (1859–1927)
It is impossible to enjoy idling

thoroughly unless one has plenty of work to do.
[*Idle Thoughts of an Idle Fellow* (1886)]

George goes to sleep at a bank from ten to four each day, except Saturdays, when they wake him up and put him outside at two.
[*Three Men in a Boat* (1889)]

JOWETT, Benjamin (1817–1893)

Research! A mere excuse for idleness; it has never achieved, and will never achieve any results of the slightest value.
[In Logan Pearsall Smith, *Unforgotten Years*]

MADAN, Geoffrey (1895–1947)

The devil finds mischief still for hands that have not learnt how to be idle.
[*Livre sans nom: Twelve Reflections* (1934)]

MARX, Karl (1818–1883)

Without doubt machinery has greatly increased the number of well-to-do idlers.
[*Das Kapital* (1867)]

MAUGHAM, William Somerset (1874–1965)

It was such a lovely day I thought it was a pity to get up.
[*Our Betters* (1923)]

NASH, Ogden (1902–1971)

I would live my life in non-chalance and insouciance
Were it not for making a living, which is rather a nouciance.
['Introspective Reflection' (1940)]

STEVENSON, Robert Louis (1850–1894)

Extreme *busyness*, whether at school or college, kirk or market, is a symptom of deficient vitality; and a faculty for idleness implies a catholic appetite and a strong sense of personal identity.
[*Virginibus Puerisque* (1881)]

THURBER, James (1894–1961)

It is better to have loafed and lost than never to have loafed at all.
[*Fables for Our Time* (1940)]

WARD, Artemus (1834–1867)

I am happiest when I am idle. I could live for months without performing any kind of labour, and at the expiration of that time I should feel fresh and vigorous enough to go right on in the same way for numerous more months.
[*Artemus Ward in London* (1867)]

ILLNESS

AUBREY, John (1626–1697)
Sciatica: he cured it, by boiling his buttock.
[*Brief Lives* (c. 1693), 'Sir Jonas Moore']

AUSTIN, Alfred (1835–1913)
[On the illness of the Prince of Wales]
Across the wires the electric message came:
'He is no better, he is much the same.'

[Attr.]

BACON, Francis (1561–1626)
The remedy is worse than the disease.
['Of Seditions and Troubles' (1625)]

CHEKHOV, Anton (1860–1904)
If many remedies are suggested for a disease, that means the disease is incurable.
[*The Cherry Orchard* (1904)]

DAVIES, Robertson (1913–1995)
Not to be healthy . . . is one of the few sins that modern society is willing to recognise and condemn.
[*The Cunning Man* (1994)]

EMERSON, Ralph Waldo (1803–1882)
A person seldom falls sick, but the bystanders are animated with a faint hope that he will die.
[*Conduct of Life* (1860)]

GALBRAITH J.K. (1908–)
Much of the world's work, it has been said, is done by men who do not feel quite well. Marx is a case in point.
[*The Age of Uncertainty*]

HELLER, Joseph (1923–)
Hungry Joe collected lists of fatal diseases and arranged them in alphabetical order so that he could put his finger without delay on any one he wanted to worry about.
[*Catch-22* (1961)]

HIPPOCRATES (c. 460–357 BC)
For extreme illnesses extreme remedies are most fitting.
[*Aphorisms*]

MCAULEY, James (1917–1976)
[After his first cancer operation; to a friend]
Well, better a semi-colon than a full stop!
[In Coleman, *The Heart of James McAuley* (1980)]

**PERELMAN, S.J.
(1904–1979)**
I've got Bright's disease and
he's got mine.

[Attr.]

SONTAG, Susan (1933–)
Illness is the night-side of life,
a more onerous citizenship.
Everyone who is born holds
dual citizenship, in the kingdom of the well and in the
kingdom of the sick. Although
we all prefer to use only the
good passport, sooner or later
each of us is obliged, at least
for a spell, to identify ourselves as citizens of that other
place.

[*Illness as Metaphor* (1978)]

**STEVENSON, Robert Louis
(1850–1894)**
Even if the doctor does not
give you a year, even if he
hesitates about a month,
make one brave push and see
what can be accomplished in
a week.

[*Virginibus Puerisque* (1881)]

See HEALTH; MEDICINE

IMAGINATION

**BLAKE, William
(1757–1827)**
What is now proved was once
only imagin'd.

['Proverbs of Hell', (c. 1793)]

**EINSTEIN, Albert
(1879–1955)**
Imagination is more important than knowledge.

[*On Science*]

ELIOT, George (1819–1880)
He said he should prefer not
to know the sources of the
Nile, and that there should be
some unknown regions pre-
served as hunting-grounds for
the poetic imagination.

[*Middlemarch* (1872)]

JOUBERT, Joseph (1754–1824)
Imagination is the eye of the
soul.

[Attr.]

KEATS, John (1795–1821)
I am certain of nothing but of
the holiness of the Heart's
affections and the truth of
Imagination – What the imagination seizes as Beauty must
be truth – whether it existed
before or not.

[Letter to Benjamin Bailey,
1817]

**ROBINSON, Roland
(1912–1992)**
Where does imagination start
but from primeval images
in man's barbaric heart?

['Mopoke']

**STEAD, Christina
(1902–1983)**
I don't know what imagin-
ation is, if not an unpruned,
tangled kind of memory.
[*Letty Fox: Her Luck* (1946)]

IMMORTALITY

ALLEN, Woody (1935-)
I don't want to achieve
immortality through my work
. . . I want to achieve it by not
dying.
[Attr.]

**BECKETT, Samuel
(1906–1989)**
Clov: Do you believe in the life
to come?
Hamm: Mine was always that.
[*Endgame* (1958)]

**BUTLER, Bishop Joseph
(1692–1752)**
That which is the foundation
of all our hopes and of all our
fears; all our hopes and fears
which are of any consideration: I mean a Future Life.
[*The Analogy of Religion*
(1736)]

**DOSTOEVSKY, Fyodor
(1821–1881)**
If you were to destroy in
mankind the belief in immortality, not only love but every

living force maintaining the
life of the world would at
once dry up. Moreover, nothing then would be immoral,
everything would be lawful,
even cannibalism.
[*The Brothers Karamazov*
(1879–1880)]

**EMERSON, Ralph Waldo
(1803–1882)**
Other world! There is no
other world! Here or nowhere
is the whole fact.
['Natural Religion']

ERTZ, Susan (1894–1985)
Someone has somewhere
commented on the fact that
millions long for immortality
who don't know what to do
with themselves on a rainy
Sunday afternoon.
[*Anger in the Sky* (1943)]

**HAZLITT, William
(1778–1830)**
No young man believes he
shall ever die.
['On the Feeling of
Immortality in Youth' (1827)]

HELLER, Joseph (1923-)
He had decided to live forever
or die in the attempt.
[*Catch-22* (1961)]

PLATO (c. 429–347 BC)
Let us be persuaded . . . to
consider that the soul is

immortal and capable of enduring all evil and all good, and so we shall always hold to the upward way and pursue justice with wisdom.

[*Republic*]

STASSINOPOULOS, Arianna (1950–)

Our current obsession with creativity is the result of our continued striving for immortality in an era when most people no longer belive in an afterlife.

[*The Female Woman* (1973)]

THOREAU, Henry (1817–1862)

[On being asked his opinion of the hereafter]
One world at a time.

[Attr.]

INCOME

AUSTEN, Jane (1775–1817)

A large income is the best recipe for happiness I ever heard of. It certainly may secure all the myrtle and turkey part of it.

[*Mansfield Park* (1814)]

DICKENS, Charles (1812–1870)

Annual income twenty pounds, annual expenditure nineteen nineteen six, result happiness. Annual income twenty pounds, annual expenditure twenty pounds ought and six, result misery.

[*David Copperfield* (1850)]

PARKINSON, C. Northcote (1909–1993)

Expenditure rises to meet income.

[Attr.]

SAKI (1870–1916)

All decent people live beyond their incomes nowadays, and those who aren't respectable live beyond other people's. A few gifted individuals manage to do both.

[*The Chronicles of Clovis* (1911)]

SAUNDERS, Ernest (1935–)

I was on a basic £100,000 a year. You don't make many savings on that.

[*The Observer*, 1987]

SMITH, Logan Pearsall (1865–1946)

There are few sorrows, however poignant, in which a good income is of no avail.

[*Afterthoughts* (1931)]

See MONEY AND WEALTH

INDECISION

**ASQUITH, Margot
(1864–1945)**
[Of Sir Stafford Cripps]
He has a brilliant mind until
he makes it up.
[In *The Wit of the Asquiths*]

**BEVAN, Aneurin
(1897–1960)**
We know what happens to
people who stay in the middle
of the road. They get run over.
[*The Observer*, 1953]

**THE BIBLE (KING JAMES
VERSION)**
How long halt ye between
two opinions?
[*I Kings*, 18:21]

JAMES, William (1842–1910)
There is no more miserable
human being than one in
whom nothing is habitual but
indecision.
[*Principles of Psychology* (1890)]

NASH, Ogden (1902–1971)
If I could but spot a conclu-
sion, I should race to it.
['All, All Are Gone, The Old
Familiar Quotations' (1952)]

SMITH, Sir Cyril (1928–)
If the fence is strong enough
I'll sit on it.
[*The Observer*, 1974]

INDEPENDENCE

AESOP (6th century BC)
The gods help those who help
themselves.
['Hercules and the Waggoner']

**EMERSON, Ralph Waldo
(1803–1882)**
It is easy in the world to live
after the world's opinion; it is
easy in solitude after our own;
but the great man is he who,
in the midst of the crowd,
keeps with perfect sweetness
the independence of solitude.
['Self-Reliance' (1841)]

**GIBBON, Edward
(1737–1794)**
The first of earthly blessings,
independence.
[*Memoirs of My Life and
Writings* (1796)]

**IBSEN, Henrik
(1828–1906)**
The strongest man in the
world is the man who stands
alone.
[*An Enemy of the People*
(1882)]

**MARRYAT, Frederick
(1792–1848)**
I think it much better that . . .
every man paddle his own
canoe.
[*Settlers in Canada* (1844)]

THOREAU, Henry (1817–1862)
I would rather sit on a pumpkin and have it all to myself than be crowded on a velvet cushion.
[*Walden* (1854)]

INDUSTRIAL RELATIONS

ANONYMOUS
In his chamber, weak and dying,
While the Norman Baron lay,
Loud, without, his men were crying,
'Shorter hours and better pay.'
['A Strike among the Poets']

COOK, A.J. (1885–1931)
Not a penny off the pay, not a minute on the day.
[Speech, 1926]

FEATHER, Vic, Baron (1906–1976)
Industrial relations are like sexual relations. It's better between two consenting parties.
[*Guardian Weekly*, 1976]

KEYNES, John Maynard (1883–1946)
There are the Trade Unionists, once the oppressed, now the tyrants, whose selfish and sectional pretensions need to be bravely opposed.
['Liberalism and Labour' (1926)]

SHINWELL, Emanuel (1884–1986)
We know that you, the organized workers of the country, are our friends . . . As for the rest, they do not matter a tinker's curse.
[Speech, 1947]

WILSON, Harold (1916–1995)
One man's wage rise is another man's price increase.
[*The Observer*, 1970]

INGRATITUDE

CHILLINGWORTH, William (1602–1644)
I once knew a man out of courtesy help a lame dog over a stile, and he for requital bit his fingers.
[*The Religion of Protestants* (1637)]

GARCÍA MÁRQUEZ, Gabriel (1928–)
There are no limits to human ingratitude.
[*No-one Writes to the Colonel* (1961)]

HUXLEY, Aldous (1894–1963)
Most human beings have an almost infinite capacity for taking things for granted.
[*Themes and Variations* (1950)]

LA ROCHEFOUCAULD (1613–1680)
Over-great haste to repay an obligation is a form of ingratitude.
[*Maximes* (1678)]

LOUIS XIV (1638–1715)
Every time I make an appointment, I make a hundred men discontented and one ungrateful.
[In Voltaire, *Siècle de Louis XIV*]

SHAKESPEARE, William (1564–1616)
Blow, blow, thou winter wind,
Thou art not so unkind
As man's ingratitude . . .
Thy tooth is not so keen,

Freeze, freeze, thou bitter sky,
That dost not bite so nigh
As benefits forgot.
[*As You Like It*, II.vii]

INSULTS

CHESTERFIELD, Lord (1694–1773)
An injury is much sooner forgotten than an insult.
[Letter to his son, 1746]

CORNEILLE, Pierre (1606–1684)
He who allows himself to be insulted, deserves to be.
[*Héraclius* (1646)]

GILBERT, W.S. (1836–1911)
I shouldn't be sufficiently degraded in my own estimation unless I was insulted with a very considerable bribe.
[*The Mikado* (1885)]

GROSSMITH, George and Weedon
I am a poor man, but I would gladly give ten shillings to find out who sent me the insulting Christmas card I received this morning.
[*Diary of a Nobody* (1894)]

SHERIDAN, Richard Brinsley (1751–1816)
If it is abuse, – why one is always sure to hear of it from one damned good-natured friend or another!
[*The Critic* (1779)]

THURBER, James (1894–1961)
A man should not insult his wife publicly, at parties. He should insult her in the privacy of the home.
[*Thurber Country* (1953)]

INTELLIGENCE

**BALDWIN, Stanley
(1867–1947)**
The intelligent are to the intelligentsia what a gentleman is
to a gent.

[Attr.]

BRENAN, Gerald (1894–1987)
Intellectuals are people who
believe that ideas are of more
importance than values. That
is to say, their own ideas and
other people's values.

[*Thoughts in a Dry Season*
(1978)]

**FREUD, Sigmund
(1856–1939)**
The voice of the intellect is a
soft one, but it does not rest
till it has gained a hearing.

[*The Future of an Illusion*]

KEATS, John (1795–1821)
The only means of strengthening one's intellect is to
make up one's mind about
nothing – to let the mind be a
thoroughfare for all thoughts.
Not a select party.

[Letter, 1819]

**LA ROCHEFOUCAULD
(1613-1680)**
The height of cleverness is to
be able to conceal it.

[*Maximes* (1678)]

**MACAULAY, Lord
(1800–1859)**
The highest intellects, like the
tops of mountains, are the
first to catch and to reflect the
dawn.

['Sir James Mackintosh'
(1843)]

**MANN, Thomas
(1875–1955)**
Every intellectual attitude is
latently political.

[*The Observer,* 1974]

**NIETZSCHE, Friedrich
(1844–1900)**
Wit is the epigram for the
death of an emotion.

[*Human, All too Human*
(1886)]

PASCAL, Blaise (1623–1662)
The more intelligence one has
the more people one finds original. Commonplace people see
no difference between men.

[*Pensées* (1670)]

**SCHOPENHAUER, Arthur
(1788–1860)**
Intellect is invisible to the
man who has none.

[*Aphorismen zur
Lebensweisheit*]

**SHAKESPEARE, William
(1564–1616)**
Brevity is the soul of wit.

[*Hamlet,* II.ii]

Look, he's winding up the watch of his wit; by and by it will strike.

[*The Tempest,* II.i]

This fellow is wise enough to play the fool;
And to do that well craves a kind of wit.

[*Twelfth Night,* III.i]

WHITEHEAD, A.N. (1861–1947)

Intelligence is quickness to apprehend as distinct from ability, which is capacity to act wisely on the thing apprehended.

[*Dialogues* (1954)]

INVENTION

EDISON, Thomas Alva (1847–1931)

To invent, you need a good imagination and a pile of junk.

[Attr.]

EMERSON, Ralph Waldo (1803–1882)

Invention breeds invention.

[*Society and Solitude* (1870)]

FRANKLIN, Benjamin (1706–1790)

[On being asked the use of a new invention]

What is the use of a new-born child?

[In Parton, *Life and Times of Benjamin Franklin* (1864)]

PROVERB

Necessity is the mother of invention.

IRELAND

ALLINGHAM, William (1824–1889)

Not men and women in an Irish street
But Catholics and Protestants you meet.

[Attr.]

BATES, Daisy May (1863–1951)

There are a few fortunate races that have been endowed with cheerfulness as their main characteristic, the Australian Aborigine and the Irish being among these.

[*The Passing of the Aborigines* (1938)]

BEHAN, Brendan (1923–1964)

Pat: He was an Anglo-Irishman.
Meg: In the blessed name of God, what's that?
Pat: A Protestant with a horse.

[*The Hostage* (1958)]

Other people have a nationality. The Irish and the Jews have a psychosis.

[*Richard's Cork Leg* (1972)]

CLINTON, Bill (1946–)

[On the IRA, shortly after they resumed their campaign of violence in February 1996]
We must not let the men of the past ruin the future of the children of Northern Ireland.

[*Daily Mail*, 1996]

DE VALERA, Eamon (1882–1975)

Whenever I wanted to know what the Irish people wanted, I had only to examine my own heart and it told me straight off what the Irish people wanted.

[*Dáil Éireann*, 1922]

DISRAELI, Benjamin (1804–1881)

A starving population, an absentee aristocracy, and an alien Church, and in addition the weakest executive in the world. That is the Irish question.

[Speech, 1844]

DOYLE, Roddy (1958–)

The Irish are the niggers of Europe . . . An' Dubliners are the niggers of Ireland . . . An' the northside Dubliners are the niggers o' Dublin – Say it loud. I'm black an' I'm proud.

[*The Commitments* (1987)]

GOGARTY, Oliver St John (1878–1957)

Politics is the chloroform of the Irish people, or rather the hashish.

[*As I Was Going Down Sackville Street* (1937)]

THE IRISH CONSTITUTION

The national territory consists of the whole island of Ireland, its islands and the territorial seas.

[Article 2]

JOHNSON, Samuel (1709–1784)

The Irish are a fair people; – they never speak well of one another.

[In Boswell, *The Life of Samuel Johnson* (1791)]

JOYCE, James (1882–1941)

Ireland is the old sow that eats her farrow.

[*A Portrait of the Artist as a Young Man* (1916)]

LEONARD, Hugh (1926–)

The problem with Ireland is that it's a country full of genius, but with absolutely no talent.

[Interview in *The Times*, 1977]

MAJOR, John (1943–)
[On the search for peace in Northern Ireland after the end of the IRA ceasefire in February 1996]
If we are pushed back, we will start again. If we are pushed back, we will start again. If we are pushed back a third time we will start again.
[*The Observer Review*, 1996]

MORRISON, Danny (1950–)
Who here really believes that we can win the war through the ballot box? But will any-one here object if with a ballot box in this hand and an Armalite in this hand we take power in Ireland.
[Provisional Sinn Féin Conference, 1981]

ROBINSON, Mary (1944–)
As the elected choice of the people of this part of our island I want to extend the hand of friendship and of love to both communities in the other part.
[Inaugural speech as President, 1991]

SMITH, Sydney (1771–1845)
The moment the very name of Ireland is mentioned, the English seem to bid adieu to common feeling, common prudence, and to common sense, and to act with the barbarity of tyrants, and the fatuity of idiots.
[*Letters of Peter Plymley* (1807)]

YEATS, W.B. (1865–1939)
Behind Ireland fierce and militant, is Ireland poetic, passionate, remembering, idyllic, fanciful, and always patriotic.
['Popular Ballad Poetry of Ireland' (1889)]

JEALOUSY

MILTON, John (1608–1674)
Nor jealousie
Was understood, the injur'd
Lover's Hell.
[*Paradise Lost* (1667)]

SAGAN, Françoise (1935–)
To jealousy nothing is more
frightful than laughter.
[Attr.]

**SHAKESPEARE, William
(1564–1616)**
O, beware, my lord, of jealousy;
It is the green-ey'd monster
which doth mock
The meat it feeds on.
[*Othello*, III.iii]

Trifles light as air
Are to the jealous confirm-
ations strong
As proofs of holy writ.
[*Othello*, III.iii]

Jealous souls will not be
answer'd so;
They are not ever jealous for
the cause,
But jealous for they are jealous.
[*Othello*, III.iv]

WELLS, H.G. (1866–1946)
Moral indignation is jealousy
with a halo.
[*The Wife of Sir Isaac Harman*
(1914)]

JUDAISM

BLUE, Rabbi Lionel (1930–)
There is always a danger in
Judaism of seeing history as a
sort of poker game played
between Jews and God, in
which the presence of others
is noted but not given much
importance.
[*The Observer*, 1982]

**HEINE, Heinrich
(1797–1856)**
It is extremely difficult for a
Jew to be converted, for how
can he bring himself to
believe in the divinity of –
another Jew?
[Attr.]

**JOHNSON, Paul
(1928–)**
For me this is a vital litmus
test: no intellectual society
can flourish where a Jew feels
even slightly uneasy.
[*The Sunday Times Magazine*,
1977]

**LAWRENCE, D.H.
(1885–1930)**
The very best that is in the
Jewish blood: a faculty for
pure disinterestedness, and
warm, physically warm love,
that seems to make the cor-
puscles of the blood glow.
[*Kangaroo* (1923)]

MARX, Groucho (1895–1977)
[When excluded, on racial grounds, from a beach club] Since my daughter is only half-Jewish, could she go into the water up to her knees?
[*The Observer*, 1977]

MILLER, Jonathan (1934–)
I'm not really a Jew; just Jew-ish, not the whole hog.
[*Beyond the Fringe* (1961)]

ROTH, Philip (1933–)
A Jewish man with parents alive is a fifteen-year-old boy, and will remain a fifteen-year-old boy until *they die*.
[*Portnoy's Complaint* (1969)]

STEIN, Gertrude (1874–1946)
The Jews have produced only three originative geniuses: Christ, Spinoza, and myself.
[In Mellow, *Charmed Circle* (1974)]

USTINOV, Sir Peter (1921–)
I believe that the Jews have made a contribution to the human condition out of all proportion to their numbers: I believe them to be an immense people. Not only have they supplied the world with two leaders of the stature of Jesus Christ and Karl Marx, but they have even indulged in the luxury of following neither one nor the other.
[*Dear Me* (1977)]

ZANGWILL, Israel (1864–1926)
No Jew was ever fool enough to turn Christian unless he was a clever man.
[*Children of the Ghetto* (1892)]

See RACE

JUDGEMENT

AUGUSTINE, Saint (354–430)
The judgement of the world is sure.
[*Contra Epistolam Parmeniani*]

THE BIBLE (KING JAMES VERSION)
Judge not, that ye be not judged.
[*Matthew*, 7:1]

He that is without sin among you, let him first cast a stone at her.
[*Luke*, 8:7]

CAMUS, Albert (1913–1960)
Don't wait for the Last Judgement. It is taking place every day.
[*The Fall* (1956)]

COMPTON-BURNETT, Dame Ivy (1884–1969)
Appearances are not held to be a clue to the truth. But we seem to have no other.
[*Manservant and Maidservant* (1947)]

COWPER, William (1731–1800)
Judgment drunk, and brib'd to lose his way,
Winks hard, and talks of darkness at noon-day.
['The Progress of Error' (1782)]

EDGEWORTH, Maria (1767–1849)
We cannot judge either of the feelings or of the characters of men with perfect accuracy, from their actions or their appearance in public; it is from their careless conversations, their half-finished sentences, that we may hope with the greatest probability of success to discover their real character.
[*Castle Rackrent* (1800)]

MONTAIGNE, Michel de (1533–1592)
It is a dangerous and serious presumption, and argues an absurd temerity, to condemn what we do not understand.
[*Essais* (1580)]

SHAKESPEARE, William (1564–1616)
What judgment shall I dread, doing no wrong?
[*The Merchant of Venice*, IV.i]

JUSTICE

BENNETT, Arnold (1867–1931)
The price of justice is eternal publicity.
[*Things That Have Interested Me*]

BINGHAM, Sir Thomas (1933–)
[Discussing the rising costs of going to law]
We cannot for ever be content to acknowledge that in England justice is open to all – like the Ritz Hotel.
[*Independent on Sunday*, 1994]

BLACKSTONE, Sir William (1723–1780)
It is better that ten guilty persons escape than one innocent suffer.
[*Commentaries on the Laws of England* (1765–1769)]

FERDINAND I (1503–1564)
Let there be justice though the world perish.
[Attr.]

FIELDING, Henry (1707-1754)
Thwackum was for doing justice, and leaving mercy to Heaven.

[*Tom Jones* (1749)]

FRANCE, Anatole (1844-1924)
To disarm the strong and arm the weak would be to change a social order which I have been commissioned to preserve. Justice is the means whereby established injustices are sanctioned.

[*Crainquebille* (1904)]

HEWART, Gordon (1870-1943)
It is not merely of some importance but is of fundamental importance that justice should not only be done, but should manifestly and undoubtedly be seen to be done.

[*Rex v. Sussex Justices*, 1923]

JUNIUS (1769-1772)
The injustice done to an individual is sometimes of service to the public.

[*Letters* (1769-1771)]

LA ROCHEFOUCAULD (1613-1680)
The love of justice in most men is no more than the fear of suffering injustice.

[*Maximes* (1678)]

LINCOLN, Abraham (1809-1865)
The probability that we may fail in the struggle ought not to deter us from the support of a cause we believe to be just.

[Speech, 1859]

MAGNA CARTA (1215)
To no one will we sell, to no one will we deny, or delay, right or justice.

[Clause 40]

MANSFIELD, Earl of (1705-1793)
[Advice given to a new colonial governor]
Consider what you think justice requires, and decide accordingly. But never give your reasons; for your judgement will probably be right, but your reasons will certainly be wrong.

[In Campbell, *Lives of the Chief Justices* (1849)]

MILTON, John (1608-1674)
Yet I shall temper so
Justice with Mercie.

[*Paradise Lost* (1667)]

ROUX, Joseph (1834-1886)
We love justice greatly, and just men but little.

[*Meditations of a Parish Priest* (1886)]

SHAKESPEARE, William (1564–1616)
What stronger breastplate
than a heart untainted?
Thrice is he arm'd that hath
his quarrel just;
And he but naked, though
lock'd up in steel,
Whose conscience with injustice is corrupted.

[*Henry VI, Part 2*, III.ii]

SHIRLEY, James (1596–1666)
Only the actions of the just
Smell sweet, and blossom in
their dust.

[*The Contention of Ajax and Ulysses* (1659)]

STOPPARD, Tom (1937–)
This is a British murder
inquiry and some degree of
justice must be seen to be
more or less done.

[*Jumpers* (1972)]

WILDE, Oscar (1854–1900)
For Man's grim Justice goes its
way,
And will not swerve aside:
It slays the weak, it slays the
strong,
It has a deadly stride.

[*The Ballad of Reading Gaol* (1898)]

See LAW

KINDNESS

BIRLEY, Mark
You never forget people who were kind to you when you were young.

[*The Observer*, 1989]

CONFUCIUS
(c. 550–c. 478 BC)
Recompense injury with justice, and recompense kindness with kindness.

[*Analects*]

DAVIES, William Henry
(1871–1940)
I love thee for a heart that's kind –
Not for the knowledge in thy mind.

['Sweet Stay-at-Home' (1913)]

GIDE, André (1869–1951)
True kindness presupposes the faculty of imagining as one's own the suffering and joy of others.

[Attr.]

JOHNSON, Samuel
(1709–1784)
Always, Sir, set a high value on spontaneous kindness. He whose inclination prompts him to cultivate your friendship of his own accord, will love you more than one whom you have been at pains to attach to you.

[In Boswell, *The Life of Samuel Johnson* (1791)]

MARSHALL, Alan
(1911–1968)
Beware of people you've been kind to.

[Remark to John Morrison]

SHAKESPEARE, William
(1564–1616)
I must be cruel, only to be kind.

[*Hamlet*, III.iv]

WILCOX, Ella Wheeler
(1850–1919)
So many gods, so many creeds,
So many paths that wind and wind,
While just the art of being kind
Is all the sad world needs.

['The World's Need' (1917)]

WILLIAMS, Tennessee
(1911–1983)
I have always depended on the kindness of strangers.

[*A Streetcar Named Desire* (1947)]

KNOWLEDGE

ADAMS, Henry (1838–1918)
They know enough who know

how to learn.
[*The Education of Henry Adams*
(1918)]

BACON, Francis (1561–1626)

Knowledge itself is power.
['Of Heresies' (1597)]

BEECHING, Rev. H.C. (1859–1919)

First come I; my name is
Jowett.
There's no knowledge but I
know it.
I am Master of this college:
What I don't know isn't
knowledge.
['The Masque of Balliol' (late
1870s)]

THE BIBLE (KING JAMES VERSION)

He that increaseth knowledge
increaseth sorrow.
[*Ecclesiastes*, 1:18]

HOLMES, Oliver Wendell (1809–1894)

It is the province of knowledge to speak and it is the
privilege of wisdom to listen.
[*The Poet at the Breakfast-
Table* (1872)]

HUXLEY, T.H. (1825–1895)

The saying that a little knowledge is a dangerous thing is,
to my mind, a very dangerous
adage. If knowledge is real

and genuine, I do not believe
that it is other than a very
valuable possession however
infinitesimal its quantity may
be. Indeed, if a little knowledge is dangerous, where is
the man who has so much as
to be out of danger?
[*Science and Culture* (1877)]

JOAD, C.E.M. (1891–1953)

There was never an age in
which useless knowledge was
more important than in ours.
[*The Observer*, 1951]

JOHNSON, Samuel (1709–1784)

Integrity without knowledge is
weak and useless, and knowledge without integrity is
dangerous and dreadful.
[*Rasselas* (1759)]

LINKLATER, Eric (1899–1974)

For the scientific acquisition
of knowledge is almost as
tedious as a routine acquisition of wealth.
[*White Man's Saga*]

MACAULAY, Lord (1800–1859)

Knowledge advances by
steps, and not by leaps.
['History' (1828)]

MILTON, John (1608–1674)

The first and wisest of them

all professd
To know this onely, that he
nothing knew.
[*Paradise Regained* (1671)]

**MUMFORD, Ethel
(1878–1940)**
Knowledge is power if you
know it about the right person.
[In Cowan, *The Wit of Women*]

**POPPER, Sir Karl
(1902–1994)**
Our knowledge can only be
finite, while our ignorance
must necessarily be infinite.
[*Conjectures and Refutations*
(1963)]

SHARPE, Tom (1928–)
His had been an intellectual

decision founded on his conviction that if a little knowledge was a dangerous thing,
a lot was lethal.
[*Porterhouse Blue* (1974)]

**SHERIDAN, Richard Brinsley
(1751–1816)**
Madam, a circulating library
in a town is an ever-green
tree of diabolical knowledge!
– It blossoms through the
year!– And depend on it, Mrs
Malaprop, that they who are
so fond of handling the
leaves, will long for the fruit
at last.
[*The Rivals* (1775)]

See LEARNING;
WISDOM

LANGUAGE

CHURCHILL, Sir Winston (1874–1965)
[Marginal comment on a document]
This is the sort of English up with which I will not put.
[In Gowers, *Plain Words* (1948)]

DAY, Clarence Shepard (1874–1935)
Imagine the Lord talking French! Aside from a few odd words in Hebrew, I took it completely for granted that God had never spoken anything but the most dignified English.
[*Life with Father* (1935)]

EMERSON, Ralph Waldo (1803–1882)
Language is fossil poetry.
['The Poet' (1844)]

FRANKLIN, Benjamin (1706–1790)
Write with the learned, pronounce with the vulgar.
[*Poor Richard's Almanac* (1738)]

GOETHE (1749–1832)
Whoever is not acquainted with foreign languages knows nothing of his own.
[*On Art and Antiquity* (1827)]

GOLDWYN, Samuel (1882–1974)
Let's have some new clichés.
[*The Observer*, 1948]

JESPERSEN, Otto (1860–1943)
In his whole life man achieves nothing so great and so wonderful as what he achieved when he learned to talk.
[*Language* (1904)]

JOHNSON, Samuel (1709–1784)
Language is the dress of thought.
[*The Lives of the Most Eminent English Poets* (1781)]

LANGLAND, William (c. 1330–c. 1400)
Grammere, that grounde is of alle.
[*The Vision of William Concerning Piers the Plowman*]

LEVI-STRAUSS, Claude (1908–)
Language is a kind of human reason, which has its own internal logic of which man knows nothing.
[*The Savage Mind* (1962)]

MACAULAY, Lord (1800–1859)
The English Bible, a book which, if everything else in our language should perish, would alone suffice to show

the whole extent of its beauty and power.

['John Dryden' (1843)]

MURROW, Edward R. (1908–1965)
[Of Churchill]
He mobilized the English language and sent it into battle to steady his fellow countrymen and hearten those Europeans upon whom the long dark night of tyranny had descended.

[Broadcast, 1954]

NARAYAN, R.K. (1907–)
English is a very adaptable language. And it's so transparent it can take on the tint of any country.

[Radio conversation, 1968]

SHAW, George Bernard (1856–1950)
England and America are two countries separated by the same language.

[*Reader's Digest*, 1942]

SIGISMUND (1368–1437)
[Responding to criticism of his Latin]
I am the Roman Emperor, and am above grammar.

[Attr.]

SPENSER, Edmund (c. 1522–1599)
So now they have made our English tongue, a gallimaufray or hodgepodge of al other speches.

[*The Shepheardes Calender* (1579)]

SULLIVAN, Annie (1866–1936)
Language grows out of life, out of its needs and experiences . . . *Language* and *knowledge* are indissolubly connected; they are interdependent.

[Speech, 1894]

TOMLIN, Lily (1939–)
Man invented language in order to satisfy his deep need to complain.

[In Pinker, *The Language Instinct* (1994)]

TUCHOLSKY, Kurt (1890–1935)
English is a simple, yet hard language. It consists entirely of foreign words pronounced wrongly.

[*Scraps* (1973)]

WEINREICH, Professor Max
A language is a dialect that has an army and a navy.

[In Rosten, *The Joys of Yiddish* (1968)]

WHORF, Benjamin (1897–1941)
We dissect nature along lines

laid down by our native language . . . Language is not simply a reporting device for experience but a defining framework for it.

[In Hoyer (ed.), *New Directions in the Study of Language* (1964)]

See WORDS

LAW

ADAMS, Richard
(1846–1908)
You have been acquitted by a Limerick jury and you may now leave the dock without any other stain on your character.

[In Healy, *The Old Munster Circuit*]

BACON, Francis (1561–1626)
One of the Seven was wont to say: 'That laws were like cobwebs; where the small flies were caught, and the great brake through.'

[*Apophthegms New and Old* (1624)]

BENTHAM, Jeremy
(1748–1832)
Lawyers are the only persons in whom ignorance of the law is not punished.

[Attr.]

BRAXFIELD, Lord
(1722–1799)
Let them bring me prisoners, and I'll find them law.

[Attr. by Cockburn]

BURKE, Edmund
(1729–1797)
People crushed by law have no hopes but from power. If laws are their enemies, they will be enemies to laws; and those who have much to hope and nothing to lose will always be dangerous more or less.

[Letter to Charles James Fox, 1777]

There is but one law for all, namely, that law which governs all law – the law of our Creator, the law of humanity, justice, equity, the law of nature, and of nations.

[Speech, 1794]

CARROLL, Lewis (1832–1898)
'I'll be judge, I'll be jury,' said cunning old Fury:
'I'll try the whole cause, and condemn you to death.'

[*Alice's Adventures in Wonderland* (1865)]

CHAPMAN, George
(c. 1559–c. 1634)
I'me asham'd the law is such an Ass.

[*Revenge for Honour* (1654)]

COETZEE, John Michael (1940–)
All we can do is to uphold the laws, all of us, without allowing the memory of justice to fade.
[*Waiting for the Barbarians* (1980)]

DENNING Lord (1899–)
To every subject of this land, however powerful, I would use Thomas Fuller's words over three hundred years ago, 'Be ye never so high, the law is above you'.
[High Court ruling against the Attorney-General, 1977]

EMERSON, Ralph Waldo (1803–1882)
Good men must not obey the laws too well.
['Politics' (1844)]

FRANCE, Anatole (1844–1924)
The law, in its majestic equality, forbids the rich as well as the poor to sleep under bridges, to beg in the streets, and to steal bread.
[*Le Lys Rouge* (1894)]

GIRAUDOUX, Jean (1882–1944)
All of us here know that there is no better way of exercising the imagination than the study of law. No poet has ever interpreted nature as freely as a lawyer interprets reality.
[*La Guerre de Troie n'aura pas lieu* (1935)]

HOLMES, Hugh (Lord Justice Holmes) (1840–1916)
An elderly pensioner on being sentenced to fifteen years' penal servitude cried 'Ah! my Lord, I'm a very old man, and I'll never do that sentence.' The judge replied, 'Well try to do as much of it as you can'.
[In Healy, *The Old Munster Circuit* (1939)]

INGRAMS, Richard (1937–)
I have come to regard the law courts not as a cathedral but rather as a casino.
[*The Guardian*, 1977]

LOCKE, John (1632–1704)
Wherever Law ends, Tyranny begins.
[*Second Treatise of Civil Government* (1690)]

MACHIAVELLI (1469–1527)
Good examples are borne out of good education, which is the outcome of good legislation; and good legislation is borne out of those uprisings which are unduly damned by so many people.
[*Discourse*]

**MAYNARD, Sir John
(1602–1690)**
[Reply to Judge Jeffreys' suggestion that he was so old he had forgotten the law]
I have forgotten more law than you ever knew, but allow me to say, I have not forgotten much.

[Attr.]

MORTIMER, John (1923–)
No brilliance is needed in the law. Nothing but common sense, and relatively clean finger nails.

[*A Voyage Round My Father* (1971)]

**POPE, Alexander
(1688–1744)**
The hungry Judges soon the sentence sign,
And wretches hang that jurymen may dine.

[*The Rape of the Lock* (1714)]

PUZO, Mario (1920–)
A lawyer with his briefcase can steal more than a thousand men with guns.

[*The Godfather* (1969)]

**RICHELIEU, Cardinal
(1585–1642)**
To pass a law and not have it enforced is to authorize the very thing you wish to prohibit.

[*Mémoires*]

**ROBESPIERRE, Maximilien
(1758–1794)**
Any law which violates the indefeasible rights of man is in essence unjust and tyrannical; it is no law.

[*Déclaration des Droits de
l'homme* (1793)]

**ROUSSEAU, Jean-Jacques
(1712–1778)**
Laws are always useful to those who have possessions, and harmful to those who have nothing.

[*Du Contrat Social* (1762)]

**SELDEN, John
(1584–1654)**
Ignorance of the law excuses no man; not that all men know the law, but because 'tis an excuse every man will plead, and no man can tell how to confute him.

[*Table Talk* (1689)]

**SMITH, F.E.
(1872–1930)**
[To a judge who complained that he was no wiser at the end than at the start of one of Smith's cases]
Possibly not, My Lord, but far better informed.

[In Birkenhead, *Life of F.E.
Smith* (1959)]

See JUSTICE

LEARNING

**ADDISON, Joseph
(1672–1719)**
The truth of it is, learning
. . . makes a silly man ten
thousand times more insuffer-
able, by supplying variety of
matter to his impertinence,
and giving him an opportunity
of abounding in absurdities.
[*The Man of the Town*]

ARISTOTLE (384–322 BC)
What we have to learn to do,
we learn by doing.
[*Nicomachean Ethics*]

**ASCHAM, Roger
(1515–1568)**
There is no such whetstone,
to sharpen a good wit and
encourage a will to learning,
as is praise.
[*The Scholemaster* (1570)]

BACON, Francis (1561–1626)
Studies serve for delight, for
ornament, and for ability.
['Of Studies' (1625)]

Crafty men contemn studies;
simple men admire them; and
wise men use them.
['Of Studies' (1625)]

**CHESTERFIELD, Lord
(1694–1773)**
Wear your learning, like your
watch, in a private pocket;
and do not merely pull it out
and strike it merely to show
you have one.
[Letter to his son, 1748]

**CONFUCIUS
(c. 550–c. 478 BC)**
Learning without thought is
labour lost; thought without
learning is perilous.
[*Analects*]

**FOOTE, Samuel
(1720–1777)**
For as the old saying is,
When house and land are
gone and spent
Then learning is most excel-
lent.
[*Taste* (1752)]

LESSING, Doris (1919–)
. . . that is what learning is.
You suddenly understand
something you've understood
all your life, but in a new way.
[*The Four-Gated City* (1969)]

MILTON, John (1608–1674)
Where there is much desire to
learn, there is of necessity will
be much arguing, much
writing, many opinions; for
opinion in good men is but
knowledge in the making.
[*Areopagitica* (1644)]

OVID (43 BC–AD 18)
Add the fact that to have dili-

gently studied the liberal arts
refines behaviour and does
not allow it to be savage.
[*Epistulae Ex Ponto*]

POPE, Alexander
(1688–1744)
A little learning is a danger-
ous thing;
Drink deep, or taste not the
Pierian spring:
There shallow draughts intox-
icate the brain,
And drinking largely sobers us
again.
[*An Essay on Criticism* (1711)]

WHITE, Patrick (1912–1990)
'I dunno,' Arthur said. 'I forget
what I was taught. I only
remember what I've learnt.'
[*The Solid Mandala* (1966)]

**See EDUCATION; KNOWL-
EDGE; SCHOOL; UNIVERSITY**

LIES

ANONYMOUS
An abomination unto the
Lord, but a very present help
in time of trouble.
[Definition of a lie]

BACON, Francis
(1561–1626)
But it is not the lie that pas-
seth through the mind, but the
lie that sinketh in, and settleth
in it, that doth the hurt.
['Of Truth' (1625)]

BELLOC, Hilaire
(1870–1953)
Matilda told such Dreadful
Lies,
It made one Gasp and Stretch
one's Eyes;
Her Aunt, who, from her
Earliest Youth,
Had kept a Strict Regard for
Truth,
Attempted to Believe Matilda:
The effort very nearly killed
her.
['Matilda' (1907)]

BUTLER, Samuel
(1835–1902)
Any fool can tell the truth, but
it requires a man of some
sense to know how to lie well.
[*The Note-Books of Samuel
Butler* (1912)]

BYRON, Lord
(1788–1824)
And, after all, what is a lie?
'Tis but
The truth in masquerade.
[*Don Juan* (1824)]

CALLAGHAN, James
(1912–)
A lie can be half-way round
the world before the truth has
got its boots on.
[Speech, 1976]

**CORNEILLE, Pierre
(1606–1684)**
One needs a good memory
after telling lies.
[*Le Menteur* (1643)]

**DAVIES, Robertson
(1913–1995)**
Better a noble lie than a miserable truth.
[In Twigg, *Conversations with
Twenty-four Canadian Writers*
(1981)]

**DISRAELI, Benjamin
(1804–1881)**
There are three kinds of lies:
lies, damned lies and statistics.
[Attr.]

EVANS, Harold (1928–)
The camera cannot lie. But it
can be an accessory to
untruth.
[Attr.]

**HAMPTON, Christopher
(1946–)**
You see, I always divide people into two groups. Those
who live by what they know
to be a lie, and those who live
by what they believe, falsely,
to be the truth.
[*The Philanthropist* (1970)]

**HERVEY, Lord
(1696–1743)**
Whoever would lie usefully

should lie seldom.
[In Croker, *Memoirs of the
Reign of George II* (1848)]

**HOUSEHOLD, Geoffrey
(1900–1988)**
It's easy to make a man confess the lies he tells to himself; it's far harder to make
him confess the truth.
[*Rogue Male* (1939)]

**IBSEN, Henrik
(1828–1906)**
Take the saving lie from the
average man and you take his
happiness away, too.
[*The Wild Duck* (1884)]

**MAUGHAM, William
Somerset (1874–1965)**
She's too crafty a woman to
invent a new lie when an old
one will serve.
[*The Constant Wife* (1927)]

**MURDOCH, Iris
(1919–)**
He led a double life. Did that
make him a liar? He did not
feel a liar. He was a man of
two truths.
[*The Sacred and Profane Love
Machine* (1974)]

**NIETZSCHE, Friedrich
(1844–1900)**
We need lies . . . in order to
live.
[*Fragments* (1880–1889)]

**PROUST, Marcel
(1871–1922)**
One of those telegrams of
which M. de Guermantes had
wittily fixed the formula:
'Cannot come, lie follows'.
[*Le Temps retrouvé* (1926)]

**SAKI
(1870–1916)**
A little inaccuracy sometimes
saves tons of explanation.
[*The Square Egg* (1924)]

**TENNYSON, Alfred, Lord
(1809–1892)**
A lie which is all a lie may be
met and fought with outright,
But a lie which is part a truth
is a harder matter to fight.
['The Grandmother' (1859)]

**VIDAL, Gore
(1925–)**
He will lie even when it is
inconvenient, the sign of the
true artist.
[Two Sisters (1970)]

**WILDE, Oscar
(1854–1900)**
The final revelation is that
Lying, the telling of beautiful
untrue things, is the proper
aim of Art.
['The Decay of Lying' (1889)]

See ART; TRUTH

ADAMS, Douglas (1952–)
The Answer to the Great
Question Of . . . Life, the
Universe and Everything . . .
Is . . . Forty-two.
[*The Hitch Hiker's Guide to the
Galaxy* (1979)]

ADAMS, Henry (1838–1918)
Chaos often breeds life, when
order breeds habit.
[*The Education of Henry Adams*
(1918)]

**AMIEL, Henri-Frédéric
(1821–1881)**
Every life is a profession of
faith, and exercises an
inevitable and silent influence.
[*Journal*, 1852]

ANKA, Paul (1941–)
And now the end is near
And so I face the final curtain,
My friends, I'll say it clear,
I'll state my case of which I'm
certain.
I've lived a life that's full, I've
travelled each and evr'y high-
way
And more, much more than
this, I did it my way.
['My Way', song, 1969]

ANONYMOUS
Be happy while y'er leevin,

For y'er a lang time deid.
[Scottish motto]

**ARNOLD, Matthew
(1822–1888)**
Is it so small a thing
To have enjoy'd the sun,
To have liv'd light in the
spring,
To have lov'd, to have
thought, to have done?
['Empedocles on Etna' (1852)]

AURELIUS, Marcus (121–180)
Remember that no one loses
any other life than this which
he now lives, nor lives any
other than this which he now
loses.

[Meditations]

BALFOUR, A.J. (1848–1930)
Nothing matters very much, and
very few things matter at all.
[Attr.]

BENNETT, Alan (1934–)
You know life . . . it's rather
like opening a tin of sardines.
We are all of us looking for
the key.
[Beyond the Fringe (1962)]

**BENTLEY, Nicolas
(1907–1978)**
One should not exaggerate
the importance of trifles. Life,
for instance, is much too short
to be taken seriously.
[Attr.]

**BLAKE, William
(1757–1827)**
For every thing that lives is
holy, life delights in life.
[America: a Prophecy (1793)]

**BRENAN, Gerald
(1894–1987)**
We should live as if we were
going to live forever, yet at
the back of our minds remember that our time is short.
[Thoughts in a Dry Season
(1978)]

**BRONTË, Charlotte
(1816-1855)**
Life, believe, is not a dream,
So dark as sages say;
Oft a little morning rain
Foretells a pleasant day!
['Life' (1846)]

**BROWNE, Sir Thomas
(1605–1682)**
Life itself is but the shadow of
death, and souls but the shadows of the living.
[The Garden of Cyrus (1658)]

The long habit of living indis-
poseth us for dying.
[Hydriotaphia: Urn Burial
(1658)]

**BUCHAN, John
(1875–1940)**
It's a great life if you don't
weaken.
[Mr Standfast (1919)]

**BUTLER, Samuel
(1835–1902)**
Life is one long process of
getting tired.
[*The Note-Books of Samuel
Butler* (1912)]

To live is like love, all reason
is against it, and all healthy
instinct for it.
[*The Note-Books of Samuel
Butler* (1912)]

**CHAMFORT, Nicolas
(1741–1794)**
Living is an illness to which
sleep provides relief every six-
teen hours. It's a palliative.
Death is the remedy.
[*Maximes et pensées* (1796)]

**CHAPLIN, Charlie
(1889–1977)**
Life is a tragedy when seen in
close-up, but a comedy in
long-shot.
[In *The Guardian*, Obituary,
1977]

CLARE, John (1793–1864)
And what is Life? – an hour
glass on the run
A mist retreating from the
morning sun
A busy bustling still repeated
dream
Its length? – A moment's
pause, a moment's thought
And happiness? A Bubble on
the stream

That in the act of seizing
shrinks to nought.
['What is Life?' (1820)]

If life had a second edition,
how I would correct the
proofs.
[Letter to a friend]

COCTEAU, Jean (1889–1963)
Life is falling sideways.
[*Opium* (1930)]

CONRAN, Shirley (1932–)
Life is too short to stuff a
mushroom.
[*Superwoman* (1975)]

CORY, William (1823–1892)
You promise heavens free
from strife,
Pure truth, and perfect change
of will;
But sweet, sweet is this
human life,
So sweet, I fain would breathe
it still;
Your chilly stars I can forgo,
This warm kind world is all I
know.
['Mimnermus in Church' (1858)]

**COUBERTIN, Pierre de
(1863–1937)**
The most important thing in
life is not the winning but the
taking part . . . The essential
thing is not conquering but
fighting well.
[Speech, 1908]

CROWFOOT (1821–1890)
What is life? It is the flash of a firefly in the night. It is the breath of a buffalo in the wintertime. It is the little shadow which runs across the grass and loses itself in the sunset.
[Last words]

DAVIES, William Henry (1871–1940)
What is this life if, full of care,
We have no time to stand and stare?
[Songs of Joy (1911)]

DISRAELI, Benjamin (1804–1881)
Next to knowing when to seize an opportunity, the most important thing in life is to know when to forego an advantage.
[Attr.]

EINSTEIN, Albert (1879–1955)
Only a life lived for others is a life worthwhile.
['Defining Success']

EMERSON, Ralph Waldo (1803–1882)
Life is good only when it is magical and musical, a perfect timing and consent, and when we do not anatomize it. You must treat the days respectfully, you must be a day yourself, and not interrogate it like

a college professor . . . You must hear the bird's song without attempting to render it into nouns and verbs.
[Society and Solitude (1870)]

FRANKLIN, Benjamin (1706–1790)
Dost thou love life? Then do not squander time, for that's the stuff life is made of.
[Poor Richard's Almanac (1746)]

GAY, John (1685–1732)
Life is a jest; and all things show it.
I thought so once; but now I know it.
['My Own Epitaph' (1720)]

GORDON, Adam Lindsay (1833–1870)
Life is mostly froth and bubble,
Two things stand like stone,
Kindness in another's trouble,
Courage in your own.
[Ye Wearie Wayfarer (1866)]

HERBERT, Sir A.P. (1890–1971)
It may be life, but ain't it slow?
['It May Be Life' (1926)]

HOBBES, Thomas (1588–1679)
No arts; no letters; no society; and which is worst of all, con-

continual fear, and danger of violent death; and the life of man, solitary, poor, nasty, brutish, and short.

[*Leviathan* (1651)]

HUBBARD, Elbert (1856–1915)
Life is just one damned thing after another.

[*Philistine*, 1909]

HUXLEY, Aldous (1894–1963)
Most of one's life . . . is one prolonged effort to prevent oneself thinking.

[*Mortal Coils* (1922)]

JAMES, Henry (1843–1916)
Live all you can; it's a mistake not to. It doesn't so much matter what you do in particular, so long as you have your life. If you haven't had that then what *have* you had?

[*The Ambassadors* (1903)]

JEANS, Sir James Hopwood (1877–1946)
Life exists in the universe only because the carbon atom possesses certain exceptional properties.

[*The Mysterious Universe* (1930)]

JOHNSON, Samuel (1709–1784)
The love of life is necessary to the vigorous prosecution of any undertaking.

[*The Rambler* (1750-1752)]

Human life is everywhere a state in which much is to be endured, and little to be enjoyed.

[*Rasselas* (1759)]

JUNG, Carl Gustav (1875–1961)
As far as we are able to understand, the only aim of human existence is to kindle a light in the darkness of mere being.

[*Memories, Dreams, Thoughts* (1962)]

KIERKEGAARD, Søren (1813–1855)
Life can only be understood backwards; but it must be lived forwards.

[*Life*]

LENNON, John (1940–1980)
Life is what happens to you when you're busy making other plans.

['Beautiful Boy', song, 1980]

LEWIS, Sir George Cornewall (1806–1863)
Life would be tolerable but for its amusements.

[In *Dictionary of National Biography*]

LONGFELLOW, Henry Wadsworth (1807–1882)
Lives of great men all remind us

We can make our lives sublime,
And, departing, leave behind
us
Footprints on the sands of
time.
                ['A Psalm of Life' (1838)]

**MANN, Thomas
(1875–1955)**
Man does not only live his
personal life as an individual,
but also, consciously or
unconsciously, the life of his
era and of his contem-
poraries.
        [*The Magic Mountain* (1924)]

**MARTIAL
(c. 40–c. 104)**
Believe me, 'I shall live' is not
the saying of a wise man.
Tomorrow's life is too late:
live today.
                        [*Epigrammata*]

**MAUGHAM, William
Somerset
(1874–1965)**
Life is too short to do anything for oneself that one can
pay others to do for one.
                [*The Summing Up* (1938)]

**MONTAIGNE, Michel de
(1533–1592)**
The value of life does not lie
in the number of years but in
the use you make of them.
                        [*Essais* (1580)]

**NASH, Ogden
(1902–1971)**
When I consider how my life
is spent,
I hardly ever repent.
                ['Reminiscent Reflection'
                                (1931)]

**NIETZSCHE, Friedrich
(1844–1900)**
Believe me! – the secret of
gathering in the greatest fruit-
fulness and the greatest
enjoyment from existence is
living dangerously!
                [*The Gay Science* (1887)]

**O'KEEFFE, Georgia
(1887–1986)**
My feeling about life is a curious kind of triumphant feeling
about seeing it bleak, knowing it is so, and walking into it
fearlessly because one has no
choice.
                                [Attr.]

**O'NEILL, Eugene
(1888–1953)**
Our lives are merely strange
dark interludes in the electric
display of God the Father!
                [*Strange Interlude* (1928)]

**PASCAL, Blaise
(1623–1662)**
The last act is bloody, however delightful the rest of the
play may be.
                        [*Pensées* (1670)]

**RUSSELL, Bertrand
(1872–1970)**
Brief and powerless is Man's
life; on him and all his race
the slow, sure doom falls piti-
less and dark.

[*Mysticism and Logic* (1918)]

**SANTAYANA, George
(1863–1952)**
There is no cure for birth and
death save to enjoy the inter-
val.

[*Soliloquies in England* (1922)]

**SHAKESPEARE, William
(1564–1616)**
All the world's a stage,
And all the men and women
merely players;
They have their exits and their
entrances;
And one man in his time
plays many parts.

[*As You Like It*, II.vii]

Life's but a walking shadow, a
poor player,
That struts and frets his hour
upon the stage,
And then is heard no more; it
is a tale
Told by an idiot, full of sound
and fury,
Signifying nothing.

[*Macbeth*, V.v]

**SHELLEY, Percy Bysshe
(1792–1822)**
Lift not the painted veil which

those who live
Call Life.

['Sonnet' (1818)]

**SMITH, Logan Pearsall
(1865–1946)**
There are two things to aim at
in life: first, to get what you
want; and, after that, to enjoy
it. Only the wisest of mankind
achieve the second.

[*Afterthoughts* (1931)]

SOCRATES (469–399 BC)
The unexamined life is not a
life worth living for a human
being.

[Attr. in Plato, *Apology*]

**STOPPARD, Tom
(1937–)**
Life is a gamble, at terrible
odds — if it was a bet, you
wouldn't take it.

[*Rosencrantz and Guildenstern
Are Dead* (1967)]

**TAYLOR, Bishop Jeremy
(1613–1667)**
As our life is very short, so it
is very miserable, and therefore it is well it is short.

[*The Rule and Exercise of Holy
Dying* (1651)]

**TERENCE
(c. 190–159 BC)**
Where there's life, there's
hope.

[*Heauton Timoroumenos*]

THOREAU, Henry David (1817–1862)
Our life is frittered away by detail . . . Simplify, simplify.
[*Walden* (1854)]

VAUVENARGUES, Marquis de (1715–1747)
In order to achieve great things we must live as though we were never going to die.
[*Réflexions et Maximes* (1746)]

VILLIERS DE L'ISLE-ADAM, Philippe-Auguste (1838–1889)
Live? The servants will do that for us.
[*Axel* (1890)]

WHITEHEAD, A.N. (1861–1947)
It is the essence of life that it exists for its own sake.
[*Nature and Life* (1934)]

WILDE, Oscar (1854–1900)
One can live for years sometimes without living at all, and then all life comes crowding into one single hour.
[*Vera, or The Nihilist* (1880)]

One's real life is so often the life that one does not lead.
['L'Envoi to Rose-Leaf and Apple-Leaf']

WODEHOUSE, P.G. (1881–1975)
I spent the afternoon musing on Life. If you come to think

of it, what a queer thing Life is! So unlike anything else, don't you know, if you see what I mean.
[*My Man Jeeves* (1919)]

See ART; DEATH

LITERATURE

CONNOLLY, Cyril (1903–1974)
Literature is the art of writing something that will be read twice; journalism what will be grasped at once.
[*Enemies of Promise* (1938)]

GOETHE (1749–1832)
National literature does not now have much significance, it is time for the era of world literature.
[*Gespräche mit Eckermann, 1827*]

HELLER, Joseph (1923–)
He knew everything about literature except how to enjoy it.
[*Catch-22* (1961)]

HORACE (65–8 BC)
In serious works and ones that promise great things, one or two purple patches are often stitched in, to glitter far and wide.
[*Ars Poetica*]

INGE, William Ralph (1860–1954)
Literature flourishes best when it is half a trade and half an art.

['The Victorian Age' (1922)]

LEWIS, Sinclair (1885–1951)
Our American professors like their literature clear, cold, pure, and very dead.

[Address to Swedish Academy, 1930]

LODGE, David (1935–)
Literature is mostly about having sex and not much about having children; life is the other way round.

[*The British Museum is Falling Down* (1965)]

LOVER, Samuel (1797–1868)
When once the itch of literature comes over a man, nothing can cure it but the scratching of a pen.

[*Handy Andy* (1842)]

NABOKOV, Vladimir (1899–1977)
Literature and butterflies are the two sweetest passions known to man.

[*Radio Times*, 1962]

NAIPAUL, V.S. (1930–1983)
Literature should be read by people privately. English should be abandoned as a silly course, and all the professors should be put out of a job.

[Attr.]

TWAIN, Mark (1835–1910)
[Definition of a classic] Something that everybody wants to have read and nobody wants to read.

['The Disappearance of Literature']

WILDE, Oscar (1854–1900)
Movement, that problem of the visible arts, can be truly realized by Literature alone. It is Literature that shows us the body in its swiftness and the soul in its unrest.

['The Critic as Artist' (1891)]

YEATS, W.B. (1865–1939)
We have no longer in any country a literature as great as the literature of the old world, and that is because the newspapers, all kinds of second-rate books, the preoccupation of men with all kinds of practical changes, have driven the living imagination out of this world.

['First Principles' (1904)]

See FICTION; POETRY; WRITING

LONELINESS

CONRAD, Joseph (1857–1924)
Who knows what true loneliness is – not the conventional word but the naked terror? To the lonely themselves it wears a mask.

[Attr.]

HAMMARSKJÖLD, Dag (1905–1961)
Pray that your loneliness may spur you into finding something to live for, great enough to die for.

[*Diaries*, 1951]

HUBBARD, Elbert (1856–1915)
Loneliness is to endure the presence of one who does not understand.

[Attr.]

SARTON, May (1912–)
Loneliness is the poverty of self; solitude is the richness of self.

[*Mrs Stevens Hears the Mermaids Singing* (1993)]

See SOLITUDE

LOVE

ANONYMOUS
Western wind, when wilt thou blow,
The small rain down can rain?
Christ, if my love were in my arms
And I in my bed again!

[*New Oxford Book of 16th-Century Verse* (1991)]

ANOUILH, Jean (1910–1987)
Love is, above all else, the gift of oneself.

[*Ardèle ou la Marguerite* (1949)]

AUDEN, W.H. (1907–1973)
When it comes, will it come without warning
Just as I'm picking my nose?
Will it knock on my door in the morning,
Or tread in the bus on my toes?
Will it come like a change in the weather?
Will its greeting be courteous or rough?
Will it alter my life altogether?
O tell me the truth about love.

['Twelve Songs']

AUSTEN, Jane (1775–1817)
All the privilege I claim for my own sex . . . is that of loving longest, when existence or when hope is gone.

[*Persuasion* (1818)]

BALZAC, Honoré de (1799–1850)
It is easier to be a lover than a

LOVE

husband, for the same reason that it is more difficult to show a ready wit all day long than to produce an occasional *bon mot*.

[Attr.]

THE BIBLE (KING JAMES VERSION)

Intreat me not to leave thee, or to return from following after thee: for whither thou goest, I will go; and where thou lodgest, I will lodge: thy people shall be my people, and thy God my God.

[*Ruth*, 1:16–17]

Greater love hath no man than this, that a man lay down his life for his friends.

[*John*, 15:13]

BICKERSTAFFE, Isaac (c. 1733–c. 1808)

Perhaps it was right to dissemble your love,
But – why did you kick me downstairs?

['An Expostulation' (1789)]

BLAKE, William (1757–1827)

Love seeketh not Itself to please,
Nor for itself hath any care.

['The Clod & the Pebble' (1794)]

BRENNAN, Christopher (1870–1932)

My heart was wandering in the sands,
a restless thing, a scorn apart;
Love set his fire in my hands,
I clasped the flame into my heart.

[*Poems* (1914)]

BRIDGES, Robert (1844–1930)

When first we met we did not guess
That Love would prove so hard a master.

['Triolet' (1890)]

BROOKE, Rupert (1887–1915)

I thought when love for you died, I should die.
It's dead. Alone, mostly strangely, I live on.

['The Life Beyond' (1910)]

BROWNING, Elizabeth Barrett (1806–1861)

How do I love thee? Let me count the ways.

[*Sonnets from the Portuguese* (1850)]

BURNS, Robert (1759–1796)

Ae fond kiss, and then we sever!
Ae fareweel, and then forever! . . .

Had we never lov'd sae kindly,
Had we never lov'd sae blindly,
Never met – or never

parted –
We had ne'er been
broken-hearted.
['Ae Fond Kiss' (1791)]

O, my luve's like a red, red,
rose
That's newly sprung in June.
O, my luve's like the melodie,
That's sweetly play'd in tune.
['A Red Red Rose' (1794)]

**BURTON, Robert
(1577-1640)**
No chord, nor cable can so
forcibly draw, or hold so fast,
as love can do with a twined
thread.
[*Anatomy of Melancholy*
(1621)]

BUTLER, Samuel (1612-1680)
For money has a power above
The stars and fate, to manage
love.
[*Hudibras* (1678)]

**BUTLER, Samuel
(1835-1902)**
'Tis better to have loved and
lost than never to have lost at
all.
[*The Way of All Flesh* (1903)]

BYRON, Lord (1788-1824)
In her first passion woman
loves her lover,
In all the others all she loves
is love.
[*Don Juan* (1824)]

**CHAMFORT, Nicolas
(1741-1794)**
Love, as it exists in society, is
nothing more than the
exchange of two fantasies and
the contact of two skins.
[*Maximes et pensées* (1796)]

**CHEVALIER, Maurice
(1888-1972)**
Many a man has fallen in love
with a girl in a light so dim he
would not have chosen a suit
by it.
[Attr.]

**COLMAN, the Elder, George
(1732-1794)**
Love and a cottage! Eh,
Fanny! Ah, give me indifference and a coach and six!
[*The Clandestine Marriage*
(1766)]

**CONGREVE, William
(1670-1729)**
In my conscience I believe the
baggage loves me, for she
never speaks well of me her
self, nor suffers any body else
to rail me.
[*The Old Bachelor* (1693)]

COPE, Wendy (1945–)
2 cures for love
1. Don't see him. Don't phone
or write a letter.
2. The easy way: get to know
him better.
[Attr.]

**DIDEROT, Denis
(1713–1784)**
They say that love takes wit
away from those who have it,
and gives it to those who
have none.
[*Paradoxe sur le Comédien*]

DONNE, John (1572–1631)
Love built on beauty, soon as
beauty dies.
[*Elegies* (c. 1595)]

I wonder by my troth, what
thou, and I
Did, till we lov'd?
[*Songs and Sonnets* (1611)]

**DOUGLAS, Lord Alfred
(1870–1945)**
I am the Love that dare not
speak its name.
['Two Loves' (1896)]

DRYDEN, John (1631–1700)
Pains of love be sweeter far
Than all other pleasures are.
[*Tyrannic Love* (1669)]

**ELLIS, Havelock
(1859–1939)**
Love is friendship plus sex.
[Attr.]

**ETHEREGE, Sir George
(c. 1635–1691)**
When love grows diseased,
the best thing we can do is
put it to a violent death; I cannot endure the torture of a
lingering and consumptive
passion.
[*The Man of Mode* (1676)]

**FARQUHAR, George
(1678–1707)**
Money is the sinews of love,
as of war.
[*Love and a Bottle* (1698)]

**FLETCHER, Phineas
(1582–1650)**
Love is like linen often
chang'd, the sweeter.
[*Sicelides* (1614)]

**FLORIAN, Jean-Pierre Claris
de (1755–1794)**
Love's pleasure only lasts a
moment; love's sorrow lasts
one's whole life long.
['Célestine' (1784)]

FORSTER, E.M. (1879–1970)
Only connect! That was the
whole of her sermon. Only
connect the prose and the
passion, and both will be
exalted, and human love will
be seen at its highest.
[*Howard's End* (1910)]

FRY, Christopher (1907–)
Try thinking of love, or some-
thing.
Amor vincit insomnia.
[*A Sleep of Prisoners* (1951)]

GAY, John (1685–1732)
Then nature rul'd, and love,

devoid of art,
Spoke the consenting language of the heart.
[*Dione* (1720)]

**GOLDSMITH, Oliver
(c. 1728–1774)**
It seemed to me pretty plain, that they had more of love than matrimony in them.
[*The Vicar of Wakefield* (1766)]

GREER, Germaine (1939–)
Love, love, love – all the wretched cant of it, masking egotism, lust, masochism, fantasy under a mythology of sentimental postures, a welter of self induced miseries and joys, blinding and masking the essential personalities in the frozen gestures of courtship, in the kissing and the dating and the desire, the compliments and the quarrels which vivify its barrenness.
[*The Female Eunuch* (1970)]

HARTLEY, L.P. (1895–1972)
Once she had loved her fellow human beings; she did not love them now, she had seen them do too many unpleasant things.
[*Facial Justice* (1960)]

HEWETT, Dorothy (1923–)
My body turns to you as the earth turns.
O for such bitter need you've taken me,
To dub me lover, friend and enemy,
Take neither one can set the other free.
But still there is a loveliness that burns
That burns between us two so tenderly.
['There is a Loveliness that Burns']

HOGG, James (1770–1835)
O, love, love, love!
Love is like a dizziness;
It winna let a poor body
Gang about his biziness!
['Love is Like a Dizziness']

HUDSON, Louise (1958–)
Now I go to films alone watch a silent telephone send myself a valentine whisper softly 'I am mine'.
['Men, Who Needs Them']

KAFKA, Franz (1883–1924)
Love is, that you are the knife which I plunge into myself.
[Letter to Milena Jesenká, 1920]

KEY, Ellen (1849–1926)
Love is moral even without legal marriage, but marriage is immoral without love.
['The Morality of Women' (1911)]

**KING, Bishop Henry
(1592–1669)**
Sleep on, my Love, in thy cold

bed,
Never to be disquieted!
My last good night! Thou wilt
not wake
Till I thy fate shall overtake:
Till age, or grief, or sickness
must
Marry my body to that dust
It so much loves; and fill the
room
My heart keeps empty in thy
tomb.
Stay for me there; I will not
fail
To meet thee in that hollow
vale . . .

But hark! My pulse like a soft
drum
Beats my approach, tells thee
I come.

['Exequy upon his Wife'
(1651)]

LAMARTINE (1790–1869)
Only one being is missing,
and your whole world is
bereft of people.

[*Premières Méditations poé-
tiques* (1820)]

LARKIN, Philip (1922–1985)
What will survive of us is
love.

['An Arundel Tomb' (1964)]

**LA ROCHEFOUCAULD
(1613–1680)**
There are very few people
who are not ashamed of having loved one another once
they have fallen out of love.

[*Maximes* (1678)]

**LINDSAY, Norman
(1879–1969)**
The best love affairs are those
we never had.

[*Bohemians of the Bulletin*
(1965)]

**LOWRY, Malcolm
(1909–1957)**
How alike are the groans of
love to those of the dying.

[*Under the Volcano* (1947)]

**MARLOWE, Christopher
(1564–1593)**
Come live with me, and be my
love,
And we will all the pleasures
prove.

['The Passionate Shepherd to
his Love']

MOLIERE (1622–1673)
One is easily taken in by what
one loves.

[*Tartuffe* (1664)]

O'BRIEN, Edna (1936–)
Oh, shadows of love, inebria-
tions of love, foretastes of
love, trickles of love, but
never yet the one true love.

[*Night* (1972)]

OVID (43 BC–AD 18)
You who seek an end to love,

love will yield to business: be busy, and you will be safe.
[*Remedia Amoris*]

PARKER, Dorothy (1893–1967)
By the time you swear you're his,
Shivering and sighing,
And he vows his passion is
Infinite, undying –
Lady, make a note of this:
One of you is lying.
['Unfortunate Coincidence' (1937)]

PARNELL, Anna (1852–1911)
Two children playing by a stream
Two lovers walking in a dream
A married pair whose dream is o'er,
Two old folks who are quite a bore.
['Love's Four Ages']

PROUST, Marcel (1871–1922)
It is wrong to speak of making a bad choice in love, since as soon as there is choice, it can only be bad.
[*La Fugitive* (1923)]

RACINE, Jean (1639–1699)
Ah, I have loved him too much not to hate him!
[*Andromaque* (1667)]

RUSSELL, Bertrand (1872–1970)
Of all forms of caution, caution in love is perhaps the most fatal to true happiness.
[*Marriage and Morals* (1929)]

SAINT–EXUPERY, Antoine de (1900–1944)
Experience shows us that love is not looking into one another's eyes but looking together in the same direction.
[*Wind, Sand and Stars* (1939)]

SEGAL, Erich (1937–)
Love means never having to say you're sorry.
[*Love Story* (1970)]

SHAKESPEARE, William (1564–1616)
Doubt thou the stars are fire;
Doubt that the sun doth move;
Doubt truth to be a liar;
But never doubt I love.
[*Hamlet*, II.ii]

The course of true love never did run smooth.
[*A Midsummer Night's Dream*, I.i]

Love looks not with the eyes, but with the mind;
And therefore is wing'd Cupid painted blind.
[*A Midsummer Night's Dream*, I.i]

My bounty is as boundless as
the sea,
My love as deep: the more I
give to thee,
The more I have, for both are
infinite.

[*Romeo and Juliet*, II.ii]

If music be the food of love,
play on,
Give me excess of it, that, sur-
feiting,
The appetite may sicken and
so die.

[*Twelfth Night*, I.i]

She never told her love,
But let concealment, like a
worm i' th' bud,
Feed on her damask cheek.
She pin'd in thought;
And with a green and yellow
melancholy
She sat like Patience on a
monument,
Smiling at grief.

[*Twelfth Night*, II.iv]

Love sought is good, but
given unsought is better.

[*Twelfth Night*, III.i]

Let me not to the marriage of
true minds
Admit impediments. Love is
not love
Which alters when it alter-
ation finds,
Or bends with the remover to
remove.

[Sonnet 116]

When my love swears that
she is made of truth,
I do believe her, though I
know she lies.

[Sonnet 138]

**SHAW, George Bernard
(1856–1950)**
The fickleness of the women I
love is only equalled by the
infernal constancy of the
women who love me.

[*The Philanderer* (1898)]

**SHELLEY, Percy Bysshe
(1792–1822)**
Familiar acts are beautiful
through love.

[*Prometheus Unbound* (1820)]

**TENNYSON, Alfred, Lord
(1809–1892)**
In the Spring a young man's
fancy lightly turns to thoughts
of love.

['Locksley Hall' (1838)]

'Tis better to have loved and
lost
Than never to have loved at
all.

[*In Memoriam A. H. H.* (1850)]

To love one maiden only,
cleave to her,
And worship her by years of
noble deeds,
Until they won her; for indeed
I knew
Of no more subtle master

under heaven
Than is the maiden passion
for a maid,
Not only to keep down the
base in man,
But teach high thought, and
amiable words
And courtliness, and the
desire of fame,
And love of truth, and all that
makes a man.
[*The Idylls of the King*]

TIBULLUS
(c. 54–19 BC)
May I be looking at you when
my last hour has come, and
as I die may I hold you with
my weakening hand.
[*Elegies*]

TOLSTOY, Leo
(1828–1910)
Love is God, and when I die it
means that I, a particle of
love, shall return to the
general and eternal source.
[*War and Peace* (1869)]

TROLLOPE, Anthony
(1815–1882)
Love is like any other luxury.
You have no right to it unless
you can afford it.
[*The Way We Live Now* (1875)]

WILCOX, Ella Wheeler
(1850–1919)
We flatter those we scarcely
know,

We please the fleeting guest,
And deal full many a thought-
less blow
To those who love us best.
['Life's Scars' (1917)]

WILDE, Oscar
(1854–1900)
Yet each man kills the thing
he loves,
By each let this be heard,
Some do it with a bitter look,
Some with a flattering word,
The coward does it with a
kiss,
The brave man with a sword!
[*The Ballad of Reading Gaol*
(1898)]

WYCHERLEY, William
(c. 1640–1716)
A mistress should be like a little country retreat near the
town, not to dwell in constantly, but only for a night
and away.
[*The Country Wife* (1675)]

YEATS, W.B.
(1865–1939)
A pity beyond all telling
Is hid in the heart of love.
['The Pity of Love' (1892)]

**See FRIENDSHIP; MAR-
RIAGE; SEPARATION**

MADNESS

**BECKETT, Samuel
(1906–1989)**
We are all born mad. Some
remain so.
[*Waiting for Godot* (1955)]

**BEERBOHM, Sir Max
(1872–1956)**
Only the insane take themselves quite seriously.
[Attr.]

**CHESTERTON, G.K.
(1874–1936)**
The madman is not the man
who has lost his reason. The
madman is the man who has
lost everything except his reason.
[*Orthodoxy* (1908)]

**DAVIES, Scrope Berdmore
(c.1783–1852)**
Babylon in all its desolation is
a sight not so awful as that of
the human mind in ruins.
[Letter to Thomas Raikes,
1835]

**DRYDEN, John
(1631–1700)**
Great wits are sure to madness near alli'd,
And thin partitions do their
bounds divide.
[*Absalom and Achitophel*
(1681)]

EURIPIDES (c. 485–406 BC)
Whom God wishes to destroy,
he first makes mad.
[Fragment]

GINSBERG, Allen (1926–1997)
I saw the best minds of my
generation destroyed by
madness, starving hysterical
naked.
[*Howl* (1956)]

GREENE, Graham (1904–1991)
Innocence is a kind of
insanity.
[*The Quiet American* (1955)]

HELLER, Joseph (1923–)
Orr was crazy and could be
grounded. All he had to do
was ask; and as soon as he
did, he would no longer be
crazy and would have to fly
more missions . . . Yossarian
was moved very deeply by the
absolute simplicity of this
clause of Catch-22 and let out
a respectful whistle.
[*Catch-22* (1961)]

JUNG, Carl Gustav (1875–1961)
Show me a sane man and I
will cure him for you.
[*The Observer*, 1975]

**KIPLING, Rudyard
(1865–1936)**
The mad all are in God's
keeping.
[*Kim* (1901)]

KYD, Thomas (1558–1594)
I am never better than when I am mad. Then methinks I am a brave fellow; then I do wonders. But reason abuseth me, and there's the torment, there's the hell.
[*The Spanish Tragedy* (1592)]

LAING, R.D. (1927–1989)
Schizophrenia cannot be understood without understanding despair.
[*The Divided Self* (1960)]

Madness need not be all breakdown. It may also be break-through. It is potential liberation and renewal as well as enslavement and existential death.
[*The Politics of Experience* (1967)]

LEE, Nathaniel (c. 1653–1692)
[Objecting to being confined in Bedlam]
They called me mad, and I called them mad, and damn them, they outvoted me.
[In Porter, *A Social History of Madness*]

PROUST, Marcel (1871–1922)
Everything great in the world is done by neurotics; they alone founded our religions and composed our masterpieces.
[*Le Côté de Guermantes* (1921)]

SHAKESPEARE, William (1564–1616)
And he repelled, a short tale to make,
Fell into a sadness, then into a fast,
Thence to a watch, thence into a weakness,
Thence to a lightness, and, by this declension,
Into the madness wherein now he raves
And all we mourn for.
[*Hamlet*, II.ii]

O, what a noble mind is here o'erthrown!
The courtier's, soldier's, scholar's, eye, tongue, sword;
Th' expectancy and rose of the fair state,
The glass of fashion and the mould of form,
Th' observ'd of all observers – quite, quite down!
[*Hamlet*, III.i]

O, let me not be mad, not mad, sweet heaven!
Keep me in temper; I would not be mad!
[*King Lear*, I.v]

SZASZ, Thomas (1920–)
Psychiatrists classify a person as neurotic if he suffers from his problems in living, and a psychotic if he makes others suffer.
[*The Second Sin* (1973)]

If you talk to God, you are praying; if God talks to you, you have schizophrenia. If the dead talk to you, you are a spiritualist; if God talks to you, you are a schizophrenic.
[*The Second Sin* (1973)]

VOLTAIRE (1694–1778)
Men will always be mad and those who think they can cure them are the maddest of all.
[Letter, 1762]

MANNERS

BRADBURY, Malcolm (1932–)
The English are polite by telling lies. The Americans are polite by telling the truth.
[*Stepping Westward* (1965)]

EASTMAN, Max (1883–1969)
[On chivalry]
It is but the courteous exterior of a bigot.
[*Woman Suffrage and Sentiment*]

EMERSON, Ralph Waldo (1803–1882)
Good manners are made up of petty sacrifices.
['Social Aims' (1875)]

JARRELL, Randall (1914–1965)
To Americans English manners are far more frightening than none at all.
[*Pictures from an Institution* (1954)]

LOUIS XVIII (1755–1824)
Punctuality is the politeness of kings.
[Attr.]

STERNE, Laurence (1713–1768)
Hail ye small sweet courtesies of life.
[*A Sentimental Journey* (1768)]

THEROUX, Paul (1941–)
The Japanese have perfected good manners and made them indistinguishable from rudeness.
[*The Great Railway Bazaar* (1975)]

TWAIN, Mark (1835–1910)
Good breeding consists in concealing how much we think of ourselves and how little we think of other persons.
[*Notebooks* (1935)]

WAUGH, Evelyn (1903–1966)
Manners are especially the need of the plain. The pretty can get away with anything.
[*The Observer*, 1962]

**WILLIAM OF WYKEHAM
(1324–1404)**
Manners maketh man.

[Attr.]

MARRIAGE

**ALBERT, Prince Consort
(1819–1861)**
Tomorrow our marriage will
be 21 years old! How many a
storm has swept over it and
still it continues green and
fresh and throws out vigorous
roots.

[Attr.]

**ASQUITH, Margot
(1864–1945)**
To marry a man out of pity is
folly; and, if you think you are
going to influence the kind of
fellow who has 'never had a
chance, poor devil,' you are
profoundly mistaken. One can
only influence the strong
characters in life, not the
weak; and it is the height of
vanity to suppose that you
can make an honest man of
anyone.

[*The Autobiography of Margot
Asquith* (1920)]

**BACON, Francis
(1561–1626)**
He that hath wife and children, hath given hostages to
fortune; for they are impediments to great enterprises,
either of virtue or mischief.

['Of Marriage and Single Life'
(1625)]

Wives are young men's mistresses, companions for middle age, and old men's nurses.

['Of Marriage and Single Life'
(1625)]

**BENNETT, Arnold
(1867–1931)**
Being a husband is a whole-
time job. That is why so many
husbands fail. They cannot
give their entire attention to
it.

[*The Title* (1918)]

**THE BIBLE (KING JAMES
VERSION)**
Therefore shall a man leave
his father and his mother, and
shall cleave unto his wife: and
they shall be one flesh.

[*Genesis*, 2:24]

**BLACKSTONE, Sir William
(1723–1780)**
Husband and wife are one,
and that one is the husband.

[In Miles, *The Women's History
of the World* (1988)]

**BURTON, Robert
(1577–1640)**
One was never married, and
that's his hell; another is, and

that's his plague.
[*Anatomy of Melancholy* (1621)]

BYRON, Lord
(1788–1824)
Though women are angels,
yet wedlock's the devil.
['To Eliza' (1806)]

CHAUCER, Geoffrey
(c. 1340–1400)
Experience, though noon
auctoritee
Were in this world, is right
ynogh for me
To speke of wo that is in
mariage.
[*The Canterbury Tales* (1387)]

COLERIDGE, Samuel Taylor
(1772–1834)
The most happy marriage I
can picture or imagine to
myself would be union of a
deaf man to a blind woman.
[In Allsop, *Recollections*
(1836)]

DISRAELI, Benjamin
(1804–1881)
Marriage is the greatest
earthly happiness when founded on complete sympathy.
[Letter to Gladstone]

FARQUHAR, George
(1678–1707)
It is a maxim that man and
wife should never have it in
their power to hang one
another.
[*The Beaux' Stratagem* (1707)]

GABOR, Zsa-Zsa (1919–)
Husbands are like fires. They
go out when unattended.
[*Newsweek*, 1960]

GOLDSMITH, Oliver
(c. 1728–1774)
I . . . chose my wife as she did
her wedding gown, not for a
fine glossy surface, but such
qualities as would wear well.
[*The Vicar of Wakefield* (1766)]

HERBERT, Sir A.P.
(1890–1971)
The critical period in matri-
mony is breakfast-time.
[*Uncommon Law* (1935)]

HUME, David (1711–1776)
I shall tell the women what it
is our sex complains of in the
married state; and if they be
disposed to satisfy us in this
particular, all the other difficulties will easily be accom-
modated. If I be not mistaken,
'tis their love of dominion.
[*Essays, Moral, Political and
Literary* (1742)]

JOHNSON, Samuel
(1709–1784)
Marriage has many pains, but
celibacy has no pleasures.
[*Rasselas* (1759)]

A gentleman who had been very unhappy in marriage married immediately after his wife died. Dr Johnson said, it was the triumph of hope over experience.
[In Boswell, *The Life of Samuel Johnson* (1791)]

Marriages would in general be as happy, and often more so, if they were all made by the Lord Chancellor . . . without the parties having any choice in the matter.
[In Boswell, *The Life of Samuel Johnson* (1791)]

KEATS, John (1795–1821)
The roaring of the wind is my wife and the Stars through the window pane are my Children.
[Letter, 1818]

LAMB, Charles (1775–1834)
Nothing to me is more distasteful than that entire complacency and satisfaction which beam in the countenance of a new-married couple.
[*Essays of Elia* (1823)]

MACNEICE, Louis (1907–1963)
So they were married – to be the more together –
And found they were never again so much together,
Divided by the morning tea,
By the evening paper,
By children and tradesmen's bills.
['Les Sylphides' (1941)]

MILL, John Stuart (1806–1873)
The moral regeneration of mankind will only really commence, when the most fundamental of the social relations [marriage] is placed under the rule of equal justice, and when human beings learn to cultivate their strongest sympathy with an equal in rights and cultivation.
[*The Subjection of Women* (1869)]

MILTON, John (1608–1674)
Flesh of Flesh,
Bone of my Bone thou art, and from thy State
Mine never shall be parted, weal or woe.
[*Paradise Lost* (1667)]

SAIKAKU, Ihara (1642–1693)
And why do people wilfully exhaust their strength in promiscuous living, when their wives are on hand from bridal night till old age – to be taken when required, like fish from a private pond.
[*The Japanese Family Storehouse* (1688)]

SAKI (1870–1916)
The Western custom of one wife and hardly any mistresses.

[*Reginald in Russia* (1910)]

SHAKESPEARE, William (1564–1616)
Let me give light, but let me not be light,
For a light wife doth make a heavy husband.

[*The Merchant of Venice*, V.i]

Thy husband is thy lord, thy life, thy keeper,
Thy head, thy sovereign; one that cares for thee,
And for thy maintenance commits his body
To painful labour both by sea and land.

[*The Taming of the Shrew*, V.ii]

SHERIDAN, Richard Brinsley (1751–1816)
'Tis safest in matrimony to begin with a little aversion.

[*The Rivals* (1775)]

STEVENSON, Robert Louis (1850–1894)
Even if we take matrimony at its lowest, even if we regard it as no more than a sort of friendship recognized by the police.

[*Virginibus Puerisque* (1881)]

Times are changed with him who marries; there are no more by-path meadows, where you may innocently linger, but the road lies long and straight and dusty to the grave.

[*Virginibus Puerisque* (1881)]

TAYLOR, Bishop Jeremy (1613–1667)
He that loves not his wife and children, feeds a lioness at home and broods a nest of sorrows.

[*XXV Sermons Preached at Golden Grove* (1653)]

WALES, Princess of (1961–)
[Referring to the Prince of Wales' relationship with Camilla Parker-Bowles]
There were three of us in this marriage, so it was a bit crowded.

[BBC television interview, 1995]

WELDON, Fay (1931–)
. . . the great wonderful construct which is marriage – a construct made up of a hundred little kindnesses, a thousand little bitings back of spite, tens of thousands of minor actions of good intent – this must not, as an institution, be brought down in ruins.

[*Splitting* (1995)]

WILDE, Oscar (1854–1900)
The real drawback to marriage is that it makes one unselfish. And unselfish people are colourless.
[*The Picture of Dorian Gray* (1891)]

Twenty years of romance make a woman look like a ruin; but twenty years of marriage make her something like a public building.
[*A Woman of No Importance* (1893)]

I am not in favour of long engagements. They give people the opportunity of finding out each other's character before marriage, which I think is never advisable.
[*The Importance of Being Earnest* (1895)]

WODEHOUSE, P.G. (1881–1975)
All the unhappy marriages come from the husbands having brains. What good are brains to a man? They only unsettle him.
[*The Adventures of Sally* (1920)]

Like so many substantial Americans, he had married young and kept on marrying, springing from blonde to blonde like the chamois of the Alps leaping from crag to crag.
[In Usborne, *Wodehouse at Work to the End* (1976)]

See LOVE

THE MEDIA

BJELKE-PETERSEN, Sir Johannes (1911–)
The greatest thing that could happen to the state and the nation is when we can get rid of all the media. Then we could live in peace and tranquillity, and no one would know anything.
[*The Spectator,* 1987]

CHOMSKY, Noam (1928–)
The Internet is an élite organization; most of the population of the world has never even made a phone call.
[*The Observer Review,* 1996]

HOWARD, Philip (1933–)
The proliferation of radio and television channels has produced a wilderness of cave-dwellers instead of the promised global village.
[*The Times,* 1992]

JACKSON, Robert (1946–)
To have open government you need mature media. It is more

difficult for people to discuss complex issues than it used to be because of the destructive power of the tabloids. The TV sound bite also makes it impossible to communicate complex arguments. It is all black and white, cut and dried, yaa-boo.
[*Independent on Sunday,* 1994]

MURDOCH, Rupert (1931–)
Monopoly is a terrible thing, till you have it.
[*The New Yorker,* 1979]

WHITLAM, Gough (1916–)
Quite small and ineffectual demonstrations can be made to look like the beginnings of a revolution if the cameraman is in the right place at the right time.
[*A Dictionary of Contemporary Quotations* (1982)]

See NEWS; TELEVISION

MEDICINE

THE BIBLE (KING JAMES VERSION)
Physician, heal thyself.
[*Luke,* 4:23]

CHEKHOV, Anton (1860–1904)
Medicine is my lawful wife but literature is my mistress.

When I'm bored with one, I spend the night with the other.
[Letter to Suvorin, 1888]

FLETCHER, John (1579–1625)
I find the medicine worse than the malady.
[*The Lover's Progress* (1623)]

FRANKLIN, Benjamin (1706–1790)
He's the best physician that knows the worthlessness of the most medicines.
[*Poor Richard's Almanac* (1733)]

GOLDWYN, Samuel (1882–1974)
Any man who goes to a psychiatrist should have his head examined.
[In Zierold, *Moguls* (1969)]

HAHNEMANN, C.F.S. (1755–1843)
Like cures like.
[Motto of homeopathic medicine]

HIPPOCRATES (c. 460–357 BC)
[Of medicine]
Life is short, science is so long to learn, opportunity is elusive, experience is dangerous, judgement is difficult.
[*Aphorisms* (c. 415 BC); often quoted as *Ars longa, vita brevis*]

**LOOS, Anita
(1893–1981)**
So then Dr Froyd said that all I needed was to cultivate a few inhibitions and get some sleep.
[*Gentlemen Prefer Blondes* (1925)]

**MCLUHAN, Marshall
(1911–1980)**
If the nineteenth century was the age of the editorial chair, ours is the century of the psychiatrist's couch.
[*Understanding Media* (1964)]

**QUARLES, Francis
(1592–1644)**
Physicians of all men are most happy; what good success soever they have, the world proclaimeth, and what faults they commit, the earth covereth.
[*Hieroglyphics of the Life of Man* (1638)]

**SHAW, George Bernard
(1856–1950)**
Optimistic lies have such immense therapeutic value that a doctor who cannot tell them convincingly has mistaken his profession.
[*Misalliance* (1914)]

**STOCKWOOD, Mervyn
(1913–)**
A psychiatrist is a man who goes to the Folies-Bergère and looks at the audience.
[*The Observer,* 1961]

SZASZ, Thomas (1920–)
Formerly, when religion was strong and science weak, men mistook magic for medicine, now, when science is strong and religion weak, men mistake medicine for magic.
[*The Second Sin* (1973)]

**WILLIAMS, Tennessee
(1911–1983)**
[On why he no longer saw his psychoanalyst]
He was meddling too much in my private life.
[Attr.]

See HEALTH; ILLNESS

MEMORY

**APOLLINAIRE, Guillaume
(1880–1918)**
Memories are hunting horns whose sound dies away in the wind.
['Cors de Chasse' (1913)]

**ARNOLD, Matthew
(1822–1888)**
And we forget because we must
And not because we will.
['Absence' (1852)]

**BRODSKY, Joseph
(1940–1996)**
What memory has in common
with art is the knack for selection, the taste for detail . . .
More than anything, memory
resembles a library in alphabetical disorder, and with no
collected works by anyone.
['In a Room and a Half' (1986)]

**CAMPBELL, Thomas
(1777–1844)**
To live in hearts we leave
behind
Is not to die.
['Hallowed Ground']

**DISRAELI, Benjamin
(1804–1881)**
Nobody is forgotten when it is
convenient to remember him.
[Attr.]

**LA ROCHEFOUCAULD
(1613–1680)**
Everyone complains of his
memory; nobody of his judgment.
[*Maximes* (1678)]

**SCHOPENHAUER, Arthur
(1788–1860)**
To expect a man to retain
everything that he has ever
read is like expecting him to
carry about in his body everything that he has ever eaten.
[*Parerga and Paralipomena*
(1851)]

**SHAW, George Bernard
(1856–1950)**
Reminiscences make one feel
so deliciously aged and sad.
[*The Irrational Knot* (1905)]

MEN

**BOMBECK, Erma
(1927–1996)**
What's wrong with you men?
Would hair stop growing on
your chest if you asked direc-
tions somewhere?
[*When You Look Like Your
Passport Photo, It's Time to Go
Home* (1991)]

**CONNOLLY, Cyril
(1903–1974)**
The true index of a man's
character is the health of his
wife.
[*The Unquiet Grave* (1944)]

COPE, Wendy (1945–)
There are so many kinds of
awful men –
One can't avoid them all. She
often said
She'd never make the same
mistake again:
She always made a new mis-
take instead.
['Rondeau Redoublé' (1986)]

DRYDEN, John (1631–1700)
Men are but children of a

larger growth;
Our appetites as apt to
change as theirs,
And full as craving too, and
full as vain.

[*All for Love* (1678)]

EMERSON, Ralph Waldo
Men are what their mothers
made them.

[*The Conduct of Life* (1860)]

FORD, Anna (1945–)
It is men who face the biggest
problems in the future, adjust-
ing to their new and complicated role.

[Remark, 1981]

FRENCH, Marilyn (1929–)
Whatever they may be in public life, whatever their relations with men, in their relations with women, all men
are rapists, and that's all they
are. They rape us with their
eyes, their laws and their
codes.

[*The Women's Room* (1977)]

FRIEDAN, Betty (1921–)
Men weren't really the enemy
– they were fellow victims suffering from an outmoded
masculine mystique that
made them feel unnecessarily
inadequate when there were
no bears to kill.

[*Christian Science Monitor*,
1974)]

**GABOR, Zsa-Zsa
(1919–)**
Never despise what it says in
the women's magazines: it
may not be subtle but neither
are men.

[*The Observer*, 1976]

HALL, Jerry (1956–)
My mother said it was simple
to keep a man, you must be a
maid in the living room, a
cook in the kitchen and a
whore in the bedroom. I said
I'd hire the other two and take
care of the bedroom bit.

[*The Observer*, 1985]

**HILL, Reginald
(1936–)**
He created a man who was
hard of head, blunt of speech,
knew which side his bread
was buttered on, and above
all took no notice of women.
Then God sent him forth to
multiply in Yorkshire.

[*Pictures of Perfection* (1994)]

**KEILLOR, Garrison
(1942–)**
Years ago, manhood was an
opportunity for achievement,
and now it is a problem to be
overcome.

[*The Book of Guys* (1994)]

**KENNEDY, Florynce R.
(1916–)**
If men could get pregnant,

abortion would be a sacrament.

[In Steinem, *The Verbal Karate of Florynce R. Kennedy, Esq.* (1973)]

MARX, Groucho (1895–1977)
A man is only as old as the woman he feels.

[Attr.]

MENCKEN, H.L. (1880–1956)
Men have a much better time of it than women. For one thing, they marry later. For another thing, they die earlier.

[*A Mencken Chrestomathy* (1949)]

NORRIS, Kathleen (1880–1966)
There are men I could spend eternity with. But not this life.

[*The Middle of the World* (1981)]

PALACIO VALDÉS, Armando (1853–1938)
When a man stops being a god for his wife, he can be sure that he's now less than a man.

[*Doctor Angélico's Papers* (1911)]

SEVIGNE, Mme de (1626–1696)
The more I see of men, the

more I admire dogs.

[Attr.]

WEST, Mae (1892–1980)
A man in the house is worth two in the street.

[*Belle of the Nineties*, film, 1934]

WEST, Dame Rebecca (1892–1983)
[Defining an anti-feminist]
The man who is convinced that his mother was a fool.

[*The Clarion*]

WHITEHORN, Katherine (1926–)
No nice men are good at getting taxis.

[*The Observer*, 1977]

MEN AND WOMEN

BURCHILL, Julie (1960–)
Men have charisma; women have vital statistics.

[*Sex and Sensibility* (1992)]

BYRON, Lord (1788–1824)
Man's love is of man's life a thing apart,
'Tis woman's whole existence.

[*Don Juan* (1824)]

The more I see of men, the less I like them. If I could but

say so of women too, all
would be well.

[*Journal*, 1814]

COLERIDGE, Samuel Taylor (1772–1834)

The man's desire is for the
woman; but the woman's
desire is rarely other than for
the desire of the man.

[*Table Talk* (1835)]

DAVIES, Robertson (1913–1995)

Women tell men things that
men are not very likely to find
out for themselves.

[In J. Madison Davis,
*Conversations with Robertson
Davies* (1989)]

DIETRICH, Marlene (1901–1992)

The average man is more
interested in a woman who is
interested in him than he is in
a woman – any woman – with
beautiful legs.

[News item, 1954]

Most women set out to try to
change a man, and when they
have changed him they do not
like him.

[Attr.]

EBNER–ESCHENBACH, Marie von (1830–1916)

A clever woman has millions

of born enemies – all stupid
men.

[*Aphorisms* (1880)]

ELIOT, George (1819–1880)

I'm not denyin' the women
are foolish: God Almighty
made 'em to match the men.

[*Adam Bede* (1859)]

GAY, John (1685–1732)

Man may escape from rope
and gun;
Nay, some have out-liv'd the
doctor's pill;
Who takes a woman must be
undone,
That basilisk is sure to kill.

[*The Beggar's Opera* (1728)]

KIPLING, Rudyard (1865–1936)

Open and obvious devotion
from any sort of man is
always pleasant to any sort of
woman.

[*Plain Tales from the Hills*
(1888)

LAVER, James (1899–1975)

Man in every age has created
woman in the image of his
own desire.

[In Neustater, *Hyenas in
Petticoats* (1989)]

LERNER, Alan Jay (1918–1986)

Why can't a woman be more

like a man?
Men are so honest, so thoroughly square;
Eternally noble, historically fair.

[*My Fair Lady* (1956)]

MEAD, Margaret (1901–1978)
Women want mediocre men, and men are working to be as mediocre as possible.

[*Quote Magazine*, 1958]

MENCKEN, H.L. (1880–1956)
Women hate revolutions and revolutionists. They like men who are docile, and well-regarded at the bank, and never late at meals.

[*Prejudices* (1922)]

POPE, Alexander (1688–1744)
Men, some to business, some to pleasure take;
But every Woman is at heart a rake:
Men, some to quiet, some to public strife;
But every lady would be queen for life.

['Epistle to a Lady' (1735)]

RAMEY, Estelle (1917–)
More and more it appears that, biologically, men are designed for short, brutal lives and women for long miserable ones.

[*The Observer*, 1985]

RHONDDA, Viscountess (1883–1958)
Women must come off the pedestal. Men put us up there to get us out of the way.

[*The Observer*, 1920]

SCHREINER, Olive (1855–1920)
It is delightful to be a woman; but every man thanks the Lord devoutly that he isn't one.

[*The Story of an African Farm* (1884)]

STEINEM, Gloria (1934–)
A woman needs a man like a fish needs a bicycle.

[Attr.]

TENNYSON, Alfred, Lord (1809–1892)
Man for the field and woman for the hearth:
Man for the sword and for the needle she:
Man with the head and woman with the heart:
Man to command and woman to obey;
All else confusion.

[*The Princess* (1847)]

WEST, Mae (1892–1980)
When women go wrong, men go right after them.

[In Weintraub, *The Wit and Wisdom of Mae West* (1967)]

WILDE, Oscar (1854–1900)
All women become like their mothers. That is their tragedy. No man does. That's his.
[*The Importance of Being Earnest* (1895)]

WODDIS, Roger
Men play the game; women know the score.
[*The Observer*, 1982]

WOOLF, Virginia (1882–1941)
Women have served all these centuries as looking-glasses possessing the magic and delicious power of reflecting the figure of man at twice its natural size.
[*A Room of One's Own* (1929)]

See FEMINISM; WOMEN

THE MIND

BRADLEY, F.H. (1846–1924)
His mind is open; yes, it is so open that nothing is retained; ideas simply pass through him.
[Attr.]

DOSTOEVSKY, Fyodor (1821–1881)
The mind is a tool, a machine, moved by spiritual fire.
[Letter to his brother, 1838]

DYER, Sir Edward (c. 1540–1607)
My mind to me a kingdom is,
Such present joys therein I find,
That it excels all other bliss
That earth affords or grows by kind.
Though much I want which most would have,
Yet still my mind forbids to crave.
['In praise of a contented mind' (1588). Attr.]

LA ROCHEFOUCAULD (1613–1680)
The mind is always fooled by the heart.
[*Maximes* (1678)]

WALPOLE, Horace (1717–1797)
When people will not weed their own minds, they are apt to be overrun with nettles.
[Letter to the Countess of Ailesbury, 1779]

WELCH, Raquel (1940–)
The mind can also be an erogenous zone.
[Attr.]

See IDEAS; THOUGHT

MODESTY

BARRIE, Sir J.M. (1860–1937)
I'm a second eleven sort of chap.
[*The Admirable Crichton* (1902)]

CHURCHILL, Sir Winston (1874–1965)
[Of Clement Attlee]
He is a modest man who has a good deal to be modest about.
[*In Chicago Sunday Tribune Magazine of Books,* 1954]

CONGREVE, William (1670–1729)
Ah! Madam, . . . you know every thing in the world but your perfections, and you only know not those, because 'tis the top of perfection not to know them.
[*Incognita* (1692)]

GILBERT, W.S. (1836–1911)
Wherever valour true is found, True modesty will there abound.
[*The Yeoman of the Guard* (1888)]

STEELE, Sir Richard (1672–1729)
These Ladies of irresistible Modesty are those who make Virtue unamiable.
[*The Tatler,* 1710]

MONEY AND WEALTH

ASTOR, John Jacob (1763–1848)
A man who has a million dollars is as well off as if he were rich.
[Attr.]

BACON, Francis (1561–1626)
And money is like muck, not good except it be spread.
['Of Seditions and Troubles' (1625)]

BEHN, Aphra (1640–1689)
Money speaks sense in a language all nations understand.
[*The Rover* (1677)]

BENCHLEY, Robert (1889–1945)
[On being told his request for a loan had been granted]
I don't trust a bank that would lend money to such a poor risk.
[Attr.]

THE BIBLE (KING JAMES VERSION)
The love of money is the root of all evil.
[*I Timothy,* 6:10]

BRENAN, Gerald (1894–1987)
Those who have some means

think that the most important thing in the world is love. The poor know that it is money.

[*Thoughts in a Dry Season* (1978)]

BURKE, Edmund (1729–1797)
If we command our wealth, we shall be rich and free: if our wealth commands us, we are poor indeed.

[*Attr.*]

BUTLER, Samuel (1835–1902)
It has been said that the love of money is the root of all evil. The want of money is so quite as truly.

[*Erewhon* (1872)]

CARNEGIE, Andrew (1835–1919)
Surplus wealth is a sacred trust which its possessor is bound to administer in his lifetime for the good of the community.

[*The Gospel of Wealth*]

DENNIS, Nigel (1912–1989)
But then one is always excited by descriptions of money changing hands. It's much more fundamental than sex.

[*Cards of Identity* (1955)]

FRANCE, Anatole (1844–1924)
In every well-governed state, wealth is a sacred thing; in democracies it is the only sacred thing.

[*Penguin Island* (1908)]

GALBRAITH, J.K. (1908–)
Money differs from an automobile, a mistress or cancer in being equally important to those who have it and those who do not.

[*Attr.*]

GETTY, J. Paul (1892–1976)
If you can actually count your money you are not really a rich man.

[In A. Barrow, *Gossip*]

GREGORY, Lady Isabella (1852–1932)
It's a good thing to be able to take up your money in your hand and to think no more of it when it slips away from you than you would of a trout that would slip back into the stream.

[*Twenty-Five*]

HORACE (65–8 BC)
Make money: make it honestly if possible; if not, make it by any means.

[*Epistles*]

HUGHES, Howard (1905–1976)
[Response when called a 'paranoid, deranged million-

aire' by a newspaper]
Goddammit, I'm a *billionaire*.
[Attr.]

HUXLEY, Sir Julian (1887–1975)
We all know how the size of
sums of money appears to
vary in a remarkable way
according as they are being
paid in or paid out.
[*Essays of a Biologist*]

ILLICH, Ivan (1926–)
Man must choose whether to
be rich in things or in the
freedom to use them.
[*Deschooling Society* (1971)]

JOHNSON, Samuel (1709–1784)
You never find people labour-
ing to convince you that you
may live very happily upon a
plentiful fortune.
[In Boswell, *The Life of Samuel
Johnson* (1791)]

LAWRENCE, D.H. (1885–1930)
Money is our madness, our
vast collective madness.
['Money-Madness' (1929)]

MILNE, A.A. (1882–1956)
For one person who dreams
of making fifty thousand
pounds, a hundred people
dream of being left fifty thousand pounds.
[*If I May*]

MORAVIA, Alberto (1907–1990)
But he died as many people
like him could die tomorrow,
running after money, and
believing that there is nothing
but money; then he was suddenly frozen by the fear of
seeing what lies behind
money.
[*Two Women* (1957)]

REINHARDT, Gottfried (1911–)
Money is good for bribing
yourself through the
inconveniences of life.
[In L. Ross, *Picture*]

RUNYON, Damon (1884–1946)
Always try to rub up against
money, for if you rub up
against money long enough,
some of it may rub off on you.
[*Furthermore* (1938)]

SCHOPENHAUER, Arthur (1788–1860)
Wealth is like sea-water; the
more we drink, the thirstier
we become.
[*Parerga and Paralipomena*
(1851)]

SICKERT, Walter (1860–1942)
Nothing knits man to man . . .
like the frequent passage from
hand to hand of cash.
['The Language of Art']

**SMITH, Logan Pearsall
(1865–1946)**
To suppose, as we all suppose, that we could be rich and not behave as the rich behave, is like supposing that we could drink all day and keep absolutely sober.
[*Afterthoughts* (1931)]

**THATCHER, Margaret
(1925–)**
Pennies do not come from heaven. They have to be earned here on earth.
[*The Sunday Telegraph,* 1982]

**TUCKER, Sophie
(1884–1966)**
From birth to eighteen, a girl needs good parents. From eighteen to thirty-five, she needs good looks. From thirty-five to fifty-five, she needs a good personality. From fifty-five on, she needs good cash.
[In Freedland, *Sophie* (1978)]

I've been poor and I've been rich. Rich is better.
[In Cowan, *The Wit of Women*]

**TWAIN, Mark
(1835–1910)**
A banker is a person who lends you his umbrella when the sun is shining and wants it back the minute it rains.
[Attr.]

**WILLIAMS, Tennessee
(1911–1983)**
You can be young without money but you can't be old without it.
[*Cat on a Hot Tin Roof* (1955)]

See INCOME

MORALITY

AYER, A.J. (1910–1989)
No morality can be founded on authority, even if the authority were divine.
[*Essay on Humanism*]

**BRECHT, Bertolt
(1898–1956)**
Feeding your face comes first, then morality.
[*The Threepenny Opera* (1928)]

**HUXLEY, Aldous
(1894–1963)**
The quality of moral behaviour varies in inverse ratio to the number of human beings involved.
[*Grey Eminence* (1941)]

**LAWRENCE, D.H.
(1885–1930)**
Morality which is based on ideas, or on an ideal, is an unmitigated evil.
[*Fantasia of the Unconscious* (1922)]

MACAULAY, Lord (1800–1859)

We know of no spectacle so ridiculous as the British public in one of its periodical fits of morality.

['Moore's *Life of Byron*' (1843)]

RUSSELL, Bertrand (1872–1970)

We have, in fact, two kinds of morality side by side: one which we preach but do not practise, and another which we practise but seldom preach.

[*Sceptical Essays* (1928)]

SHAW, George Bernard (1856–1950)

An Englishman thinks he is moral when he is only uncomfortable.

[*Man and Superman* (1903)]

SPENCER, Herbert (1820–1903)

Absolute morality is the regulation of conduct in such a way that pain shall not be inflicted.

['Prison Ethics' (1891)]

STEVENSON, Robert Louis (1850–1894)

If your morals make you dreary, depend upon it, they are wrong.

[*Across the Plains* (1892)]

WILDE, Oscar (1854–1900)

Morality is simply the attitude we adopt towards people whom we personally dislike.

[*An Ideal Husband* (1895)]

See GOOD AND EVIL; GOODNESS; VIRTUE

MORTALITY

ANONYMOUS

Gaudeamus igitur,
Juvenes dum sumus
Post jucundam juventutem,
Post molestam senectutem,
Nos habebit humus.
Let us be happy while we are young, for after carefree youth and careworn age, the earth will hold us also.

['Gaudeamus Igitur', 13th century]

BEHN, Aphra (1640–1689)

Faith, Sir, we are here today and gone tomorrow.

[*The Lucky Chance* (1687)]

THE BIBLE (KING JAMES VERSION)

All flesh is grass, and all the goodliness thereof is as the flower of the field.

[*Isaiah*, 40:6]

DOWSON, Ernest (1867–1900)

They are not long, the days of

wine and roses;
Out of a misty dream
Our path emerges for a while,
then closes
Within a dream.

['Vitae Summa Brevis Spem
Nos Vetat Incohare Longam'
(1896)]

**HERRICK, Robert
(1591–1674)**
Gather ye Rose-buds while ye
may,
Old Time is still aflying:
And this same flower that
smiles today,
Tomorrow will be dying.

[*Hesperides* (1648)]

HORACE (65–8 BC)
Believe every day that has
dawned is your last.

[*Epistles*]

**MARVELL, Andrew
(1621–1678)**
But at my back I always hear
Time's wingèd chariot
hurrying near.
And yonder all before us lie
Deserts of vast eternity.
Thy beauty shall no more be
found;
Nor, in thy marble vault, shall
sound
My echoing song: then worms
shall try
That long preserved virginity:
And your quaint honour turn
to dust;

And into ashes all my lust.
The grave's a fine and private
place,
But none I think do there
embrace.

['To His Coy Mistress' (1681)]

**MILLAY, Edna St Vincent
(1892–1950)**
After all, my erstwhile dear,
My no longer cherished,
Need we say it was not love,
Just because it perished?

['Passer Mortuus Est' (1921)]

**MONTAIGNE, Michel de
(1533–1592)**
One should always have one's
boots on and be ready to
leave.

[*Essais* (1580)]

MOTHERS

**ALCOTT, Louisa May
(1832–1888)**
What *do* girls do who haven't
any mothers to help them
through their troubles?

[*Little Women* (1868)]

BALLANTYNE, Sheila (1936–)
I acknowledge the cold truth
of her death for perhaps the
first time. She is truly gone,
forever out of reach, and I
have become my own judge.

[*Imaginary Crimes* (1982)]

**BARKER, George
(1913–1991)**
Seismic with laughter,
Gin and chicken helpless in
her Irish hand,
Irresistible as Rabelais, but
most tender for
The lame dogs and hurt birds
that surround her.
['Sonnet: To My Mother'
(1944)]

BARZAN, Gerald
Mother always said that
honesty was the best policy,
and money isn't everything.
She was wrong about other
things too.
[Attr.]

**BOMBECK, Erma
(1927–1996)**
My mother phones daily to
ask, 'Did you just try to reach
me?' When I reply, 'No', she
adds, 'So, if you're not too
busy, call me while I'm still
alive,' and hangs up.
[*The 1992 Erma Bombeck
Calendar*]

**CAMPBELL, David Gordon
(1915–1979)**
The cruel girls we loved
Are over forty,
Their subtle daughters
Have stolen their beauty;
And with a blue stare
Of cool surprise
They mock their anxious mothers

With their mothers' eyes.
['Mothers and Daughters'
(c. 1965)]

**DAWE, (Donald) Bruce
(1930–)**
Mum, you would have loved
the way you went!
one moment, at a barbecue in
the garden
– the next, falling out of your
chair,
hamburger in one hand,
and a grandson yelling.
['Going' (1970)]

ELLIS, Alice Thomas (1932–)
Claudia . . . remembered that
when she'd had her first baby
she had realized with aston-
ishment that the perfect
couple consisted of a mother
and child and not, as she had
always supposed, a man and
woman.
[*The Other Side of the Fire*]

**FISHER, Dorothy Canfield
(1879–1958)**
A mother is not a person to
lean on but a person to make
leaning unnecessary.
[*Her Son's Wife* (1926)]

**FRIDAY, Nancy
(1937–)**
Blaming mother is just a negative way of clinging to her
still.
[*My Mother/My Self* (1977)]

HUBBARD, Kin (1868–1930)
The old-time mother who used to wonder where her boy was now has a grandson who wonders where his mother is.

[Attr.]

LAWRENCE, D.H. (1885–1930)
[On his relationship with his mother]
We have loved each other, almost with a husband and wife love, as well as filial and maternal . . . It has been rather terrible and has made me, in some respects, abnormal.

[Attr.]

MAUGHAM, William Somerset (1874–1965)
Few misfortunes can befall a boy which bring worse consequences than to have a really affectionate mother.

[*A Writer's Notebook* (1949)]

OLSEN, Tillie (1913–)
More than in any other human relationship, overwhelmingly more, motherhood means being instantly interruptible, responsive, responsible.

[*Silences: When Writers Don't Write* (1965)]

RILEY, Janet Mary (1915–)
The role of mother is probably the most important career a woman can have.

[*The Times-Picayune*, 1986]

SCOTT-MAXWELL, Florida (1884–1979)
No matter how old a mother is, she watches her middle-aged children for signs of improvement.

[*The Measure of My Days* (1968)]

SHAKESPEARE, William (1564–1616)
Thou art thy mother's glass, and she in thee
Calls back the lovely April of her prime.

[Sonnet 3]

STEAD, Christina (1902–1983)
A mother! What are we really? They all grow up whether you look after them or not.

[*The Man Who Loved Children*]

STEFANO, Joseph (1922–)
A boy's best friend is his mother.

[*Psycho*, screenplay, 1960]

WALLACE, William Ross (c. 1819–1881)
The hand that rocks the cradle
Is the hand that rules the world.

['What Rules the World' (c. 1865)]

WOOD, Mrs Henry
(1814–1887)
Dead! and . . . never called
me mother.
[*East Lynne* (stage adaptation,
1874)]

MUSIC

ADDISON, Joseph (1672–1719)
Music, the greatest good that
mortals know,
And all of heaven we have
below.
['Song for St Cecilia's Day'
(1694)]

ADE, George (1866–1944)
The music teacher came twice
a week to bridge the awful gap
between Dorothy and Chopin.
[Attr.]

ANDERSEN, Hans Christian
(1805–1875)
[Of the music to be played at
his funeral]
Most of the people who walk
after me will be children;
make the beat keep time with
little steps.
[In Godden, *Hans Christian
Andersen* (1955)]

APPLETON, Sir Edward
Victor (1892–1965)
I do not mind what language
an opera is sung in so long as

it is a language I don't understand.
[*The Observer*, 1955]

ARMSTRONG, Louis
(1900–1971)
[When asked how he felt
about people copying his
style]
A lotta cats copy the Mona
Lisa, but people still line up to
see the original.
[Attr.]

BEECHAM, Sir Thomas
(1879–1961)
There are two golden rules for
an orchestra: start together
and finish together. The public
doesn't give a damn what
goes on in between.
[In Atkins and Newman,
Beecham Stories (1978)]

BEETHOVEN, Ludwig Van
(1770–1827)
[Said to a violinist complaining that a passage was
unplayable]
When I composed that, I was
conscious of being inspired by
God Almighty. Do you think I
can consider your puny little
fiddle when He speaks to me?
[Attr.]

BIRTWISTLE, Harrison
(1934–)
I get someone to write the

programme notes. Then I know what the piece is about.

[*The Observer*, 1996]

BURNEY, Fanny (1752–1840)
All the delusive seduction of martial music.

[*Diary*, 1802]

CONGREVE, William (1670–1729)
Music has charms to soothe a savage breast.

[*The Mourning Bride* (1697)]

COWARD, Sir Noël (1899–1973)
Extraordinary how potent cheap music is.

[*Private Lives* (1930)]

DRYDEN, John (1631–1700)
What passion cannot Music raise and quell?

['A Song for St. Cecilia's Day' (1687)]

GASKELL, Elizabeth (1810–1865)
We were none of us musical, though Miss Jenkyns beat time, out of time, by way of appearing to be so.

[*Cranford* (1853)]

GELDOF, Bob (1954–)
I'm into pop because I want to get rich, get famous and get laid.

[Attr.]

HOLST, Gustav (1874–1934)
Never compose anything unless the not composing of it becomes a positive nuisance to you.

[Letter to W.G. Whittaker]

HUXLEY, Aldous (1894–1963)
Since Mozart's day composers have learned the art of making music throatily and palpitatingly sexual.

[*Along the Road* (1925)]

JOHNSON, Samuel (1709–1784)
Of music Dr Johnson used to say that it was the only sensual pleasure without vice.

[In *European Magazine*, 1795]

PARKER, Charlie (1920–1955)
Music is your own experience, your thoughts, your wisdom. If you don't live it, it won't come out of your horn.

[In Shapiro and Hentoff, *Hear Me Talkin' to Ya* (1955)]

RANDOLPH, David
[On *Parsifal*]
The kind of opera that starts at six o'clock and after it has been going three hours, you look at your watch and it says 6.20.

[In *The Frank Muir Book* (1976)]

**ROSSINI, Gioacchino
(1792–1868)**
Give me a laundry-list and I
will set it to music.

[Attr.]

SATIE, Erik (1866–1925)
[Direction on one of his piano
pieces]
To be played with both hands
in the pocket.

[Attr.]

SCHNABEL, Artur (1882–1951)
The notes I handle no better
than many pianists. But the
pauses between the notes –
ah, that is where the art
resides.

[*Chicago Daily News*, 1958]

SCHUBERT, Franz (1797–1828)
My compositions spring from
my sorrows. Those that give
the world the greatest delight
were born of my deepest
griefs.

[*Diary*, 1824]

**SHAKESPEARE, William
(1564–1616)**
In sweet music is such art,
Killing care and grief of heart
Fall asleep or hearing die.

[*Henry VIII*, III.i]

Music oft hath such a charm
To make bad good and good
provoke to harm.

[*Measure For Measure*, IV.i]

How sour sweet music is
When time is broke and no
proportion kept!
So is it in the music of men's
lives.

[*Richard II*, V.v]

**SHAW, George Bernard
(1856–1950)**
At every one of those concerts
in England you will find rows
of weary people who are
there, not because they really
like classical music, but
because they think they ought
to like it.

[*Man and Superman* (1903)]

**STEVENS, Wallace
(1879–1955)**
Just as my fingers on these
keys
Make music, so the self-same
sounds
On my spirit make a music, too.

Music is feeling, then, not
sound.
And thus it is what I feel,
Here in this room, desiring
you.
Thinking of your blue-
shadowed silk,
Is music.

['Peter Quince at the Clavier'
(1923)]

**TENNYSON, Alfred, Lord
(1809–1892)**
Music that gentlier on the

spirit lies,
Than tir'd eyelids upon tir'd
eyes.
['The Lotos-Eaters' (1832)]

**THOMAS, Irene
(1920–)**
The cello is not one of my
favourite instruments. It has

such a lugubrious sound, like
someone reading a will.

[Attr.]

**WILLIAMSON, Malcolm
(1931–)**
Lloyd Webber's music is
everywhere, but so is Aids.

[Attr.]

NATIONS

**INGE, William Ralph
(1860–1954)**
A nation is a society united by
a delusion about its ancestry
and by a common hatred of
its neighbours.
[In Sagittarius and George,
The Perpetual Pessimist]

KUBRICK, Stanley (1928–)
The great nations have always
acted like gangsters, and the
small nations like prostitutes.
[The Guardian, 1963]

**PARNELL, Charles Stewart
(1846–1891)**
No man has a right to fix the
boundary of the march of a
nation: no man has a right to
say to his country – thus far
shalt thou go and no further.
[Speech, 1885]

**WILSON, Woodrow
(1856–1924)**
No nation is fit to sit in judgement upon any other nation.
[Speech, 1915]

NATURE

**THE BIBLE (KING JAMES
VERSION)**
While the earth remaineth,
seedtime and harvest, and
cold and heat, and summer
and winter, and day and night
shall not cease.
[Genesis, 8:22]

**BRIDGES, Robert
(1844–1930)**
Man masters nature not by
force but by understanding.
[Attr.]

**BROWNE, Sir Thomas
(1605–1682)**
All things are artificial, for
nature is the art of God.
[Religio Medici (1643)]

**CHESTERTON, G.K.
(1874–1936)**
Is ditchwater dull? Naturalists
with microscopes have told
me that it teems with quiet
fun.
[The Listener, 1936]

CLARKE, Marcus (1846–1881)
In Australia alone is to be
found the Grotesque, the
Weird, the strange scribblings
of nature learning how to
write.
[Preface to A.L. Gordon, Sea
Spray and Smoke Drift (1867)]

CURIE, Marie (1867–1934)
All my life through, the new
sights of Nature made me
rejoice like a child.
[Pierre Curie]

**DARWIN, Charles
(1809–1882)**
What a book a devil's chaplain might write on the clumsy, wasteful, blundering, low, and horribly cruel works of nature!
[Letter to J.D. Hooker, 1856]

**GRACIÁN, Baltasar
(1601–1658)**
Art is not essential where Nature is sufficient.
[The Hero (1637)]

GREY OWL (1888–1938)
Civilisation says, 'Nature belongs to man.' The Indian says, 'No, man belongs to nature.'
[Address at Norwich]

HORACE (65–8 BC)
You may drive out Nature with a pitchfork, but she always comes hurrying back.
[Epistles]

HUGO, Victor (1802–1885)
Nature is unforgiving; she will not agree to withdraw her flowers, her music, her scents or her rays of light before the abominations of man.
[Ninety-three (1874)]

**INGERSOLL, Robert Greene
(1833–1899)**
In nature there are neither rewards nor punishments –

there are consequences.
[Some Reasons Why (1881)]

**LINNAEUS, Carl
(1707–1778)**
Nature does not make progress by leaps and bounds.
[Philosophia Botanica]

MILTON, John (1608–1674)
In those vernal seasons of the yeer, when the air is calm and pleasant, it were an injury and sullennesse against nature not to go out, and see her riches, and partake in her rejoycing with heaven and earth.
[Of Education: To Master Samuel Hartlib (1644)]

**RABELAIS, François
(c. 1494–c. 1553)**
Nature abhors a vacuum.
[Gargantua (1534)]

**SHAKESPEARE, William
(1564–1616)**
In nature's infinite book of secrecy
A little I can read.
[Antony and Cleopatra, I.ii]

**SMITH, Alexander
(1830–1867)**
Nature, who makes the perfect rose and bird,
Has never made the full and perfect man.
[City Poems (1857), 'Horton']

THOREAU, Henry (1817–1862)
I frequently tramped eight or
ten miles through the deepest
snow to keep an appointment
with a beech-tree, or a yellow
birch, or an old acquaintance
among the pines.
[*Walden* (1854)]

UVAVNUK
The arch of sky and mighti-
ness of storms
Have moved the spirit within me,
Till I am carried away
Trembling with joy.
[In Rasmussen, *Intellectual
Culture of the Igulik Eskimos*
(1929)]

**VOLTAIRE
(1694–1778)**
Know that the secret of the
arts is to correct nature.
[*Epîtres*, 'A M. de Verrière']

**WHITMAN, Walt
(1819–1892)**
After you have exhausted
what there is in business, politics, conviviality, and so on
–have found that none of
these finally satisfy, or perma-
nently wear – what remains?
Nature remains.
[*Specimen Days and Collect*
(1882)]

**WORDSWORTH, William
(1770–1850)**
Nature never did betray

The heart that loved her.
['Tintern Abbey' (1798)]

One impulse from a vernal
wood
May teach you more of man,
Of moral evil and of good,
Than all the sages can . . .

Sweet is the lore which
Nature brings;
Our meddling intellect
Misshapes the beauteous
forms of things:
We murder to dissect.
['The Tables Turned' (1798)]

THE NAVY

**CAMPBELL, Thomas
(1777–1844)**
Britannia needs no bulwarks,
No towers along the steep;
Her march is o'er the moun-
tain waves,
Her home is on the deep.
With thunders from her native
oak
She quells the floods below.
['Ye Mariners of England' (1801)]

**CHURCHILL, Sir Winston
(1874–1965)**
Don't talk to me about naval
tradition. It's nothing but rum,
sodomy and the lash.
[In Gretton, *Former Naval
Person* (1968)]

COVENTRY, Thomas (1578–1640)
The dominion of the sea, as it is an ancient and undoubted right of the crown of England, so it is the best security of the land. The wooden walls are the best walls of this kingdom.

[Speech in Star Chamber, 1635]

MACAULAY, Lord (1800–1859)
There were gentlemen and there were seamen in the navy of Charles the Second. But the seamen were not gentlemen; and the gentlemen were not seamen.

[History of England (1849), I]

NEIGHBOURS

AUSTEN, Jane (1775–1817)
For what do we live, but to make sport for our neighbours, and laugh at them in our turn?

[Pride and Prejudice (1813)]

THE BIBLE (KING JAMES VERSION)
Thou shalt love thy neighbour as thyself.

[Leviticus, 19:18]

BRADLEY, F.H. (1846–1924)
The propriety of some persons seems to consist in having improper thoughts about their neighbours.

[Aphorisms (1930)]

CHESTERTON, G.K. (1874–1936)
We make our friends, we make our enemies; but God makes our next-door neighbour.

[Heretics (1905)]

CLEESE, John (1939–)
Loving your neighbour as much as yourself is practically bloody impossible . . . You might as well have a Commandment that states, 'Thou shalt fly'.

[The Times, 1993]

PROVERB
Good fences make good neighbours.

NEWS

AUSTEN, Jane (1775–1817)
Lady Middleton . . . exerted herself to ask Mr Palmer if there was any news in the paper.
'No, none at all,' he replied, and read on.

[Sense and Sensibility (1811)]

**BENNETT, Arnold
(1867–1931)**
Journalists say a thing that they know isn't true, in the hope that if they keep on saying it long enough it *will* be true.

[*The Title* (1918)]

**BEVAN, Aneurin
(1897–1960)**
I read the newspapers avidly. It is my one form of continuous fiction.

[*The Observer*, 1960]

CANTONA, Eric (1966–)
[Commenting on the interest taken by the press in the outcome of his court case]
When the seagulls follow the trawler, it is because they think sardines will be thrown into the sea.

[*The Observer*, 1995]

**CARLYLE, Thomas
(1795–1881)**
Burke said there were Three Estates in Parliament; but, in the Reporters' Gallery yonder, there sat a *Fourth Estate* more important far than they all.

['The Hero as Man of Letters' (1841)]

**CHESTERTON, G.K.
(1874–1936)**
It's not the world that's got so much worse but the news

coverage that's got so much better.

[Attr.]

CURZON Lord (1859–1925)
I hesitate to say what the functions of the modern journalist may be; but I imagine that they do not exclude the intelligent anticipation of facts even before they occur.

[Speech, 1898]

**DANA, Charles Anderson
(1819–1897)**
When a dog bites a man that is not news, but when a man bites a dog that is news.

[*New York Sun*, 1882]

**DRAYTON, Michael
(1563–1631)**
Ill news hath wings, and with the wind doth go,
Comfort's a cripple and comes ever slow.

[*The Barrons' Wars* (1603)]

**FAIRBURN, A.R.D.
(1904–1957)**
The press: slow dripping of water on mud;
thought's daily bagwash, ironing out opinion,
scarifying the edges of ideas.

[*Collected Poems* (1966)]

**GARCÍA MÁRQUEZ, Gabriel
(1928–)**
Journalism is a literary genre

very similar to that of the novel, and has the great advantage that the reporter can invent things. And that is completely forbidden to the novelist.

[Speech, 1994]

HEPWORTH, John (1921–)
Most journalists of my generation died early, succumbing to one or other of the two great killers in the craft – cirrhosis or terminal alimony.

[National Review, 1974]

IGNATIEFF, Michael (1947–)
News is a genre as much as fiction or drama: it is a regime of visual authority, a coercive organization of images according to a stopwatch.

[Daedalus, 1988]

KIPLING, Rudyard (1865–1936)
[Of newspaper barons] Power without responsibility – the prerogative of the harlot throughout the ages.

[Remark, quoted by Baldwin in 1931]

KRAUS, Karl (1874–1936)
To have no thoughts and be able to express them – that's what makes a journalist.

[Pro domo et mundo (1912)]

LONGFORD, Lord (1905–)
On the whole I would not say

that our Press is obscene. I would say that it trembles on the brink of obscenity.

[The Observer, 1963]

MACCARTHY, Sir Desmond (1878–1952)
[Journalists are] more attentive to the minute hand of history than to the hour hand.

[In Tynan, Curtains (1961)]

MAILER, Norman (1923–)
Once a newspaper touches a story, the facts are lost forever, even to the protagonists.

[The Presidential Papers (1976)]

MARQUIS, Don (1878–1937)
The art of newspaper paragraphing is to stroke a platitude until it purrs like an epigram.

[In Anthony, O Rare Don Marquis (1962)]

MILLER, Arthur (1915–)
A good newspaper, I suppose, is a nation talking to itself.

[The Observer, 1961]

MURDOCH, Rupert (1931–)
I think the important thing is that there be plenty of newspapers with plenty of people controlling them so there can be choice.

[Film interview, 1967]

**MURRAY, David
(1888–1962)**
A reporter is a man who has
renounced everything in life
but the world, the flesh, and
the devil.

[*The Observer*, 1931]

**SCOTT, C.P.
(1846–1932)**
Comment is free, but facts are
sacred.

[*Manchester Guardian*, 1921]

**TOMALIN, Nicholas
(1931–1973)**
The only qualities essential for
real success in journalism are
rat-like cunning, a plausible
manner, and a little literary
ability.

[*The Sunday Times Magazine*,
1969]

**WOLFE, Humbert
(1886–1940)**
You cannot hope
To bribe or twist,
thank God! the
British journalist.
But, seeing what
the man will do
unbribed, there's
no occasion to.

['Over the Fire' (1930)]

**See MEDIA;
TELEVISION**

NOSTALGIA

AUGIER, Emile (1820–1889)
La nostalgie de la boue.
Homesickness for the gutter.

[*Le Mariage d'Olympe* (1855)]

BYRON, Lord (1788–1824)
Ah! happy years! once more
who would not be a boy?

[*Childe Harold's Pilgrimage*
(1818)]

The 'good old times' – all
times when old are good –
Are gone.

['The Age of Bronze' (1823)]

**HOUSMAN, A.E.
(1859–1936)**
That is the land of lost con-
tent,
I see it shining plain,
The happy highways where I
went
And cannot come again.

[*A Shropshire Lad* (1896)]

LAMB, Charles (1775–1834)
All, all are gone, the old familiar faces.

['The Old Familiar Faces']

**ORWELL, George
(1903–1950)**
Before the war, and especially
before the Boer War, it was
summer all the year round.

[*Coming Up for Air* (1939)]

**TENNYSON, Alfred, Lord
(1809–1892)**
Tears, idle tears, I know not
what they mean,
Tears from the depth of some
divine despair
Rise in the heart, and gather
to the eyes,
In looking on the happy
Autumn-fields,
And thinking of the days that
are no more.
[*The Princess* (1847)]

**THOMAS, Dylan
(1914–1953)**
Years and years and years
ago, when I was a boy, when
there were wolves in Wales,
and birds the colour of red-
flannel petticoats whisked
past the harp-shaped hills ...
when we rode the daft and
happy hills bareback, it
snowed and it snowed.
[*A Child's Christmas in Wales*
(1954)]

YEATS, W.B. (1865–1939)
In the Junes that were warmer
than these are, the waves
were more gay,
When I was a boy with never
a crack in my heart.
['The Meditation of the Old
Fisherman' (1886)]

OBSTINACY

ARISTOTLE (384–322 BC)
Obstinate people may be sub-divided into the opinionated, the ignorant, and the boorish.
[*Nicomachean Ethics*]

MACNEICE, Louis (1907–1963)
One must not dislike people . . . because they are intransi-gent. For that could be only playing their own game.
[*Zoo* (1938)]

MAUGHAM, William Somerset (1874–1965)
Like all weak men he laid an exaggerated stress on not changing one's mind.
[*Of Human Bondage* (1915)]

PROVERB
None so deaf as those who will not hear.

STERNE, Laurence (1713–1768)
'Tis known by the name of perseverance in a good cause – and of obstinacy in a bad one.
[*Tristram Shandy* (1767)]

OPINIONS

BAEZ, Joan (1941–)
I've never had a humble opinion. If you've got an opin-ion, why be humble about it.
[*Scotland on Sunday*, 1992]

CONGREVE, William (1670–1729)
I am always of the opinion with the learned, if they speak first.
[*Incognita* (1692)]

HALSEY, Margaret (1910–)
The English think of an opinion as something which a decent person, if he has the misfortune to have one, does all he can to hide.
[*With Malice Toward Some* (1938)]

LOCKE, John (1632–1704)
New opinions are always sus-pected, and usually opposed, without any reason but because they are not already common.
[*Essay concerning Human Understanding* (1690)]

MACKINTOSH, Sir James (1765–1832)
Men are never so good or so bad as their opinions.
['Jeremy Bentham' (1830)]

**MAISTRE, Joseph de
(1753–1821)**
Wrong opinions are like
counterfeit coins, which are
first minted by great wrong-
doers, then spent by decent
people who perpetuate the
crime without knowing what
they are doing.
[*Les soirées de
Saint-Pétersbourg*]

**MILL, John Stuart
(1806–1873)**
If all mankind minus one, were
of one opinion, and only one
person were of the contrary
opinion, mankind would be no
more justified in silencing that
one person, than he, if he had
the power, would be justified
in silencing mankind.
[*On Liberty* (1859)]

**SPENCER, Herbert
(1820–1903)**
Opinion is ultimately determined by the feelings, and not
by the intellect.
[*Social Statics* (1850)]

OPTIMISM

**CABELL, James Branch
(1879–1958)**
The optimist proclaims that
we live in the best of all
possible worlds; and the
pessimist fears this is true.
[*The Silver Stallion* (1926)]

**SHORTER, Clement King
(1857–1926)**
The latest definition of an
optimist is one who fills up
his crossword puzzle in ink.
[*The Observer*, 1925]

USTINOV, Sir Peter (1921–)
I am an optimist, unrepentant
and militant. After all, in order
not to be a fool an optimist
must know how sad a place
the world can be. It is only the
pessimist who finds this out
anew every day.
[*Dear Me* (1977)]

VOLTAIRE (1694–1778)
Everything is for the best in
the best of all possible worlds.
[*Candide* (1759)]

See PESSIMISM

PARENTS

**BUTLER, Samuel
(1835–1902)**
Parents are the last people on earth who ought to have children.

[Attr.]

**COMPTON-BURNETT, Dame
Ivy (1884–1969)**
Don't be too hard on parents. You may find yourself in their place.

[*Elders and Betters* (1944)]

**LARKIN, Philip
(1922–1985)**
They fuck you up, your mum and dad.
They may not mean to, but they do.
They fill you with the faults they had.
And add some extra, just for you.

['This be the Verse' (1974)]

**SHAW, George Bernard
(1856–1950)**
Parentage is a very important profession; but no test of fitness for it is ever imposed in the interest of the children.

[*Everybody's Political What's What* (1944)]

SPARK, Muriel (1918–)
Parents learn a lot from their children about coping with life.

[*The Comforters* (1957)]

See CHILDREN

PASSION

**JUNG, Carl Gustav
(1875–1961)**
A man who has not gone through the hell of his passions has never overcome them either.

[*Memories, Dreams, Thoughts* (1962)]

**LA ROCHEFOUCAULD
(1613–1680)**
If we resist our passions, it is more because of their weakness than because of our strength.

[*Maximes*]

**L'ESTRANGE, Sir Roger
(1616–1704)**
It is with our passions as it is with fire and water, they are good servants, but bad masters.

[Translation of *Aesop's Fables*]

**SHAKESPEARE, William
(1564–1616)**
Give me that man
That is not passion's slave, and I will wear him

In my heart's core, ay, in my
heart of heart,
As I do thee.

[*Hamlet*, III.ii]

THE PAST

**BEERBOHM, Sir Max
(1872–1956)**
There is always something
rather absurd about the past.

[Attr.]

COLETTE (1873–1954)
But the past, the beautiful
past striped with sunshine,
grey with mist, childish,
blooming with hidden joy,
bruised with sweet sorrow . . .
Ah! if only I could resurrect
one hour of that time, one
alone – but which one?

[*Paysages et portraits* (1958)]

**HARTLEY, L.P.
(1895–1972)**
The past is a foreign country:
they do things differently
there.

[*The Go-Between* (1953)]

**ONDAATJE, Michael
(1943–)**
The past is still, for us, a place
that is not yet safely settled.

[*The Faber Book of
Contemporary Canadian Short
Stories* (1990)]

**SANTAYANA, George
(1863–1952)**
Those who cannot remember
the past are condemned to
repeat it.

[*The Life of Reason* (1906)]

**TERTZ, Abram
(1925–1997)**
In the past, people did not
cling to life quite as much,
and it was easier to breathe.

[*A Voice From the Chorus*
(1973)]

**WAIN, John
(1925–)**
Keep off your thoughts from
things that are past and done;
For thinking of the past wakes
regret and pain.

[*Resignation*, translated from
the Chinese of Po-Chü-I]

PATIENCE

**BIERCE, Ambrose
(1842–c. 1914)**
Patience: A minor form of
despair, disguised as a virtue.

[*The Cynic's Word Book* (1906)]

**FONTAINE, Jean de la
(1621–1695)**
Patience and time do more
than force and rage.

['Le lion et le rat']

**MASSINGER, Philip
(1583–1640)**
Patience, the beggar's virtue.
[*A New Way to Pay Old Debts*
(1633)]

**SHAKESPEARE, William
(1564–1616)**
How poor are they that have
not patience!
What wound did ever heal but
by degrees?
[*Othello*, II.iii]

**TAYLOR, Elizabeth
(1912–1975)**
It is very strange . . . that the
years teach us patience; that
the shorter our time, the
greater our capacity for
waiting.
[*A Wreath of Roses* (1950)]

PATRIOTISM

CAVELL, Edith (1865–1915)
[Said on the eve of her
execution]
Standing, as I do, in view of
God and eternity I realize that
patriotism is not enough. I
must have no hatred or bitter-
ness towards anyone.
[*The Times*, 1915]

**CHESTERTON, G.K.
(1874–1936)**
'My country, right or wrong,'
is a thing that no patriot
would think of saying except
in a desperate case. It is like
saying, 'My mother, drunk or
sober'.
[*The Defendant* (1901)]

**DECATUR, Stephen
(1779–1820)**
Our country! In her intercourse with foreign nations,
may she always be in the
right; but our country, right or
wrong.
[In Mackenzie, *Life of Decatur*
(1846)]

DRYDEN, John (1631–1700)
Never was patriot yet, but was
a fool.
[*Absalom and Achitophel*
(1681)]

**FORSTER, E.M.
(1879–1970)**
I hate the idea of causes, and
if I had to choose between
betraying my country and
betraying my friend, I hope I
should have the guts to betray
my country.
[*Two Cheers for Democracy*
(1951)]

**GASKELL, Elizabeth
(1810–1865)**
That kind of patriotism which
consists in hating all other
nations.
[*Sylvia's Lovers* (1863)]

**GOLDSMITH, Oliver
(c. 1728–1774)**
Such is the patriot's boast,
where'er we roam,
His first best country ever is at
home.
['The Traveller' (1764)]

HORACE (65–8 BC)
*Dulce et decorum est pro patria
mori.*
It is sweet and honourable to
die for one's country.
[*Odes*]

**JOHNSON, Samuel
(1709–1784)**
Patriotism is the last refuge of
a scoundrel.
[In Boswell, *The Life of Samuel
Johnson* (1791)]

KINNOCK, Neil (1942–)
[Of nuclear disarmament]
I would die for my country but
I could never let my country
die for me.
[Speech, 1987]

OWEN, Wilfred (1893–1918)
If you could hear, at every jolt,
the blood
Come gargling from the froth-
corrupted lungs,
Obscene as cancer, bitter as
the cud
Of vile, incurable sores on
innocent tongues, –
My friend, you would not tell
with such high zest
To children ardent for some
desperate glory,
The old Lie: *Dulce et decorum
est
Pro patria mori.*
['Dulce et decorum est'
(1917)]

PLOMER, William (1903–1973)
Patriotism is the last refuge of
the sculptor.
[Attr.]

**RUSSELL, Bertrand
(1872–1970)**
Patriots always talk of dying
for their country, and never of
killing for their country.
[Attr.]

SCHURZ, Carl (1829–1906)
Our country, right or wrong!
When right, to be kept right;
when wrong, to be put right!
[Speech, 1872]

SCOTT, Sir Walter (1771–1832)
Breathes there the man, with
soul so dead,
Who never to himself hath said,
This is my own, my native
land!
[*The Lay of the Last Minstrel*
(1805)]

**SMOLLETT, Tobias
(1721–1771)**
True Patriotism is of no Party.
[*The Adventures of Sir
Launcelot Greaves* (1762)]

TROTSKY, Leon (1879–1940)

Patriotism to the Soviet State is a revolutionary duty, whereas patriotism to a bourgeois State is treachery.

[In Fitzroy Maclean, *Disputed Barricade*]

PEACE

ANONYMOUS

Since wars begin in the minds of men, it is in the minds of men that the defences of peace must be constructed.

[Constitution of UNESCO]

BELLOC, Hilaire (1870–1953)

Pale Ebenezer thought it wrong to fight,
But Roaring Bill (who killed him) thought it right.

['The Pacifist' (1938)]

BRECHT, Bertolt (1898–1956)

Don't tell me that peace has broken out.

[*Mother Courage* (1939)]

EINSTEIN, Albert (1879–1955)

Peace cannot be kept by force. It can only be achieved by understanding.

[*Notes on Pacifism*]

GANDHI (1869–1948)

I wanted to avoid violence. Non-violence is the first article of my faith. It is also the last article of my creed.

[Speech, 1922]

IZETBEGOVIC, Alija (1925–)

[On signing the peace accord in Paris, December 1995]
I feel like a man who is drinking a bitter but useful medicine.

[*The Observer Review*, 1995]

JERROLD, Douglas William (1803–1857)

We love peace, as we abhor pusillanimity; but not peace at any price.

['Peace' (1859)]

LIE, Trygve (1896–1968)

Now we are in a period which I can characterize as a period of cold peace.

[*The Observer*, 1949]

MILTON, John (1608–1674)

Peace hath her victories
No less renowned than war.

['To the Lord General Cromwell' (1652)]

RUSSELL, Lord John (1792–1878)

If peace cannot be maintained with honour, it is no longer peace.

[Speech, 1853]

TACITUS (AD c. 56–c. 120)
They create a desert, and call it peace.

[*Agricola*]

WALPOLE, Horace (1717–1797)
When will the world know that peace and propagation are the two most delightful things in it?

[Letter to Sir Horace Mann, 1778]

WILSON, Woodrow (1856–1924)
There is a price which is too great to pay for peace, and that price can be put in one word. One cannot pay the price of self-respect.

[Speech, 1916]

It must be a peace without victory . . . only a peace between equals can last.

[Speech, 1917]

See WAR AND PEACE

THE PEOPLE

ALCUIN (735–804)
Nor should those be heeded who are wont to say 'The voice of the people is the voice of God', since popular uproar is always akin to madness.

[Letter to Charlemagne]

BURKE, Edmund (1729–1797)
It is a general popular error to imagine the loudest complainers for the public to be the most anxious for its welfare.

[*Observations on 'The Present State of the Nation'* (1769)]

The people never give up their liberties but under some delusion.

[Speech, 1784]

CONFUCIUS (c. 550–c. 478 BC)
The people may be made to follow a course of action, but they may not be made to understand it.

[*Analects*]

CROMWELL, Oliver (1599–1658)
[Referring to a cheering crowd]
The people would be just as noisy if they were going to see me hanged.

[Attr.]

DICKENS, Charles (1812–1870)
'But suppose there are two mobs?' suggested Mr Snodgrass. 'Shout with the largest,' replied Mr Pickwick.

[*The Pickwick Papers* (1837)]

PESSIMISM

DRYDEN, John (1631–1700)
Nor is the people's judgement
always true:
The most may err as grossly
as the few.

[*Absalom and Achitophel*
(1681)]

HITLER, Adolf (1889–1945)
The broad mass of a people . . .
falls victim to a big lie more
easily than to a small one.

[*Mein Kampf* (1925)]

JUVENAL (c. 60–130)
Two things only the people
anxiously desire: bread and
circuses.

[*Satires*]

**KENNEDY, Robert F.
(1925–1968)**
One fifth of the people are
against everything all the
time.

[*The Observer*, 1964]

**LINCOLN, Abraham
(1809–1865)**
You can fool some of the
people all of the time, and all
of the people some of the
time, but you cannot fool all
of the people all the time.

[Attr.]

SCHULZ, Charles (1922–)
I love mankind – it's people I
can't stand.

[*Go Fly a Kite, Charlie Brown*]

**BENNETT, Arnold
(1867–1931)**
Pessimism, when you get
used to it, is just as agreeable
as optimism.

[*Things That Have Interested
Me*]

**BEVERIDGE, William Henry
(1879–1963)**
Scratch a pessimist, and you
find often a defender of privilege.

[*The Observer*, 1943]

**LOWELL, Robert
(1917–1977)**
If we see light at the end of
the tunnel,
It's the light of the oncoming
train.

['Since 1939' (1977)]

MALLET, Robert (1915–)
How many pessimists end up
by desiring the things they
fear, in order to prove that
they are right.

[*Apostilles*]

**MEIR, Golda
(1898–1978)**
Pessimism is a luxury that a
Jew can never allow himself.

[*The Observer*, 1974]

PETER, Laurence J. (1919–1990)
A pessimist is a man who looks both ways before crossing a one-way street.

[Attr.]

See OPTIMISM

PHILOSOPHY

AYER, A.J. (1910–1989)
The principles of logic and metaphysics are true simply because we never allow them to be anything else.

[*Language, Truth and Logic* (1936)]

BOWEN, Lord (1835–1894)
On a metaphysician: A blind man in a dark room – looking for a black hat – which isn't there.

[Attr.]

CICERO (106–43 BC)
But somehow there is nothing so absurd that some philosopher has not said it.

[*De Divinatione*]

EDWARDS, Oliver (1711–1791)
I have tried too in my time to be a philosopher; but, I don't

know how, cheerfulness was always breaking in.
[In Boswell, *The Life of Samuel Johnson* (1791)]

HUXLEY, T.H. (1825–1895)
I doubt if the philosopher lives, or has ever lived, who could know himself to be heartily despised by a street boy without some irritation.

[*Evolution and Ethics* (1893)]

MACNEICE, Louis (1907–1963)
Good-bye now, Plato and Hegel,
The shop is closing down;
They don't want any philosopher-kings in England,
There ain't no universals in this man's town.

[*Autumn Journal* (1939)]

NIETZSCHE, Friedrich (1844–1900)
What I understand philosophers to be: a terrible explosive, in the presence of which everything is in danger.

[*Ecce Homo* (1888)]

PASCAL, Blaise (1623–1662)
To ridicule philosophy is truly to philosophize.

[*Pensées* (1670)]

RUSSELL, Bertrand (1872–1970)
Organic life, we are told, has

developed gradually from the protozoon to the philosopher, and this development, we are assured, is indubitably an advance. Unfortunately it is the philosopher, not the protozoon, who gives us this assurance.

[*Mysticism and Logic* (1918)]

SHAKESPEARE, William (1564–1616)
There are more things in heaven and earth, Horatio, Than are dreamt of in your philosophy.

[*Hamlet*, I.v]

VOLTAIRE (1694–1778)
In philosophy, we must distrust the things we understand too easily as well as the things we don't understand.

[*Lettres philosophiques* (1734)]

Superstition sets the whole world on fire; philosophy quenches the flames.

[*Dictionnaire philosophique* (1764)]

WHITEHEAD, A.N. (1861–1947)
Philosophy is the product of wonder.

[*Nature and Life* (1934)]

BIERCE, Ambrose (1842–c. 1914)
Plagiarize: To take the thought or style of another writer whom one has never, never read.

[*The Enlarged Devil's Dictionary* (1961)]

MIZNER, Wilson (1876–1933)
When you steal from one author, it's plagiarism; if you steal from many, it's research.

[Attr.]

MONTAIGNE, Michel de (1533–1592)
One could say of me that in this book I have only made up a bunch of other men's flowers, providing of my own only the string to tie them together.

[*Essais* (1580)]

MORE, Hannah (1745–1833)
He lik'd those literary cooks Who skim the cream of others' books; And ruin half an author's graces By plucking bon-mots from their places.

[*Florio* (1786)]

SHERIDAN, Richard Brinsley (1751–1816)
All that can be said is, that two people happened to hit on the same thought – and Shakespeare made use of it first, that's all.

[*The Critic* (1779)]

STRAVINSKY, Igor (1882–1971)
A good composer does not imitate; he steals.

[In Yates, *Twentieth Century Music* (1967)]

SULLIVAN, Sir Arthur (1842–1900)
[Accused of plagiarism]
We all have the same eight notes to work with.

[Attr.]

PLEASURE

ALCOTT, Bronson (1799–1888)
A sip is the most that mortals are permitted from any goblet of delight.

[*Table Talk* (1877)]

AUSTEN, Jane (1775–1817)
One half of the world cannot understand the pleasures of the other.

[*Emma* (1816)]

BIERCE, Ambrose (1842–c. 1914)
Debauchee: One who has so earnestly pursued pleasure that he has had the misfortune to overtake it.

[*The Cynic's Word Book* (1906)]

BURKE, Edmund (1729–1797)
I am convinced that we have a degree of delight, and that no small one, in the real misfortunes and pains of others.

[*A Philosophical Enquiry* (1757)]

BURNS, Robert (1759–1796)
But pleasures are like poppies spread:
You seize the flow'r, its bloom is shed;
Or like the snow falls in the river,
A moment white – then melts for ever.

['Tam o' Shanter' (1790)]

BYRON, Lord (1788–1824)
Pleasure's a sin, and sometimes sin's a pleasure.

[*Don Juan* (1824)]

CABELL, James Branch (1879–1958)
A man possesses nothing certainly save a brief loan of his own body: and yet the body of man is capable of much curious pleasure.

[*Jurgen* (1919)]

COWPER, William
(1731–1800)
Remorse, the fatal egg by
pleasure laid.
> ['The Progress of Error'
> (1782)]

HUNT, Leigh
(1784–1859)
A pleasure so exquisite as
almost to amount to pain.
> [Letter, 1848]

JOHNSON, Samuel
(1709–1784)
Pleasure is very seldom found
where it is sought; our
brightest blazes of gladness
are commonly kindled by
unexpected sparks.
> [*The Idler* (1758–1760)]

No man is a hypocrite in his
pleasures.
> [In Boswell, *The Life of Samuel
> Johnson* (1791)]

LAMB, Charles
(1775–1834)
The greatest pleasure I know,
is to do a good action by
stealth, and to have it found
out by accident.
> ['Table Talk by the Late Elia']

MOLIERE (1622–1673)
Heaven forbids certain pleasures, it is true, but one can
arrive at certain compromises.
> [*Tartuffe* (1664)]

O'ROURKE, P.J. (1947–)
After all, what is your hosts'
purpose in having a party?
Surely not for you to enjoy
yourself; if that were their sole
purpose, they'd have simply
sent champagne and women
over to your place by taxi.
> [Attr.]

SHAKESPEARE, William
(1564–1616)
These violent delights have
violent ends.
> [*Romeo and Juliet*, II.vi]

WOOLLCOTT, Alexander
(1887–1943)
All the things I really like to
do are either immoral, illegal,
or fattening.
> [In Drennan, *Wit's End* (1973)]

POETRY

BYRON, Lord (1788–1824)
Nothing so difficult as a
beginning
In poesy, unless perhaps the
end.
> [*Don Juan* (1824)]

What is poetry? – The feeling
of a Former world and Future.
> [Journal, 1821]

CAGE, John (1912–1992)
I have nothing to say, I am

saying it, and that is poetry.
[*Silence* (1961)]

**COLERIDGE, Samuel Taylor
(1772–1834)**
I wish our clever young poets
would remember my homely
definitions of prose and poetry; that is prose = words in
their best order; poetry = the
best words in the best order.
[*Table Talk* (1835)]

Poetry is certainly something
more than good sense, but it must
be good sense at all events; just
as a palace is more than a house,
but it must be a house, at least.
[*Table Talk* (1835)]

EWART, Gavin (1916–1995)
Good light verse is better than
bad heavy verse any day of
the week.
[*Penultimate Poems* (1989)]

**FARQUHAR, George
(1678–1707)**
Poetry's a mere drug, Sir.
[*Love and a Bottle* (1698)]

FROST, Robert (1874–1963)
Poetry is a way of taking life
by the throat.
[In Sergeant, *Robert Frost: the
Trial by Existence* (1960)]

**GRANVILLE-BARKER, Harley
(1877–1946)**
Rightly thought of there is

poetry in peaches . . . even
when they are canned.
[*The Madras House*]

**HOPKINS, Gerard Manley
(1844–1889)**
The poetical language of an
age should be the current
language heightened.
[Letter to Robert Bridges,
1879]

**HOUSMAN, A.E.
(1859–1936)**
Even when poetry has a
meaning, as it usually has, it
may be inadvisable to draw it
out . . . perfect understanding
will sometimes almost
extinguish pleasure.
['The Name and Nature of
Poetry' (1933)]

**JARRELL, Randall
(1914–1965)**
Some poetry seems to have
been written on typewriters
by other typewriters.
[Attr.]

KEATS, John (1795–1821)
If Poetry comes not as naturally as Leaves to a tree it had
better not come at all.
[Letter to John Taylor, 1818]

**KLOPSTOCK, Friedrich
(1724–1803)**
[Of one of his poems]
God and I both knew what it

meant once; now God alone knows.

[Attr.]

MACAULAY, Lord (1800–1859)
As civilization advances, poetry almost necessarily declines.

[*Collected Essays* (1843)]

PAZ, Octavio (1914–)
Poetry is nothing but time, ceaselessly creative rhythm.

[*The Bow and the Lyre* (1956)]

PRESTON, Keith (1884–1927)
Of all the literary scenes
Saddest this sight to me:
The graves of little magazines
Who died to make verse free.

['The Liberators']

SHELLEY, Percy Bysshe (1792–1822)
[Poetry] lifts the veil from the hidden beauty of the world, and makes familiar objects be as if they were not familiar.

[*A Defence of Poetry* (1821)]

THOMAS, Dylan (1914–1953)
These poems, with all their crudities, doubts, and confusions, are written for the love of Man and in praise of God, and I'd be a damn' fool if they weren't.

[*Collected Poems* (1952), Note]

VALERY, Paul (1871–1945)
My poems mean what people take them to mean.

[*Variety* (1924)]

WAIN, John (1925–)
Poetry is to prose as dancing is to walking.

[BBC broadcast, 1976]

WILDE, Oscar (1854–1900)
There seems to be some curious connection between piety and poor rhymes.

[In Lucas, *A Critic in Pall Mall* (1919)]

WORDSWORTH, William (1770–1850)
I have said that poetry is the spontaneous overflow of powerful feelings: it takes its origin from emotion recollected in tranquillity.

[*Lyrical Ballads* (1802)]

See LITERATURE; WRITING

POETS

AUDEN, W.H. (1907–1973)
It is a sad fact about our culture that a poet can earn much more money writing or talking about his art than he can by practising it.

[*The Dyer's Hand* (1963)]

**BLAKE, William
(1757–1827)**
The reason Milton wrote in
fetters when he wrote of
Angels & God, and at liberty
when of Devils & Hell, is
because he was a true Poet
and of the Devil's party without knowing it.
['The Voice of the Devil']

**COLERIDGE, Samuel Taylor
(1772–1834)**
No man was ever yet a great
poet, without being at the
same time a profound
philosopher.
[Biographia Literaria (1817)]

**CONGREVE, William
(1670–1729)**
It is the business of a comic
poet to paint the vices and
follies of human kind.
[The Double Dealer (1694)]

ELIOT, T.S. (1888–1965)
The business of the poet is
not to find new emotions, but
to use the ordinary ones and,
in working them up into
poetry, to express feelings
which are not in actual
emotions at all.
['Tradition and the Individual
Talent' (1919)]

**GRAVES, Robert
(1895–1985)**
To be a poet is a condition
rather than a profession.
[Questionnaire in Horizon]

**PESSOA, Fernando
(1888–1935)**
Being a poet is not an
ambition of mine.
It is my way of being alone.
[The Guardian of Flocks
(1914)]

PLATO (c. 429–347 BC)
Poets utter great and wise
things which they do not
themselves understand.
[Republic]

**POPE, Alexander
(1688–1744)**
Sir, I admit your gen'ral Rule
That every Poet is a Fool;
But you yourself may serve to
show it,
That every Fool is not a Poet.
['Epigram from the French'
(1732)]

**WALLER, Edmund
(1606–1687)**
Poets lose half the praise they
should have got,
Could it be known what they
discreetly blot.
['On Roscommon's
Translation of Horace']

**WOOLF, Virginia
(1882–1941)**
I would venture to guess that
Anon, who wrote so many

poems without signing them, was often a woman.
[A Room of One's Own (1929)]

YEATS, W.B. (1865–1939)
The poet finds and makes his mask in disappointment, the hero in defeat.
['Anima Hominis']

POLITICIANS

ADAMS, Franklin P. (1881–1960)
The trouble with this country is that there are too many politicians who believe, with a conviction based on experience, that you can fool all of the people all of the time.
[Nods and Becks (1944)]

ALLEN, Dave (1936–)
If John Major was drowning, his whole life would pass in front of him and he wouldn't be in it.
[On stage, 1991]

ASQUITH, Margot (1864–1945)
[Of Lloyd George]
He couldn't see a belt without hitting below it.
[As I Remember, 1967]

BARNARD, Robert (1936–)
Early on in his stint as a junior minister a newspaper had called him 'the thinking man's Tory', and the label had stuck, possibly because there was so little competition.
[Political Suicide (1986)]

BELLOCH, Juan Alberto (1950–)
Judges are guided by the law; politicians by expediency.
[El país: edición internacional, 1994]

BRIGHT, John (1811–1889)
[Of Disraeli]
He is a self-made man, and worships his creator.
[Remark, c.1868]

BROWN, Tina (1953–)
[Of Richard Crossman]
[He] has the jovial garrulity and air of witty indiscretion that shows he intends to give nothing away.
[Loose Talk (1979)]

BUCHWALD, Art (1925–)
[Of Richard Nixon]
I worship the quicksand he walks in.
[Attr.]

CAMERON, Simon (1799–1889)
An honest politician is one who, when he is bought, will stay bought.
[Remark]

CAMPBELL, Menzies (1941–)
[Of John Smith, leader of the Labour Party]
He had all the virtues of a Scottish Presbyterian, but none of the vices.
[*The Guardian*, 1994]

CRITCHLEY, Julian (1930–)
The only safe pleasure for a parliamentarian is a bag of boiled sweets.
[*The Listener*, 1982]

CUMMINGS, e. e. (1894–1962)
a politician is an arse upon which everyone has sat except a man
[*1 x 1* (1944), no. 10]

DE GAULLE, Charles (1890–1970)
Since a politician never believes what he says, he is quite surprised to be taken at his word.
[Attr.]

DOUGLAS-HOME, Sir Alec (1903–1995)
There are two problems in my life. The political ones are insoluble and the economic ones are incomprehensible.
[*Speech*, 1964]

FOLEY, Rae (1900–1978)
He had the misleading air of open-hearted simplicity that people have come to demand of their politicians.
[*The Hundredth Door* (1950)]

FORD, Gerald R. (1913–)
[Referring to his own appointment as President]
I guess it proves that in America anyone can be President.
[In Reeves, *A Ford Not a Lincoln*]

GAREL-JONES, Tristan (1941–)
My profession does not allow me to go swanning around buying pints of milk.
I wouldn't be of sufficient service to my constituents if I went into shops.
[*The Independent*, 1994]

GUINAN, Texas (1884–1933)
A politician is a fellow who will lay down your life for his country.
[Attr.]

HEALEY, Denis (1917–)
[On Geoffrey Howe's attack on his Budget proposals]
Like being savaged by a dead sheep.
[*Speech*, 1978]

HOGGART, Simon (1946–)
Reagan was probably the first modern president to treat the

post as a part-time job, one way of helping to fill the otherwise blank days of retirement.

[*America 1990*]

HOWAR, Barbara (1934–)

There are no such things as good politicians and bad politicians. There are only politicians, which is to say, they all have personal axes to grind, and all too rarely are they honed for the public good.

[*Laughing All the Way* (1973)]

KHRUSHCHEV, Nikita (1894–1971)

Politicians are the same everywhere. They promise to build a bridge even when there's no river.

[Remark to journalists in the USA, 1960]

LE GUIN, Ursula (1929–)

He had grown up in a country run by politicians who sent the pilots to man the bombers to kill the babies to make the world safe for children to grow up in.

[*The Lathe of Heaven* (1971)]

LYNNE, Liz (1948–)

[On the behaviour of MPs] It was like a bunch of 11-year-olds at their first secondary school.

[*The Independent*, 1992]

MACMILLAN, Harold (1894–1986)

If people want a sense of purpose they should get it from their archbishop. They should certainly not get it from their politicians.

[In Fairlie, *The Life of Politics* (1968)]

MAJOR, John (1943–)

People with vision usually do more harm than good.

[*The Economist*, 1993]

MUGGERIDGE, Malcolm (1903–1990)

[Of Anthony Eden] He was not only a bore; he bored for England.

[*Tread Softly For You Tread on My Jokes* (1966)]

NIXON, Richard (1913–1994)

There can be no whitewash at the White House.

[*The Observer*, 1973]

PARKER, Dorothy (1893–1967)

[Response to news that President Calvin Coolidge had died] How could they tell?

[In Keats, *You Might As Well Live* (1970)]

**POMPIDOU, Georges
1911–1974)**
A statesman is a politician
who places himself at the service of a nation. A politician is
a statesman who places the
nation at his service.
[*The Observer*, 1973]

**ROOSEVELT, Franklin
Delano (1882–1945)**
A radical is a man with both
feet firmly planted in the air.
[Radio broadcast, 1939]

**ROOSEVELT, Theodore
1858–1919)**
The most successful politician
is he who says what everybody is thinking most often
and in the loudest voice.
[In Andrews, *Treasury of
Humorous Quotations*]

AHL, Mort (1927–)
Washington could not tell a
lie; Nixon could not tell the
truth; Reagan cannot tell the
difference.
[*The Observer*, 1987]

[Of President Nixon]
Would you buy a second-hand
car from this man?
[Attr.]

SHORTEN, Caroline
Most Conservatives believe
that a creche is something
that happens between two

Range Rovers in Tunbridge
Wells.
[*The Independent*, 1993]

SMITH, F.E. 1872–1930
Winston [Churchill] has
devoted the best years of his
life to preparing his
impromptu speeches.
[Attr.]

THATCHER, Carol (1953–)
[Of her mother, Margaret
Thatcher]
Reality hasn't really inter-
vened in my mother's life
since the seventies.
[*Daily Mail*, 1996]

**THATCHER, Margaret
(1925–)**
U-turn if you want to. The
lady's not for turning.
[Speech, 1980]

I don't mind how much my
Ministers talk – as long as
they do what I say.
[*The Observer*, 1980]

**TROLLOPE, Anthony
(1815–1882)**
It has been the great fault of
our politicians that they have
all wanted to do something.
[*Phineas Finn* (1869)]

**TRUMAN, Harry S.
(1884–1972)**
[Referring to Vice-President

Nixon's nomination for President]
You don't set a fox to watching the chickens just because he has a lot of experience in the hen house.
[Speech, 1960]

TWAIN, Mark (1835–1910)
The radical invents the views. When he has worn them out, the conservative adopts them.
[Notebooks (1935)]

WALPOLE, Robert (1676–1745)
[Of fellow-parliamentarians] All those men have their price.
[In Coxe, Memoirs of Sir Robert Walpole (1798)]

WHITEHORN, Katherine (1926–)
It is a pity, as my husband says, that more politicians are not bastards by birth instead of vocation.
[The Observer, 1964]

POLITICS

ABBOTT, Diane (1953–)
Being an MP is the sort of job all working-class parents want for their children – clean, indoors and no heavy lifting.
[The Observer, 1994]

ADAMS, Henry (1838–1918)
Politics, as a practice, whatever its professions, has always been the systematic organization of hatreds.
[The Education of Henry Adams (1918)]

ANONYMOUS
Don't tell my mother I'm in politics – she thinks I play the piano in a whorehouse.
[American saying from the Depression]

ARENDT, Hannah (1906-1975)
Truthfulness has never been counted among the political virtues, and lies have always been regarded as justifiable tools in political dealings.
[Crises of the Republic (1972)]

ARISTOTLE (384–322 BC)
Man is by nature a political animal.
[Politics]

ASTOR, Nancy (1879–1964)
Women are young at politics, but they are old at suffering; soon they will learn that through politics they can prevent some kinds of suffering.
[My Two Countries (1923)]

BIERCE, Ambrose (1842–c. 1914)
Nepotism: Appointing your

grandfather to office for the good of the party.

> [*The Enlarged Devil's Dictionary* (1961)]

BISMARCK, Prince Otto von (1815–1898)
Politics is the art of the possible.

> [Remark, 1863]

BURKE, Edmund (1729–1797)
The conduct of a losing party never appears right: at least it never can possess the only infallible criterion of wisdom to vulgar judgments – success.

> [*Letter to a Member of the National Assembly* (1791)]

CAMUS, Albert (1913–1960)
Politics and the fate of mankind are shaped by men without ideals and without greatness. Men who have greatness within them don't concern themselves with politics.

> [*Notebooks, 1935–1942*]

CLARK, Alan (1928–)
There are no true friends in politics. We are all sharks circling and waiting, for traces of blood to appear in the water.

> [*Diary*, 1990]

DE GAULLE, Charles (1890–1970)
I have come to the conclusion that politics are too serious a matter to be left to the politicians.

> [Attr.]

DERBY, Earl of (*19th century*)
The Conservatives are the weakest among the intellectual classes: as is natural.

> [Letter to Disraeli]

DISRAELI, Benjamin (1804–1881)
Damn your principles! Stick to your party.

> [Attr.]

EINSTEIN, Albert (1879–1955)
An empty stomach is not a good political adviser.

> [*Cosmic Religion* (1931)]

FIELDS, W.C. (1880–1946)
Hell, I never vote *for* anybody. I always vote *against*.

> [In Taylor, *W. C. Fields* (1950)]

FISHER, H.A.L. (1856–1940)
Politics is the art of human happiness.

> [*History of Europe* (1935)]

FOUCAULT, Michel (1926–1984)
Marxism exists in nineteenth-

century thought in the same way as a fish exists in water; that is, it stops breathing anywhere else.
[In Eribon, *Michel Foucault* (1989)]

FROST, Robert (1874–1963)
I never dared be radical when young
For fear it would make me conservative when old.
['Precaution' (1936)]

A liberal is a man too broad-minded to take his own side in a quarrel.
[Attr.]

GAITSKELL, Hugh (1906–1963)
All terrorists, at the invitation of the Government, end up with drinks at the Dorchester.
[Letter to *The Guardian*, 1977]

GALBRAITH, J.K. (1908–)
There are times in politics when you must be on the right side and lose.
[*The Observer*, 1968]

HAVEL, Václav (1936–)
Ideology is a special way of relating to the world. It offers human beings the illusion of an identity, of dignity, and of morality, while making it easier for them to part with it.
[*Living in Truth* (1987)]

HIGHTOWER, Jim (1933–)
Only things in the middle of the road are yellow lines and dead armadillos.
[Attr.]

HITLER, Adolf (1889–1945)
What is essential is the formation of the political will of the entire nation: that is the starting point for political actions.
[Speech, 1932]

HORNE, Donald Richmond (1921–)
Politics is both fraud and vision.
[*The Legend of King O'Malley*]

JENKINS, Roy (1920–)
[Used in connection with the SDP, established in 1981]
Breaking the mould of British politics.
[Attr.]

JOHNSON, Samuel (1709–1784)
Politics are now nothing more than a means of rising in the world.
[In Boswell, *The Life of Samuel Johnson* (1791)]

LA BRUYERE, Jean de (1645–1696)
Party loyalty brings the greatest of men down to the petty level of the masses.
[*Les caractères ou les moeurs de ce siècle* (1688)]

MCCARTHY, Senator Eugene (1916–)
Being in politics is like being a football coach. You have to be smart enough to understand the game and dumb enough to think it's important.
[Interview, 1968]

MACMILLAN, Harold (1894–1986)
[On the life of a Foreign Secretary]
Forever poised between a cliché and an indiscretion.
[Newsweek, 1956]

As usual the Liberals offer a mixture of sound and original ideas. Unfortunately none of the sound ideas is original and none of the original ideas is sound.
[The Observer, 1961]

I have never found in a long experience of politics that criticism is ever inhibited by ignorance.
[Attr.]

MAO TSE-TUNG (1893–1976)
All reactionaries are paper tigers.
[Quotations from Chairman Mao Tse-Tung]

MILL, John Stuart (1806–1873)
A party of order or stability, and a party of progress or reform, are both necessary elements of a healthy state of political life.
[On Liberty (1859)]

MILLIGAN, Spike (1918–)
[Remark made about a pre-election poll]
One day the don't-knows will get in, and then where will we be?
[Attr.]

NAPOLEON I (1769–1821)
[To Josephine in 1809, on divorcing her for reasons of state]
I still love you, but in politics there is no heart, only head.
[Attr.]

ORWELL, George (1903–1950)
No book is genuinely free from political bias. The opinion that art should have nothing to do with politics is itself a political attitude.
['Why I Write' (1946)]

PANKHURST, Emmeline (1858–1928)
The argument of the broken pane of glass is the most valuable argument in modern politics.
[Attr.]

PARRIS, Matthew (1949–)
Being an MP feeds your vanity

and starves your self-respect.
[*The Times*, 1994]

POWELL, Enoch
(1912–)
Above any other position of
eminence, that of Prime
Minister is filled by fluke.
[*The Observer*, 1987]

REAGAN, Ronald (1911–)
Politics is supposed to be the
second oldest profession. I
have come to understand that
it bears a very close resem-
blance to the first.
[Remark at a conference,
1977]

Politics is not a bad profession. If you succeed there are
many rewards, if you disgrace
yourself you can always write
a book.
[Attr.]

RUSK, Dean (1909–)
[Of the Cuban missile crisis]
We're eye-ball to eye-ball and
I think the other fellow just
blinked.
[Remark, 1962]

SHAW, George Bernard
(1856–1950)
He knows nothing; and he
thinks he knows everything.
That points clearly to a political career.
[*Major Barbara* (1907)]

SOMOZA, Anastasio
(1925–1980)
You won the elections. But I
won the count.
[*The Guardian*, 1977]

SOPER, Donald (1903–)
[On the quality of debate in
the House of Lords]
It is, I think, good evidence of
life after death.
[*The Listener*, 1978]

STEVENSON, Adlai
(1900–1965)
I will make a bargain with the
Republicans. If they will stop
telling lies about Democrats,
we will stop telling the truth
about them.
[Speech, 1952]

STEVENSON, Robert Louis
(1850–1894)
Politics is perhaps the only
profession for which no
preparation is thought necessary.
[*Familiar Studies of Men and
Books* (1882)]

STOPPARD, Tom (1937–)
The House of Lords, an illusion to which I have never
been able to subscribe –
reponsibility without power,
the prerogative of the eunuch
throughout the ages.
[*Lord Malquist and Mr Moon*
(1966)]

THATCHER, Margaret (1925–)
Victorian values . . . were the values when our country became great.

[Television interview, 1982]

No one would have remembered the Good Samaritan if he'd only had good intentions. He had money as well.

[*The Observer*, 1980]

THORPE, Jeremy (1929–)
[Remark on Macmillan's Cabinet purge, 1962]
Greater love hath no man than this, that he lay down his friends for his life.

[Speech, 1962]

TONER, Pauline (1935–1989)
[The credo of the first woman Minister in the history of the Parliament of Victoria, Australia]
Why join a women's group to lobby government ministers when you can become a minister yourself?

[*Australian Women's Weekly*, 1982]

VALERY, Paul (1871–1945)
Politics is the art of preventing people from becoming involved in affairs which concern them.

[*As Such 2* (1943)]

VIDAL, Gore (1925–)
Any American who is prepared to run for President should automatically, by definition, be disqualified from ever doing so.

[Attr.]

WALDEN, George (1939–)
[On John Major's policy of non-cooperation with Europe over the export ban on British beef]
Patriots are not supposed to make fools of their own people.

[*The Times*, May 1996]

WILSON, Harold (1916–1995)
The Labour Party is like a stage-coach. If you rattle along at great speed everybody inside is too exhilarated or too seasick to cause any trouble. But if you stop everybody gets out and argues about where to go next.

[In L. Smith, *Harold Wilson, The Authentic Portrait*]

ZAPPA, Frank (1940–1993)
Politics is the entertainment branch of industry.

[Attr.]

See CAPITALISM; COMMUNISM; FASCISM; SOCIALISM

POVERTY

BAGEHOT, Walter (1826–1877)
Poverty is an anomaly to rich people. It is very difficult to make out why people who want dinner do not ring the bell.

[*Literary Studies* (1879)]

BEHN, Aphra (1640–1689)
Come away; poverty's catching.

[*The Rover* (1677)]

THE BIBLE (KING JAMES VERSION)
The poor always ye have with you.

[*John*, 12:8]

BLAKE, William (1757–1827)
Is this a holy thing to see,
In a rich and fruitful land,
Babes reduc'd to misery,
Fed with cold and usurous hand?

['Holy Thursday' (1794)]

CHAMFORT, Nicolas (1741–1794)
The poor are the negroes of Europe.

[*Maximes et Pensées* (1796)]

COBBETT, William (1762–1835)
To be poor and independent is very nearly an impossibility.

[*Advice to Young Men* (1829)]

COWPER, William (1731–1800)
[Of a burglar]
He found it inconvenient to be poor.

['Charity' (1782)]

CRABBE, George (1754–1832)
The murmuring poor, who will not fast in peace.

[*The Newspaper* (1785)]

FARQUHAR, George (1678–1707)
'Tis still my maxim, that there is no scandal like rags, nor any crime so shameful as poverty.

[*The Beaux' Stratagem* (1707)]

GELDOF, Bob (1954–)
I'm not interested in the bloody system! Why has he no food? Why is he starving to death?

[In Care, *Sayings of the Eighties* (1989)]

JOHNSON, Samuel (1709–1784)
Resolve not to be poor: whatever you have, spend less. Poverty is a great enemy to human happiness; it certainly destroys liberty, and it makes some virtues impracticable

and others extremely difficult.
[Letter to Boswell, 1782]

JUVENAL (c. 60-130)
Rarely they rise by virtue's aid, who lie
Plung'd in the depths of help-less poverty.
[*Satires*; trans. Dryden]

SHAW, George Bernard (1856-1950)
The greatest of our evils and the worst of our crimes is poverty.
[*Major Barbara* (1907)]

TERESA, Mother (1910-)
. . . the poor are our brothers and sisters . . . people in the world who need love, who need care, who have to be wanted.
[*Time*, 1975]

TRACY, Spencer (1900-1967)
[Of leaner times in his life] There were times my pants were so thin I could sit on a dime and tell if it was heads or tails.
[In Swindell, *Spencer Tracy*]

WILDE, Oscar (1854-1900)
We are often told that the poor are grateful for charity. Some of them are, no doubt, but the best amongst the poor are never grateful. They are

ungrateful, discontented, dis-obedient, and rebellious. They are quite right to be so.
['The Soul of Man under Socialism' (1891)]

POWER

ACTON, Lord (1834-1902)
Power tends to corrupt, and absolute power corrupts absolutely. Great men are almost always bad men.
[Letter, 1887]

AMIS, Kingsley (1922-1995)
Generally, nobody behaves decently when they have power.
[*Radio Times*, 1992]

ANDREOTTI, Giulio (1919-)
Power wears down the man who doesn't have it.
[In Biagi, *The Good and the Bad* (1989)]

AUNG SAN SUU KYI
Concepts such as truth, jus-tice, compassion are often the only bulwarks which stand against ruthless power.
[*Index on Censorship*, 1994]

BURKE, Edmund (1729-1797)
Those who have been once intoxicated with power, and

have derived any kind of emolument from it, even though but for one year, never can willingly abandon it.

[*Letter to a Member of the National Assembly* (1791)]

CLARE, Dr Anthony (1942–)
Apart from the occasional saint, it is difficult for people who have the smallest amount of power to be nice.

[In Care, *Sayings of the Eighties* (1989)]

FAUST, Beatrice (1939–)
Women's Liberationists are both right and wrong when they say that rape is not about sex but about power: for men, sex is power, unless culture corrects biology.

[*Women, Sex and Pornography* (1980)]

GOERING, Hermann (1893–1946)
Guns will make us powerful; butter will only make us fat.

[Broadcast, 1936]

HITLER, Adolf (1889–1945)
Germany will either be a world power or will not exist at all.

[*Mein Kampf* (1927)]

JONES, Sir William (1746–1794)
My opinion is, that power

should always be distrusted, in whatever hands it is placed.

[In Teignmouth, *Life of Sir W. Jones* (1835)]

KISSINGER, Henry (1923–)
Power is the ultimate aphrodisiac.

[Attr.]

MAO TSE-TUNG (1893–1976)
Every Communist must grasp the truth. Political power grows out of the barrel of a gun.

[Speech, 1938]

MILL, John Stuart (1806–1873)
The only purpose for which power can be rightfully exercised over any member of a civilized community, against his will, is to prevent harm to others. His own good, either physical or moral, is not sufficient warrant.

[*On Liberty* (1859)]

RENAN, J. Ernest (1823–1892)
'Knowledge is power' is the finest idea ever put into words.

[*Dialogues et fragments philosophiques* (1876)]

STEVENSON, Adlai (1900–1965)
Power corrupts, but lack of

power corrupts absolutely.
[*The Observer*, 1963]

TURENNE, Henri, Vicomte (1611–1675)
God is always on the side of the big battalions.

[Attr.]

PRAISE

BIERCE, Ambrose (1842–c. 1914)
Eulogy: Praise of a person who has either the advantages of wealth and power, or the consideration to be dead.
[*The Enlarged Devil's Dictionary* (1961)]

GAY, John (1685–1732)
Praising all alike, is praising none.
['A Letter to a Lady' (1714)]

LA ROCHEFOUCAULD (1613–1680)
Refusal of praise reveals a desire to be praised twice over.
[*Maximes* (1678)]

MARTIAL (c. 40–c. 104)
They praise those works but they read something else.
[*Epigrammata*]

PROVERB
Self-praise is no recommendation.

SMITH, Sydney (1771–1845)
Praise is the best diet for us, after all.

[In Holland, *A Memoir of the Reverend Sydney Smith* (1855)]

THE PRESENT

CLARE, John (1793–1864)
The present is the funeral of the past,
And man the living sepulchre of life.

['The Past' (1845)]

EMERSON, Ralph Waldo (1803–1882)
Write it on your heart that every day is the best day in the year. No man has learned anything rightly until he knows that every day is Doomsday.
[*Society and Solitude* (1870)]

FRANKLIN, Benjamin (1706–1790)
The golden age never was the present age.
[*Poor Richard's Almanac* (1750)]

HORACE (65–8 BC)
Carpe diem.
Seize the day.

[*Odes*]

**MALLARME, Stéphane
(1842–1898)**
That virgin, vital, beautiful
day: today.
[*Plusieurs sonnets* (1881)]

**SHAKESPEARE, William
(1564–1616)**
Past and to come seems best;
things present, worst.
[*Henry IV, Part 2*, I.iii]

PRINCIPLES

**ADLER, Alfred
(1870–1937)**
It is easier to fight for one's
principles than to live up to
them.
[Attr.]

**BALDWIN, Stanley
(1867–1947)**
I would rather be an oppor-
tunist and float than go to the
bottom with my principles
round my neck.
[Attr.]

**MACKENZIE, Sir Compton
(1883–1972)**
I don't believe in principles.
Principles are only excuses for
what we want to think or
what we want to do.
[*The Adventures of Sylvia
Scarlett* (1918)]

**MELBOURNE, Lord
(1779–1848)**
Nobody ever did anything very
foolish except from some
strong principle.
[Attr.]

**ROOSEVELT, Franklin
Delano (1882–1945)**
To stand upon the ramparts
and die for our principles is
heroic, but to sally forth to
battle and win for our
principles is something more
than heroic.
[Speech, 1928]

**SADE, Marquis de
(1740–1814)**
All universal moral principles
are idle fancies.
[*The 120 Days of Sodom*
(1784)]

PRISON

**BRONTË, Emily
(1818–1848)**
Oh dreadful is the check –
intense the agony –
When the ear begins to hear
and the eye begins to see;
When the pulse begins to
throb, the brain to think
again;
The soul to feel the flesh and
the flesh to feel the chain!
['The Prisoner' (1846)]

DOWLING, Basil Cairns
[On prisons]
Prisoners and warders – we
are all of one blood.
They're much alike, except for
a different coat
And a different hat;
And they all seem decent,
kindly fellows enough
As they work and chat:
How can it be that men like
this have been hanged
By men like that?
[In Burton, *In Prison* (1945)]

FRANK, Otto
(1889-1980)
When you have survived life
in a concentration camp you
have ceased to count yourself
as a member of the human
race. You will forever be outside the experience of the rest
of mankind.
[In the *Daily Mail*, 1996]

HAWTHORNE, Nathaniel
(1804-1864)
The black flower of civilized
society, a prison.
[*The Scarlet Letter* (1850)]

INGRAMS, Richard (1937-)
[On the prospect of going to
gaol, 1976]
The only thing I really mind
about going to prison is the
thought of Lord Longford
coming to visit me.
[Attr.]

LOVELACE, Richard
(1618-1658)
Stone walls do not a prison
make
Nor iron bars a cage;
Minds innocent and quiet take
That for an hermitage;
If I have freedom in my love,
And in my soul am free;
Angels alone, that soar above,
Enjoy such liberty.
['To Althea, From Prison'
(1649)]

RALEIGH, Sir Walter
(c. 1552-1618)
But now close kept, as cap-
tives wonted are:
That food, that heat, that light
I find no more;
Despair bolts up my doors,
and I alone
Speak to dead walls, but
those hear not my moan.
[Untitled poem]

WAUGH, Evelyn
(1903-1966)
Anyone who has been to an
English public school will
always feel comparatively at
home in prison.
[*Decline and Fall* (1928)]

WILDE, Oscar
(1854-1900)
The vilest deeds like poison-
weeds
Bloom well in prison-air;
It is only what is good in Man

That wastes and withers there.

[*The Ballad of Reading Gaol* (1898)]

PROGRESS

ANONYMOUS
We've made great medical progress in the last generation. What used to be merely an itch is now an allergy.

BLAKE, William (1757–1827)
Without Contraries is no progression.
Attraction and Repulsion, Reason and Energy, Love and Hate, are necessary to Human existence.

[*The Marriage of Heaven and Hell* (c. 1793)]

BORGES, Jorge Luis (1899–1986)
We have stopped believing in progress. What progress that is!

[*Ibarra, Borges et Borges*]

BUTLER, Samuel (1835–1902)
All progress is based upon a universal innate desire on the part of every organism to live beyond its income.

[*The Note-Books of Samuel Butler* (1912)]

CLIFFORD, William Kingdon (1845–1879)
. . . scientific thought is not an accompaniement or condition of human progress, but human progress itself.

[*Aims and Instruments of Scientific Thought* (1872)]

COMTE, Auguste (1798–1857)
Love our principle, order our foundation, progress our goal.

[*Système de politique positive*]

DE KLERK, F.W. (1936–)
A man of destiny knows that beyond this hill lies another and another. The journey is never complete.

[*The Observer,* 1994]

DOUGLASS, Frederick (c. 1818–1895)
If there is no struggle, there is no progress.

[Attr.]

ELLIS, Havelock (1859–1939)
What we call 'Progress' is the exchange of one nuisance for another nuisance.

[*Impressions and Comments* (1914)]

FREUD, Sigmund (1856–1939)
What progress we are making. In the Middle Ages they

would have burned me. Now they are content with burning my books.

[Letter, 1933]

**GIBBON, Edward
(1737–1794)**
All that is human must retrograde if it does not advance.
[Decline and Fall of the Roman Empire (1776–88)]

**HEGEL, Georg Wilhelm
(1770–1831)**
The history of the world is none other than the progress of the consciousness of freedom.
[Philosophy of History]

**HUBBARD, Elbert
(1856–1915)**
The world is moving so fast these days that the man who says it can't be done is generally interrupted by someone doing it.
[Attr.]

**LINDBERGH, Anne Morrow
(1906–)**
Why do progress and beauty have to be so opposed?
[Hour of Gold, Hour of Lead (1973)]

**SAINT–EXUPERY, Antoine de
(1900–1944)**
Man's 'progress' is but a gradual discovery that his questions have no meaning.
[The Wisdom of the Sands]

**SHAW, George Bernard
(1856–1950)**
The reasonable man adapts himself to the world: the unreasonable one persists in trying to adapt the world to himself. Therefore all progress depends on the unreasonable man.
[Man and Superman (1903)]

**THURBER, James
(1894–1961)**
Progress was all right; only it went on too long.
[Attr.]

**VIGNEAUD, Vincent de
(1901–1978)**
Nothing holds up the progress of science so much as the right idea at the wrong time.
[Most Secret War (1978)]

**WALKER, Alice
(1944–)**
People tend to think that life really does progress for everyone eventually, that people progress, but actually only *some* people progress. The rest of the people don't.
[In C. Tate (ed.), Black Women Writers at Work (1983)]

PROPERTY

**DICKENS, Charles
(1812–1870)**
Get hold of portable property.
[*Great Expectations* (1861)]

**DRUMMOND, Thomas
(1797–1840)**
Property has its duties as well
as its rights.
[Letter, 1838]

**EMERSON, Ralph Waldo
(1803–1882)**
A man builds a fine house;
and now he has a master, and
a task for life; he is to furnish,
watch, show it, and keep it in
repair, the rest of his days.
[*Society and Solitude* (1870)]

**INGERSOLL, Robert Greene
(1833–1899)**
Few rich men own their own
property. The property owns
them.
[Address, 1896]

**JAMES, Henry
(1843–1916)**
The black and merciless
things that are behind the
great possessions.
[*The Ivory Tower* (1917)]

LOOS, Anita (1893–1981)
Kissing your hand may make
you feel very very good but a

diamond and safire bracelet
lasts forever.
[*Gentlemen Prefer Blondes*
(1925)]

**PROUDHON, Pierre-Joseph
(1809–1865)**
If I were asked to answer the
following question: 'What is
slavery?' and I replied in one
word, 'Murder!' my meaning
would be understood at once
. . . Why, then, to this other
question: 'What is property?'
may I not likewise answer
'Theft'?
[*Qu'est-ce que la propriété?*
(1840)]

PUNISHMENT

ARENDT, Hannah (1906–1975)
No punishment has ever pos-
sessed enough power of
deterrence to prevent the
commission of crimes.
[*Eichmann in Jerusalem* (1963)]

**BENTHAM, Jeremy
(1748–1832)**
All punishment is mischief: all
punishment in itself is evil.
[*An Introduction to the
Principles of Morals and
Legislation* (1789)]

GILBERT, W.S. (1836–1911)
My object all sublime

I shall achieve in time –
To let the punishment fit the crime –
The punishment fit the crime.
[*The Mikado* (1885)]

HALIFAX, Lord (1633–1695)
Men are not hang'd for stealing Horses, but that Horses may not be stolen.
['Of Punishment' (1750)]

HUBBARD, Elbert (1856–1915)
Men are not punished for their sins, but by them.
[*A Thousand and One Epigrams* (1911)]

JUVENAL (c. 60–130)
The chief punishment is this: that no guilty man is acquitted in his own judgement.
[*Satires*]

KARR, Alphonse (1808–1890)
If we want to abolish the death penalty, let our friends the murderers take the first step.
[*Les Guêpes* (1849)]

KEY, Ellen (1849–1926)
Corporal punishment is as humiliating for him who gives it as for him who receives it; it is ineffective besides. Neither shame nor physical pain have

any other effect than a hardening one.
[*The Century of the Child* (1909)]

SALMON, George (1819–1904)
[On hearing a colleague claiming to have been caned only once in his life, and that, for telling the truth]
Well, it certainly cured you, Mahaffy.
[Attr.]

SHAKESPEARE, William (1564–1616)
Use every man after his desert, and who shall scape whipping?
[*Hamlet*, II.ii]

STOWE, Harriet Beecher (1811–1896)
Whipping and abuse are like laudanum; you have to double the dose as the sensibilities decline.
[*Uncle Tom's Cabin* (1852)]

VIDAL, Gore (1925–)
[When asked for his views about corporal punishment]
I'm all for bringing back the birch, but only between consenting adults.
[TV interview with David Frost]

See CRIME

QUOTATIONS

CHURCHILL, Sir Winston (1874–1965)
It is a good thing for an uneducated man to read books of quotations
[*My Early Life* (1930)]

EMERSON, Ralph Waldo (1803-1882)
Every man is a borrower and a mimic, life is theatrical and literature a quotation.
[*Society and Solitude* (1870)]

Next to the originator of a good sentence is the first quoter of it.
[*Letters and Social Aims* (1875)]

MONTAGUE, C.E. (1867–1928)
To be amused at what you read – that is the great spring of happy quotation.
[*A Writer's Notes on his Trade* (1930)]

PEARSON, Hesketh (1887–1964)
A widely-read man never quotes accurately . . .
Misquotation is the pride and privilege of the learned.
[*Common Misquotations* (1937)]

Misquotations are the only quotations that are never misquoted.
[*Common Misquotations* (1937)]

RIBBLESDALE, Lord (1854-1925)
It [is] gentlemanly to get one's quotations very slightly wrong. In that way one unprigs oneself and allows the company to correct one.
[In Cooper, *The Light of Common Day* (1959)]

SHAW, George Bernard (1856-1950)
I often quote myself. It adds spice to the conversation.
[*Readers Digest* (1959)]

STOPPARD, Tom (1937-)
It is better to be quotable than to be honest.
[*The Guardian*]

WILLIAMS, Kenneth (1926-1988)
The nicest thing about quotes is that they give us a nodding acquaintance with the originator which is often socially impressive.
[*Acid Drops* (1980)]

YOUNG, Edward (1683-1765)
Some, for renown, on scraps of learning dote,
And think they grow immortal as they quote.
[*Love of Fame* (1728)]

RACE

BIKO, Steve (1946–1977)
We wanted to remove him
[the white man] from our
table, strip the table of all the
trappings put on it by him,
decorate it in true African
style, settle down and then
ask him to join us if he liked.
[Speech, 1971]

**DE BLANK, Joost
(1908–1968)**
I suffer from an incurable disease – colour blindness.
[Attr.]

**DISRAELI, Benjamin
(1804–1881)**
All is race; there is no other
truth.
[Tancred (1847)]

**EINSTEIN, Albert
(1879–1955)**
If my theory of relativity is
proven successful, Germany
will claim me as a German
and France will declare that I
am a citizen of the world.
Should my theory prove
untrue, France will say that I
am a German and Germany
will declare that I am a Jew.
[Address, c. 1929]

FANON, Frantz (1925–1961)
For the black man there is
only one destiny. And it is
white.
[Black Skin, White Masks]

GORDIMER, Nadine (1923–)
The force of white men's
wills, which dispensed and
withdrew life, imprisoned and
set free, fed or starved, like
God himself.
[Six Feet of the Country (1956)]

HITLER, Adolf (1889–1945)
Whoever is not racially pure
in this world is chaff.
[Mein Kampf (1925)]

**KING, Martin Luther
(1929–1968)**
I want to be the white man's
brother, not his brother-in-
law.
[New York Journal, 1962]

LESSING, Doris (1919–)
[Referring to South Africa]
When old settlers say 'One
has to understand the country', what they mean is, 'You
have to get used to our ideas
about the native.' They are
saying, in effect, 'Learn our
ideas, or otherwise get out;
we don't want you.'
[The Grass is Singing (1950)]

MANDELA, Nelson (1918–)
I have fought against white
domination, and I have fought
against black domination. I

have cherished the ideal of a democratic and free society in which all persons will live together in harmony and with equal opportunities. It is an ideal which I hope to live for and achieve. But, if needs be, it is an ideal for which I am prepared to die.
[Statement in the dock, 1964]

MENAND, Louis
The evil of modern society isn't that it creates racism but that it creates conditions in which people who don't suffer from injustice seem incapable of caring very much about people who do.
[The New Yorker, 1992]

MENCKEN, H.L.
(1880–1956)
One of the things that makes a Negro unpleasant to white folk is the fact that he suffers from their injustice. He is thus a standing rebuke to them.
[Notebooks (1956)]

MILLER, Arthur (1915–)
If there weren't any anti-semitism, I wouldn't think of myself as Jewish.
[The Observer, 1995]

PATON, Alan (1903–1988)
I have one great fear in my heart, that one day when they [whites] are turned to loving,

they will find we [blacks] are turned to hating.
[Cry, the Beloved Country (1948)]

PLOMER, William
(1903–1973)
The warm heart of any human that saw the black man first not as a black but as a man.
[Turbott Wolfe (1926)]

POWELL, Enoch (1912–)
[On race relations in Britain] As I look ahead I am filled with foreboding. Like the Roman I seem to see 'The River Tiber foaming with much blood'.
[Speech, 1968]

SHERIDAN, Philip Henry
(1831–1888)
The only good Indian is a dead Indian.
[Attr.]

TECUMSEH
(d. 1812)
Where today are the Pequot? Where are the Narragansett, the Mohican, the Pokanoket, and many other once powerful tribes of our people? They have vanished before the avarice and the oppression of the White Man, as snow before a summer sun.
[In Brown, Bury My Heart at Wounded Knee (1971)]

TOMASCHEK, Rudolphe
(b. c. 1895)
Modern Physics is an instrument of Jewry for the destruction of Nordic science . . .
True physics is the creation of the German spirit.
[In Shirer, *The Rise and Fall of the Third Reich* (1960)]

TUTU, Archbishop Desmond
(1931–)
It is very difficult now to find anyone in South Africa who ever supported apartheid.
[*The Observer*, 1994]

X, Malcolm (1925–1965)
I believe in the brotherhood of all men, but I don't believe in wasting brotherhood on anyone who doesn't want to practise it with me.
[Speech, 1964]

ZANGWILL, Israel
(1864–1926)
The law of dislike for the unlike will always prevail. And whereas the unlike is normally situated at a safe distance, the Jews bring the unlike into the heart of *every milieu*, and must therefore defend a frontier line as large as the world.
[Speech, 1911]

DESCARTES, René
(1596–1650)
The reading of all good books is like a conversation with the finest men of past centuries.
[*Discours de la Méthode* (1637)]

DISRAELI, Benjamin
(1804–1881)
[His customary reply to those who sent him unsolicited manuscripts]
Thank you for the manuscript; I shall lose no time in reading it.
[Attr.]

FLAUBERT, Gustave
(1821–1880)
Do not read, as children do, for the sake of entertainment, or like the ambitious, for the purpose of instruction. No, read in order to live.
[Letter, 1857]

FRANKLIN, Benjamin
(1706–1790)
[On being asked what condition of man he considered the most pitiable]
A lonesome man on a rainy day who does not know how to read.
[In Shriner, *Wit, Wisdom, and Foibles of the Great*]

REALISM

HAMERTON, P.G. (1834–1894)
The art of reading is to skip judiciously.
[*The Intellectual Life* (1873)]

HANDKE, Peter (1942–)
The most unthinking person of all: the one who only flicks through every book.
[*The Weight of the World. A Diary* (1977)]

HELPS, Sir Arthur (1813–1875)
Reading is sometimes an ingenious device for avoiding thought.
[*Friends in Council* (1849)]

JOHNSON, Samuel (1709–1784)
A man ought to read just as inclination leads him; for what he reads as a task will do him little good.
[In Boswell, *The Life of Samuel Johnson* (1791)]

MAO TSE-TUNG (1893–1976)
To read too many books is harmful.
[*The New Yorker,* 1977]

ORTON, Joe (1933–1967)
Reading isn't an occupation we encourage among police officers. We try to keep the paper work down to a minimum.
[*Loot* (1967)]

SMITH, Logan Pearsall (1865–1946)
People say that life is the thing, but I prefer reading.
[*Afterthoughts* (1931)]

STERNE, Laurence (1713–1768)
Digressions, incontestably, are the sunshine; – they are the life, the soul of reading; – take them out of this book for instance, – you might as well take the book along with them.
[*Tristram Shandy*]

WILDE, Oscar (1854–1900)
I never travel without my diary. One should always have something sensational to read in the train.
[*The Importance of Being Earnest* (1895)]

See BOOKS

REALISM

BACON, Francis (1561–1626)
We are much beholden to Machiavel and others, that write what men do, and not what they ought to do.
[*The Advancement of Learning* (1605)]

DÜRRENMATT, Friedrich (1921–1990)
Whoever is faced with the paradoxical exposes himself to reality.
[*The Physicists* (1962)]

ELIOT, T.S. (1888–1965)
Human kind
Cannot bear very much reality.
[*Four Quartets* (1944)]

HEGEL, Georg Wilhelm (1770–1831)
What is rational is real, and what is real is rational.
[*Basis of Legal Philosophy* (1820)]

KHRUSHCHEV, Nikita (1894–1971)
If you cannot catch a bird of paradise, better take a wet hen.
[Attr.]

TWAIN, Mark (1835–1910)
Don't part with your illusions. When they are gone, you may still exist, but you have ceased to live.
[*Pudd'nhead Wilson's Calendar* (1894)]

WILDE, Oscar (1854–1900)
Cecily: When I see a spade I call it a spade.
Gwendolen: I am glad to say that I have never seen a spade. It is obvious that our social spheres have been widely different.
[*The Importance of Being Earnest* (1895)]

See ART

REBELLION

ARNOLD, Thomas (1795–1842)
As for rioting, the old Roman way of dealing with that is always the right one; flog the rank and file, and fling the ringleaders from the Tarpeian rock.
[Letter, written before 1828]

BRADSHAW, John (1602–1659)
Rebellion to tyrants is obedience to God.
[In Randall, *Life of Jefferson* (1865)]

BURKE, Edmund (1729–1797)
Make the Revolution a parent of settlement, and not a nursery of future revolutions.
[*Reflections on the Revolution in France* (1790)]

CAMUS, Albert (1913–1960)
Every revolutionary ends as an oppressor or a heretic.
[*The Rebel* (1951)]

All modern revolutions have led to a reinforcement of the power of the State.
[*The Rebel* (1951)]

CONRAD, Joseph (1857–1924)
The scrupulous and the just, the noble, humane, and devoted natures; the unselfish and the intelligent may begin a movement – but it passes away from them. They are not the leaders of a revolution. They are its victims.
[*Under Western Eyes* (1911)]

DURRELL, Lawrence (1912–1990)
No one can go on being a rebel too long without turning into an autocrat.
[*Balthazar* (1958)]

ENGELS, Friedrich (1820–1895)
The proletariat has nothing to lose but its chains in this revolution. It has a world to win. Workers of the world, unite!
[*The Communist Manifesto* (1848)]

HILL, Reginald (1936–)
The first thing revolutionaries of the left or right give up is their sense of humour. The second thing is other people's rights.
[In Winks (ed.), *Colloquium on Crime* (1986)]

JEFFERSON, Thomas (1743–1826)
A little rebellion now and then is a good thing.
[Letter to James Madison, 1787]

SHAKESPEARE, William (1564–1616)
Rebellion lay in his way, and he found it.
[*Henry IV, Part 1*, V.i]

STORR, Dr Anthony (1920–)
It is harder to rebel against love than against authority.
[Attr.]

TROTSKY, Leon (1879–1940)
Insurrection is an art, and like all arts it has its laws.
[*History of the Russian Revolution* (1933)]

WEIL, Simone (1909–1943)
Nowadays we think of revolution not as the solution to problems posed by current developments but as a miracle which releases us from the obligation to solve these problems.
[*Oppression and Freedom* (1955)]

WELLINGTON, Duke of (1769–1852)
Beginning reform is beginning revolution.
[In Mrs Arbuthnot's Journal, 1830]

RELIGION

**ADDISON, Joseph
(1672–1719)**
We have in England a particular bashfulness in every thing that regards religion.
[*The Spectator*, 1712]

**ARNOLD, Matthew
(1822–1888)**
The true meaning of religion is thus not simply morality, but morality touched by emotion.
[*Literature and Dogma* (1873)]

**BARRIE, Sir J.M.
(1860–1937)**
One's religion is whatever he is most interested in, and yours is Success.
[*The Twelve-Pound Look*]

**BEHAN, Brendan
(1923–1964)**
Pound notes are the best religion in the world.
[*The Wit of Brendan Behan* (1968)]

**BLAKE, William
(1757–1827)**
I went to the Garden of Love, And saw what I never had seen:
A Chapel was built in the midst, Where I used to play on the green.

And the gates of this Chapel were shut,
And 'Thou shalt not' writ over the door . . .

And Priests in black gowns were walking their rounds,
And binding with briars my joys & desires.
['The Garden of Love' (1794)]

**BROWNE, Sir Thomas
(1605–1682)**
Persecution is a bad and indirect way to plant religion.
[*Religio Medici* (1643)]

**BURKE, Edmund
(1729–1797)**
Nothing is so fatal to religion as indifference, which is, at least, half infidelity.
[Letter to William Smith, 1795]

**BURTON, Robert
(1577–1640)**
One religion is as true as another.
[*Anatomy of Melancholy* (1621)]

BUTLER, Samuel (1835–1902)
To be at all is to be religious more or less.
[*The Note-Books of Samuel Butler* (1912)]

**COLTON, Charles Caleb
(c. 1780–1832)**
Men will wrangle for religion;

write for it; fight for it; anything but – live for it.
[*Lacon* (1820)]

DIOGENES (THE CYNIC)
(c. 400–325 BC)
I do not know whether there
are gods, but there ought to be.
[In Tertullian, *Ad Nationes*]

DIX, George (1901–1952)
It is no accident that the sym-
bol of a bishop is a crook, and
the sign of an archbishop is a
double-cross.
[Letter to *The Times*, 1977]

ELLIS, Havelock
(1859–1939)
The whole religious com-
plexion of the modern world
is due to the absence from
Jerusalem of a lunatic asylum.
[*Impressions and Comments*
(1914)]

EMERSON, Ralph Waldo
(1803–1882)
The religions we call false
were once true.
['Character' (1866)]

I have heard with admiring
submission the experience of
the lady who declared that
'the sense of being well-dressed
gives a feeling of inward
tranquillity which religion is
powerless to bestow.'
['Social Aims' (1875)]

FREUD, Sigmund
(1856–1939)
Religion is an illusion and it
derives its strength from the
fact that it falls in with our
instinctual desires.
[*New Introductory Lectures on
Psychoanalysis* (1933)]

HOOTON, Harry (1908–1961)
Psychology is the theology of
the twentieth century.
['Inhuman Race']

JERROLD, Douglas William
(1803–1857)
Religion's in the heart, not in
the knees.
[*The Devil's Ducat* (1830)]

MARLOWE, Christopher
(1564–1593)
I count religion but a childish
toy,
And hold there is no sin but
ignorance.
[*The Jew of Malta* (c. 1592)]

MARX, Karl (1818–1883)
Religion . . . is the opium of
the people.
[*A Contribution to the Critique
of Hegel's Philosophy of Right*
(1844)]

MELBOURNE, Lord
(1779–1848)
[On listening to an evangelical
sermon]
Things have come to a pretty

pass when religion is allowed to invade the sphere of private life.

[In Russell, *Collections and Recollections* (1898)]

O'CASEY, Sean
(1880–1964)

There's no reason to bring religion into it. I think we ought to have as great a regard for religion as we can, so as to keep it out of as many things as possible.

[*The Plough and the Stars* (1926)]

RUNCIMAN, Sir Steven
(1903–)

Unlike Christianity, which preached a peace that it never achieved, Islam unashamedly came with a sword.

[*A History of the Crusades* (1954)]

SHAW, George Bernard
(1856–1950)

I can't talk religion to a man with bodily hunger in his eyes.

[*Major Barbara* (1907)]

SWIFT, Jonathan
(1667–1745)

We have just enough religion to make us hate, but not enough to make us love one another.

[*Thoughts on Various Subjects* (1711)]

WEBB, Beatrice
(1858–1943)

Religion is love; in no case is it logic.

[*My Apprenticeship* (1926)]

ZANGWILL, Israel
(1864–1926)

Let us start a new religion with one commandment, 'Enjoy thyself'.

[*Children of the Ghetto* (1892)]

REPUTATION

BURNEY, Fanny
(1752–1840)

Nothing is so delicate as the reputation of a woman; it is at once the most beautiful and most brittle of all human things.

[*Evelina* (1778)]

MITCHELL, Margaret
(1900–1949)

Until you've lost your reputation, you never realize what a burden it was or what freedom really is.

[*Gone with the Wind* (1936)]

SHAKESPEARE, William
(1564–1616)

Good name in man and woman, dear my lord,
Is the immediate jewel of their souls:

Who steals my purse steals
trash; 'tis something, nothing;
'Twas mine, 'tis his, and has
been slave to thousands;
But he that filches from me
my good name
Robs me of that which not
enriches him
And makes me poor indeed.
[*Othello*, III.iii]

WASHINGTON, George
(1732–1799)
Associate yourself with men
of good quality if you esteem
your own reputation; for 'tis
better to be alone than in bad
company.
[*Rules of Civility and Decent
Behaviour*]

See CHARACTER

REVENGE

ATWOOD, Margaret
(1939–)
An eye for an eye leads only
to more blindness.
[*Cat's Eye* (1988)]

BACON, Francis
(1561–1626)
Revenge is a kind of wild justice, which the more man's
nature runs to, the more
ought law to weed it out.
['Of Revenge' (1625)]

A man that studieth revenge
keeps his own wounds green.
['Of Revenge' (1625)]

THE BIBLE (KING JAMES
VERSION)
Vengeance is mine; I will
repay, saith the Lord.
[*Romans*, 12:19]

CYRANO DE BERGERAC
(1619–1655)
The universe may perish, so
long as I have my revenge.
[*La Mort d'Agrippine* (1654)]

MILTON, John (1608–1674)
Revenge, at first though
sweet,
Bitter ere long back on it self
recoils.
[*Paradise Lost* (1667)]

SHAKESPEARE, William
(1564–1616)
Let's make us med'cines of
our great revenge
To cure this deadly grief.
[*Macbeth*, IV.iii]

RIDICULE

ALBEE, Edward (1928–)
I have a fine sense of the
ridiculous, but no sense of
humour.
[*Who's Afraid of Virginia Woolf?*
(1962)]

NAPOLEON I (1769–1821)
It is only one step from the sublime to the ridiculous.

[Attr.]

SCOTT, Sir Walter (1771–1832)
Ridicule often checks what is absurd, and fully as often smothers that which is noble.

[*Quentin Durward* (1823)]

RIGHTS

CONDORCET, Antoine-Nicolas de (1743–1794)
Either none of mankind possesses genuine rights, or everyone shares them equally; whoever votes against another's rights, whatever his religion, colour or sex, forswears his own.

[In Vansittart (ed.), *Voices of the Revolution* (1989)]

JEFFERSON, Thomas (1743–1826)
We hold these truths to be self-evident: that all men are created equal; that they are endowed by their Creator with certain unalienable rights; that among these are life, liberty, and the pursuit of happiness.

[Declaration of Independence, 1776]

JOHNSON, Samuel (1709–1784)
I have got no further than this: Every man has a right to utter what he thinks truth, and every other man has a right to knock him down for it. Martyrdom is the test.

[In Boswell, *The Life of Samuel Johnson* (1791)]

MAGNA CARTA (1215)
No free man shall be taken or imprisoned or dispossessed, or outlawed or exiled, or in any way destroyed, nor will we go upon him, nor will we send against him, except by the lawful judgement of his peers or by the law of the land.

[Clause 39]

PANKHURST, Emmeline (1858–1928)
Women had always fought for men, and for their children. Now they were ready to fight for their own human rights. Our militant movement was established.

[*My Own Story* (1914)]

UNIVERSAL DECLARATION OF HUMAN RIGHTS
All human beings are born free and equal in dignity and rights.

[Article 1]

ROYALTY

ARCHER, Lord Jeffrey
(1940–)
An entire family of divorcees, and they're head of the Church of England. It's going to make the person out there wonder if it's all worth it.
[Comment on the Royal Family, 1992]

BURCHILL, Julie
(1960–)
[Of Princess Diana]
She is Madonna crossed with Mother Theresa – a glorious totem of Western ideals.
[*Sex and Sensibility* (1992)]

ELIZABETH I
(1533–1603)
[Of the approaching Armada]
I know I have the body of a weak and feeble woman, but I have the heart and stomach of a king, and of a king of England too; and think foul scorn that Parma or Spain, or any prince of Europe, should dare to invade the borders of my realm.
[Speech, 1588]

Though God hath raised me high, yet this I count the glory of my crown: that I have reigned with your loves.
[The Golden Speech, 1601]

GEORGE VI
(1895–1952)
We're not a family; we're a firm.
[Attr. in Lane, *Our Future King*]

MACHIAVELLI
(1469–1527)
In order to keep his people united and faithful, a prince must not be concerned with being reputed as a cruel man.
[*The Prince* (1532)]

SHAKESPEARE, William
(1564–1616)
Uneasy lies the head that wears a crown.
[*Henry IV, Part 2*, III.i]

I think the King is but a man as I am: the violet smells to him as it doth to me.
[*Henry V*, IV.i]

WORSTHORNE, Sir Peregrine
(1923–)
A little more willingness to bore, and much less eagerness to entertain, would do the monarchy no end of good.
[*The Sunday Telegraph*, 1993]

SCHOOL

CLARK, Lord Kenneth (1903–1983)
[On boarding schools]
This curious, and, to my mind, objectionable feature of English education was maintained solely in order that parents could get their children out of the house.
[*Another Part of the Wood* (1974)]

DAVIES, Robertson (1913–1995)
The most strenuous efforts of the most committed educationalists in the years since my boyhood have been quite unable to make a school into anything but a school, which is to say a jail with educational opportunities.
[*The Cunning Man* (1994)]

FIELDING, Henry (1707–1754)
Public schools are the nurseries of all vice and immorality.
[*Joseph Andrews* (1742)]

FORSTER, E.M. (1879–1970)
[Of public schoolboys]
They go forth into it [the world] with well-developed bodies, fairly developed minds, and undeveloped hearts.
[*Abinger Harvest* (1936)]

WELLINGTON, Duke of (1769–1852)
The battle of Waterloo was won on the playing fields of Eton.
[Attr.]

See EDUCATION; TEACHERS

SCIENCE

AUDEN, W. H. (1907–1973)
The true men of action in our time, those who transform the world, are not the politicians and statesmen, but the scientists.
[*The Dyer's Hand* (1963)]

BAINBRIDGE, Kenneth (1904–)
Now we are all sons of bitches.
[Remark after directing the first atomic test, 1945]

BRONOWSKI, Jacob (1908-1974)
Science has nothing to be ashamed of, even in the ruins of Nagasaki.
[*Science and Human Values*]

CHOMSKY, Noam (1928–)
As soon as questions of will or decision or reason or choice of action arise, human science is at a loss.
[Television interview, 1978]

CLARKE, Arthur C. (1917–)
Technology, sufficiently
advanced, is indistinguishable
from magic.

[*The Times*, 1996]

**CRONENBERG, David
(1943–)**
A virus is only doing its job.

[*The Sunday Telegraph*, 1992]

DAGG, Fred (1948–)
I can see . . . why a man who
lives in Colorado is so anxious
for all this nuclear activity to
go on in Australia, an area
famed among nuclear scientists for its lack of immediate
proximity to their own resi-
dential areas.

[*Dagshead Revisited* (1989)]

**DÜRRENMATT, Friedrich
(1921–1990)**
Our science has become terrible, our research dangerous,
our knowledge fatal.

[*The Physicists* (1962)]

**EDDINGTON, Sir Arthur
(1882–1944)**
We used to think that if we
knew one, we knew two,
because one and one are two.
We are finding that we must
learn a great deal more about
'and'.

[In Mackay, *The Harvest of a
Quiet Eye* (1977)]

**EINSTEIN, Albert
(1879–1955)**
A theory can be proved by
experiment; but no path leads
from experiment to the birth
of a theory.

[In Mackay, *The Harvest of a
Quiet Eye* (1977)]

When a man sits with a pretty
girl for an hour, it seems like
a minute. But let him sit on a
hot stove for a minute – and
it's longer than any hour.
That's relativity.

[Attr.]

**HEISENBERG, Werner
(1901–1976)**
Natural science does not simply describe and explain
nature, it is part of the interplay
between nature and ourselves.

[Attr.]

HUXLEY, T.H. (1825–1895)
The great tragedy of Science –
the slaying of a beautiful
hypothesis by an ugly fact.

[*British Association Annual
Report* (1870)]

**JEANS, Sir James Hopwood
(1877–1946)**
Science should leave off making pronouncements: the river
of knowledge has too often
turned back on itself.

[*The Mysterious Universe*
(1930)]

MONTAIGNE, Michel de (1533–1592)
Science without conscience is but death of the soul.

[In Simcox, *Treasury of Quotations*]

NEWTON, Sir Isaac (1642–1727)
If I have seen further it is by standing on the shoulders of giants.

[Letter to Robert Hooke, 1675–76]

OPPENHEIMER, J. Robert (1904–1967)
[On the consequences of the first atomic test]
The physicists have known sin; and this is a knowledge which they cannot lose.

[Lecture, 1947]

PASTEUR, Louis (1822–1895)
In the field of observation, chance favours only the prepared mind.

[Lecture, 1854]

PEACOCK, Thomas Love (1785–1866)
I almost think it is the ultimate destiny of science to exterminate the human race.

[*Gryll Grange* (1861)]

PORTER, Sir George (1920–)
Should we force science down the throats of those that have no taste for it? Is it our duty to drag them kicking and screaming into the twenty-first century? I am afraid that it is.

[Speech, 1986]

ROUX, Joseph (1834–1886)
Science is for those who learn; poetry, for those who know.

[*Meditations of a Parish Priest* (1886)]

STENHOUSE, David (1932–)
[On the conservation of biological resources]
I know a man who has a device for converting solar energy into food. Delicious stuff he makes with it, too. Being doing it for years . . . It's called a farm.

[*Crisis in Abundance* (1966)]

SZENT-GYÖRGYI, Albert von (1893–1986)
Discovery consists of seeing what everybody has seen and thinking what nobody has thought.

[In Good (ed.), *The Scientist Speculates* (1962)]

SCOTLAND

BARRIE, Sir J.M. (1860–1937)
There are few more impres-

sive sights in the world than a
Scotsman on the make.
[*What Every Woman Knows*
(1908)]

BOORDE, Andrew
(c. 1490–1549)

Trust your no Skott.
[Letter to Thomas Cromwell,
1536]

The devellysche dysposicion
of a Scottysh man, not to love
nor favour an Englishe man.
[Letter to Thomas Cromwell,
1536]

BURNS, Robert (1759–1796)

My heart's in the Highlands,
my heart is not here,
My heart's in the Highlands a-
chasing the deer,
A-chasing the wild deer and
following the roe –
My heart's in the Highlands,
wherever I go!
['My Heart's in the Highlands'
(1790)]

The story of Wallace poured a
Scottish prejudice in my veins
which will boil along there till
the flood-gates of life shut in
eternal rest.
[Letter to Dr Moore, 1787]

CLEVELAND, John
(1613–1658)

Had Cain been Scot, God
would have changed his
doom,
Nor forced him wander, but
confined him home.
['The Rebel Scot' (1647)]

EWART, Gavin (1916–1995)

The Irish are great talkers
Persuasive and disarming,
You can say lots and lots
Against the Scots –
But at least they're never
charming!
[*The Complete Little Ones*
(1986)]

HAMILTON, Ian (1925–)

[On the performance of
Scottish National Party MPs in
Westminster]

Courage is a quality Scots lack
only when they become MPs.
They should be twisting the
lion's tail until it comes out by
the roots.
[*Daily Mail*, 1996]

JENKINS, Robin
(1912–)

Football has taken the place
of religion in Scotland.
[*A Would-Be Saint*]

JOHNSON, Samuel
(1709–1784)

A Scotchman must be a very
sturdy moralist who does not
love Scotland better than
truth.
[*A Journey to the Western
Islands of Scotland* (1775)]

KEILLOR, Garrison (1942–)
Lutherans are like Scottish
people, only with less frivolity.
[*The Independent*, 1992]

**MACDIARMID, Hugh
(1892–1978)**
It's easier to lo'e Prince
Charlie
Than Scotland – mair's the
shame!
['Bonnie Prince Charlie' (1930)]

The rose of all the world is
not for me
I want for my part
Only the little white rose of
Scotland
That smells sharp and sweet
– and breaks the heart.
['The Little White Rose']

NICHOLSON, Emma (1941–)
England treats Scotland as if it
was an island off the coast of
West Africa in the 1830s.
[*Daily Mail*, 1996]

**NORTH, Christopher
(1785–1854)**
Minds like ours, my dear
James, must always be above
national prejudices, and in all
companies it gives me true
pleasure to declare, that, as a
people, the English are very
little indeed inferior to the
Scotch.
[*Blackwood's Edinburgh
Magazine*, 1826]

OGILVY, James (1663–1730)
[On signing the Act of Union]
Now there's an end of ane old
song.

[Remark, 1707]

**SCOTT, Sir Walter
(1771–1832)**
Still from the sire the son
shall hear
Of the stern strife, and car-
nage drear,
Of Flodden's fatal field,
Where shiver'd was fair
Scotland's spear,
And broken was her shield!
[*Marmion* (1808)]

**WODEHOUSE, P.G.
(1881–1975)**
It is never difficult to distinguish between a Scotsman
with a grievance and a ray of
sunshine.
[*Blandings Castle and
Elsewhere* (1935)]

THE SEA

AESCHYLUS (525–456 BC)
The ceaseless twinkling
laughter of the waves of the
sea.

[*Prometheus Bound*]

BYRON, Lord (1788–1824)
Dark-heaving – boundless,
endless, and sublime,

The image of eternity.
[*Childe Harold's Pilgrimage*
(1818)]

CARSON, Rachel
(1907–1964)
In its mysterious past, it encompasses all the dim origins of life and receives in the end . . . the dead husks of that same life. For all at last return to the sea – to Oceanus, the ocean river, like the ever-flowing stream of time, the beginning and the end.
[*The Sea Around Us* (1951)]

CHOPIN, Kate (1851–1904)
The voice of the sea speaks to the soul. The touch of the sea is sensuous, enfolding the body in its soft, close embrace.
[*The Awakening* (1899)]

CLAYTON, Keith (1928–)
[Of sewage]
You can do far worse than putting it into a deep and well-flushed sea. As far as poisoning the fish are concerned, that's rubbish. The sewage has probably kept the poor fish alive.
[*The Times*, 1992]

COLERIDGE, Samuel Taylor
(1772–1834)
As idle as a painted ship
Upon a painted ocean.

Water, water, every where,
And all the boards did shrink;
Water, water, every where
Nor any drop to drink.
['The Rime of the Ancient
Mariner' (1798)]

CONRAD, Joseph
(1857–1924)
This could have occurred nowhere but in England, where men and sea interpenetrate, so to speak.
[*Youth* (1902)]

The sea has never been friendly to man. At most it has been the accomplice of human restlessness.
[Attr.]

CUNNINGHAM, Allan
(1784–1842)
A wet sheet and a flowing sea,
A wind that follows fast
And fills the white and rustling sail
And bends the gallant mast.
['A Wet Sheet and a Flowing
Sea' (1825)]

DICKENS, Charles
(1812–1870)
I want to know what it says . . . The sea, Floy, what it is that it keeps on saying?
[*Dombey and Son* (1848)]

DONNE, John (1572–1631)
The sea is as deepe in a
calme as in a storme.
[*Sermons*]

**FLECKER, James Elroy
(1884–1915)**
The dragon-green, the luminous, the dark, the serpent-
haunted sea.
[*The Golden Journey to
Samarkand* (1913)]

JOYCE, James (1882–1941)
The snotgreen sea. The scro-
tumtightening sea.
[*Ulysses* (1922)]

**MASEFIELD, John
1878–1967)**
I must go down to the seas
again, to the lonely sea and
the sky,
And all I ask is a tall ship and
a star to steer her by,
['Sea Fever' (1902)]

**RIMBAUD, Arthur
1854–1891)**
I have bathed in the Poem
Of the Sea, steeped in stars,
milky,
Devouring the green azures.
['Le Bâteau ivre' (1870)]

**ROSSETTI, Dante Gabriel
1828–1882)**
The sea hath no king but God
alone.
['The White Ship']

SYNGE, J.M. (1871–1909)
'A man who is not afraid of
the sea will soon be
drownded,' he said, 'for he
will be going out on a day he
shouldn't. But we do be afraid
of the sea, and we do only be
drownded now and again.'
[*The Aran Islands* (1907)]

UVAVNUK
The great sea
Has set me adrift
It moves me as the weed in
the river,
Earth and the great weather
Move me,
Have carried me away
And move my inward parts
with joy.
[In Rasmussen, *Intellectual
Culture of the Igulik Eskimos*
(1929)]

**WHITING, William
(1825–1878)**
Eternal Father, strong to save,
Whose arm hath bound the
restless wave,
. . . O hear us when we cry to
Thee
For those in peril on the sea.
[Hymn, 1869]

THE SEASONS

ADAMS, Richard (1920–)
Many human beings say that

they enjoy the winter, but what they really enjoy is feeling proof against it.
[*Watership Down* (1974)]

COLERIDGE, Samuel Taylor (1772–1834)
Summer has set in with its usual severity.
[*Letters of Charles Lamb* (1888)]

HOLMES, Oliver Wendell (1809–1894)
For him in vain the envious seasons roll
Who bears eternal summer in his soul.
['The Old Player' (1861)]

HOOD, Thomas (1799–1845)
I saw old Autumn in the misty morn
Stand shadowless like Silence, listening
To silence.
['Ode: Autumn' (1823)]

SANTAYANA, George (1863–1952)
To be interested in the changing seasons is, in this middling zone, a happier state of mind than to be hopelessly in love with spring.
[*Little Essays* (1920)]

SHAKESPEARE, William (1564–1616)
At Christmas I no more desire a rose
Than wish a snow in May's new-fangled shows;
But like of each thing that in season grows.
[*Love's Labour's Lost*, I.i]

WALPOLE, Horace (1717–1797)
The way to ensure summer in England is to have it framed and glazed in a comfortable room.
[Letter to William Cole, 1774]

See WEATHER

SECRETS

ACTON, Lord (1834–1902)
Everything secret degenerates . . . nothing is safe that does not show how it can bear discussion and publicity.
[Attr.

CERVANTES (1547–1616)
Brazenness and public liberties do much more harm to a woman's honour than secret wickedness.
[*Don Quixote* (1615)

CONGREVE, William (1670–1729)
I know that's a secret, for it's whispered everywhere.
[*Love for Love* (1695)

DRYDEN, John (1631–1700)
For secrets are edged tools,
And must be kept from children and from fools.
[*Sir Martin Mar-All* (1667)]

FRANKLIN, Benjamin (1706–1790)
Three may keep a secret, if two of them are dead.
[*Poor Richard's Almanac* (1735)]

FRANKS, Oliver, Baron (1905–1992)
It is a secret in the Oxford sense: you may tell it to only one person at a time.
[*Sunday Telegraph*, 1977]

FROST, Robert (1874–1963)
We dance round in a ring and suppose,
But the Secret sits in the middle and knows.
['The Secret Sits' (1942)]

SELF

ARNOLD, Matthew (1822–1888)
Resolve to be thyself; and know, that he,
Who finds himself, loses his misery!
['Self–Dependence' (1852)]

BRONTË, Emily (1818–1848)
He is more myself than I am.
[*Wuthering Heights* (1847)]

BURNS, Robert (1759–1796)
O wad some Power the giftie gie us
To see oursels as ithers see us!
['To a Louse' (1786)]

CARLYLE, Thomas (1795–1881)
A certain inarticulate Self-consciousness dwells dimly in us . . . Hence, too, the folly of that impossible precept, *Know thyself*; till it be translated into this partially possible one, *Know what thou canst work at*.
[*Sartor Resartus* (1834)]

EMERSON, Ralph Waldo (1803–1882)
All sensible people are selfish, and nature is tugging at every contract to make the terms of it fair.
[*Conduct of Life* (1860)]

HILLEL, 'The Elder' (c. 60 BC–c. 10 AD)
If I am not for myself who is for me; and being for my own self what am I? If not now when?
[In Taylor (ed.), *Sayings of the Jewish Fathers* (1877)]

HUXLEY, Aldous (1894–1963)
There's only one corner of the universe you can be certain of improving, and that's your own self.
[*Time Must Have a Stop* (1944)]

JOAD, C.E.M. (1891–1953)
Whenever I look inside myself I am afraid.
[*The Observer*, 1942]

KEMPIS, Thomas à (c. 1380–1471)
The humble knowledge of thyself is a surer way to God than the deepest search after learning.
[*De Imitatione Christi* (1892)]

LA ROCHEFOUCAULD (1613–1680)
Self-love is the greatest flatterer of all.
[*Maximes* (1678)]

Self-interest speaks every kind of language, and plays every role, even that of disinterestedness.
[*Maximes* (1678)]

MANSFIELD, Katherine (1888–1923)
[On human limitations]
To have the courage of your excess – to find the limit of yourself.
[*Journal of Katherine Mansfield* (1954)]

MOLIERE (1622–1673)
We should look long and carefully at ourselves before we consider judging others.
[*Le Misanthrope* (1666)]

MONTAIGNE, Michel de (1533–1592)
The greatest thing in the world is to know how to belong to oneself.
[*Essais* (1580)]

POWELL, Anthony (1905–)
He fell in love with himself at first sight and it is a passion to which he has always remained faithful. Self-love seems so often unrequited.
[*The Acceptance World* (1955)]

RUSSELL, Bertrand (1872–1970)
Man is not a solitary animal, and so long as social life survives, self-realization cannot be the supreme principle of ethics.
[*A History of Western Philosophy* (1946)]

SHAKESPEARE, William (1564–1616)
This above all – to thine own self be true,
And it must follow, as the night the day,
Thou canst not then be false to any man.
[*Hamlet*, I.iii]

**SHAW, George Bernard
(1856–1950)**
It is easy – terribly easy – to
shake a man's faith in himself.
To take advantage of that to
break a man's spirit is devil's
work.

[*Candida* (1898)]

**TOLSTOY, Leo
(1828–1910)**
I am always with myself, and
it is I who am my own tor-
mentor.
[*Memoirs of a Madman* (1943)]

**TROLLOPE, Anthony
(1815–1882)**
Never think that you're not
good enough yourself. A man
should never think that. My
belief is that in life people will
take you very much at your
own reckoning.
[*The Small House at Allington*
(1864)]

**WHITMAN, Walt
(1819–1892)**
Behold, I do not give lectures
or a little charity,
When I give I give myself.
['Song of Myself' (1855)]

**WILDE, Oscar
(1854–1900)**
Other people are quite dreadful. The only possible society
is oneself.
[*An Ideal Husband* (1895)]

**BAYLY, Thomas Haynes
(1797–1839)**
Absence makes the heart
grow fonder,
Isle of Beauty, Fare thee well!
['Isle of Beauty', song, 1830]

**BRENNAN, Christopher
(1870–1932)**
I am shut out of mine own
heart
because my love is far from
me.
['I Am Shut Out of Mine Own
Heart' (1914)]

**BUSSY-RABUTIN, Comte de
(1618–1693)**
Absence is to love what the
wind is to fire; it extinguishes
the small, it kindles the great.
[*Histoire Amoureuse des Gaules*
(1665)]

COPE, Wendy (1945–)
The day he moved out was
terrible –
That evening she went
through hell.
His absence wasn't a problem
But the corkscrew had gone
as well.
['Loss' (1992)]

**JAGO, Rev. Richard
(1715–1781)**
With leaden foot time creeps

along
While Delia is away.

[*Absence*]

KEATS, John (1795–1821)
I wish you could invent some
means to make me at all
happy without you. Every
hour I am more and more
concentrated in you; every
thing else tastes like chaff in
my Mouth.
[Letter to Fanny Brawne, 1820]

POUND, Ezra (1885–1972)
And if you ask how I regret
that parting:
It is like the flowers falling at
Spring's end
Confused, whirled in a tangle.
What is the use of talking, and
there is no end of talking,
There is no end of things in
the heart.

['Exile's Letter' (1915)]

**SCHOPENHAUER, Arthur
(1788–1860)**
Every separation gives a foretaste of death, – and every
reunion a foretaste of resurrection.
[*Parerga und Paralipomena* (1851)]

**SHAKESPEARE, William
(1564–1616)**
Parting is such sweet sorrow
That I shall say good night till
it be morrow.

[*Romeo and Juliet*, II.ii]

ALLEN, Woody (1935–)
Hey, don't knock mastur-
bation! It's sex with someone
I love.

[*Annie Hall*, film, 1977]

On bisexuality: It immediately
doubles your chances for a
date on Saturday night.
[*New York Times*, 1975]

ANONYMOUS
Post coitum omne animal triste.
After coition every animal is
sad.

[Post-classical saying]

AUGUSTINE, Saint (354–430)
Give me chastity and conti-
nence, but not yet.
[*Confessions* (398)]

**BANKHEAD, Tallulah
(1903–1968)**
[To an admirer]
I'll come and make love to
you at five o'clock. If I'm late
start without me.
[In Morgan, *Somerset
Maugham* (1980)]

BURCHILL, Julie (1960–)
Sex, on the whole, was meant
to be short, nasty and brutish.
If what you want is cuddling,
you should buy a puppy.
[*Sex and Sensibility* (1992)]

CAMPBELL, Mrs Patrick (1865–1940)
I don't mind where people make love, so long as they don't do it in the street and frighten the horses.

[Attr.]

CHESTERFIELD, Lord (1694–1773)
[On sex]
The pleasure is momentary, the position ridiculous, and the expense damnable.

[Attr.]

COMFORT, Alex (1920–)
A woman who has the divine gift of lechery will always make a superlative partner.

[Attr.]

COOGAN, Tim Pat (1935–)
[Describing the Catholic Church's rulings on sexual morality]
It's rather like teaching swimming from a book without ever having got wet oneself.

[*Disillusioned Decades* (1987)]

DAVIES, Robertson (1913–1995)
Sex that is not an evidence of a strong human tie is just like blowing your nose; it's not a celebration of a splendid relationship.

[Interview, 1974]

DONNE, John (1572–1631)
Licence my roving hands, and let them go,
Before, behind, between, above, below.
O my America! my new-found-land,
My kingdom, safeliest when one man mann'd.
['To His Mistress Going to Bed' (c. 1595)]

DURRELL, Lawrence (1912–1990)
No more about sex, it's too boring.

[*Tunc* (1968)]

DWORKIN, Andrea (1946–)
Intercourse as an act often expresses the power men have over women.

[*Intercourse* (1987)]

Seduction is often difficult to distinguish from rape. In seduction, the rapist often bothers to buy a bottle of wine.

[*The Independent*, 1992]

FAIRBAIRN, Sir Nicholas (1933–1995)
Most cases of rape are reported as an act of vengeance because the fellow has got himself another woman. Or guilt.

[*Daily Mail*, 1993]

SEX

**FIGES, Eva
(1932–)**
When modern woman discovered the orgasm it was (combined with modern birth control) perhaps the biggest single nail in the coffin of male dominance.

[In Morgan, *The Descent of Woman* (1972)]

**GWYN, Nell
(1650–1687)**
[On prostitution]
As for me, it is my profession, I do not pretend to anything better.

[In Miles, *The Women's History of the World* (1988)]

**HERRICK, Robert
(1591–1674)**
Night makes no difference 'twixt the Priest and Clark; Jone as my Lady is as good i' th' dark.

[*Hesperides* (1648)]

**HILLINGDON, Lady Alice
(1857–1940)**
I am happy now that Charles calls on my bedchamber less frequently than of old. As it is, I now endure but two calls a week and when I hear his steps outside my door I lie down on my bed, close my eyes, open my legs and think of England.

[*Journal* (1912)]

**HUXLEY, Aldous
(1894–1963)**
'Bed,' as the Italian proverb succinctly puts it, 'is the poor man's opera.'

[*Heaven and Hell* (1956)]

LANDERS, Ann (1918–)
Women complain about sex more often than men. Their gripes fall into two major categories: (1) Not enough (2) Too much.

[*Ann Landers Says Truth Is Stranger Than . . .* (1968)]

**LAWRENCE, D.H.
(1885–1930)**
How wonderful sex can be, when men keep it powerful and sacred, and it fills the world! Like sunshine through and through you!

[*The Plumed Serpent* (1926)]

It's all this cold-hearted fucking that is death and idiocy.

[*Lady Chatterley's Lover* (1928)]

**LONGFORD, Lord
(1905–)**
No sex without responsibility.

[*The Observer*, 1954]

**MACLAINE, Shirley
(1934–)**
The more sex becomes a non-issue in people's lives, the happier they are.

[Attr.]

MIKES, George (1912–1987)
Continental people have sex life; the English have hot-water bottles.
[*How to be an Alien* (1946)]

MILLER, Henry (1891–1980)
Sex is one of the nine reasons for reincarnation . . . The other eight are unimportant.
[*Big Sur and the Oranges of Hieronymus Bosch*]

MONTGOMERY, Viscount (1887–1976)
[Comment on a bill to relax the laws against homosexuals]
This sort of thing may be tolerated by the French, but we are British – thank God.
[Speech, 1965]

MUGGERIDGE, Malcolm (1903–1990)
An orgy looks particularly alluring seen through the mists of righteous indignation.
[*The Most of Malcolm Muggeridge* (1966)]

The orgasm has replaced the Cross as the focus of longing and the image of fulfilment.
[*The Most of Malcolm Muggeridge* (1966)]

NASH, Ogden (1902–1971)
Home is heaven and orgies are vile
But you *need* an orgy, once in a while.
['Home, Sweet Home' (1935)]

NEWBY, P.H. (1918–)
He felt that he could love this woman with the greatest brutality. The situation between them was electric. When he was in a room with her the only thing he could think of was sex.
[*A Journey to the Interior* (1945)]

ORTON, Joe (1933–1967)
You were born with your legs apart. They'll send you to the grave in a Y-shaped coffin.
[*What the Butler Saw* (1969)]

PHILIP, Prince, Duke of Edinburgh (1921–)
I don't think a prostitute is more moral than a wife, but they are doing the same thing.
[*The Observer*, 1988]

PINTER, Harold (1930–)
I tend to believe that cricket is the greatest thing that God ever created on earth . . . certainly greater than sex, although sex isn't too bad either.
[Interview in *The Observer*, 1980]

SALINGER, J.D. (1919–)
Sex is something I really don't understand too hot. You never

know *where* the hell you are. I keep making up these sex rules for myself, and then I break them right away.
[*The Catcher in the Rye* (1951)]

SAYERS, Dorothy L. (1893–1957)

As I grow older and older,
And totter towards the tomb,
I find that I care less and less
Who goes to bed with whom.
[In Hitchman, *Such a Strange Lady* (1975)]

SCOTT, Valerie

[Toronto prostitute-by-choice] We don't sell our bodies. Housewives do that. What we do is *rent* our bodies for sexual services.
[*The Toronto Star,* 1989]

SHAKESPEARE, William (1564–1616)

Is it not strange that desire should so many years outlive performance?
[*Henry IV, Part 2,* II.iv]

STEINEM, Gloria (1934–)

[On transsexualism] If the shoe doesn't fit, must we change the foot?
[*Outrageous Acts and Everyday Rebellions* (1984)]

STEWART, Rod (1945–)

[On his sexual partners] The most memorable is always the current one; the rest just merge into a sea of blondes.
[Attr.]

SZASZ, Thomas (1920–)

Traditionally, sex has been a very private, secretive activity. Herein perhaps lies its powerful force for uniting people in a strong bond. As we make sex less secretive, we may rob it of its power to hold men and women together.
[*The Second Sin* (1973)]

THURBER, James (1894–1961)

[On being accosted at a party by a drunk woman who claimed she would like to have a baby by him] Surely you don't mean by unartificial insemination!
[Attr.]

VIDAL, Gore (1925–)

[On being asked if his first sexual experience had been heterosexual or homosexual] I was too polite to ask.
[*Forum,* 1987]

VOLTAIRE (1694–1778)

It is one of the superstitions of the human mind to have imagined that virginity could be a virtue.
['The Leningrad Notebooks' (c. 1735–1750)]

WAX, Ruby (1953-)
This 'relationship' business is one big waste of time. It is just Mother Nature urging you to breed, breed, breed. Learn from nature. Learn from our friend the spider. Just mate once and then kill him.

[*Spectator*, 1994]

SHAKESPEARE

AUBREY, John (1626–1697)
He was a handsome, well-shaped man: very good company, and of a very ready and pleasant smooth wit.

[*Brief Lives* (c. 1693)]

AUSTEN, Jane (1775–1817)
We all talk Shakespeare, use his similes, and describe with his descriptions.

[*Mansfield Park* (1814)]

DARWIN, Charles (1809–1882)
I have tried lately to read Shakespeare, and found it so intolerably dull that it nauseated me.

[*Autobiography* (1877)]

ELIOT, T.S. (1888–1965)
We can say of Shakespeare, that never has a man turned so little knowledge to such great account.

[Lecture, 1942]

GRAVES, Robert (1895–1985)
The remarkable thing about Shakespeare is that he is really very good – in spite of all the people who say he is very good.

[*The Observer*, 1964]

OLIVIER, Laurence (1907–1989)
Shakespeare – the nearest thing in incarnation to the eye of God.

[*Kenneth Harris Talking To*: 'Sir Laurence Olivier']

PHILIP, Prince, Duke of Edinburgh (1921-)
A man can be forgiven a lot if he can quote Shakespeare in an economic crisis.

[Attr.]

POWYS, John Cowper (1872–1963)
He combined scepticism of everything with credulity about everything . . . and I am convinced this is the true Shakespearian way wherewith to take life.

[*Autobiography*]

WALPOLE, Horace (1717–1797)
One of the greatest geniuses that ever existed, Shakespeare, undoubtedly wanted taste.

[Letter, 1764]

ANONYMOUS
Can't act, can't sing, slightly bald. Can dance a little.
> [Comment by a Hollywood executive on Fred Astaire's first screen test]

BROOKS, Mel (1926–)
That's it, baby, if you've got it, flaunt it.
> [*The Producers*, film, 1968]

CHASEN, Dave
Bogart's a helluva nice guy until 11.30 p.m. After that he thinks he's Bogart.
> [In Halliwell, *The Filmgoer's Book of Quotes* (1973)]

CHER (1946–)
Mother told me a couple of years ago, 'Sweetheart, settle down and marry a rich man.' I said, 'Mom, I am a rich man.'
> [*The Observer Review*, 1995]

COCHRAN, Charles B. (1872–1951)
I still prefer a good juggler to a bad Hamlet.
> [*The Observer*, 1943]

DAVIS, Bette (1908–1989)
[Of a starlet]
I see – she's the original good time that was had by all.
> [In Halliwell, *Filmgoer's Book of Quotes* (1973)]

DAVIS, Sammy, Junior (1925–1990)
Being a star has made it possible for me to get insulted in places where the average Negro could never hope to get insulted.
> [*Yes I can* (1965)]

GARBO, Greta (1905–1990)
I never said, 'I want to be alone.' I only said, 'I want to be *let* alone.' There is all the difference.
> [In Colombo, *Wit and Wisdom of the Moviemakers*]

GARLAND, Judy (1922–1969)
I was born at the age of twelve on a Metro-Goldwyn-Mayer lot.
> [*The Observer*, 1951]

GOLDWYN, Samuel (1882–1974)
Directors [are] always biting the hand that lays the golden egg.
> [In Zierold, *Moguls* (1969)]

I'll give you a definite maybe.
> [In Colombo, *Wit and Wisdom of the Moviemakers*]

In two words: im possible.
[Attr.; in Zierold, *Moguls*
(1969)]

What we want is a story that starts with an earthquake and works its way up to a climax.
[Attr.]

GRADE, Lew (1906–1994)
All my shows are great. Some of them are bad. But they are all great.
[*The Observer*, 1975]

HELPMAN, Sir Robert (1909–1986)
[After the opening night of *Oh, Calcutta!*]
The trouble with nude dancing is that not everything stops when the music stops.
[In *The Frank Muir Book* (1976)]

LEVANT, Oscar (1906–1972)
Strip the phony tinsel off Hollywood and you'll find the real tinsel underneath.
[In Halliwell, *Filmgoer's Book of Quotes* (1973)]

MONROE, Marilyn (1926–1962)
Hollywood is a place where they'll pay you $50,000 for a kiss and 50 cents for your soul.
[Attr.]

REED, Rex (1938–)
In Hollywood, if you don't have happiness you send out for it.
[In Colombo, *Colombo's Hollywood*]

RICHARD, Cliff (1940–)
Stars who debauch themselves, get addicted to drugs then kick them get all the praise. Wouldn't you think that people who have never been addicted should be praised all the more?
[*The Observer Review*, 1996]

SHAW, George Bernard (1856–1950)
The trouble, Mr Goldwyn, is that you are only interested in art and I am only interested in money.
[In Johnson, *The Great Goldwyn* (1937)]

SOUTHERN, Terry (1924–)
She says, 'Listen, who do I have to fuck to get *off* this picture?'
[*Blue Movie* (1970)]

THOMAS, Irene (1920–)
It was the kind of show where the girls are not auditioned – just measured.
[Attr.]

**TRACY, Spencer
(1900–1967)**
[Explaining what he looked for in a script]
Days off.

[*Attr.*]

**WELLES, Orson
(1915–1985)**
I began at the top and I've been working my way down ever since.
[In Colombo, *Wit and Wisdom of the Moviemakers*]

See CINEMA

SILENCE

**AUSTEN, Jane
(1775–1817)**
From politics, it was an easy step to silence.
[*Northanger Abbey* (1818)]

**BACON, Francis
(1561–1626)**
Silence is the virtue of fools.
[*The Advancement of Learning* (1623)]

**HOLMES, Oliver Wendell
(1809–1894)**
And silence, like a poultice, comes
To heal the blows of sound.
['The Music-Grinders' (1836)]

**LA ROCHEFOUCAULD
(1613–1680)**
Silence is the safest policy for the man who distrusts himself.
[*Maximes* (1678)]

**LINCOLN, Abraham
(1809–1865)**
Better to remain silent and be thought a fool than to speak out and remove all doubt.
[*Attr.*]

**MANDELSTAM, Nadezhda
(1899–1980)**
If nothing else is left, one must scream. Silence is the real crime against humanity.
[*Hope Against Hope* (1970)]

**SAINTE-BEUVE
(1804–1869)**
Silence is the supreme contempt.
['Mes Poisons']

**SIDNEY, Sir Philip
(1554–1586)**
Shallow brookes murmur moste,
Depe sylent slyde away.
[*Old Arcadia* (1581)]

**TUPPER, Martin
(1810–1889)**
Well-timed silence hath more eloquence than speech.
[*Proverbial Philosophy* (1838)]

VIRGIL (70–19 BC)
Through the friendly silence of the soundless moonlight.
[*Aeneid*]

WITTGENSTEIN, Ludwig (1889–1951)
What can be said at all can be said clearly; and whereof one cannot speak, thereon one must keep silent.
[*Tractatus Logico-Philosophicus* (1922)]

See CONVERSATION

SIN

AUDEN, W.H. (1907–1973)
All sin tends to be addictive, and the terminal point of addiction is what is called damnation.
[*A Certain World* (1970)]

THE BIBLE (KING JAMES VERSION)
Be sure your sin will find you out.
[*Numbers*, 32:23]

He that is without sin among you, let him first cast a stone.
[*John*, 8:7]

The wages of sin is death.
[*Romans*, 6:23]

BULGAKOV, Mikhail (1891–1940)
Cowardice is, without a doubt, one of the greatest sins.
[*The Master and Margarita* (1967)]

BUNYAN, John (1628–1688)
One leak will sink a ship, and one sin will destroy a sinner.
[*The Pilgrim's Progress* (1678)]

COOLIDGE, Calvin (1872–1933)
[On being asked what had been said by a clergyman who preached on sin]
He said he was against it.
[Attr.]

COWLEY, Abraham (1618–1667)
Lukewarmness I account a sin As great in love as in religion.
['The Request' (1647)]

EDDY, Mary Baker (1821–1910)
Sin brought death, and death will disappear with the disappearance of sin.
[*Science and Health* (1875)]

JUVENAL (c. 60–130)
Count it the greatest sin to put life before honour, and for the sake of life to lose the reasons for living.
[*Satires*]

**QUEVEDO Y VILLEGAS,
Francisco Gómez de
(1580–1645)**
So blind am I to my mortal
entanglement
that I dare not call upon thee,
Lord, for fear
that thou wouldst take me
away from my sin.
[*Christian Heraclitus* (1613)]

**ROOSEVELT, Theodore
(1858–1919)**
The worst sin towards our fellow creatures is not to hate
them, but to be indifferent to
them: that's the essence of
inhumanity.
[*The Devil's Disciple* (1901)]

**SHAKESPEARE, William
(1564–1616)**
Plate sin with gold,
And the strong lance of justice
hurtless breaks;
Arm it in rags, a pigmy's
straw does pierce it.
[*King Lear,* IV.vi]

Few love to hear the sins they
love to act.
[*Pericles, Prince of Tyre,* I.i]

Nothing emboldens sin so
much as mercy.
[*Timon of Athens,* III.v]

WILDE, Oscar (1854–1900)
It has been said that the great
events of the world take place

in the brain. It is in the brain,
and the brain only, that the
great sins of the world take
place.
[*The Picture of Dorian Gray*
(1891)]

See EVIL

SLAVERY

**GANDHI
(1869–1948)**
The moment the slave
resolves that he will no longer
be a slave, his fetters fall. He
frees himself and shows the
way to others. Freedom and
slavery are mental states.
[*Non-Violence in Peace and
War* (1949)]

**GILL, Eric
(1882–1940)**
That state is a state of Slavery
in which a man does what he
likes to do in his spare time
and in his working time that
which is required of him.
['Slavery and Freedom'
(1929)]

**JOHNSON, Samuel
(1709–1784)**
How is it that we hear the
loudest yelps for liberty
among the drivers of negroes?
[*Taxation No Tyranny* (1775)]

**LINCOLN, Abraham
(1809–1865)**
In giving freedom to the
slave, we assure freedom to
the free – honourable alike in
what we give and what we
preserve.

[Speech, 1862]

**STANTON, Elizabeth Cady
(1815–1902)**
The prolonged slavery of
woman is the darkest page in
human history.
[In Anthony and Gage, *History
of Woman Suffrage* (1881)]

**WEDGWOOD, Josiah
(1730–1795)**
Am I not a man and a
brother?
Motto adopted by Anti-
Slavery Society]

SLEEP

**BROWNE, Sir Thomas
(1605–1682)**
Sleep is a death, O make me
try,
By sleeping what it is to die.
And as gently lay my head
On my grave, as now my bed.
[*Religio Medici* (1643)]

**CERVANTES, Miguel de
(1547–1616)**
God bless whoever invented
sleep, the cloak that covers all
human thoughts. It is the food
that satisfies hunger, the
water that quenches thirst,
the fire that warms cold, the
cold that reduces heat, and,
lastly, the common currency
which can buy anything, the
balance and compensating
weight that makes the shepherd equal to the king, and
the simpleton equal to the
sage.

[*Don Quixote* (1615)]

**DICKENS, Charles
(1812–1870)**
It would make any one go to
sleep, that bedstead would,
whether they wanted to or
not.
[*The Pickwick Papers* (1837)]

**HENRI IV OF FRANCE
(1553–1610)**
Great eaters and great
sleepers are not capable of
doing anything great.
[Attr.]

**NIETZSCHE, Friedrich
(1844–1900)**
Sleeping is no mean art: it is
necessary to stay awake for it
all day.
[*Thus Spake Zarathustra*
(1884)]

SHAKESPEARE, William (1564–1616)

Methought I heard a voice cry
'Sleep no more;
Macbeth does murder sleep' –
the innocent sleep,
Sleep that knits up the ravell'd
sleave of care,
The death of each day's life,
sore labour's bath,
Balm of hurt minds, great
nature's second course,
Chief nourisher in life's feast.

[*Macbeth*, II.ii]

SOUTHEY, Robert (1774–1843)

Thou hast been call'd, O
Sleep! the friend of Woe,
But 'tis the happy who have
called thee so.

[*The Curse of Kehama* (1810)]

TERTZ, Abram (1925–1997)

Sleep is the watering place of
the soul to which it hastens at
night to drink at the sources
of life.
In sleep we receive confirm-
ation . . . that we must go
on living.

[*A Voice From the Chorus* (1973)]

SMOKING

CALVERLEY, C.S. (1831–1884)

How they who use fusees
All grow by slow degrees
Brainless as chimpanzees,
Meagre as lizards:
Go mad, and beat their wives;
Plunge (after shocking lives)
Razors and carving knives
Into their gizzards.

['Ode to Tobacco' (1861)]

ELIZABETH I (1533–1603)

[To Sir Walter Raleigh]
I have known many persons
who turned their gold into
smoke, but you are the first to
turn smoke into gold.

[In Chamberlin, *The Sayings of
Queen Elizabeth* (1923)]

HELPS, Sir Arthur (1813–1875)

What a blessing this smoking
is! perhaps the greatest that
we owe to the discovery of
America.

[*Friends in Council* (1859)]

JAMES VI OF SCOTLAND AND I OF ENGLAND (1566–1625)

A custom loathesome to the
eye, hateful to the nose,
harmful to the brain, dangerous to the lungs, and in the
black, stinking fume thereof,
nearest resembling the horrible Stygian smoke of the pit
that is bottomless.

[*A Counterblast to Tobacco*
(1604)]

KIPLING, Rudyard (1865–1936)
And a woman is only a woman, but a good cigar is a Smoke.
['The Betrothed' (1886)]

LAMB, Charles (1775–1834)
Dr Parr . . . asked him, how he had acquired his power of smoking at such a rate? Lamb replied, 'I toiled after it, sir, as some men toil after virtue.'
[In Talfourd, *Memoirs of Charles Lamb* (1892)]

NAPOLEON III (1808–1873)
[On being asked to ban smoking] This vice brings in one hundred million francs in taxes every year. I will certainly forbid it at once – as soon as you can name a virtue that brings in as much revenue.
[In Hoffmeister, *Anekdotenschatz*]

SATIE, Erik (1866–1925)
My doctor has always told me to smoke. He explains himself thus: 'Smoke, my friend. If you don't, someone else will smoke in your place.'
[*Mémoires d'un amnésique* (1924)]

TWAIN, Mark (1835–1910)
[Saying how easy it is to give up smoking]
I've done it a hundred times!
[Attr.]

WILDE, Oscar (1854–1900)
A cigarette is the perfect type of a perfect pleasure. It is exquisite, and it leaves one unsatisfied. What more can one want?
[*The Picture of Dorian Gray* (1891)]

SOCIALISM

BENNETT, Alan (1934–)
Why is it always the intelligent people who are socialists?
[*Forty Years On* (1969)]

BEVAN, Aneurin (1897–1960)
The language of priorities is the religion of Socialism.
[Attr.]

DURANT, Will (1885–1982)
There is nothing in Socialism that a little age or a little money will not cure.
[Attr.]

KEYNES, John Maynard (1883–1946)
Marxian Socialism must always remain a portent to the historians of opinion – how a doctrine so illogical and so dull can have exercised so powerful and enduring an influence over the

minds of men, and, through them, the events of history.
['The End of Laissez-Faire' (1926)]

KINNOCK, Neil (1942–)
The idea that there is a model Labour voter, a blue-collar council house tenant who belongs to a union and has 2.4 children, a five-year-old car and a holiday in Blackpool, is patronizing and politically immature.
[Speech, 1986]

ORWELL, George (1903–1950)
As with the Christian religion, the worst advertisement for Socialism is its adherents.
[*The Road to Wigan Pier* (1937)]

STOPPARD, Tom (1937–)
Socialists treat their servants with respect and then wonder why they vote Conservative.
[*Lord Malquist and Mr Moon* (1966)]

THATCHER, Margaret (1925–)
State socialism is totally alien to the British character.
[*The Times*, 1983]

WARREN, Earl (1891–1974)
Many people consider the things which government

does for them to be social progress, but they consider the things government does for others as socialism.
[*Peter's Quotations*]

See CAPITALISM

SOCIETY

ARISTOTLE (384–322 BC)
A person who cannot live in society, or does not need to because he is self-sufficient, is either a beast or a god.
[*Politics*]

AURELIUS, Marcus (121–180)
What is not good for the bee-hive, cannot be good for the bees.
[*Meditations*]

BACON, Francis (1561–1626)
Man seeketh in society comfort, use, and protection.
[*The Advancement of Learning* (1605)]

CICERO (106–43 BC)
O tempora! O mores!
What times! What manners!
[*In Catilinam*]

CLAUDEL, Paul (1868–1955)
The only living societies are

those which are animated by inequality and injustice.

[*Conversations dans le Loir-et-Cher*]

COUNIHAN, Noel Jack (1913–1986)
In human society the warmth is mainly at the bottom.

[*Age*, 1986]

EMERSON, Ralph Waldo (1803–1882)
Society everywhere is in con-spiracy against the manhood of every one of its members.

['Self-Reliance' (1841)]

GALBRAITH, J.K. (1908–)
In the affluent society, no sharp distinction can be made between luxuries and necessaries.

[*The Affluent Society* (1958)]

HUME, Basil (1923–)
[On the killing of London headmaster Philip Lawrence]
We have really lost in our society the sense of the sacredness of life.

[*The Observer Review*, 1995]

JENKINS, Roy (1920–)
The permissive society has been allowed to become a dirty phrase. A better phrase is the civilized society.

[Speech, 1969]

MANDELA, Nelson (1918–)
We enter into a covenant that we shall build the society in which all South Africans, both black and white, will be able to walk tall, without any fear in their hearts, assured of their inalienable right to human dignity – a rainbow nation at peace with itself and the world.

[Inaugural Address, 1994]

ROOSEVELT, Theodore (1858–1919)
The men with the muck-rakes are often indispensable to the well-being of society; but only if they know when to stop raking the muck.

[Speech, 1906]

SMITH, Adam (1723–1790)
No society can surely be flour-ishing and happy, of which the far greater part of the members are poor and miser-able.

[*Wealth of Nations* (1776)]

SPENCER, Herbert (1820–1903)
No one can be perfectly free till all are free; no one can be perfectly moral till all are moral; no one can be per-fectly happy till all are happy.

[*Social Statics* (1850)]

**SPINOZA, Baruch
(1632–1677)**
Man is a social animal.
[*Ethics* (1677)]

**THACKERAY, William
Makepeace (1811–1863)**
It is impossible, in our con-
dition of Society, not to be
sometimes a Snob.
[*The Book of Snobs* (1848)]

**THATCHER, Margaret
(1925–)**
There is no such thing as
society. There are individual
men and women and there
are families.
[Attr.]

WILDE, Oscar (1854–1900)
[Of society]
To be in it is merely a bore.
But to be out of it simply a
tragedy.
[*A Woman of No Importance*
(1893)]

SOLITUDE

**COWPER, William
(1731–1800)**
I praise the Frenchman, his
remark was shrewd –
How sweet, how passing
sweet, is solitude!
But grant me still a friend in
my retreat,

Whom I may whisper – solitude is sweet.
['Retirement' (1782)]

ECO, Umberto (1932–)
Solitude is a kind of freedom.
[*The Observer Review,* 1995]

**GIBBON, Edward
(1737–1794)**
I was never less alone than
when by myself.
[*Memoirs of My Life and
Writings* (1796)]

**MANN, Thomas
(1875–1955)**
Solitude gives rise to what is
original, to what is daringly
and displeasingly beautiful, to
poetry. Solitude however also
gives rise to what is wrong,
excessive, absurd and forbidden.
[*Death in Venice* (1912)]

**MONTAIGNE, Michel de
(1533–1592)**
We should keep for ourselves
a little back shop, all our own,
untouched by others, in which
we establish our true freedom
and chief place of seclusion
and solitude.
[*Essais* (1580)]

**SASSOON, Siegfried
(1886–1967)**
Alone . . . The word is life
endured and known.

It is the stillness where our
spirits walk
And all but inmost faith is
overthrown.
[*The Heart's Journey* (1928)]

SCHOPENHAUER, Arthur (1788–1860)

Solitude is the fate of all outstanding minds: it will at
times be deplored; but it will
always be chosen as the
lesser of two evils.
['Aphorisms for Wisdom' (1851)]

SCHREINER, Olive (1855–1920)

She thought of the narrow-
ness of the limits within
which a human soul may
speak and be understood by
its nearest of mental kin, of
how soon it reaches that solitary land of the individual
experience in which no fellow
footfall is ever heard.
[*The Story of an African Farm* (1884)]

THOREAU, Henry (1817–1862)

I never found the companion
that was so companionable as
solitude.
[*Walden* (1854)]

See LONELINESS

THE SOUL

THE BIBLE (KING JAMES VERSION)

What is a man profited, if he
shall gain the whole world,
and lose his own soul?
[*Matthew*, 16:26]

CRABBE, George (1754–1832)

It is the soul that sees; the
outward eyes
Present the object, but the
mind descries.
[*The Lover's Journey*]

DICKINSON, Emily (1830–1886)

The Soul selects her own
Society –
Then – shuts the Door –
To her divine Majority –
Present no more . . .

I've known her – from an
ample nation –
Choose One –
Then – close the Valves of her
attention –
Like Stone.
['The Soul selects her own Society' (c. 1862)]

KEATS, John (1795–1821)

A man should have the fine
point of his soul taken off to
become fit for this world.
[Letter to J.H. Reynolds, 1817]

LUCRETIUS (c. 95–55 BC)
What has this bugbear death
to frighten man
If souls can die as well as
bodies can?
[*De Rerum Natura*; trans.
Dryden]

**MCAULEY, James Philip
(1917–1976)**
The soul must feed on something for its dreams,
In those brick suburbs, and
there wasn't much:
It can make do with little, so it
seems.
['Wisteria' (1971)]

**MEREDITH, George
(1828–1909)**
There is nothing the body suffers the soul may not profit by.
[*Modern Love* (1862)]

**SMITH, Logan Pearsall
(1865–1946)**
Most people sell their souls,
and live with a good con-
science on the proceeds.
[*Afterthoughts* (1931)]

**STERNE, Laurence
(1713–1768)**
I am positive I have a soul;
nor can all the books with
which materialists have
pestered the world ever convince me to the contrary.
[*A Sentimental Journey* (1768)]

**WEBSTER, John
(c. 1580–c. 1625)**
My soul, like to a ship in a
black storm,
Is driven, I know not whither.
[*The White Devil* (1612)]

See IMMORTALITY

SPACE

**ADDISON, Joseph
(1672–1719)**
The spacious firmament on
high,
With all the blue ethereal sky,
And spangled heavens, a
shining frame,
Their great Original proclaim.
[*The Spectator*, 1712]

ALFONSO X (1221–1284)
[On the Ptolemaic system of
astronomy]
If the Lord Almighty had con-
sulted me before embarking
upon Creation, I should have
recommended something sim-
pler.
[Attr.]

ARMSTRONG, Neil (1930–)
[On stepping on to the moon]
That's one small step for a
man, one giant leap for
mankind.
[*New York Times*, 1969]

SPORT AND GAMES

THE BIBLE (KING JAMES VERSION)
The heavens declare the glory of God; and the firmament sheweth his handywork.

[*Psalms*, 19:1]

BYRON, Lord (1788–1824)
Ye stars! which are the poetry of heaven!

[*Childe Harold's Pilgrimage* (1818)]

DE VRIES, Peter (1910–)
Anyone informed that the universe is expanding and contracting in pulsations of eighty billion years has a right to ask, 'What's in it for me?'

[*The Glory of the Hummingbird* (1974)]

FROST, Robert (1874–1963)
They cannot scare me with their empty spaces
Between stars – on stars
where no human race is.
I have it in me so much nearer home
To scare myself with my own desert places.

['Desert Places' (1936)]

FULLER, Richard Buckminster (1895–1983)
I am a passenger on the spaceship, Earth.

[*Operating Manual for Spaceship Earth* (1969)]

HOLMES, Rev. John H. (1879–1964)
This universe is not hostile, nor yet is it friendly. It is simply indifferent.

[*A Sensible Man's View of Religion* (1932)]

HOPKINS, Gerard Manley (1844–1889)
Look at the stars! look, look up at the skies!
Oh look at all the fire-folk sitting in the air!
The bright boroughs, the circle-citadels there!

['The Starlight Night' (1877)]

VIRGIL (70–19 BC)
And when the rising sun has first breathed on us with his panting horses, over there the glowing evening-star is lighting his late lamps.

[*Georgics*]

SPORT AND GAMES

ALI, Muhammad (1942–)
Float like a butterfly, sting like a bee.

[Catchphrase]

ALLISON, Malcolm (1927–)
Professional football is no longer a game. It's a war. And it brings out the same

primitive instincts that go back thousands of years.
[*The Observer*, 1973]

ANONYMOUS

Shooting is a popular sport in the countryside . . . Unlike many other countries, the outstanding characteristic of the sport has been that it is not confined to any one class.
[The Northern Ireland Tourist Board, 1969]

'Well, what sort of sport has Lord – had?'
'Oh, the young Sahib shot divinely, but God was very merciful to the birds.'
[In Russell, *Collections and Recollections* (1898)]

ARCHER, Mark

In the case of almost every sport one can think of, from tennis to billiards, golf to skittles, it was royalty or the aristocracy who originally developed, codified and popularised the sport, after which it was taken up by the lower classes.
[*The Spectator*, 1996]

BALL, Alan (1943-)

[After making a substitution which enabled his team to win a key relegation battle]
I thought if we were going to lose it, we might as well lose it by trying to win it.
[*Daily Mail*, 1996]

BARBARITO, Luigi (1922–)

[Papal emissary, commenting on a sponsored snooker competition at a convent]
Playing snooker gives you firm hands and helps to build up character. It is the ideal recreation for dedicated nuns.
[*The Daily Telegraph*, 1989]

BARNES, Simon (1951–)

Sport is something that does not matter, but is performed as if it did. In that contradiction lies its beauty.
[*The Spectator*, 1996]

BELASCO, David (1853–1931)

Boxing is showbusiness with blood.
[Attr., 1915]

BENNETT, Alan (1934–)

If you think squash is a competitive activity, try flower arrangement.
[*Talking Heads* (1988)]

BROWN, Rita Mae (1944–)

Sport strips away personality, letting the white bone of character shine through.
[*Sudden Death* (1983)]

BYRON, H.J. (1834–1884)

Life's too short for chess.

[*Our Boys*]

CANTERBURY, Tom

The trouble with referees is that they just don't care which side wins.

[*The Guardian*, 1980]

COLEMAN, David (1926–)

That's the fastest time ever run – but it's not as not as the world record.

[In Fantoni, *Private Eye's Colemanballs (3)* (1986)]

COWPER, William (1731–1800)

[Of hunting]

Detested sport,

That owes its pleasures to another's pain.

[*The Task* (1785)]

DAVIS, Steve (1957–)

Sport is cut and dried. You always know when you succeed . . . You are not an actor: you don't wonder 'did my performance go down all right?' You've lost.

[Remark]

DEMPSEY, Jack (1895–1983)

Kill the other guy before he kills you.

[Motto]

DUFFY, Jim

[Of goalkeeper Andy Murdoch]

He has an answerphone installed on his six-yard line and the message says: 'Sorry, I'm not in just now, but if you'd like to leave the ball in the back of the net, I'll get back to you as soon as I can.'

[In *Umbro Book of Football Quotations* (1993)]

EUBANK, Chris (1966–)

Any boxer who says he loves boxing is either a liar or a fool. I'm not looking for glory . . . I'm looking for money. I'm looking for readies.

[*The Times*, 1993]

FITZSIMMONS, Robert (1862–1917)

[Remark before a boxing match, 1900]

The bigger they come, the harder they fall.

[Attr.]

FORD, Henry (1863–1947)

Exercise is bunk. If you are healthy, you don't need it: if you are sick, you shouldn't take it.

[Attr.]

GASCOIGNE, Paul (1967–)

I get on a train and sit in second class and people think, 'tight bastard. Money he's got and he sits in second class.'

So I think, '**** them' and I
go in first class and then they
say, 'look at that ****'ing flash
bastard in first class'.
[*The Herald*, 1995]

GRACE, W.G. (1848–1915)
[Refusing to leave the crease
after being bowled first ball in
front of a large crowd]
They came to see me bat not
to see you bowl.
[Attr.]

HEMINGWAY, Ernest (1898–1961)
Bullfighting is the only art in
which the artist is in danger of
death and in which the degree
of brilliance in the performance is left to the fighter's
honour.
[*Death in the Afternoon* (1932)]

HUISTRA, Peter (1967–)
Soccer in Japan is interesting,
in Glasgow it's a matter of life
and death.
[*Daily Mail*, 1996]

INGHAM, Bernard (1932–)
Blood sport is brought to its
ultimate refinement in the
gossip columns.
[Remark, 1986]

JOHNSON, Samuel (1709–1784)
It is very strange, and very
melancholy, that the paucity
of human pleasures should
persuade us ever to call
hunting one of them.
[In Piozzi, *Anecdotes of the
Late Samuel Johnson* (1786)]

KINGLAKE, Edward (1864–1935)
Every Australian worships the
Goddess of Sport with profound adoration, and there is
no nation in the world which
treats itself to so many holidays.
[*The Australian at Home*]

LAMB, Charles (1775–1834)
Man is a gaming animal. He
must always be trying to get
the better in something or
other.
['Mrs Battle's Opinions on
Whist' (1823)]

LOUIS, Joe (1914–1981)
[Referring to the speed of an
opponent, Billy Conn]
He can run, but he can't hide.
[Attr.]

MCGUIGAN, Barry (1961–)
The gladiators and champions
through the ages confirm
quite clearly that aggressive
competition is part of the
human makeup. For the sport
of professional boxing to be
banned would be the most
terrible error.
[*The Observer*, 1994]

MOURIE, Graham (1952–)
Nobody ever beats Wales at
rugby, they just score more
points.
[In Keating, *Caught by Keating*]

O'ROURKE, P.J. (1947–)
The sport of skiing consists of
wearing three thousand dollars' worth of clothes and
equipment and driving two
hundred miles in order to
stand around at a bar
and get drunk.
[*Modern Manners* (1984)]

**ORWELL, George
(1903–1950)**
Serious sport has nothing to
do with fair play. It is bound
up with hatred, jealousy,
boastfulness, disregard for all
rules and sadistic pleasure in
witnessing violence; in other
words it is war minus the
shooting.
[*Shooting an Elephant* (1950)]

OVETT, Steve (1955–)
There is no way sport is so
important that it can be
allowed to damage the rest of
your life.
[Remark at the Olympic
Games, 1984]

**RICE, Grantland
(1880–1954)**
For when the One Great
Scorer comes to mark against

your name,
He marks – not that you won
or lost – but how you played
the Game.
['Alumnus Football' (1941)]

SEAL, Christopher
Hunting people tend to be
churchgoers on a higher level
than ordinary folk. One has a
religious experience in the
field.
[*The Times*, 1993]

**SHANKLY, Bill
(1914–1981)**
Some people think football is
a matter of life and death. I
don't like that attitude. I can
assure them it is much more
serious than that.
[Remark on BBC TV, 1981]

**SHAW, George Bernard
(1856–1950)**
I take athletic competitive
sports very seriously indeed . . .
as they seem to produce more
bad feeling, bad manners and
international hatred than any
other popular movement.
[*Auckland Star*, 1934]

**SNAGGE, John
(1904–1996)**
I don't know who's ahead –
it's either Oxford or
Cambridge.
[Radio commentary on the
Boat Race, 1949]

**STUBBES, Philip
(c. 1555–1610)**
Football . . . causeth fighting,
brawling, contention, quarrel
picking, murder, homicide and
great effusion of blood, as
daily experience teacheth.
[*Anatomy of Abuses* (1583)]

WALTON, Izaak (1593–1683)
As no man is born an artist,
so no man is born an angler.
[*The Compleat Angler* (1653)]

WILDE, Oscar (1854–1900)
The English country gentleman galloping after a fox –
the unspeakable in full pursuit
of the uneatable.
[*A Woman of No Importance*
(1893)]

**WODEHOUSE, P.G.
(1881–1975)**
The least thing upset him on
the links. He missed short
putts because of the uproar of
the butterflies in the adjoining
meadows.
[*The Clicking of Cuthbert*
(1922)]

THE STATE

**BOUTROS-GHALI, Boutros
(1922–)**
The time of absolute and
exclusive national sovereignty
has passed.
[*Scotland on Sunday,* 1992]

**BURKE, Edmund
(1729–1797)**
A state without the means of
some change is without the
means of its conservation.
[*Reflections on the Revolution
in France* (1790)]

**CROMWELL, Oliver
(1599–1658)**
The State, in choosing men to
serve it, takes no notice of
their opinions. If they be
willing faithfully to serve it,
that satisfies.
[Said before the Battle of
Marston Moor, 1644]

**INGE, William Ralph
(1860–1954)**
The nations which have put
mankind and posterity most
in their debt have been small
states – Israel, Athens,
Florence, Elizabethan
England.
[*Outspoken Essays: Second
Series* (1922)]

**LANDOR, Walter Savage
(1775–1864)**
States, like men, have their
growth, their manhood, their
decrepitude, their decay.
[*Imaginary Conversations*
(1876)]

LENIN, V.I. (1870–1924)
So long as the state exists
there is no freedom. When
there is freedom there will be
no state.
[*The State and Revolution*
(1917)]

**MILL, John Stuart
(1806–1873)**
The worth of a State, in the
long run, is the worth of the
individuals composing it.
[*On Liberty* (1859)]

PLATO (c. 429–347 BC)
It is the rulers of the state, if
anybody, who may lie in
dealing with citizens or enemies, for reasons of state.
[*Republic*]

RUSKIN, John (1819–1900)
I hold it for indisputable, that
the first duty of a State is to
see that every child born
therein shall be well housed,
clothed, fed and educated, till
it attain years of discretion.
[*Time and Tide by Weare and
Tyne* (1867)]

**STALIN, Joseph
(1879–1953)**
The state is a machine in the
hands of the ruling class for
suppressing the resistance of
its class enemies.
[*Foundations of Leninism*
(1924)]

STYLE

**ARNOLD, Matthew
(1822–1888)**
People think that I can teach
them style. What stuff it all is!
Have something to say, and
say it as clearly as you can.
That is the only secret of style.
[In Russell, *Collections and
Recollections* (1898)]

**BUFFON, Comte de
(1707–1788)**
These things [subject matter]
are external to the man; style
is the essence of man.
['Discours sur le Style' (1753)]

**CAMUS, Albert
(1913–1960)**
Style, like sheer silk, too often
hides eczema.
[*The Fall* (1956)]

**RENARD, Jules
(1864–1910)**
Poor style reflects imperfect
thought.
[*Journal*, 1898]

**WESLEY, Samuel
(1662–1735)**
Style is the dress of thought; a
modest dress,
Neat, but not gaudy, will true
critics please.
['An Epistle to a Friend concerning Poetry' (1700)]

WILDE, Oscar (1854–1900)
In matters of grave importance, style, not sincerity, is the vital thing.
[*The Importance of Being Earnest* (1895)]

SUCCESS

BROOKNER, Anita (1928–)
[On the myth of the tortoise and the hare]
In real life, of course, it is the hare who wins. Every time. Look around you. And in any case it is my contention that Aesop was writing for the tortoise market . . . Hares have no time to read. They are too busy winning the game.
[*Hotel du Lac* (1984)]

BROWNING, Robert (1812–1889)
A minute's success pays the failure of years.
['Apollo and the Fates' (1887)]

DEWAR, Lord (1864–1930)
The road to success is filled with women pushing their husbands along.
[Epigram]

DICKINSON, Emily (1830–1886)
Success is counted sweetest By those who ne'er succeed.

To comprehend a nectar Requires sorest need.
['Success is counted sweetest' (c. 1859)]

JAMES, William (1842–1910)
The moral flabbiness born of the exclusive worship of the bitch-goddess *success*. That – with the squalid cash interpretation put on the word success – is our national disease.
[Letter to H.G. Wells, 1906]

LA ROCHEFOUCAULD (1613–1680)
To succeed in the world we do all we can to appear successful.
[*Maximes* (1678)]

RENOIR, Jean (1894–1979)
Is it possible to succeed without betrayal?
[*My Life and My Films* (1974)]

VIDAL, Gore (1925–)
It is not enough to succeed. Others must fail.
[In Irvine, *Antipanegyric for Tom Driberg* (1976)]

VIRGIL (70–19 BC)
To these success gives heart: they can because they think they can.
[*Aeneid*]

SUFFERING

ANONYMOUS
Three things one does not
recover from –
oppression that knows the
backing of brute force,
poverty that knows the desti-
tution of one's home,
and being deprived of children.
[Somali poem]

AUDEN, W.H. (1907–1973)
About suffering they were
never wrong,
The Old Masters: how well
they understood
Its human position; how it
takes place
While someone else is eating
or opening a window or just
walking dully along.
['Musée des Beaux Arts']

AUSTEN, Jane (1775–1817)
One does not love a place the
less for having suffered in it,
unless it has all been suffering, nothing but suffering.
[Persuasion (1818)]

BOETHIUS (c. 475–524)
Nothing is miserable unless
you think it so; conversely,
every lot is happy to one who
is content with it.
[De Consolatione Philosophiae
(c. 524)]

**BONO, Edward de
(1933–)**
Unhappiness is best defined
as the difference between our
talents and our expectations.
[The Observer, 1977]

**BROWNING, Elizabeth
Barrett
(1806–1861)**
For frequent tears have run
The colours from my life.
[Sonnets from the Portuguese
(1850)]

**CHAUCER, Geoffrey
(c. 1340–1400)**
For of fortunes sharpe adver-
sitee
The worste kynde of infortune
is this,
A man to han ben in prosperi-
tee,
And it remembren, whan it
passed is.
[Troilus and Criseyde]

**CORNEILLE, Pierre
(1606–1684)**
Telling one's sorrows often
brings comfort.
[Polyeucte (1643)]

**COWPER, William
(1731–1800)**
But misery still delights to
trace
Its semblance in another's
case.
['The Castaway' (1799)]

**DICKINSON, Emily
(1830–1886)**
After great pain, a formal feeling comes –
The Nerves sit ceremonious,
like Tombs –
The stiff Heart questions was
it He, that bore,
And Yesterday, or Centuries
before?
['After great pain, a formal
feeling comes' (c. 1862)]

GAY, John (1685–1732)
A moment of time may make
us unhappy forever.
[The Beggar's Opera (1728)]

**HAZLITT, William
(1778–1830)**
The least pain in our little finger gives us more concern
and uneasiness, than the
destruction of millions of our
fellow-beings.
[Edinburgh Review, 1829]

**HEMINGWAY, Ernest
(1898–1961)**
The world breaks everyone
and afterward many are
strong at the broken places.
[A Farewell to Arms (1929)]

**HOGG, James
(1770–1835)**
How often does the evening
cup of joy lead to sorrow in
the morning!
[Attr.]

**JOHNSON, Samuel
(1709–1784)**
There is no wisdom in useless
and hopeless sorrow.
[Letter to Mrs. Thrale, 1781]

**KEMPIS, Thomas à
(c. 1380–1471)**
If you bear the cross willingly,
it will bear you.
[De Imitatione Christi (1892 ed.)]

**LA ROCHEFOUCAULD
(1613–1680)**
One is never as unhappy as
one thinks, or as happy as
one hopes to be.
[Maximes (1664)]

We are all strong enough to
bear the sufferings of others.
[Maximes (1678)]

**LOWELL, James Russell
(1819–1891)**
The misfortunes hardest to
bear are those which never
come.
['Democracy' (1887)]

**MONTAIGNE, Michel de
(1533–1592)**
A man who fears suffering is
already suffering from what
he fears.
[Essais (1580)]

NIETZSCHE, Friedrich (1844–1900)
What actually fills you with indignation as regards suffering is not suffering in itself but the pointlessness of suffering.
[*On the Genealogy of Morals* (1881)]

SAKI (1870–1916)
He's simply got the instinct for being unhappy highly developed.
[*The Chronicles of Clovis* (1911)]

SHAKESPEARE, William (1564–1616)
When sorrows come, they come not single spies,
But in battalions.
[*Hamlet*, IV.v]

Misery acquaints a man with strange bedfellows.
[*The Tempest*, II.ii]

SHAW, George Bernard (1856–1950)
The secret of being miserable is to have leisure to bother about whether you are happy or not.
[*Misalliance* (1914)]

VERLAINE, Paul (1844–1896)
Tears fall in my heart as rain falls on the city.
[*Romances sans paroles* (1874)]

WHITTIER, John Greenleaf (1807–1892)
For all sad words of tongue or pen,
The saddest are these: 'It might have been!'
['Maud Muller' (1854)]

WILDE, Oscar (1854–1900)
Where there is sorrow, there is holy ground.
[*De Profundis* (1897)]

SUICIDE

GREER, Germaine (1939–)
Suicide is an act of narcissistic manipulation and deep hostility.
[*The Observer Review*, 1995]

NIETZSCHE, Friedrich (1844–1900)
The thought of suicide is a great comfort: it's a good way of getting through many a bad night.
[*Beyond Good and Evil* (1886)]

PARKER, Dorothy (1893–1967)
Razors pain you;
Rivers are damp;
Acids stain you;
And drugs cause cramp.
Guns aren't lawful;
Nooses give;
Gas smells awful;

You might as well live.
['Résumé' (1937)]

SANDERS, George
(1906–1972)
Dear World, I am leaving you
because I am bored. I am
leaving you with your worries.
Good luck.

[Suicide note]

TENNYSON, Alfred, Lord
(1809–1892)
Nor at all can tell
Whether I mean this day to
end myself,
Or lend an ear to Plato where
he says,
That men like soldiers may
not quit the post
Allotted by the Gods.
['Lucretius' (1868)]

SUPERSTITION

BACON, Francis
(1561–1626)
There is a superstition in
avoiding superstition.
['Of Superstition' (1625)]

BARRIE, Sir J.M.
(1860–1937)
Every time a child says 'I don't
believe in fairies,' there is a
little fairy somewhere that
falls down dead.
[*Peter Pan* (1904)]

BOHR, Niels
(1885–1962)
[Explaining why he had a
horseshoe on his wall]
Of course I don't believe in it.
But I understand that it brings
you luck whether you believe
in it or not.
[Attr.]

BROWNE, Sir Thomas
(1605–1682)
For my part, I have ever
believed, and do now know,
that there are witches.
[*Religio Medici* (1643)]

BURKE, Edmund
(1729–1797)
Superstition is the religion of
feeble minds.
[*Reflections on the Revolution
in France* (1790)]

GOETHE
(1749–1832)
Superstition is the poetry of
life.
['Literature and Language'
(1823)]

JOHNSON, Samuel
(1709–1784)
[Of ghosts]
All argument is against it; but
all belief is for it.
[In Boswell, *The Life of Samuel
Johnson* (1791)]

TASTE

**BENNETT, Arnold
(1867–1931)**
Good taste is better than bad taste, but bad taste is better than no taste.
[*The Observer,* 1930]

**FITZGERALD, Edward
(1809–1883)**
Taste is the feminine of genius.
[Letter to J.R. Lowell, 1877]

**REYNOLDS, Sir Joshua
(1723–1792)**
Taste does not come by chance: it is a long and laborious task to acquire it.
[In Northcote, *Life of Sir Joshua Reynolds* (1818)]

VALERY, Paul (1871–1945)
Taste is created from a thousand distastes.
[*Unsaid Things*]

TAXES

**BURKE, Edmund
(1729–1797)**
To tax and to please, no more than to love and to be wise, is not given to men.
[*Speech on American Taxation* (1774)]

**DICKENS, Charles
(1812–1870)**
'It was as true,' said Mr Barkis, . . . as taxes is. And nothing's truer than them.'
[*David Copperfield* (1850)]

**MITCHELL, Margaret
(1900–1949)**
Death and taxes and childbirth? There's never any convenient time for any of them!
[*Gone with the Wind* (1936)]

**OTIS, James
(1725–1783)**
Taxation without representation is tyranny.
[Attr.]

**SHAW, George Bernard
(1856–1950)**
A government which robs Peter to pay Paul can always depend on the support of Paul.
[*Everybody's Political What's What* (1944)]

**SMITH, Adam
(1723–1790)**
There is no art which one government sooner learns of another than that of draining money from the pockets of the people.
[*Wealth of Nations* (1776)]

TEACHERS

AUDEN, W.H. (1907–1973)
A professor is one who talks in someone else's sleep.
[Attr.]

BERLIOZ, Hector (1803–1869)
Time is a great teacher, but unfortunately it kills all its pupils.
[Attr.]

CHURCHILL, Sir Winston (1874–1965)
Headmasters have powers at their disposal with which Prime Ministers have never yet been invested.
[*My Early Life* (1930)]

MONTESSORI, Maria (1870–1952)
We teachers can only help the work going on, as servants wait upon a master.
[*The Absorbent Mind*]

SHAW, George Bernard (1856–1950)
He who can, does. He who cannot, teaches.
[*Man and Superman* (1903)]

TROLLOPE, Anthony (1815–1882)
[Of his headmaster]
He must have known me had he seen me as he was wont to see me, for he was in the habit of flogging me constantly. Perhaps he did not recognize me by my face.
[*Autobiography* (1883)]

WAUGH, Evelyn (1903–1966)
We schoolmasters must temper discretion with deceit.
[*Decline and Fall* (1928)]

YEATMAN, Robert (1897–1968)
For every person wishing to teach there are thirty not wanting to be taught.
[*And Now All This* (1932)]

See EDUCATION; LEARNING; SCHOOL; UNIVERSITY

TELEVISION

BAKEWELL, Joan (1933–)
The BBC is full of men appointing men who remind them of themselves when young, so you get the same backgrounds, the same education, and the same programmes.
[*The Observer*, 1993]

BIAGI, Enzo (1920–)
Television has done more for

the unification of Italy than Garibaldi and Cavour did; it has given us a communal custom and language.

[*The Good and the Bad* (1989)]

COREN, Alan (1938–)
Television is more interesting than people. If it were not, we should have people standing in the corners of our rooms.

[Attr.]

COWARD, Sir Noël (1899–1973)
Television is for appearing on, not looking at.

[Attr.]

DEBRAY, Régis (1942–)
The darkest spot in modern society is a small luminous screen.

[*Teachers, Writers, Celebrities*]

ECO, Umberto (1932–)
Television doesn't present, as an ideal to aspire to, the superman but the everyman. Television puts forward, as an ideal, the absolutely average man.

[*Diario Minimo*]

FROST, David (1939–)
Television is an invention that permits you to be entertained in your living room by people you wouldn't have in your home.

[Remark, 1971]

HITCHCOCK, Alfred (1899–1980)
Television has brought murder back into the home – where it belongs.

[*The Observer*, 1965]

MCLUHAN, Marshall (1911–1980)
Television brought the brutality of war into the comfort of the living room. Vietnam was lost in the living rooms of America – not on the battle fields of Vietnam.

[Montreal *Gazette*, 1975]

PARRIS, Matthew (1949–)
Television lies. All television lies. It lies persistently, instinctively and by habit . . . A culture of mendacity surrounds the medium, and those who work there live it, breathe it and prosper by it. . . . I know of no area of public life – no, not even politics – more saturated by professional cynicism.

[*The Spectator*, 1996]

SCOTT, C.P. (1846–1932)
Television? The word is half Latin and half Greek. No good can come of it.

[Attr.]

See MEDIA; NEWS

TEMPTATION

BECKFORD, William (1760–1844)
I am not over-fond of resisting temptation.
[*Vathek* (1787)]

GRAHAM, Clementina (1782–1877)
The best way to get the better of temptation is just to yield to it.
[*Mystifications* (1859)]

JERROLD, Douglas William (1803–1857)
Honest bread is very well – it's the butter that makes the temptation.
[*The Catspaw* (1850)]

WILDE, Oscar (1854–1900)
I couldn't help it. I can resist everything except temptation.
[*Lady Windermere's Fan* (1892)]

THEATRE

ADAMOV, Arthur (1908–1970)
The reason why Absurdist plays take place in No Man's Land with only two characters is primarily financial.
[Attr.]

ADDISON, Joseph (1672–1719)
A perfect tragedy is the noblest production of human nature.
[*The Spectator,* 1711]

ARISTOTLE (384–322 BC)
The plot is the first principle and, as it were, the soul of tragedy; character comes second.
[*Poetics*]

BANKHEAD, Tallulah (1903–1968)
It's one of the tragic ironies of the theatre that only one man in it can count on steady work – the night watchman.
[*Tallulah* (1952)]

BERNARD, Tristan (1866–1947)
In the theatre the audience want to be surprised – but by things that they expect.
[Attr.]

BROOKS, Mel (1926–)
Tragedy is if I cut my finger. Comedy is if I walk into an open sewer and die.
[*The New Yorker,* 1978]

BURNEY, Fanny (1752–1840)
'Do you come to the play without knowing what it is?'
'Oh, yes, sir, yes, very fre-

quently. I have no time to read play-bills. One merely comes to meet one's friends, and show that one's alive.'

[*Evelina* (1778)]

BYRON, Lord
(1788–1824)
All tragedies are finish'd by a death,
All comedies are ended by a marriage.

[*Don Juan* (1824)]

COOK, Peter
(1937–1995)
You know, I go to the theatre to be entertained . . . I don't want to see plays about rape, sodomy and drug addiction . . . I can get all that at home.

[*The Observer*, cartoon caption, 1962]

CRAIG, Sir Gordon
(1872–1966)
Farce is the essential theatre. Farce refined becomes high comedy: farce brutalized becomes tragedy.

[Attr.]

GWENN, Edmund
(1875–1959)
[Reply on his deathbed, when someone said to him, 'It must be very hard']
It is. But not as hard as farce.

[*Time*, 1984]

HITCHCOCK, Alfred
(1899–1980)
What is drama but life with the dull bits cut out?

[*The Observer*,1960]

HUXLEY, Aldous
(1894–1963)
We participate in a tragedy; at a comedy we only look.

[*The Devils of Loudun* (1952)]

KEMBLE, John Philip
(1757–1823)
[Said during a play which was continually interrupted by a crying child]
Ladies and gentlemen, unless the play is stopped, the child cannot possibly go on.

[Attr.]

PINTER, Harold (1930–)
I've never regarded myself as the one authority on my plays just because I wrote the damned things.

[*The Observer*, 1993]

SHAW, George Bernard
(1856–1950)
You don't expect me to know what to say about a play when I don't know who the author is, do you? . . . If it's by a good author, it's a good play, naturally. That stands to reason.

[*Fanny's First Play* (1911)]

STOPPARD, Tom (1937–)
The bad end unhappily, the good unluckily. That is what tragedy means.
[*Rosencrantz and Guildenstern Are Dead* (1967)]

See ACTORS

THOUGHT

BIERCE, Ambrose (1842–c. 1914)
Brain: An apparatus with which we think that we think.
[*The Cynic's Word Book* (1906)]

CONFUCIUS (c. 550–c. 478 BC)
Learning without thought is labour lost; thought without learning is perilous.
[*Analects*]

DESCARTES, René (1596–1650)
I think, therefore I am.
[*Discours de la Méthode* (1637)]

EMERSON, Ralph Waldo (1803–1882)
Beware when the great God lets loose a thinker on this planet. Then all things are at risk.
['Circles' (1841)]

GOETHE (1749–1832)
Everything worth thinking has already been thought, our concern must only be to try to think it through again.
['Thought and Action' (1829)]

HAZLITT, William (1778–1830)
The most fluent talkers or most plausible reasoners are not always the justest thinkers.
[*Atlas* (1830), 'On Prejudice']

HORVÁTH, Ödön von (1901–1938)
Thinking hurts.
[*A Child of our Time* (1938)]

JAMES, William (1842–1910)
A great many people think they are thinking when they are merely rearranging their prejudices.
[Attr.]

LUTHER, Martin (1483–1546)
Thoughts are not subject to duty.
[*On Worldly Authority* (1523)]

MILL, John Stuart (1806–1873)
No great improvements in the lot of mankind are possible, until a great change takes place in the fundamental

constitution of their modes of thought.

[*Autobiography* (1873)]

REITH, Lord (1889–1971)
You can't think rationally on an empty stomach, and a whole lot of people can't do it on a full one either.

[Attr.]

RUSKIN, John (1819–1900)
The purest and most thoughtful minds are those which love colour the most.

[*The Stones of Venice*, II (1853)]

RUSSELL, Bertrand (1872–1970)
Many people would sooner die than think. In fact they do.

[In Flew, *Thinking about Thinking* (1975)]

SARTRE, Jean-Paul (1905–1980)
My thought is *me*: that is why I cannot stop. I exist by what I think . . . and I can't prevent myself from thinking.

[*Nausea* (1938)]

SHAKESPEARE, William (1564–1616)
There is nothing either good or bad, but thinking makes it so.

[*Hamlet*, II.ii]

SHELLEY, Percy Bysshe (1792–1822)
A single word even may be a spark of inextinguishable thought.

[*A Defence of Poetry* (1821)]

VALERY, Paul (1871–1945)
A gloss on Descartes:
Sometimes I think: and sometimes I am.

[*The Faber Book of Aphorisms* (1962)]

VAUVENARGUES, Marquis de (1715–1747)
Great thoughts come from the heart.

[*Réflexions et Maximes* (1746)]

VOLTAIRE (1694–1778)
People use thought only to justify their injustices, and they use words only to disguise their thoughts.

[*Dialogues* (1763)]

See IDEAS; MIND

TIME

AURELIUS, Marcus (121–180)
Time is like a river made up of the things which happen, and its current is strong; no sooner does anything appear than

it is carried away, and another comes in its place, and will be carried away too.

[*Meditations*]

BASHÓ, Matsuo (1644–1694)

Days and months are itinerants on an eternal journey; the years that pass by are also travellers.

['Narrow Roads of Oku' (1703)]

THE BIBLE (KING JAMES VERSION)

To every thing there is a season, and a time to every purpose under the heaven.

[*Ecclesiastes*, 3:1–8]

BOUCICAULT, Dion (1822–1890)

Men talk of killing time, while time quietly kills them.

[*London Assurance* (1841)]

COMPTON-BURNETT, Dame Ivy (1884–1969)

Time has too much credit . . . I never agree with the compliments paid to it. It is not a great healer. It is an indifferent and perfunctory one. Sometimes it does not heal at all. And sometimes when it seems to, no healing has been necessary.

[*Darkness and Day* (1951)]

COWARD, Sir Noël (1899–1973)

Time is the reef upon which all our frail mystic ships are wrecked.

[*Blithe Spirit* (1941)]

DISRAELI, Benjamin (1804–1881)

Time is the great physician.

[*Henrietta Temple* (1837)]

DOBSON, Henry Austin (1840–1921)

Time goes, you say? Ah no! Alas, Time stays, *we* go.

['The Paradox of Time' (1877)]

EMERSON, Ralph Waldo (1803–1882)

A day is a miniature eternity.

[*Journals*]

FRAME, Janet (1924–)

There is no past present or future. Using tenses to divide time is like making chalk marks on water.

[*Faces in the Water* (1961)]

MCLUHAN, Marshall (1911–1980)

For tribal man space was the uncontrollable mystery. For technological man it is time that occupies the same role.

[*The Mechanical Bridge* (1951)]

MAXWELL, Gavin
(1914–1969)
Yet while there is time, there
is the certainty of return.
[*Ring of Bright Water* (1960)]

PERICLES (c. 495–429)
Wait for that wisest of coun-
sellors, Time.
[In Plutarch, *Life*]

ROGERS, Will (1879–1935)
Half our life is spent trying to
find something to do with the
time we have rushed through
life trying to save.
[*The New York Times*, 1930]

SHAKESPEARE, William
(1564–1616)
Come what come may,
Time and the hour runs
through the roughest day.
[*Macbeth*, I.iii]

I wasted time, and now doth
time waste me.
[*Richard II*, V.v]

STOPPARD, Tom (1937–)
Eternity's a terrible thought. I
mean, where's it all going to
end?
[*Rosencrantz and Guildenstern
Are Dead* (1967)]

THOMAS, Dylan
(1914–1953)
Oh as I was young and easy
in the mercy of his means,

Time held me green and dying
Though I sang in my chains
like the sea.
['Fern Hill' (1946)]

VAUGHAN, Henry
(1622–1695)
I saw Eternity the other night
Like a great Ring of pure and
endless light,
All calm, as it was bright,
And round beneath it, Time in
hours, days, years
Driv'n by the spheres
Like a vast shadow mov'd, in
which the world
And all her train were hurl'd.
[*Silex Scintillans*]

WATTS, Isaac
(1674–1748)
Time, like an ever-rolling
stream,
Bears all its sons away;
They fly forgotten, as a dream
Dies at the opening day.
[*The Psalms of David Imitated*
(1719)]

YOUNG, Edward
(1683–1765)
Procrastination is the Thief of
Time.
[*Night-Thoughts on Life, Death
and Immortality*]

See CHANGE

TOLERANCE

THE BIBLE (KING JAMES VERSION)
For ye suffer fools gladly, seeing ye yourselves are wise.
[*Paul, 3:67*]

BROWNE, Sir Thomas (1605–1682)
No man can justly censure or condemn another, because indeed no man truly knows another.
[*Religio Medici* (1643)]

BURKE, Edmund (1729–1797)
There is, however, a limit at which forbearance ceases to be a virtue.
[*Observations*]

SADE, Marquis de (1740–1814)
Tolerance is the virtue of the weak.
[*La nouvelle Justine* (1797)]

STAËL, Mme de (1766–1817)
Understanding everything makes one very tolerant.
[*Corinne* (1807)]

TROLLOPE, Anthony (1815–1882)
It is because we put up with bad things that hotel-keepers continue to give them to us.
[*Orley Farm* (1862)]

TRADITION

BOOK OF COMMON PRAYER
There was never any thing by the wit of man so well devised, or so sure established, which in continuance of time hath not been corrupted.
[*The Preface*]

COKE, Sir Edward (1552–1634)
How long soever it hath continued, if it be against reason, it is of no force in law.
['Commentary upon Littleton']

DISRAELI, Benjamin (1804–1881)
A precedent embalms a principle.
[Attr.]

HARDY, Thomas (1840–1928)
Five decades hardly modified the cut of a gaiter, the embroidery of a smock-frock, by the breadth of a hair. Ten generations failed to alter the turn of a single phrase. In these Wessex nooks the busy outsider's ancient times are only old; his old times are still new; his present is futurity.
[*Far From the Madding Crowd* (1874)]

TRAVEL

**ARNOLD, Matthew
(1822–1888)**
A wanderer is man from his
birth.
He was born in a ship
On the breast of the river of
Time.
['The Future']

**COLERIDGE, Samuel Taylor
(1772–1834)**
From whatever place I write
you will expect that part of my
'Travels' will consist of excur-
sions in my own mind.
[*Satyrane's Letters* (1809)]

**COWPER, William
(1731–1800)**
How much a dunce that has
been sent to roam
Excels a dunce that has been
kept at home.
['The Progress of Error' (1782)]

DIDION, Joan (1934–)
Certain places seem to exist
mainly because someone has
written about them.
[*The White Album* (1979)]

DREW, Elizabeth (1887–1965)
Too often travel, instead of
broadening the mind, merely
lengthens the conversation.
[*The Literature of Gossip*
(1964)]

ELIOT, T.S. (1888–1965)
The first condition of understanding a foreign country is
to smell it.
[Attr.]

**EMERSON, Ralph Waldo
(1803–1882)**
Travelling is a fool's paradise.
Our first journeys discover to
us the indifference of places.
['Self-Reliance' (1841)]

GEORGE VI (1895–1952)
Abroad is bloody.
[In Auden, *A Certain World*
(1970)]

**JOHNSON, Amy
(1903–1941)**
Had I been a man I might
have explored the Poles or
climbed Mount Everest, but as
it was my spirit found an out-
let in the air.
[In Margot Asquith (ed.),
Myself When Young]

**JOHNSON, Samuel
(1709–1784)**
[Of the Giant's Causeway]
Worth seeing? yes; but not
worth going to see.
[In Boswell, *The Life of Samuel
Johnson* (1791)]

**KILVERT, Francis
(1840–1879)**
Of all noxious animals, too,
the most noxious is a tourist.

And of all tourists, the most vulgar, ill-bred, offensive and loathsome is the British tourist.

[*Diary*, 1870]

KIPLING, Rudyard (1865–1936)

Down to Gehenna or up to the Throne,
He travels the fastest who travels alone.

['The Winners' (1888)]

MACAULAY, Dame Rose (1881–1958)

The great and recurrent question about abroad is, is it worth getting there?

[Attr.]

MANSFIELD, Katherine (1888–1923)

Whenever I prepare for a journey I prepare as though for death. Should I never return, all is in order. That is what life has taught me.

[*Journal of Katherine Mansfield* (1954)]

MOORE, George (1852–1933)

A man travels the world over in search of what he needs and returns home to find it.

[*The Brook Kerith* (1916)]

SACKVILLE-WEST, Vita (1892–1962)

Travel is the most private of pleasures. There is no greater bore than the travel bore. We do not in the least want to hear what he has seen in Hong Kong.

[*Passenger to Tehran* (1926)]

STARK, Dame Freya (1893–)

The beckoning counts, and not the clicking latch behind you.

[*The Sunday Telegraph*, 1993]

STERNE, Laurence (1713–1768)

A man should know something of his own country too, before he goes abroad.

[*Tristram Shandy* (1767)]

STEVENSON, Robert Louis (1850–1894)

To travel hopefully is a better thing than to arrive, and the true success is to labour.

[*Virginibus Puerisque* (1881)]

But all that I could think of, in the darkness and the cold,
Was that I was leaving home and my folks were growing old.

['Christmas at Sea' (1890)]

There's nothing under Heav'n so blue

That's fairly worth the travelling to.
['A Song of the Road' (1896)]

VIZINCZEY, Stephen (1933–)
I was told I am a true cosmopolitan. I am unhappy everywhere.
[*The Guardian*, 1968]

See FOREIGNERS

TRUST

CAMUS, Albert (1913–1960)
It is very true that we seldom confide in those who are better than ourselves.
[*The Fall* (1956)]

FIELDING, Henry (1707–1754)
Never trust the man who hath reason to suspect that you know that he hath injured you.
[*Jonathan Wild* (1743)]

JEFFERSON, Thomas (1743–1826)
When a man assumes a public trust, he should consider himself as public property.
[Remark, 1807]

PITT, William (1708–1778)
I cannot give them my confidence; pardon me, gentlemen,

confidence is a plant of slow growth in an aged bosom: youth is the season of credulity.
[Speech, 1766]

SHERIDAN, Richard Brinsley (1751–1816)
There is no trusting appearances.
[*The School for Scandal* (1777)]

WILLIAMS, Tennessee (1911–1983)
We have to distrust each other. It's our only defence against betrayal.
[*Camino Real* (1953)]

TRUTH

BACON, Francis (1561–1626)
What a man had rather were true he more readily believes.
[*The New Organon* (1620)]

BALDWIN, Stanley (1867–1947)
A platitude is simply a truth repeated until people get tired of hearing it.
[Attr.]

BERKELEY, Bishop George (1685–1753)
Truth is the cry of all, but the game of the few.
[*Siris* (1744)]

THE BIBLE (KING JAMES VERSION)
Great is Truth, and mighty above all things.
[Apocrypha, *I Esdras*, 4:41]

And ye shall know the truth, and the truth shall make you free.
[*John*, 8:32]

BLAKE, William (1757–1827)
A truth that's told with bad intent
Beats all the Lies you can invent.
['Auguries of Innocence' (c. 1803)]

BOLINGBROKE, Henry (1678–1751)
Plain truth will influence half a score of men at most in a nation, or an age, while mystery will lead millions by the nose.
[Letter, 1721]

BOWEN, Elizabeth (1899–1973)
Nobody speaks the truth when there's something they must have.
[*The House in Paris* (1935)]

BRAQUE, Georges (1882–1963)
Truth exists; only lies are invented.
[*Day and Night, Notebooks* (1952)]

COWPER, William (1731–1800)
And diff'ring judgments serve but to declare
That truth lies somewhere, if we knew but where.
['Hope' (1782)]

DARLING, Charles (1849–1936)
Much truth is spoken, that more may be concealed.
[*Scintillae Juris* (1877)]

DOYLE, Sir Arthur Conan (1859–1930)
It is an old maxim of mine that when you have excluded the impossible, whatever remains, however improbable, must be the truth.
['The Beryl Coronet' (1892)]

DRYDEN, John (1631–1700)
I never saw any good that came of telling truth.
[*Amphitryon* (1690)]

FRAME, Janet (1924–)
In an age of explanation one can always choose varieties of truth.
[*Living in the Maniototo* (1979)]

HUXLEY, T.H. (1825–1895)
Irrationally held truths may be more harmful than reasoned errors.
[*Science and Culture, and Other Essays* (1881)]

IBSEN, Henrik (1828–1906)
A man should never have his best trousers on when he goes out to battle for freedom and truth.
    [*An Enemy of the People* (1882)]

JOHNSON, Samuel (1709–1784)
[On sceptics]
Truth, Sir, is a cow which will yield such people no more milk, and so they are gone to milk the bull.
    [In Boswell, *The Life of Samuel Johnson* (1791)]

LEACOCK, Stephen (1869–1944)
A half truth in argument, like a half brick, carries better.
    [In Flesch, *The Book of Unusual Quotations*]

LE GALLIENNE, Richard (1866–1947)
[Of Oscar Wilde]
Paradox with him was only Truth standing on its head to attract attention.
    [*The Romantic 90s*]

NIXON, Richard (1913–1994)
Let us begin by committing ourselves to the truth, to see it like it is and to tell it like it is, to find the truth, to speak the truth and live with the truth. That's what we'll do.
    [Speech, 1968]

PROUST, Marcel (1871–1922)
A truth which is clearly understood can no longer be written with sincerity.
    ['Senancour c'est moi']

SAMUEL, Lord (1870–1963)
A truism is on that account none the less true.
    [*A Book of Quotations* (1947)]

SOLZHENITSYN, Alexander (1918–)
When truth is discovered by someone else, it loses something of its attractiveness.
    [*Candle in the Wind*]

TWAIN, Mark (1835–1910)
When in doubt, tell the truth.
    [*Pudd'nhead Wilson's New Calendar*]

WHITEHEAD, A.N. (1861–1947)
There are no whole truths; all truths are half-truths. It is trying to treat them as whole truths that plays the devil.
    [*Dialogues* (1954), Prologue]

WILDE, Oscar (1854–1900)
If one tells the truth, one is sure, sooner or later, to be found out.
    [*The Chameleon*, 1894]

WRIGHT, Frank Lloyd (1869–1959)
The truth is more important than the facts.
[In Simcox, *Treasury of Quotations*]

YELTSIN, Boris (1931–)
Truth is truth, and the truth will overcome the left, the right and the centre.
[Interview in *Newsweek*, 1994]

See ART; ERROR; LIES

TYRANNY

ARENDT, Hannah (1906–1975)
Under conditions of tyranny it is far easier to act than to think.
[In Auden, *A Certain World* (1970)]

BIKO, Steve (1946–1977)
The most potent weapon in the hands of the oppressor is the mind of the oppressed.
[Address to students, 1971]

BROWNING, Robert (1812–1889)
Oppression makes the wise man mad.
[*Luria* (1846)]

BURKE, Edmund (1729–1797)
Bad laws are the worst sort of tyranny.
[*Speech at Bristol* (1780)]

DEFOE, Daniel (c. 1661–1731)
Nature has left this tincture in the blood,
That all men would be tyrants if they could.
['The Kentish Petition' (1713)]

HERRICK, Robert (1591–1674)
'Twixt Kings & Tyrants there's this difference known;
Kings seek their Subjects good: Tyrants their owne.
[*Hesperides* (1648)]

MANDELA, Nelson (1918–)
Never, never and never again shall it be that this beautiful land will again experience the oppression of one by another and suffer the indignity of being the skunk of the world.
[Inauguration speech, 1994]

MILL, John Stuart (1806–1873)
Whatever crushes individuality is despotism, by whatever name it may be called.
[*On Liberty* (1859)]

**NIEMÖLLER, Martin
(1892–1984)**
In Germany, the Nazis came
for the Communists and I
didn't speak up because I was
not a Communist. Then they
came for the Jews and I didn't
speak up because I was not a
Jew. Then they came for the
trade unionists and I didn't
speak up because I was not a
trade unionist. Then they
came for the Catholics and I
was a Protestant so I didn't
speak up. Then they came for
me . . . By that time there was
no one to speak up for anyone.
[In Neil, *Concise Dictionary of
Religious Quotations*]

PITT, William (1708–1778)
Where law ends, there tyran-
ny begins.
[Speech, 1770]

See CENSORSHIP

UNIVERSITY

**BATESON, Mary Catherine
(1939–)**
Most higher education is devoted to affirming the traditions and origins of an existing elite and transmitting them to new members.
[*Composing a Life* (1989)]

**FRY, Stephen
(1957–)**
The competitive spirit is an ethos which it is the business of universities . . . to subdue and neutralise.
[*Paperweight* (1992)]

HODSON, Peregrine
He probably doesn't understand what he's looking at but he's reluctant to ask, because this is Japan and the student doesn't ask questions but waits to be told by the teacher.
[*A Circle Round The Sun*]

JOHNSON, Paul (1928–)
In a growing number of countries everyone has a qualified right to attend a university . . . The result is the emergence of huge caravanserais . . . where higher education is doled out rather like gruel in a soup kitchen.
[*The Spectator*, 1996]

**LODGE, David
(1935–)**
Universities are the cathedrals of the modern age. They shouldn't have to justify their existence by utilitarian criteria.
[*Nice Work*]

**MCLUHAN, Marshall
(1911–1980)**
The reason universities are so full of knowledge is that the students come with so much and they leave with so little.
[*Antigonish Review*, 1988]

**NABOKOV, Vladimir
(1899–1977)**
Like so many ageing college people, Pnin had long ceased to notice the existence of students on the campus.
[*Pnin* (1957)]

**O'CONNOR, Flannery
(1925–1964)**
Everywhere I go I'm asked if I think the university stifles writers. My opinion is that they don't stifle enough of them. There's many a best-seller that could have been prevented by a good teacher.
[In Fitzgerald, *The Nature and Aim of Fiction*]

**OZICK, Cynthia
(1928–)**
It is the function of a liberal

university not to give the right
answers, but to ask right
questions.
                    ['Women and Creativity'
                              (1969)]

WALKER, Alice (1944–)
Ignorance, arrogance and
racism have bloomed as

Superior Knowledge in all too
many universities.
                    [*In Search of our Mothers'
                              Gardens* (1983)]

**See EDUCATION; LEARN-
ING; SCHOOL; TEACHERS**

VIOLENCE

**ASIMOV, Isaac
(1920–1992)**
Violence is the last refuge of
the incompetent.
[*Foundation* (1951)]

BRIEN, Alan (1925–)
Violence is the repartee of the
illiterate.
[*Punch*, 1973]

**BRIGHT, John
(1811–1889)**
Force is not a remedy.
[Speech, 1880]

**BRONOWSKI, Jacob
(1908–1974)**
The wish to hurt, the momentary intoxication with pain, is
the loophole through which
the pervert climbs into the
minds of ordinary men.
[*The Face of Violence* (1954)]

HORACE (65–8 BC)
Brute force without judgement
collapses under its own
weight.
[*Odes*]

**INGE, William Ralph
(1860–1954)**
A man may build himself a
throne of bayonets, but he
cannot sit upon it.
[*Philosophy of Plotinus* (1923)]

**KING, Martin Luther
(1929–1968)**
A riot is at bottom the
language of the unheard.
[*Chaos or Community* (1967)]

KORAN
Let there be no violence in
religion.
[Chapter 2]

**MACKENZIE, Sir Compton
(1883–1972)**
There is little to choose
morally between beating up a
man physically and beating
him up mentally.
[*On Moral Courage* (1962)]

MILTON, John (1608–1674)
Who overcomes
By force, hath overcome but
half his foe.
[*Paradise Lost* (1667)]

**ROOSEVELT, Theodore
(1858–1919)**
There is a homely old adage
which runs, 'Speak softly and
carry a big stick; you will go
far.'
[Speech, 1903]

**SAINT-PIERRE, Bernardin de
(1737–1814)**
Women are false in countries
where men are tyrants.
Violence everywhere leads to
deception.
[*Paul et Virginie* (1788)]

UNAMUNO, Miguel de (1864–1936)
To conquer is not to convince.
[Speech, 1936]

VIRTUE

ARISTOTLE (384–322 BC)
Moral virtues we acquire through practice like the arts.
[Nicomachean Ethics]

BAGEHOT, Walter (1826–1877)
Nothing is more unpleasant than a virtuous person with a mean mind.
[Literary Studies (1879)]

BROWNE, Sir Thomas (1605–1682)
There is no road or ready way to virtue.
[Religio Medici (1643)]

CONFUCIUS (c. 550–c. 478 BC)
To be able to practise five things everywhere under heaven constitutes perfect virtue . . . gravity, generosity of soul, sincerity, earnestness, and kindness.
[Analects]

FLETCHER, John (1579–1625)
'Tis virtue, and not birth that makes us noble:
Great actions speak great minds, and such should govern.
[The Prophetess (1622)]

GOLDSMITH, Oliver (c. 1728–1774)
The virtue which requires to be ever guarded, is scarce worth the sentinel.
[The Vicar of Wakefield (1766)]

LA ROCHEFOUCAULD (1613–1680)
Greater virtues are needed to sustain good fortune than bad.
[Maximes (1678)]

MILTON, John (1608–1674)
Most men admire
Virtue, who follow not her lore.
[Paradise Regained (1671)]

MOLIERE (1622–1673)
Virtue, in this world, should be accommodating.
[Le Misanthrope (1666)]

POPE, Alexander (1688–1744)
For Virtue's self may too much zeal be had;.
The worst of Madmen is a Saint run mad.
[Imitations of Horace (1738)]

SHAKESPEARE, William (1564–1616)
Dost thou think, because thou art virtuous, there shall be no more cakes and ale?

[*Twelfth Night*, II.iii]

WALPOLE, Horace (1717–1797)
Tell me, ye divines, which is the most virtuous man, he who begets twenty bastards, or he who sacrifices an hundred thousand lives?

[Letter, 1778]

WASHINGTON, George (1732–1799)
Few men have virtue to withstand the highest bidder.

[*Moral Maxims*]

See GOOD AND EVIL; GOODNESS; MORALITY

WAR

ANONYMOUS
To save the town, it became necessary to destroy it.
[American officer, during the Vietnam War, 1968]

AUSTEN, Jane (1775–1817)
Of the Battle of Albuera in 1811]
How horrible it is to have so many people killed! – And what a blessing that one cares for none of them!
[Letter to Cassandra Austen, 1811]

BARUCH, Bernard M. (1870–1965)
Let us not be deceived – we are today in the midst of a cold war.
[Speech, 1947]

BENNETT, Alan (1934–)
I have never understood this liking for war. It panders to instincts already catered for within the scope of any respectable domestic establishment.
[Forty Years On (1969)]

THE BIBLE (KING JAMES VERSION)
All they that take the sword shall perish with the sword.
[Matthew, 26:52]

BORGES, Jorge Luis (1899–1986)
[On the Falklands War of 1982]
The Falklands thing was a fight between two bald men over a comb.
[Time, 1983]

BRADLEY, Omar Nelson (1893–1981)
[On a proposal to carry the Korean war into China]
The wrong war, at the wrong place, at the wrong time, and with the wrong enemy.
[Senate inquiry, 1951]

BRIGHT, John (1811–1889)
[Referring to the Crimean War]
The angel of death has been abroad throughout the land; you may almost hear the beating of his wings.
[Speech, 1855]

CHRISTIE, Dame Agatha (1890–1976)
One is left with the horrible feeling now that war settles *nothing*; that to *win* a war is as disastrous as to lose one!
[An Autobiography (1977)]

CHURCHILL, Sir Winston (1874–1965)
[On RAF pilots in the Battle of Britain]
Never in the field of human

conflict was so much owed by so many to so few.

[Speech, 1940]

CICERO (106–43 BC)
Laws are silent in war.
[*Pro Milone*]

CLAUSEWITZ, Karl von (1780–1831)
War is nothing but a continuation of politics by other means.

[*On War* (1834)]

CORNFORD, Frances Crofts (1886–1960)
How long ago Hector took off his plume,
Not wanting that his little son should cry,
Then kissed his sad
Andromache goodbye –
And now we three in Euston waiting-room.

['Parting in Wartime' (1948)]

ELLIS, Havelock (1859–1939)
In many a war it has been the vanquished, not the victor, who has carried off the finest spoils.

[*The Soul of Spain* (1908)]

ERASMUS (c. 1466–1536)
War is sweet to those who do not fight.

[*Adagia* (1500)]

GOLDWATER, Barry (1909–)
You've got to forget about this civilian. Whenever you drop bombs, you're going to hit civilians.

[Speech, 1967]

HAIG, Earl (1861–1928)
Every position must be held to the last man: there must be no retirement. With our backs to the wall, and believing in the justice of our cause, each one of us must fight on to the end.

[Order to British forces on the Western Front, 1918]

HANRAHAN, Brian (1949–)
[Reporting the British attack on Port Stanley airport, during the Falklands war]
I'm not allowed to say how many planes joined the raid but I counted them all out and I counted them all back.

[BBC report, 1 May 1982]

HIROHITO, Emperor (1901–1989)
The war situation has developed not necessarily to Japan's advantage.

[Announcing Japan's surrender, 15 August 1945]

HITLER, Adolf (1889–1945)
[Said in 1939]
In starting and waging a war

it is not right that matters, but victory.
[In Shirer, *The Rise and Fall of the Third Reich* (1960)]

HOBBES, Thomas (1588–11679
Force, and fraud, are in war the two cardinal virtues.
[*Leviathan* (1651)]

HOPE, Alec (1907–)
[An ironic parody of the Greek epitaph commemorating the Spartans who died at Thermopylae in 480 BC]
Go tell those old men, safe in bed,
We took their orders and are dead.
['Inscription for Any War']

JARRELL, Randall (1914–1965)
From my mother's sleep I fell into the State,
And I hunched in its belly till my wet fur froze.
Six miles from earth, loosed from its dream of life,
I woke to black flak and the nightmare fighters.
When I died they washed me out of the turret with a hose.
['The Death of the Ball Turret Gunner' (1969)]

JOHNSON, Hiram (1866–1945)
The first casualty when war comes is truth.
[Speech, US Senate, 1917]

KEY, Ellen (1849–1926)
Everything, everything in war is barbaric . . . But the worst barbarity of war is that it forces men collectively to commit acts against which individually they would revolt with their whole being.
[*War, Peace, and the Future* (1916)]

LLOYD GEORGE, David (1863–1945)
[Referring to the popular opinion that World War I would be the last major war]
This war, like the next war, is a war to end war.
[Attr.]

MACDONALD, Ramsay (1866–1937)
We hear war called murder. It is not: it is suicide.
· [*The Observer*, 1930]

MAO TSE-TUNG (1893–1976)
We are advocates of the abolition of war, we do not want war; but war can only be abolished through war, and in order to get rid of the gun it is necessary to take up the gun.
[*Quotations from Chairman Mao Tse-Tung*]

MEIR, Golda (1898–1978)
A leader who doesn't hesitate before he sends his nation into battle is not fit to be a leader.
[Shenker, *As Good as Golda* (1943)]

MICHAELIS, John H. (1912–1985)
[Said to his regiment during the Korean War]
You're not here to die for your country. You're here to make those – die for theirs.
[Attr.]

MOLTKE, Helmuth von (1800–1891)
Eternal peace is a dream, and not even a pleasant one; and war is an integral part of the way God has ordered the world . . . Without war, the world would sink in the mire of materialism.
[Letter, 1880]

MONTAGUE, C.E. (1867–1928)
War hath no fury like a non-combatant.
[*Disenchantment* (1922)]

OWEN, Wilfred (1893–1918)
What passing-bells for these who die as cattle?
Only the monstrous anger of the guns.
Only the stuttering rifles' rapid rattle

Can patter out their hasty orisons.
['Anthem for Doomed Youth' (1917)]

PYRRHUS (319–272 BC)
[After a hard-won battle]
If we are victorious against the Romans in one more battle we shall be utterly ruined.
[In Plutarch, *Lives*]

RABELAIS, François (c. 1494–c. 1553)
Money is the sinews of battle.
[*Gargantua* (1534)]

ROOSEVELT, Franklin Delano (1882–1945)
More than an end to war, we want an end to the beginnings of all wars.
[Speech, 1945]

SANDBURG, Carl (1878–1967)
Sometime they'll give a war and nobody will come.
[*The People, Yes* (1936)]

SASSOON, Siegfried (1886–1967)
[From the statement sent to his commanding officer, July 1917]
I am making this statement as an act of wilful defiance of military authority, because I believe that the War is being deliberately prolonged by

those who have the power to end it . . . I have seen and endured the sufferings of the troops, and I can no longer be a party to prolong these sufferings for ends which I believe to be evil and unjust.
[*Memoirs of an Infantry Officer* (1930)]

SHAKESPEARE, William (1564–1616)
Once more unto the breach, dear friends, once more;
Or close the wall up with our English dead.
In peace there's nothing so becomes a man
As modest stillness and humility;
But when the blast of war blows in our ears,
Then imitate the action of the tiger:
Stiffen the sinews, summon up the blood,
Disguise fair nature with hard-favour'd rage;
Then lend the eye a terrible aspect.
[*Henry V*, III.i]

STRACHEY, Lytton (1880–1932)
[Reply when asked by a Tribunal what he, as a conscientious objector, would do if he saw a German soldier trying to rape his sister]
I should try and come

between them.
[In Holroyd, *Lytton Strachey: A Critical Biography* (1968)]

UREY, Harold (1893–1981)
The next war will be fought with atom bombs and the one after that with spears.
[*The Observer*, 1946]

VULLIAMY, Ed
[A pacifist until the war in the Balkans forced him to change his convictions]
Ironically, the horrors of war have taught me that there are things that are worse than war, and against them determined and careful war should be waged, in the name of the innocent and the weak.
[*The Weekend Guardian*, 1992]

WAUGH, Evelyn (1903–1966)
When the war broke out she took down the signed photograph of the Kaiser and, with some solemnity, hung it in the menservants' lavatory; it was her one combative action.
[*Vile Bodies* (1930)]

WELLINGTON, Duke of (1769–1852)
[Refusing permission to shoot at Napoleon during the Battle of Waterloo]
It is not the business of generals to shoot one another.
[Attr.]

**WILSON, Woodrow
(1856–1924)**
Once lead this people into
war and they'll forget there
ever was such a thing as tolerance.
[In Dos Passos, *Mr Wilson's
War* (1917)]

See PEACE

WAR AND PEACE

**CHURCHILL, Sir Winston
(1874–1965)**
In war, resolution; in defeat,
defiance; in victory, magna-
nimity; in peace, goodwill.
[*The Gathering Storm*]

**CLEMENCEAU, Georges
(1841–1929)**
It is easier to make war than
to make peace.
[Speech, 1919]

KETTLE, Thomas (1880–1916)
If I live, I mean to spend the
rest of my life working for
perpetual peace. I have seen
war and faced artillery and
know what an outrage it is
against simple men.
[*Poems and Parodies*]

**VEGETIUS RENATUS,
Flavius (fl. c. 375)**
Let him who desires peace be

prepared for war.
[*Epitoma Rei Militaris*]

**WILDER, Thornton
(1897–1975)**
When you're at war you think
about a better life; when
you're at peace you think
about a more comfortable
one.
[*The Skin of Our Teeth* (1942)]

See PEACE; WAR

THE WEATHER

**AUSTEN, Jane
(1775–1817)**
What dreadful hot weather we
have! It keeps me in a continual state of inelegance.
[Letter, 1796]

**CHEKHOV, Anton
(1860–1904)**
He who doesn't notice
whether it is winter or summer is happy.
[*The Three Sisters* (1901)]

**ELLIS, George
(1753–1815)**
Snowy, Flowy, Blowy,
Showery, Flowery, Bowery,
Hoppy, Croppy, Droppy,
Breezy, Sneezy, Freezy.
['The Twelve Months']

**GOGARTY, Oliver St John
(1878–1957)**
In my best social accent I
addressed him. I said, 'It is
most extraordinary weather
for this time of year!' He
replied, 'Ah, it isn't this time
of year at all.'
[*It Isn't This Time of Year at All*
(1954)]

**LODGE, David
(1935–)**
The British, he thought, must
be gluttons for satire: even
the weather forecast seemed
to be some kind of spoof, predicting every possible combi-
nation of weather for the next
twenty-four hours without
actually committing itself to
anything specific.
[*Changing Places* (1975)]

**MACAULAY, Dame Rose
(1881–1958)**
Owing to the weather, English
social life must always have
largely occurred either
indoors, or, when out of
doors, in active motion.
['Life Among The English'
(1942)]

**POUND, Ezra
(1885–1972)**
Winter is icummen in,
Lhude sing Goddamn,
Raineth drop and staineth
slop,

And how the wind doth
ramm!
Sing: Goddamn.
['Ancient Music' (1916)]

**SMITH, Logan Pearsall
(1865–1946)**
Thank heavens, the sun has
gone in, and I don't have to
go out and enjoy it.
[*All Trivia* (1933), 'Last Words']

See SEASONS

WISDOM

AESCHYLUS (525–456 BC)
It is a fine thing even for an
old man to learn wisdom.
[*Fragments*]

**ARISTOPHANES
(c. 445–385 BC)**
One may learn wisdom even
from one's enemies.
[*Birds*]

BACON, Francis (1561–1626)
A wise man will make more
opportunities than he finds.
['Of Ceremonies and Respects'
(1625)]

**CHESTERFIELD, Lord
(1694–1773)**
Be wiser than other people if
you can; but do not tell them so.
[Letter to his son, 1745]

COWPER, William (1731–1800)
Knowledge is proud that he has learn'd so much;
Wisdom is humble that he knows no more.
[*The Task* (1785)]

EMERSON, Ralph Waldo (1803–1882)
Now that is the wisdom of a man, in every instance of his labor, to hitch his wagon to a star, and see his chore done by the gods themselves.
[*Society and Solitude* (1870)]

HORACE (65–8 BC)
To have made a beginning is half of the business; dare to be wise.
[*Epistles*]

HUTCHESON, Francis (1694–1746)
Wisdom denotes the pursuing of the best ends by the best means.
[*An Inquiry into the Original of our Ideas of Beauty and Virtue* (1725)]

LEVI-STRAUSS, Claude (1908–)
The wise man is not the man who gives the right answers; he is the one who asks the right questions.
[*The Raw and the Cooked*]

PLATO (c. 429–347 BC)
That man is wisest who, like Socrates, has realized that in truth his wisdom is worth nothing.
[*The Apology of Socrates*]

QUARLES, Francis (1592–1644)
Be wisely worldly, not worldly wise.
[*Emblems*, II (1635)]

ROOSEVELT, Theodore (1858–1919)
Nine-tenths of wisdom is being wise in time.
[Speech, 1917]

SMOLLETT, Tobias (1721–1771)
Some folks are wise, and some are otherwise.
[*The Adventures of Roderick Random* (1748)]

SWIFT, Jonathan (1667–1745)
No wise man ever wished to be younger.
[*Thoughts on Various Subjects* (1711)]

SZASZ, Thomas (1920–)
The stupid neither forgive nor forget; the naive forgive and forget; the wise forgive but do not forget.
[*The Second Sin* (1973)]

See KNOWLEDGE

WOMEN

ANONYMOUS
In particular, the State recognises that by her life within the home, woman gives to the State a support without which the common good cannot be achieved.
[*The Irish Constitution*]

AUSTEN, Jane (1775–1817)
Where people wish to attach, they should always be ignorant. To come with a well-informed mind, is to come with an inability of administering to the vanity of others, which a sensible person would always wish to avoid. A woman especially, if she have the misfortune of knowing any thing, should conceal it as well as she can.
[*Northanger Abbey* (1818)]

In nine cases out of ten, a woman had better show more affection than she feels.
[Letter]

BEAUVOIR, Simone de (1908–1986)
One is not born a woman: one becomes a woman.
[*The Second Sex* (1950)]

BURNET, Sir Frank Macfarlane (1899–1985)
In an affluent society most healthy women would like to have four healthy children.
[*Dominant Mammal* (1970)]

BUTLER, Samuel (1612–1680)
The souls of women are so small,
That some believe they've none at all.
[*Miscellaneous Thoughts*]

BUTLER, Samuel (1835–1902)
Brigands demand your money or your life; women require both.
[Attr.]

BYRON, Lord (1788–1824)
There is something to me very softening in the presence of a woman, – some strange influence, even if one is not in love with them – which I cannot at all account for, having no very high opinion of the sex.
[Journal, 1814]

CATULLUS (84–c. 54 BC)
But what a woman says to her eager lover, she ought to write in the wind and the running water.
[*Carmina*]

CERVANTES, Miguel de (1547–1616)
An honest woman and a broken leg should be at home; and for a decent maiden, working is her holiday.
[*Don Quixote* (1615)]

EKLAND, Britt (1942–)
As a single woman with a child, I would love to have a wife.
[*The Independent*, 1994]

ELIOT, George (1819–1880)
I should like to know what is the proper function of women, if it is not to make reasons for husbands to stay at home, and still stronger reasons for bachelors to go out.
[*The Mill on the Floss* (1860)]

FRAYN, Michael (1933–)
No woman so naked as one you can see to be naked underneath her clothes.
[*Constructions*]

FREUD, Sigmund (1856–1939)
The great question . . . which I have not been able to answer, despite my thirty years of research into the feminine soul, is 'What does a woman want?'
[In Robb, *Psychiatry in American Life*]

GRANVILLE, George (1666–1735)
Of all the plagues with which the world is curst,
Of every ill, a woman is the worst.
[*The British Enchanters*]

HAKIM, Catherine
The unpalatable truth is that a substantial proportion of women still accept the sexual division of labour which sees home-making as women's principal activitiy and income-earning as men's principal activity in life.
[*The Observer Review*, 1996]

HARMAN, Sir Jeremiah (1930–)
I've always thought there were only three kinds of women: wives, whores and mistresses.
[Attr. in *Daily Mail*, 1996]

IRVING, Washington (1783–1859)
A woman's whole life is a history of the affections.
[*The Sketch Book* (1820)]

JOHNSON, Samuel (1709–1784)
Sir, a woman's preaching is like a dog's walking on his hinder legs. It is not done well; but you are surprised to find it done at all.
[In Boswell, *The Life of Samuel Johnson* (1791)]

**LA ROCHEFOUCAULD
(1613–1680)**
One can find women who
have never had a love affair,
but it is rare to find a woman
who has only had one.
                    [*Maximes* (1678)]

**LOOS, Anita
(1893–1981)**
So this gentleman said a girl
with brains ought to do something with them besides think.
[*Gentlemen Prefer Blondes* (1925)]

**MCCARTHY, Abigail
(c. 1914–)**
For those of us whose lives
have been defined by others –
by wifehood and motherhood
– there is no individual
achievement to measure, only
the experience of life itself.
              [*Private Faces/Public Places*
                                    (1972)]

**MASEFIELD, John
(1878–1967)**
To get the whole world out of
bed
And washed, and dressed,
and warmed, and fed,
To work, and back to bed
again,
Believe me, Saul, costs worlds
of pain.
                [‘The Everlasting Mercy’
                                    (1911)]

**MAUGHAM, William
Somerset (1874–1965)**
A woman will always sacrifice
herself if you give her the
opportunity. It is her favourite
form of self-indulgence.
                    [*The Circle* (1921)]

**MILTON, John
(1608–1674)**
. . . nothing lovelier can be
found
In Woman, than to studie
household good,
And good works in her
Husband to promote.
                [*Paradise Lost* (1667)]

**NASH, Ogden
(1902–1971)**
Women would rather be right
than reasonable.
                  [‘Frailty, Thy Name is a
                            Misnomer’ (1942)]

**NIETZSCHE, Friedrich
Wilhelm (1844–1900)**
Everything to do with women
is a mystery, and everything
to do with women has one
solution: it's called pregnancy.
                [*Thus Spake Zarathustra*
                                    (1884)]

NIN, Anais (1903–1977)
Women (and I, in this Diary)
have never separated sex
from feeling, from love of the
whole man.
                    [*Delta of Venus* (1977)]

POPE, Alexander (1688–1744)
Most Women have no Characters at all.
['Epistle to a Lady' (1735)]

RACINE, Jean (1639–1699)
She wavers, she hesitates; in a word, she is a woman.
[Athalie (1691)]

ROWLAND, Helen (1875–1950)
It takes a woman twenty years to make a man of her son, and another woman twenty minutes to make a fool of him.
[Reflections of a Bachelor Girl (1909)]

RUBINSTEIN, Helena (c. 1872–1965)
There are no ugly women, only lazy ones.
[My Life for Beauty (1965)]

SCHOPENHAUER, Arthur (1788–1860)
One needs only to see the way she is built to realize that woman is not intended for great mental labour.
[Attr.]

SHAKESPEARE, William (1564–1616)
Frailty, thy name is woman!
[Hamlet, I.ii]

She's beautiful, and therefore to be woo'd;
She is a woman, therefore to be won.
[Henry VI, Part 1, V.iii]

SOUTHEY, Robert (1774–1843)
What will not woman, gentle woman, dare,
When strong affection stirs her spirit up?
[Madoc (1805)]

STOCKS, Mary, Baroness (1891–1975)
It is clearly absurd that it should be possible for a woman to qualify as a saint with direct access to the Almighty while she may not qualify as a curate.
[Attr.]

VANBRUGH, Sir John (1664–1726)
Once a woman has given you her heart you can never get rid of the rest of her.
[The Relapse (1696)]

WELLS, H.G. (1866–1946)
There's no social differences – till women come in.
[Kipps: the Story of a Simple Soul (1905)]

WOLFF, Charlotte (1904–1986)
Women have always been the guardians of wisdom and

humanity which makes them natural, but usually secret, rulers. The time has come for them to rule openly, but together with and not against men.

[*Bisexuality: A Study*]

WYNNE-TYSON, Esme (1898–1972)
Scheherazade is the classical example of a woman saving her head by using it.

[Attr.]

See FEMINISM; MEN AND WOMEN

WORDS

AESCHYLUS (525–456 BC)
Words are physic to the distempered mind.

[*Prometheus Bound*]

CONFUCIUS (c. 550–c. 478 BC)
Without knowing the force of words, it is impossible to know men.

[*Analects*]

ELIOT, T.S. (1888–1965)
Words strain,
Crack and sometimes break, under the burden,
Under the tension, slip, slide, perish,
Decay with imprecision, will not stay in place,
Will not stay still.

[*Four Quartets* (1944)]

EMERSON, Ralph Waldo (1803–1882)
Words are also actions, and actions are a kind of words.

['The Poet' (1844)]

HOBBES, Thomas (1588–1679)
Words are wise men's counters, they do but reckon by them; but they are the money of fools.

[*Leviathan* (1651)]

HUXLEY, Aldous (1894–1963)
Thanks to words, we have been able to rise above the brutes; and thanks to words, we have often sunk to the level of the demons.

[*Adonis and the Alphabet* (1956)]

KIPLING, Rudyard (1865–1936)
Words are, of course, the most powerful drug used by mankind.

[Speech, 1923]

LYDGATE, John (c. 1370–c. 1451)
Woord is but wynd; leff woord and tak the dede.

['Secrets of Old Philosophers']

**POPE, Alexander
(1688–1744)**
Words are like leaves; and
where they most abound,
Much fruit of sense beneath is
rarely found.
[*An Essay on Criticism* (1711)]

**SHAKESPEARE, William
(1564–1616)**
But words are words: I never
yet did hear
That the bruis'd heart was
pierced through the ear.
[*Othello*, I.iii]

**SPENCER, Herbert
(1820–1903)**
How often misused words
generate misleading thoughts.
[*Principles of Ethics* (1879)]

**See CONVERSATION;
LANGUAGE**

WORK

**ACHESON, Dean
(1893–1971)**
[Remark made on leaving his
post as Secretary of State,
1952]
I will undoubtedly have to
seek what is happily known
as gainful employment, which
I am glad to say does not
describe holding public office.
[Attr.]

ANONYMOUS
Laborare est orare.
Work is prayer.
[Unknown origin]

The working class can kiss
my arse –
I've got the boss's job at last.
[Australian Labor movement,
traditional folk saying]

BALDWIN, James (1924–1987)
The price one pays for pursuing any profession or calling
is an intimate knowledge of
its ugly side.
[*Nobody Knows My Name*
(1961)]

**THE BIBLE (KING JAMES
VERSION)**
The labourer is worthy of his
hire.
[*Luke*, 10:7]

If any would not work, neither
should he eat.
[*II Thessalonians*, 3:10]

**BUTLER, Samuel
(1835–1902)**
Every man's work, whether it
be literature or music or pictures or architecture or anything else, is always a portrait
of himself.
[*The Way of All Flesh* (1903)]

CARLYLE, Thomas (1795–1881)
Work is the grand cure of all

the maladies and miseries that ever beset mankind.
[Speech, 1886]

CLARKE, John (fl. 1639)
He that would thrive
Must rise at five;
He that hath thriven
May lie till seven.
[*Paraemiologia Anglo-Latina* (1639)]

COLERIDGE, Samuel Taylor (1772–1834)
Work without hope draws nectar in a sieve,
And hope without an object cannot live.
['Work Without Hope' (1828)]

COLLINGWOOD, Robin George (1889–1943)
Perfect freedom is reserved for the man who lives by his own work and in that work does what he wants to do.
[*Speculum Mentis* (1924)]

COWARD, Sir Noël (1899–1973)
Work is much more fun than fun.
[*The Observer*, 1963]

CURIE, Marie (1867–1934)
One never notices what has been done; one can only see what remains to be done.
[Letter to her brother, 1894]

GEORGE, Henry (1839–1897)
The man who gives me employment, which I must have or suffer, that man is my master, let me call him what I will.
[*Social Problems* (1884)]

JEROME, Jerome K. (1859–1927)
I like work; it fascinates me. I can sit and look at it for hours. I love to keep it by me: the idea of getting rid of it nearly breaks my heart.
[*Three Men in a Boat* (1889)]

KOLLWITZ, Käthe (1867–1945)
For the last third of life there remains only work. It alone is always stimulating, rejuvenating, exciting and satisfying.
[*Diaries and Letters* (1955)]

LANG, Ian (1940–)
Job insecurity is a state of mind.
[*The Observer Review*, 1995]

LARKIN, Philip (1922–1985)
Why should I let the toad work
Squat on my life?
Can't I use my wit as a pitchfork
And drive the brute off?
['Toads' (1955)]

PARKINSON, C. Northcote (1909–1993)
Work expands so as to fill the time available for its completion.

[*Parkinson's Law* (1958)]

PETER, Laurence J. (1919–1990)
In a hierarchy every employee tends to rise to his level of incompetence.

[*The Peter Principle* (1969)]

REAGAN, Ronald (1911–)
They say hard work never hurt anybody, but I figure why take the chance.

[Attr.]

ROOSEVELT, Theodore (1858–1919)
No man needs sympathy because he has to work . . . Far and away the best prize that life offers is the chance to work hard at work worth doing.

[Address, 1903]

ROWLAND, Helen (1875–1950)
When you see what some girls marry, you realize how they must hate to work for a living.

[*Reflections of a Bachelor Girl* (1909)]

RUSSELL, Bertrand (1872–1970)
One of the symptoms of approaching nervous breakdowns is the belief that one's work is terribly important. If I were a medical man, I should prescribe a holiday to any patient who considered his work important.

[Attr.]

SHAKESPEARE, William (1564–1616)
The labour we delight in physics pain.

[*Macbeth*, II.iii]

STANTON, Elizabeth Cady (1815–1902)
Woman has been the great unpaid laborer of the world.
[In Anthony and Gage, *History of Woman Suffrage* (1881)]

TEBBITT, Norman (1931–)
[Of his father who had grown up during the 1930s]
He didn't riot. He got on his bike and looked for work and he kept looking till he found it.

[Speech, 1981]

WATTS, Isaac (1674–1748)
In works of labour, or of skill, I would be busy too;

For Satan finds some mischief
still
For idle hands to do.
['Against Idleness and
Mischief' (1715)]

WILDE, Oscar (1854–1900)
Work is the curse of the
drinking classes.
[In Pearson, *Life of Oscar
Wilde* (1946)]

YEATS, W.B. (1865–1939)
The intellect of man is forced
to choose
Perfection of the life, or of the
work.
['The Choice' (1933)]

THE WORLD

**BALFOUR, A.J.
(1848–1930)**
This is a singularly ill–
contrived world, but not so
ill–contrived as all that.
[Attr.]

**BROWNE, Sir Thomas
(1605–1682)**
The created world is but a
small parenthesis in eternity.
[*Christian Morals* (1716)]

**CLOUGH, Arthur Hugh
(1819–1861)**
This world is bad enough,
may-be,
We do not comprehend it;
But in one fact can all agree,
God won't, and we can't
mend it.
[*Dipsychus* (1865)]

**DIDEROT, Denis
(1713–1784)**
What a fine comedy this
world would be if one did not
play a part in it!
[*Letters to Sophie Volland*]

**FERLINGHETTI, Lawrence
(1920–)**
The world is a beautiful place
to be born into
if you don't mind some people
dying
all the time
or maybe only starving
some of the time
which isn't half so bad
if it isn't you.
[*Pictures of the Gone World*
(1955)]

**FIRBANK, Ronald
(1886–1926)**
The world is disgracefully
managed, one hardly knows
to whom to complain.
[*Vainglory* (1915)]

**HEMINGWAY, Ernest
(1898–1961)**
The world is a fine place and
worth the fighting for.
[*For Whom the Bell Tolls*
(1940)]

KAFKA, Franz (1883–1924)
In the struggle between you and the world, support the world.

[*Reflections* (1953)]

MCLUHAN, Marshall (1911–1980)
The new electronic interdependence recreates the world in the image of a global village.

[*The Gutenberg Galaxy* (1962)]

MACNEICE, Louis (1907–1963)
World is crazier and more of it than we think,
Incorrigibly plural. I peel and portion
A tangerine and spit the pips and feel
The drunkenness of things being various.

['Snow' (1935)]

SARTRE, Jean-Paul (1905–1980)
The world can survive very well without literature. But it can survive even more easily without man.

[*Situations*]

SHAKESPEARE, William (1564–1616)
How many goodly creatures are there here!
How beauteous mankind is! O brave new world
That has such people in't!

[*The Tempest*, V.i]

SMOLLETT, Tobias (1721–1771)
I consider the world as made for me, not me for the world: it is my maxim therefore to enjoy it while I can, and let futurity shift for itself.

[*The Adventures of Roderick Random* (1748)]

TRAHERNE, Thomas (c. 1637–1674)
You never enjoy the world aright, till the sea itself floweth in your veins, till you are clothed with the heavens, and crowned with the stars: and perceive yourself to be the sole heir of the whole world, and more than so, because men are in it who are every one sole heirs as well as you.

[*Centuries of Meditations*]

WRITERS

AUDEN, W.H. (1907–1973)
No poet or novelist wishes he were the only one who ever lived, but most of them wish they were the only one alive, and quite a number fondly believe their wish has been granted.

[*The Dyer's Hand* (1963)]

AUSTEN, Jane (1775–1817)
I think I may boast myself to be, with all possible vanity, the most unlearned and uninformed female who ever dared to be an authoress.
[Letter, 1815]

BAGEHOT, Walter (1826–1877)
Writers, like teeth, are divided into incisors and grinders.
['The First Edinburgh Reviewers' (1858)]

BEAUVOIR, Simone de (1908–1986)
Writers who stand out, as long as they are not dead, are always scandalous.
[*The Second Sex* (1950)]

BENNETT, Alan (1934–)
We were put to Dickens as children but it never quite took. That unremitting humanity soon had me cheesed off.
[*The Old Country* (1978)]

BERNARD, Jeffrey (1932–)
Writers as a rule don't make fighters, although I would hate to have to square up to Taki or Andrea Dworkin.
[*Spectator*, 1992]

CANETTI, Elias (1905–1994)
He lays sentences like eggs, but he forgets to incubate them.
[*The Human Province. Notes from 1942 to 1972*]

CHATEAUBRIAND (1768–1848)
The original writer is not the one who refrains from imitating others, but the one who can be imitated by none.
[*The Beauties of Christianity* (1802)]

CONNOLLY, Cyril (1903–1974)
Better to write for yourself and have no public, than write for the public and have no self.
[In Pritchett (ed.), *Turnstile One*]

EMERSON, Ralph Waldo (1803–1882)
Talent alone cannot make a writer. There must be a man behind the book.
['Goethe; or, the Writer' (1850)]

FAULKNER, William (1897–1962)
The writer's only responsibility is to his art . . . If a writer has to rob his mother, he will not hesitate; the 'Ode on a Grecian Urn' is worth any number of old ladies.
[*Paris Review*, 1956]

FROST, Robert (1874–1963)
No tears in the writer, no tears in the reader.
[*Collected Poems* (1939)]

GORDIMER, Nadine (1923–)
The tension between standing apart and being fully involved; that is what makes a writer.
[*Selected Stories* (1975)]

HOBBES, Thomas (1588–1679)
The praise of ancient authors, proceeds not from the reverence of the dead, but from the competition, and mutual envy of the living.
[*Leviathan* (1651)]

JOHNSON, Samuel (1709–1784)
The greatest part of a writer's time is spent in reading, in order to write: a man will turn over half a library to make one book.
[In Boswell, *The Life of Samuel Johnson* (1791)]

JOSEPH, Michael (1897–1958)
Authors are easy to get on with – if you're fond of children.
[*The Observer*, 1949]

KOESTLER, Arthur (1905–1983)
A writer's ambition should be . . . to trade a hundred contemporary readers for ten readers in ten years' time and for one reader in a hundred years' time.
[*New York Times Book Review*, 1951]

LAMB, Lady Caroline (1785–1828)
[Of Byron]
Mad, bad, and dangerous to know.
[*Journal*, 1812]

LANDOR, Walter Savage (1775–1864)
Clear writers, like clear fountains, do not seem so deep as they are; the turbid look the most profound.
[*Imaginary Conversations* (1824)]

MACDIARMID, Hugh (1892–1978)
Our principal writers have nearly all been fortunate in escaping regular education.
[*The Observer*, 1953]

MACMANUS, Michael (1888–1951)
But my work is undistinguished
And my royalties are lean
Because I never am obscure
And not at all obscene.
['An Author's Lament']

SINGER, Isaac Bashevis (1904–1991)
When I was a little boy they called me a liar but now that I am a grown up they call me a writer.

[*The Observer*, 1983]

VIDAL, Gore (1925–)
American writers want to be not good but great; and so are neither.

[*Two Sisters* (1970)]

YEATS, W.B. (1865–1939)
It's not a writer's business to hold opinions.

[Attr.]

WRITING

ANONYMOUS
Inspiration is the act of drawing up a chair to the writing desk.

ATWOOD, Margaret (1939–)
Writing . . . is an act of faith: I believe it's also an act of hope, the hope that things can be better than they are.

[Attr.]

AUSTEN, Jane (1775–1817)
Let other pens dwell on guilt and misery.

[*Mansfield Park* (1814)]

BOILEAU-DESPREAUX, Nicolas (1636–1711)
He who does not know how to limit himself does not know how to write.

[*L'Art Poétique* (1674)]

BULWER-LYTTON, Edward (1803–1873)
Beneath the rule of men entirely great
The pen is mightier than the sword.

[*Richelieu* (1839)]

DE VRIES, Peter (1910–)
I write when I'm inspired, and I see to it that I'm inspired at nine o'clock every morning.

[*The Observer*, 1980]

ELIOT, T.S. (1888–1965)
[On his ideal of writing]
The common word exact without vulgarity, the formal word precise but not pedantic, the complete consort dancing together.

[*The Sunday Telegraph*, 1993]

FROST, Robert (1874–1963)
Writing free verse is like playing tennis with the net down.

[Address, 1935]

GORKY, Maxim (1868–1936)
You must write for children just as you do for adults, only better.

[Attr.]

JOHNSON, Samuel (1709–1784)
The only end of writing is to enable the readers better to enjoy life, or better to endure it.

[*Works* (1787)]

KEATS, John (1795–1821)
I am convinced more and more day by day that fine writing is next to fine doing, the top thing in the world.

[Letter to J.H. Reynolds, 1819]

LAWRENCE, D.H. (1885–1930)
I like to write when I feel spiteful: it's like having a good sneeze.

[Letter to Lady Cynthia Asquith, 1913]

ORWELL, George (1903–1950)
Good prose is like a window pane.

['Why I Write' (1946)]

PASCAL, Blaise (1623–1662)
The last thing one finds out when constructing a work is what to put first.

[*Pensées* (1670)]

RENARD, Jules (1864–1910)
The profession of letters is, after all, the only one in which one can make no money without being ridiculous.

[*Journal*]

SIDNEY, Sir Philip (1554–1586)
Byting my tongue and penne, beating my selfe for spite:
'Foole,' saide My muse to mee, 'looke in thy heart and write'.

[*Astrophel and Stella* (1591)]

SIMENON, Georges (1903–1989)
Writing is not a profession but a vocation of unhappiness.

[*Writers at Work* (1958)]

See CRITICISM; FICTION; LITERATURE; POETRY

YOUTH

**ASQUITH, Herbert
(1852–1928)**
Youth would be an ideal state
if it came a little later in life.
[*The Observer*, 1923]

**BULWER-LYTTON, Edward
(1803–1873)**
In the lexicon of youth, which
Fate reserves
For a bright manhood, there is
no such word
As – *fail*!
[*Richelieu* (1839)]

CHANEL, Coco (1883–1971)
Youth is something very new:
twenty years ago no one
mentioned it.
[In Haedrich, *Coco Chanel, Her
Life, Her Secrets* (1971)]

CRISP, Quentin (1908–)
The young always have the
same problem – how to rebel
and conform at the same
time. They have now solved
this by defying their parents
and copying one another.
[*The Naked Civil Servant*
(1968)]

**DISRAELI, Benjamin
(1804–1881)**
Youth is a blunder; Manhood
a struggle; Old Age a regret.
[*Coningsby* (1844)]

GAY, John (1685–1732)
Youth's the season made for
joys,
Love is then our duty.
[*The Beggar's Opera* (1728)]

**JOHNSON, Samuel
(1709–1784)**
Young men have more virtue
than old men; they have more
generous sentiments in every
respect.
[In Boswell, *The Life of Samuel
Johnson* (1791)]

**OSBORNE, John
(1929–1994)**
I keep looking back, as far as I
can remember, and I can't
think what it was like to feel
young, really young.
[*Look Back in Anger* (1956)]

PORTER, Hal (1911–1984)
How ruthless and hard and
vile and right the young are.
[*The Watcher on the Cast-iron
Balcony* (1963)]

**SHAW, George Bernard
(1856–1950)**
Youth, which is forgiven
everything, forgives itself
nothing; age, which forgives
itself everything, is forgiven
nothing.
[*Man and Superman* (1903)]

It's all that the young can do
for the old, to shock them and

keep them up to date.
[*Fanny's First Play* (1911)]

SMITH, Logan Pearsall (1865–1946)
The old know what they want; the young are sad and bewildered.
['Last Words' (1933)]

THATCHER, Margaret (1925–)
Young people ought not to be idle. It is very bad for them.
[*The Times*, 1984]

WILDE, Oscar (1854–1900)
The old-fashioned respect for the young is fast dying out.
[*The Importance of Being Earnest* (1895)]

WILSON, Woodrow (1856–1924)
Generally young men are regarded as radicals. This is a popular misconception. The most conservative persons I ever met are college undergraduates.
[Speech, 1905]

See AGE

INDEX OF SOURCES